MANAGEMENT METHODOLOGY FOR SOFTWARE PRODUCT ENGINEERING

MANAGEMENT METHODOLOGY FOR SOFTWARE PRODUCT ENGINEERING

RICHARD C. GUNTHER

Manager
Product Planning
and Market Analysis
Amdahl Corporation

A Wiley-Interscience Publication
JOHN WILEY & SONS
New York   Chichester   Brisbane   Toronto

Library of Congress Cataloging in Publication Data:

Gunther, Richard C., 1937–
    Management methodology for software product engineering.

    "A Wiley-Interscience publication."
    Bibliography: p.
    Includes index.
    1. Computer programming management.   I. Title.

QA76.6.G85   658′.05   78-711
ISBN 0-471-33600-9

Printed in the United States of America

10 9 8 7 6 5 4 3 2 1

IN MEMORY OF

MY FATHER

If we wish our science to be complete, those matters which promote the end we have in view must one and all be scrutinized by a movement of thought which is continuous and nowhere interrupted; they must also be included in an enumeration which is both adequate and methodical.

from *Rules for the Direction of the Mind*

René Descartes, circa 1629

PREFACE

Back in 1620 Francis Bacon challenged the Aristotelian view of the sciences as unrelated collections of aphorisms. In his *New Organon* he introduced a method of induction whereby he iterated from observed facts to derived axioms to further experiments and then to new axioms. Through this method he discovered underlying principles common to many sciences. Simultaneously, René Descartes codified the procedures of science into self-consistent systems of theory.

We who call ourselves software engineers have taken a similar approach. We challenge the view that the production of software is fundamentally different from the production of anything else. We observe the facts accumulated over several years of software production, compare them with other facts from our environment, and exploit similarities to determine underlying principles. While we still share Bacon's uncertainty about the exact character of abstractions, our experience shows us that there do exist general principles, and that adherence to them improves our ability to produce software on time, within budget, and according to specification.

In this book you will find a methodology for managing the planning, design, construction, evaluation, documentation, distribution, and maintenance of software. This methodology exploits the high correlation between phases in the life cycle of a software system and the functions that must be performed throughout the cycle. You will see how top-down design, management by objectives, configuration management, and other principles can be integrated through a self-consistent set of documents and procedures that continually reinforce one another.

This book emphasizes the product concept; the concept of heavy-duty software—software to be used by a vast, perhaps little known body of users and to be promoted, maintained, and enhanced over a long period of time. It presents techniques and tools tailored for managing such heavy-duty software. You can select from among them those that meet your needs, whether you are a data processing manager, a defense system project leader, a software company product manager, or a director of software development for a hardware manufacturer. The methodology presented is fully compatible with structured programming and with chief programmer teams, but it works equally well with or without them.

The book is divided into five parts: background, techniques, tools, appendix, and references. In the first part you are introduced to concepts that are fundamental to the rest of the book: software as a product, the life cycle, the phase-function matrix, hierarchical decomposition. A sample company and a sample software product are introduced. This company and product are featured throughout the book to demonstrate how highly correlated the concepts are and how self-consistent the documents and procedures are. In the second part each function involved in software production is discussed separately. The role of each function in every phase of a product's life cycle is explored. This organization enhances the book's value for reference: you can easily review a single function or you can review a single phase by studying a selected section of each chapter. The third part discusses in great detail the semantics and syntax you will need to implement the book's methodology in self-consistent plans, specifications, and reports. Particular emphasis is placed on an integrated set of design documents that observe a rigorous decomposition of substance and by life cycle phase. Finally, the fourth part includes a complete example of the master plan for development of a software product and the fifth part has a list of references you can use to amplify the text.

Every technique and tool presented in this book has been successfully employed somewhere and many can be employed independently of one another. They are fully compatible with structured programming and chief programmer team concepts. They are based on top-down, modular design. Because they are tightly correlated, the more you employ them together the more you will benefit from synergism as they reinforce one another. Where necessary, you are cautioned to avoid introducing critical elements too soon or too late or too fast for assimilation.

Why should you read *Management Methodology for Software Product Engineering* instead of or in addition to any of a number of other books on the management of programming? First, because you want to produce heavy-duty software and because of that you have complex communication problems to overcome which texts without a product orientation fail to acknowledge. Second, because you want assurance that as you adopt each technique or tool, it will still work after you introduce other techniques and tools. Not only will it continue to work; it will work better. Lastly, because you want to adopt a methodology that is founded on sound planning, documentation, and review principles that assure at the beginning of a development project you will not overlook something and have to take costly corrective action in midstream.

This book is the result of many years of evolution, beginning with the early work of Kenneth W. Kolence, who first kindled my interest in software engineering management and later inspired me to undertake the task of writing the book. As a practitioner of the subject I found it difficult to make time available for the project, and I owe thanks to Clair E. Miller and Kornel Spiro for their understanding and encouragement over the years it took to complete the work. Most of all I am indebted to my family, who allowed me many evenings and weekends to work, and especially to my wife Suzanne, who more than anyone else made it possible for me to finish.

RICHARD C. GUNTHER

Palo Alto, California
January 1978

CONTENTS

Chapter 1   About This Book   1

    1.1   What This Book Is and Is Not, 1
    1.2   Where To Look for Information Not in
          This Book, 5
    1.3   How To Read This Book, 6
    1.4   How To Apply This Book, 7

PART I   BACKGROUND

Chapter 2   Software as a Product   13

    2.1   The Product Concept, 14
    2.2   The Life Cycle of a Software Product, 16
    2.3   Life Cycle Phases and Organizational
          Functions, 20
    2.4   External Design and Internal Design, 21
    2.5   Hierarchical Decomposition, 22
    2.6   Development Tools and Product End
          Items, 23

Chapter 3   The Sample Company: The ABC Corporation   26

    3.1   History and Markets of ABC, 27
    3.2   Organization of the ABC Corporation, 27
    3.3   Organization of the ABC Computers
          Company, 29
    3.4   Organization of Research and
          Development, 31
    3.5   Organization of the Software Products
          Department, 32

3.6   Stereotype Functions in a Real
         Organization, 32

Chapter 4   The Sample Product: A$K   34

         4.1   How the Product Came To Be, 34
         4.2   The Need for A$K: What It Is, 36
         4.3   A$K as Heavy-Duty Software, 36
         4.4   Treatment of A$K in This Book, 37

PART II TECHNIQUES OF SOFTWARE PRODUCT
         ENGINEERING MANAGEMENT

Chapter 5   Managing Software Product Management   41

         5.1   The Product Concept as a Communications
                  Tool, 41
         5.2   A Top-Down View of Software Product
                  Management, 42
         5.3   Interface Management, 45
         5.4   Setting and Meeting Objectives, 46
         5.5   Personnel Selection and Training, 48

Chapter 6   Managing Software Product Planning   52

         6.1   Types of Plans, 53
         6.2   Plans Decomposition, 56
         6.3   Organizing for the Planning Function, 57
         6.4   Plans for Software Products, 60
         6.5   Pilot Systems, 63
         6.6   Managing Software Product Planning in the
                  Analysis Phase, 64
         6.7   Managing Software Product Planning in the
                  Feasibility Phase, 67
         6.8   Managing Software Product Planning in the
                  Design and Programming Phases, 69
         6.9   Managing Software Product Planning in the
                  Evaluation and Use Phases, 69
         6.10   Planning's Review and Approval
                  Responsibility, 70

Chapter 7   Managing Software Product Development   76

    7.1   Organizing for the Development
           Function, 77
    7.2   Chief Programmer Teams, 79
    7.3   Time and Cost Estimating, 82
    7.4   Project Management, 85
    7.5   Managing Software Product Development
           in the Analysis Phase, 87
    7.6   Managing Software Product Development
           in the Feasibility Phase, 91
    7.7   Managing Software Product Development
           in the Design Phase, 93
    7.8   Managing Software Product Development
           in the Programming Phase, 97
    7.9   Managing Software Product Development
           in the Evaluation Phase, 100
    7.10 Project Termination, 102
    7.11 Development's Review and Approval
           Responsibility, 103

Chapter 8   Managing Software Product Services   105

    8.1   The Definition of Services, 105
    8.2   Organizing for the Services Function, 106
    8.3   Managing Software Product Services in the
           Analysis Phase, 107
    8.4   Managing Software Product Services in the
           Feasibility and Design Phases, 109
    8.5   Managing Software Product Services in the
           Programming Phase, 111
    8.6   Managing Software Product Services in the
           Evaluation Phase, 111
    8.7   Managing Software Product Services in the
           Use Phase, 114
    8.8   Services' Review and Approval
           Responsibility, 117

Chapter 9   Managing Software Product Publications   119

    9.1   Organizing for the Publications Function, 119
    9.2   Standards and Practices, 122

9.3   Managing Software Product Publications in
       the Analysis Phase, 124
9.4   Managing Software Product Publications in
       the Feasibility Phase, 126
9.5   Managing Software Product Publications in
       the Design Phase, 126
9.6   Managing Software Product Publications in
       the Programming Phase, 128
9.7   Managing Software Product Publications in
       the Evaluation Phase, 130
9.8   Managing Software Product Publications in
       the Use Phase, 131
9.9.   Publications' Review and Approval
       Responsibility, 131

Chapter 10   Managing Software Product Test   133

10.1   The State of the Art in Assuring Quality, 133
10.2   Types of Software Product Test, 135
10.3   Organizing for the Test Function, 138
10.4   Managing Software Product Test in the
       Analysis Phase, 142
10.5   Managing Software Product Test in the
       Feasibility Phase, 142
10.6   Managing Software Product Test in the
       Design Phase, 144
10.7   Managing Software Product Test in the
       Programming Phase, 147
10.8   Managing Software Product Test in the
       Evaluation Phase, 149
10.9   Managing Software Product Test in the
       Use Phase, 153
10.10 Test's Review and Approval
       Responsibility, 153

Chapter 11   Managing Software Product Support   155

11.1   Organizing for the Support Function, 156
11.2   Managing Software Product Support in the
       Analysis and Feasibility Phases, 159
11.3   Managing Software Product Support in the
       Design and Programming Phases, 160

11.4 Managing Software Product Support in the
Evaluation Phase, 164
11.5 Managing Software Product Support in the
Use Phase, 166
11.6 Support's Review and Approval
Responsibility, 168

Chapter 12 Managing Software Product Maintenance 170

12.1 Organizing for the Maintenance
Function, 171
12.2 Managing Software Product Maintenance in
the Analysis and Feasibility Phases, 173
12.3 Managing Software Product Maintenance in
the Design Phase, 175
12.4 Managing Software Product Maintenance in
the Programming and Evaluation Phases, 175
12.5 Managing Software Product Maintenance in
the Use Phase, 177
12.6 Maintenance's Review and Approval
Responsibility, 178

PART III TOOLS FOR SOFTWARE PRODUCT
ENGINEERING MANAGEMENT

Chapter 13 Requirements Contract 183

13.1 Requirements Contract Format, 184
13.2 Requirements Contract Contents, 184

Chapter 14 Other Plans 210

14.1 Budget, 210
14.2 Budget Allocation, 216
14.3 Individual Work Plan, 222
14.4 Manpower Summary, 225
14.5 Configurator, 229
14.6 Network Plan, 239
14.7 Schedule Notice, 246

Chapter 15   Specifications   **250**

15.1   External Specification, 251
15.2   Internal Specification, 267
15.3   Maintenance Specification, 279
15.4   Release Specification, 284

Chapter 16   Reports   **290**

16.1   Budget Allocation Summary, 290
16.2   Schedule Notice Summary, 293
16.3   Milestones Due Report, 297
16.4   Project Progress Report, 299
16.5   Trend Charts, 301
16.6   Maintenance Request, 305
16.7   Maintenance Request Summaries, 311

Chapter 17   Procedures   **317**

17.1   Why Procedures Are Needed, 317
17.2   Policies Versus Formats Versus
       Procedures, 319
17.3   Procedures Handbook, 320
17.4   Procedures Versus Standards, 320
17.5   Configuration Management, 321
17.6   Programming Standards, 333
17.7   Publications Standards, 333
17.8   Ownership, 335
17.9   Licenses and Contracts, 338

Chapter 18   Review Boards   **340**

18.1   The Need for Formal Boards, 340
18.2   Interdisciplinary Board, 341
18.3   Technical Review Board, 343
18.4   Enhancement Board, 344

Appendix:
Product Objectives and Requirements for A$K   **347**

References   **367**

Index   **373**

MANAGEMENT METHODOLOGY FOR SOFTWARE PRODUCT ENGINEERING

Chapter

1

About This Book

The title of this book, *Management Methodology for Software Product Engineering,* suggests that it is a book about managing software engineering—which it is. But what is software engineering? The term originated with, or at least was popularized by, the two conferences sponsored by the North Atlantic Treaty Organization in 1968 and 1969 (1). The science of **software engineering** has progressed since then to the point where now, according to Yeh (2), it is an engineering approach to computer software development encompassing programming methodology, software reliability, performance and design evaluations, software project management, and program development tools and standards.

1.1 WHAT THIS BOOK IS AND IS NOT

While this book does not claim to cover all of the above mentioned topics, it does provide planning and control techniques and tools that discourage poor and encourage good programming methodology and software reliability, ensure comprehensive and timely design evaluations, and improve and simplify project management. Thus it does provide an engineering approach to software reliability, design evaluation, and project management. It does not address itself to programming methodology, performance evaluation, or program development tools and standards except to make occasional recommendations and to point to appropriate references for more information.

This is a book about software products and begins with the assumption that there is a difference between a computer program or a system of computer programs and a software product. A **software product** is a computer program plus all of the planning, documentation, testing, publications, training, distribution, maintenance, and control that comprise the aggregate heavy-duty software—software to be installed at more than one site, for use by people not known by the developers, in ways not anticipated by the developers. Many good books and articles have been written about the development of software systems (not software products) for an audience that is the institutional or corporate data processing or information systems department. Such works make one or more of the following assumptions:

- The developer is the user or is at least organizationally related to the user.
- The user specifies his requirements directly to the developer.
- The user participates in design reviews.
- The software must run on only one or on a very limited range of hardware configurations.
- The developer installs the software for the user.
- Problems in using the software are resolved by direct interaction between the user and the developer/maintainer.

Except in the limited case where it is developed on contract for a single customer, none of the above assumptions is likely to apply to a software product. Therefore, this book makes assumptions that are essentially contrary to those above:

- The developer is unacquainted with the user.
- User requirements either are deduced by the developer or are presented to him by an intermediary, such as a marketing support organization.
- Users do not participate in design reviews, except possibly when represented by an intermediary.
- The software must run on a wide range of hardware configurations, in a wide range of software environments.
- Users install the software themselves or have someone other than the developer do it for them.
- Problems are resolved by correspondence, sometimes through an intermediary.

This book, then, is written mainly for an audience interested in providing and maintaining software for multiple and diverse users who are continually at arms' length from the developers and maintainers. All of these assumptions apply to computer manufacturers and software vendors. Although there is close and frequent interaction between providers and users of software systems, institutions and corporations with widely distributed computer processing requirements face many of the distribution, reliability, and control problems addressed in this book. The data processing manager who serves a limited, well-known user community can also benefit from this book. The more of its systems he employs, the better he will serve his users and the easier it will be for him to expand his services, adding one system after another.

This book, then, is about software products. About what else is it or is it not? Well, it is a book on management, not on programming. It is a book on software engineering, but on how to manage it rather than on how to practice it. Again, there are many excellent works on programming, documenting, and testing. There is no attempt to duplicate them here, although several of them are referenced so that you can find information that is consistent with the management systems presented here. Consistency is emphasized because it is a key concept in this book. The book is a collection of management principles, concepts, and practices that have been proven to work somewhere at some time. But it is much more because each idea embodied in the book has been designed or reworked to fit an overall grand design in which all of the tools and techniques reinforce one another. Each can be taken from the book and used by itself, but if they are taken all together they synergistically produce a system far more productive than the sum of the parts.

In a thought-provoking article (3), Nolan hypothesizes a stage theory for managing computer resources. A stage theory premises that a system—economic, sociological, galactic—evolves through distinct stages that can be abstracted into a taxonomy. Such a stage theory appears to apply to the way the production of heavy-duty software is evolving. If Mr. Nolan were to study the methodology of heavy-duty software production as he studied the use of computers, he might derive a chart like the one shown in Figure 1.1. This figure hypothesizes three stages: the Age of Programming, the Age of Software Development, and the Age of Software Engineering. While an observer of the computer industry might conclude that the industry as a whole traversed these stages in the periods indicated in Figure 1.1, he would, observing one heavy-duty software supplier at a time, see each supplier traverse the three stages in sequence no matter when the supplier entered the first stage. Said another way, a stage theory predicts that if the theory applies to a system, it applies to each member of the system. An objective of this book is to shorten

Attribute	Age of Programming	Age of Software Development	Age of Software Engineering
Principal period	1950–1962	1963–1971	1972–?
What is generated	Computer programs	Software	Software products
Generation or selection sequence	Hardware first	Parallel	Software first
Construction method	Monolithic	Modular	Structured
Design process	Bottom-up	Top-down	Top-down
Construction process	Bottom-up	Bottom-up	Top-down
Quality assurance	None	By developer	Independent
Production organization	Individual effort	Project team	Chief programmer team
Maintainability and reliability	Not considered	Afterthought	Designed-in
Maintenance	None	By developer	By specialists
Users	Few, sophisticated	Many, initiated	Very many, uninitiated
Use of development support libraries	None	Occasional	Mandatory
Language used	Assembly	Assembly, higher-level	Higher-level implementation
Design documentation telling			
Why?	None	None	Before construction
What?	Before construction	Before construction	Before construction
How?	None	After construction	During construction
Project control	None	Critical path methods	Critical path methods and management by objectives

Figure 1.1   A possible stage hypothesis for heavy-duty software development.

the time for you, as a supplier of heavy-duty software, to get from the Age of Programming to the Age of Software Engineering by describing and rationalizing many attributes of software engineering. While following this book's methodology is not a necessary condition for reaching the Age of Software Engineering, it is a sufficient condition.

A prominent secondary theme in this book is project management. Organization of the development function into projects is now so widely accepted that it is taken for granted here. The concept of chief programmer teams that became popular in the early 1970s is encompassed, but is not a prerequisite. So, in addition to being a general treatise on software product management, this book is a book on project management.

1.2 WHERE TO LOOK FOR INFORMATION NOT IN THIS BOOK

As noted previously, there are many writings on managing software development and on computer programming. Few on either subject deal with heavy-duty software, but the percentage of new writings on these subjects that does deal with heavy-duty software is increasing. Assuming the trend continues, watch for new titles to appear in the software engineering series of technical publishers. Watch also the proceedings of the National Computer Conferences sponsored by the American Federation of Information Processing Societies, and conferences sponsored by individual societies such as the Association for Computing Machinery and the Institute of Electrical and Electronics Engineers (IEEE). The conferences on software reliability sponsored by IEEE are particularly good. These societies are also setting up special interest groups on software engineering that publish papers and sponsor meetings. Organizations like the American Management Associations are becoming more active in software engineering. Project management and consulting firms in particular, are presenting training courses that emphasize the integration of many of the concepts set forth here. University curricula are still weak on software engineering; but indeed, according to Mills (4), "universities have no experience in even knowing what to teach." Structured programming and reliability engineering are becoming more popular in degree programs, and extension programs now offer courses in management. Teaching management in extension courses probably will continue to predominate, since the time when such training is most useful to the recipient is not while he is pursuing a degree but after he has plied his science for a few years and has made his way into management.

Many of the really valuable references for software product development belong to such producers of software products as IBM, Univac, Computer Sciences, SDC, and Applied Data Research. The list of references in this book is therefore small. But fortunately it is quite good. Emphasis in this list is placed first on primacy of the source and second on ease of retrieving it.

1.3 HOW TO READ THIS BOOK

You can read this book from cover to cover and come away with a thorough understanding of a methodology for software product engineering management. Unless you are concerned with all aspects of software product management, however, you may not want to read the whole book. Part Two is therefore organized by functional discipline so that you can study one function at a time—Planning, Development, Services, Publications, Test, Support, and Maintenance. The book has a vocabulary very much its own, but key terms are printed in bold-face type where they are defined and those definitions are referenced in the index. Each chapter also has pointers to in-depth discussions of related topics to enhance the use of the book for reference.

In addition to breaking down software engineering by function, the book breaks it down by phase. Most authors writing on software development acknowledge phases, but there is yet no standard for phase naming nor even for the number of phases (5). In this book there are six phases: Analysis, Feasibility, Design, Programming, Evaluation, and Use. If you read Part Two from beginning to end, you will be introduced to the role of each function in each phase, in the natural order of the phases. If you are particularly interested in one phase at a time, you will find subheadings in each chapter dealing with each phase. Thus, for reference, you can reread the subsections from each chapter dealing with each phase.

Another organizational attribute of the book is the division between techniques and tools. Part Two describes the techniques employed by the functions to fulfill their roles in each phase; Part Three describes the management tools they use. You may find Part Three particularly useful in establishing or revising your systems and procedures.

Two common threads are woven through the book to make it as readable as possible. These threads are a fictitious company and a fictitious product that appear again and again as illustrative examples. They both demonstrate the self-consistency of the techniques and tools presented, and provide a familiar base of reference as you move from topic to topic.

The easiest way to read the book is to read all of Part One first. Chapter 2 in Part One introduces the key concepts of product, life cycle, phase, function, external design, and internal design. Chapters 3 and 4 introduce the sample company and the sample product to establish a context for all future references to them. After reading Part One, select chapters from Part Two for reading in the order of greatest interest to you. If you read them in the order of presentation, you will read about each function in the most probable order of its primary involvement in a product's life cycle. You can comfortably branch to a section of Part Three from Part Two when a new tool is introduced. Otherwise, use Part Three primarily for reference. Part Three is followed by an appendix containing an example of a complete product master plan, called a requirements contract.

1.4 HOW TO APPLY THIS BOOK

Having read this far you have probably discovered that you have a need either to import or to export heavy-duty software. Quite possibly it was never before perceived as such. A university is a good example of an organization that imports heavy-duty software. Aware that computer services are too vital in their day-to-day operations many universities no longer look to their computer science department to provide those services as a byproduct of their experimentation. They are realizing that they need stable, reliable facilities and that to get them they must employ professional management, proven hardware, and heavy-duty software. You may observe that heavy-duty software is being built by your organization, either for its own consumption or for export, but that there is something less than a satisfactory provision for it in your milieu. This is particularly common in smaller organizations where the ability to communicate informally contributes to a too-relaxed attitude toward documentation, coordination, procedures—all of that "red tape" which the founders of your organization may have hoped to leave behind when they went into business for themselves. If your organization is small or if you are in that awkward transition state when your organization is getting so large that informal communication is no longer effective, this book may be just what you need to establish a software product development methodology that will produce satisfactory results, no matter how large you grow. Finally, if you are in a very large or very old organization, there may indeed be too much structure, too many controls, too much reporting. It may not be able to produce software products with the speed or technical soundness necessary to achieve desired results. Software product organizations do exist that are encumbered by too many procedures, by an inability to waive inappropriate procedures, or by other red tape. Here again, this book has something to offer.

This book is written with many reminders that some of its features are optional or adaptable. On the other hand, the book stresses the reasons for doing some things in a specific way where all known alternatives seem inferior. You will find many techniques and tools for your use. Assuming you are not now using all of them, where should you begin or in what order should you adopt them? There is no one answer, but here are a few tips.

If you begin by applying hierarchical decomposition to your plans and to your product designs, many of the other concepts will readily fall into place. The keystone of a good structure is a master plan, a development contract that clearly establishes, before a project starts, why you should undertake the project, what the project entails, and how it will be executed. You will find such a contract, called a requirements contract, described and referenced throughout this book. You will find a complete example of one in the Appendix. You should introduce it into your methodology before anything else.

A good product requires a good design and a good design demands good documentation so that the design can be understood and followed as product development proceeds. In the case where many people must understand and communicate a heavy-duty software design, that design is only as good as its documentation. Thus, to be a successful supplier of software products you must have documents that cover all aspects of development. Once you have instituted the requirements contract concept, make sure your product specifications meet the needs of the several functions who depend on them, namely, Development, Test, Publications, etc. And they will if you next implement the external specifications concept described in this book.

A document is useful only if it is current and available. This requires configuration management. Implement the identification, revision control, cataloging, and distribution control techniques presented in this book at the earliest possible time. If you are an advocate of structured programming, you probably recall that one element of configuration management, the development support librarian (6), is the first technique to implement if you want to use chief programmer teams.

There are very good reasons for separating from one another some of the functions that contribute to a successful product. By the time you have the above techniques and tools working, you will definitely be ready to make this separation. Firstly, assure that the Test Function is independent from and therefore cannot be overruled by Development. Secondly, separate out Services so that all other functions can draw upon them equally, with no preference given to any one function. Organize Planning, Support, Documentation, and Maintenance however they can best meet your needs. Do not hesitate to reorganize them as your needs change. Thus prepared, enter the Age of Software Engineering and practice its management as it should be and is being practiced, in whole or in part, by successful managers.

Part One
BACKGROUND

Chapter

2

Software as a Product

Sound principles for managing software products follow rather naturally from a full acceptance of the idea that software should be treated like any other product. Indeed, the principles expounded in this book apply in the main to the management of many high-technology products.

But surely, you may argue, not all software should be subjected to the rigorous controls of planning, documenting, designing, and testing required for other products. What about the accountant who codes a program to prepare a one-of-a-kind report from the monthly accounts receivable data base? Or what about the statistician who writes a program to search for an obscure repetitive pattern in a data stream or time series? Should these pieces of software be treated as products? Clearly they should not.

The type of software that is best managed like a product is **heavy-duty software**; that is, software that will be replicated many times and installed at many different sites; software that will be used by many different people in different ways, and in ways not anticipated by the developers; software whose users won't have access to the developers. The clearest examples are most, if not all, systems software, and applications software that is independently licensed for a fee.

Once you have fully accepted the idea that heavy-duty software is a product, it seems so simple and natural that you wonder how it was overlooked for so long. It wasn't until the mid-1960s that the idea really began to take hold. Perhaps one reason is that software has no unique physical embodiment. You cannot touch, smell, or weigh it. It seems ethereal. Another reason may be that programming is easily learned, and a good student can build his own software after a four-week programming course. It seems too easy. A third related reason may be that nearly all of the early software developers were programmers who came from disciplines such as mathematics, and few came from engineering disciplines that teach the product concept.

Unbundling—the separate pricing of hardware, software, and services—which began around 1970, more than anything else hardened the concept of software as a product. Now the really heavy-duty software is scrutinized for its return on investment and planned carefully to keep costs within line of realizable profits. Specifications are reviewed more carefully with regard to customer needs. After all, if you pay for what you get, you can afford to be more choosey!

Judging from the sales of software packages, software products are here to stay. According to International Computer Programs, Inc. (7), three software packages had each achieved sales of at least $20 million as of early 1977. At least 227 packages had reached sales of $1 million and three products had been installed at 3000 or more sites!

2.1   THE PRODUCT CONCEPT

Products do not just happen. They are planned and designed to meet certain specifications and are built because there has been management recognition of needs that can profitably be fulfilled by them.

Whatever else a product may be, it is something that performs a useful function for someone. Also many copies of it can be made, manufactured, or replicated so that there is normally a large base of users or clients for the product. Above all it is supported—with promotion, training, and maintenance.

One of the important attributes of a product is that it has very concrete external specifications. Documentation is usually supplied with the product that describes in detail the functions that it performs and tells you how to use it to perform the desired functions.

Frequently a product is part of a system of products and must be assembled and installed either by the end user or by a specialist representing the supplier. Additional documentation is normally supplied to assist in this installation.

Training may accompany a product if it is very new, very different from other products, or quite intricate to operate. Training may be carried out through self-instruction, or in the case of more complex products, through formal classroom instruction arranged by the supplier. The training may cover the same two topics that the documentation cited above covers: how to install the product and how to use the product.

This documentation and training cover the external features of the product. Other documentation and training cover features internal to the product: how it works, how it was built, what its parts are. For manufactured products this includes manufacturing drawings and specifications, bills of materials, and sources of supply for parts and raw materials. For software it includes specifications, listings, program and data generators, and again, bills of materials. More internal documentation is needed for maintenance of the product. This includes enough of the principles of operation of the product to satisfy the needs of the person performing maintenance. It includes specific instructions for troubleshooting and for repairing common malfunctions. During the useful life of a product the user must also have access to maintenance service or be prepared to maintain the product himself.

For a product that is expected to have a long and useful life, the documentation may also include enough internal description of its operation to permit modification of the product, either by the end user himself or by his technical agent. The automotive market is a prime example of this product attribute. Auto enthusiasts need considerable internal documentation to make performance enhancements or to exchange engines. Such documentation is used to tailor or customize the product for a unique use. It also is used to enhance or upgrade the product when design changes come about through experience gained in using the product or when new features are developed by the manufacturer. An example of this occurs in the aircraft industry: worn-out engines often are replaced with new designs.

Quality control is an important product attribute. The product must behave reliably and predictably as described in the documentation, and identical copies of the product must behave in exactly the same way.

In most respects software products are similar to other computer products. But there is one significant difference between them: a software product is easy to manufacture or replicate. As a result the cost and lead time of manufacturing software are negligible in the context of overall computer use.

An analogy may explain why many managers in the computer industry still fail to see software as a product. They regard software as a coat of paint on the hardware. What they fail to see is that the hardware to which that paint is applied is like a street sign. It is useless without that coat of paint! Furthermore, the paint on that street sign must be durable, highly visible, in sharply contrasting colors, and perhaps reflective. The cost of the paint applied to the sign is low, the time necessary to apply it is short, and it can be changed easily. But what about the research and development that made the paint durable and visible and made the graphics of the sign meaningful? The same paint and graphics applied to a piece of cardboard convey most of the sign's utility without any metal. The intrinsic value of the sign, therefore, is not in the hardware at all, but in the software! So, too, with computers.

2.2 THE LIFE CYCLE OF A SOFTWARE PRODUCT

Like a living organism, a product has a life cycle. It begins at birth (or perhaps at conception) and ends with death or disposal. This notion has been well developed and has proven to be quite useful in product management. You can distinguish several phases of a product's existence during its life cycle. These may overlap, even as the child-hood phase of a person overlaps the youth phase. And as this example suggests, the beginning and end of a phase cannot be pinpointed precisely in time.

What is the life cycle of a software product and what are its phases? There is not as much difference of opinion on this subject as you might think. Benjamin (5) summarizes several phase decompositions and you can surely recall others that are similar. There are six distinct phases shown in Figure 2.1 that appear again and again throughout this book. Whether this particular six-partition decomposition is better than others is not a key issue: what is important is recognizing that phases exist and organizing your thinking to account for them.

The **Analysis Phase** begins when the need for a product is acknowledged by your management. This acknowledgment is usually accompanied by an intent, perhaps tentative or provisional, to develop the product. It might be included in a plan, for example. In the Analysis Phase your attention and energy are focused on under-standing the role the proposed product would play. The work that takes place in this phase is the planning and coordinating needed to prepare a formal written set of requirements for the product. The phase ends when you have crystallized requirements to the point where they can be reviewed, modified as necessary, and approved by the management personnel responsible. The Analysis Phase generally takes 4 to 10 weeks.

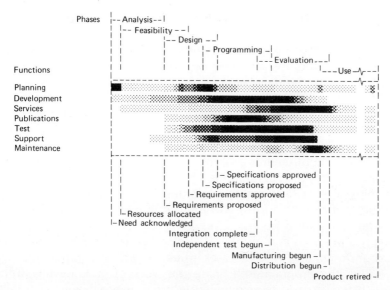

Figure 2.1   The phase-function matrix.

The **Feasibility Phase** is the technical part of the Analysis Phase. It begins when your management intent has firmed to the point where you authorize and initiate a project and allocate resources (manpower) to it. The work involved is a study of the proposed product to develop enough understanding to determine a reasonable estimate of feasibility. You may be in the habit of thinking of a feasibility study as a purely technical analysis used to determine if the proposed activity can be carried out; that is, to determine if the proposed product can be developed. But it goes beyond that. There is operational feasibility: will the product work well in practice, performing its intended function in an expeditious manner? There is economic feasibility: can it be developed for a reasonable cost? How much? Will it be a cost-effective tool when it finally gets into the hands of the ultimate user? There is marketing feasibility: will it be attractive, salable, installable, and serviceable; and can it easily be explained and taught? These and other similar questions you address in the Feasibility Phase, primarily during the review of the requirements mentioned above.

The Feasibility Phase ends when the requirements are approved, generally 1 to 10 weeks after the end of the Analysis Phase. Frequently your conclusion at this time is to stop further development.

The **Design Phase** usually starts early in the Feasibility Phase, as soon as you have committed some provisional objectives to paper. You perform as much early design prior to completion of the Feasibility Phase as you require to confirm probable feasibility of the proposed objectives and to restate them firmly as requirements.

When your requirements are approved, the Design Phase is in high gear. You record your design in a formal specification for the product. The Design Phase ends when that specification has been formally approved. The Design Phase may be completed within a week of the approval of requirements or it may continue for 10 weeks or longer.

You initiate the **Programming Phase** as early in the Design Phase as meaningful specifications for portions of the product are available, but not prior to the approval of the requirements. This overlapping of Programming and Design saves total development time, which is usually a precious commodity. It also serves as a check on the validity of your design and in some cases influences key design decisions.

During the Programming Phase the work of building the product takes place. It consists of detailed internal designing of the software, as well as flow-charting, documenting, coding, and debugging it. The Programming Phase is complete when the developers have finished documenting, debugging, and integrating and have successfully handed the resulting software to an independent unit for evaluation.

The Programming Phase generally takes from 2 to 10 months to complete. If you anticipate that it will take a year or longer, then you may have tried to package more software into one product than is wise. You may be able to improve the manageability of the product if you decompose it into a set of several smaller products.

The **Evaluation Phase** of the product's life cycle is a buffer zone between the start of integrated testing and the beginning of live use of the product. In the Evaluation Phase you subject your product to rigorous testing by a group of people other than the developers. This is done to ensure that the product meets requirements and specifications; that it performs as it should in a user environment; that all the necessary documentation is available, accurately and completely describing the software; that the product can be installed using the installation instructions; and that it is adequately free of defects. The phase begins as soon as all components are in place and running. It ends when the test organization certifies that your product has passed all tests and is ready for live use. The Evaluation Phase generally lasts as long as the Programming Phase, but structured programming techniques may reduce it to as little as a third of the Programming Phase (see Figure 2.2).

Traditional Programming System Development Life Cycle:

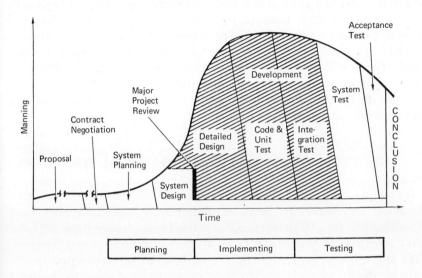

Structured Programming (Top Down) System Development Life Cycle:

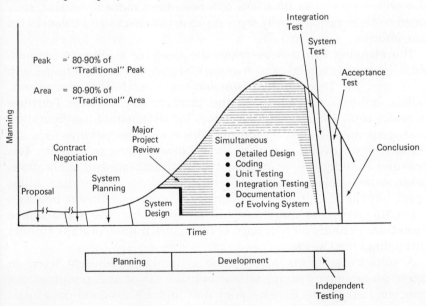

Figure 2.2 Phase length differences in traditional and structured programming system development life cycles. (Reprinted, by permission, from (8), pp. 216–217.)

The **Use Phase** begins when your product enters the distribution system and generally lasts two to six years. This is the time during which the product is in active and productive use. Your activities in the Use Phase include training, installation, tuning, maintenance, and possibly product enhancement. The phase ends when your product is retired and the above activities stop. Note, however, that your product may still be in use by someone long after the Use Phase as herein defined is completed, because that someone can productively use the product even without your training, installation, tuning, maintenance, and enhancement.

2.3 LIFE CYCLE PHASES AND ORGANIZATIONAL FUNCTIONS

Refer again to Figure 2.1. The organizational functions listed there are: Planning, Development, Services, Publications, Test, Support, and Maintenance. In a large organization developing heavy-duty software you can expect to find organizational units with these or similar titles. They represent ongoing functions that have to be performed for all software products, and it makes good organizational sense to charter a unit to perform each unique function, since each type of activity and the skills required to do it are different. Even more important, they need to be organizationally separate to act as checks and balances for one another.

The **Planning Function** identifies the need for a software product, establishes its feasibility, and monitors its progress through to the end of its use. The **Development Function** specifies, designs, documents, builds, debugs, and integrates the product. The **Services Function** provides tools and computing services for all functions, configuration management, distribution, and miscellaneous administrative support. **Publications** provides user manuals and other reference material. **Test** provides an independent evaluation of both software and publications prior to their release to users. **Support** promotes the product, trains users, installs the product, and provides continual liaison between other functions and users. Last but far from least, the **Maintenance Function** provides error correction and minor enhancements throughout the Use Phase.

A software products organization is markedly different from an open programming shop, where virtually all of the resources are concentrated in the development unit and are assigned on a rotational basis to client programming projects. In such a circumstance, however, the software being developed is not heavy-duty as defined in this methodology. If you were to impose these other functions in such a situation you would probably find your clients resenting them as unnecessary, costly, and time-consuming red tape. And your clients would most likely be correct.

In Part Two of this book there are a number of chapters devoted to techniques of software product management. Each chapter deals with the management of one of the organizational functions and presents techniques peculiar to managing that particular function. Each covers all relevant phases of the product life cycle, with emphasis on particular phases varying from chapter to chapter, depending on how much the given function is involved with the product in each phase. The shading in Figure 2.1 suggests the degree of involvement of each function in each of the phases.

2.4   EXTERNAL DESIGN AND INTERNAL DESIGN

One of the life cycle phases is called the Design Phase. It might well have been called the External Design Phase to emphasize the fact that only the external attributes of the design—what the product is—are being fixed and recorded in the product specification. All interfaces with other products are specified: calling sequences and parameters, tables and arrays, entries and exits, input and output files, and functions performed. Only what is needed to clarify the external design is said about internal design.

Internal design specifies how the product is to function. Modules, subprograms, overlay structures, dynamic tables, flow charts, and decision tables are the stuff of internal design. Good internal design techniques, and good techniques for the management of the internal design process comprise the programming methodology part of software engineering, a subject matter complete unto itself. Perhaps it is better to say that they comprise several subject matters complete unto themselves, for what is good design practice in one type of software (accounting programs, for example) will be inappropriate for other types of software (compilers, say). In any case, the subject is highly technical, is beyond the scope of this book, and is covered by many other excellent writings.

Internal design is an activity of the Development Function and is performed in the Programming Phase. Good internal design techniques and good techniques for the management of the internal design process are essential to the management of the Development Function. Their brief treatment in this book should not suggest otherwise to you.

2.5 HIERARCHICAL DECOMPOSITION

As you read this book you will continually encounter the term **hierarchical decomposition**, meaning the subdivision of a complex topic into several more manageable, smaller subtopics, followed by the further subdivision of each subtopic until every necessary detail is expressed in a comprehensible context. The concept of hierarchical decomposition is so innate we often fail to realize how often it occurs. It derives from the human need to deal with a manageable number of discrete stimuli and to "chunk" data together until the number of discrete items to be dealt with at once is about seven (9). This same need for cognitive convenience is expressed in the limit of a person's management span of control which is discussed in Chapter 7. Indeed, the noted psychologist Miller has suggested that "a hierarchical structure is the basic form of organization in human problem-solving" (10).

A rigid hierarchical decomposition follows several rules. First, a plan or design is complete at every level in the hierarchy; that is, complete in the sense of covering all aspects at the same level of detail. Secondly, at any level in the hierarchy, each subdivision fully encompases a single function or topic at the same level of detail. For example, if there are two functions definable at level four and only one of them can sensibly be further decomposed to a fifth, bottom level, then the other fourth-level function should be described at the level of detail appropriate to the fifth level.

Some of the forms of hierarchical decomposition you will encounter are top-down management (Chapter 5), plans decomposition (Chapter 6), design decomposition (Chapter 7), and the structuring of product plans and specifications (particularly Chapter 13 and Sections 15.1–15.3). You have probably seen several formal hierarchical decompositions elsewhere: stepwise refinement (11), levels of abstraction (12), hierarchy of documentation (13), top-down programming (14), modular decomposition (15), composite design (16), and structured design (17). Alexander offers a particularly stimulating presentation in his *Notes on the Synthesis of Form* (18). In this little gem of a book he presents a philosophical discussion of design analysis and synthesis followed by a mathematical technique for the decomposition of a set of constraints into subsets such that their interactions are minimized. His work and the works of Böhm (19), Hoare (20), Mills (21), and others as yet unpublished are making major contributions to software engineering by quantifying software design and proof of correctness.

If as you read this book you begin to feel there are natural laws underlying the selection, arrangement, and adaptation of management tools and techniques in software engineering, it is because there are and we are only just beginning to discover, analyze, and obey them. In particular, as we understand hierarchical decomposition better, much of what is presented in this book as the result of applied intuition and natural selection may one day be restated as manifestations of natural laws. Remember, software engineering is truly in its infancy, having been recognized as a discipline unto itself only since about 1968 (1).

2.6 DEVELOPMENT TOOLS AND PRODUCT END ITEMS

Another view of the development process may help you see the many facets of a software product. Figure 2.3 shows several of the key tools used to develop a software product and some of the end items that comprise the product. Elements are located in the figure according to the functions primarily responsible for them and according to the times in a product's life cycle when they come into being. Tools are enclosed by circles; end items are enclosed by rectangles. Lines connecting elements represent primary flows of information. By stretching your imagination, you should be able to overlay Figures 2.1 and 2.3 (the juxtaposition of the functions in Figure 2.3 is different from that in Figure 2.1 only to make the information flow lines easy to follow).

The nomenclature used in Figure 2.3 is used throughout this book. Most of the tools referenced are specific examples of generic tools you need. Since it is much easier to deal with specifics than generics, and since the specifics used here have all proven themselves over several years of use in several environments, you should find them easy to understand and to apply if you wish to do so.

Figure 2.3 should be read from left to right, consistent with the passing of time. Figure 2.3 begins with a **product line plan** that proposes a system solution to a complex user need or a complex of user needs. It may well include hardware as well as software. The first recording of the need for a specific product marks the beginning of the Analysis Phase. Such a product line plan is likely to be the first recording. Product line plans often spawn several **product plans**, each of which deals in greater detail with a single product than does the product line plan. The ultimate affirmation of a product line or product plan occurs when it is restated in a **budget** which encumbers resources to fulfill

24

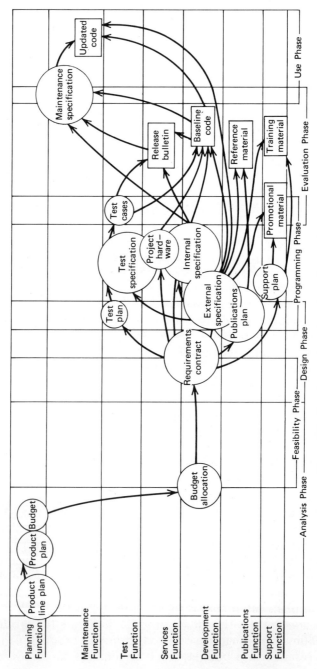

Figure 2.3 Development tools and product end items.

the plan. All of these tools are used primarily by the Planning Function.

After a budget is approved, resources are committed through a budget allocation to initiate the Feasibility Phase. The first activity of this phase is to determine the requirements and objectives of a product—the reasons *why* it should be built—and to record them in a **requirements contract**. In preparing and reviewing a requirements contract enough analysis is performed to affirm feasibility. Approval of a requirements contract ends the Feasibility Phase. It also gives rise to several other activities: production of publications, test, and support plans. In addition it generates external and internal specifications of design. The approval of an **external specification**, which is a complete and rigorous statement of *what* a product is, completely constrains the product's design and thus ends the Design Phase.

Product development activity peaks in the Programming Phase when test plans are expanded into test specifications. The internal design is completely recorded in an **internal specification** that tells *how* the product is built, a support plan is generated, and hardware resources are made available. While the Development Function transforms the external and internal design into **baseline code**, the initial embodiment of a product, the Test Function transforms its test specification into test cases; the Publications Function generates reference material; and the Support Function generates promotional and training material. These latter activities run from the second half of the Programming Phase through most of the Evaluation Phase. At the very end of the Evaluation Phase, Services prepares an installation guide called a **release bulletin** and Maintenance pulls together into a maintenance specification everything it will need in the future. The Use Phase begins when a product is declared ready for release to its users. What remains after that in Figure 2.3 is the occasional production of updated code to correct errors found by users and to keep the product in tune with its environment.

Figure 2.3 and this verbal summary of it are a greatly simplified overview of the software product engineering process. The chapters that follow cover everything above in suitable detail and fill in the many gaps that are deliberately left open here.

Chapter

3

The Sample Company: The ABC Corporation

Many of the ideas in this book are illustrated and made concrete through the use of a specific fictitious software product, described in detail in the next chapter, and through the use of a specific, though also fictitious, company. The company serves as a concrete environment in which the product is born, developed, used, and eventually retired so that you can follow the product through its life cycle.

The sample company could have been a major industrial corporation that uses computers extensively, and hence would be in the business of making and using heavy-duty software products for its own in-house computers. It might have been a large software house or a large systems house; or a small one, for that matter. The concepts you find in this book apply equally well to all. They apply especially well to a computer manufacturer, such as the sample company, the ABC Corporation.

3.1 HISTORY AND MARKETS OF ABC

During the early days of computing, the company was known as the Allied Business Computing Machines Company, and its products became established and referred to as ABC Machines. Later the company name was changed to The ABC Corporation to capitalize on the familiar expression "ABC Machines."

The company has some penetration in most markets where computers are sold and has several product lines to serve these markets. During the past decade corporate policy has been to concentrate on accounting and commercial data processing for medium-size industrial firms. The company has been successful in increasing its share of this market by aggressive marketing combined with vigorous, properly focused product development. The company is respected for its growth in this market, and now enjoys a large and loyal customer base therein.

The computer product line sold primarily in this market is the ABC Stella series. It has a good performance record, and after years of evolutionary upgrading, is now reasonably mature. Old hardware components have been replaced with new ones, new peripherals have been added to the line, and old software products are being replaced with new higher performing ones. The company is now enhancing its support of communications, with the goal to make that support invisible to user applications software.

Those in the top management of the company believe that the computer business will gradually become a service business, and that the selling of services in large computer networks will be the sector of largest growth in the computer business, particularly for the market area where it is doing best, medium-size industrial firms. To strengthen its thrust in the services sector it has established the ABC Services Company. It is a self-contained company selling a variety of computing services—using, of course, ABC Stella machines in several configurations.

3.2 ORGANIZATION OF THE ABC CORPORATION

Within the ABC Corporation, it is the task of the ABC Computers Company to develop, build, and sell computer systems world-wide. It is a profit center, and the major contributor of both sales and profits to the family of companies affiliated with the ABC Corporation. It is constrained by general policy guidance from the parent ABC Corporation, particularly with regard to its relations with sister companies, but it is otherwise free to pursue new markets.

The ABC Services Company sells services: over-the-counter batch computing with Stella 100s in major United States and European cities; remote batch computing on the same machines, via the very successful ABC Telcoscope 33 remote batch terminal installed at customer sites; time-sharing computing in two major cities on the Stella 100 computer, via ABC Telcoscope 43 conversational terminals; and totally packaged applications services, both remote and local, notably in accounting. It buys its computer products from the ABC Computers Company, in line with corporate policy. It supplies funding to the ABC Computers Company for the development of special computer products it needs in the pursuit of its mission.

Relations between Computers and Services have at times been strained due to the fact that Services is at the mercy of Computers for its major products. In the view of the management of Services, Computers has been unresponsive on occasion to the needs of Services. A case in point was the early Telcoscope 42 conversational terminal, which was not compatible with other industry terminals in use by clients of the Services Company. The problem was compounded because the terminal was unreliable and expensive to acquire (all terminals are currently manufactured for ABC Computers by another company). The Research Division was called in by corporate management and they helped the development engineers in the Computers Company draw up specifications for a new version of Telcoscope, the Model 43, which was acceptable to Services and turned out to be a winner for Computers as well.

Figure 3.1 shows the organizational relations described above and also indicates the main tasks of each organization. The other divisions and companies of the ABC Corporation are not described here because they do not play a role in the development of software products. One other observation worth making about the corporation is that it is not market centered. **Market centered** (22) means organized to best meet customer needs, as contrasted to functional needs of the corporation. ABC is **product centered**, that is, organized around products (computers, services, etc.). This is beginning to hamper both ABC Computers and ABC Services in trying to meet competition with separate marketing forces. Some of the conflicts

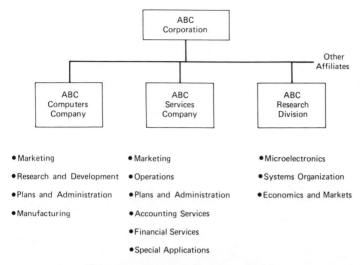

Figure 3.1   Corporate structure of ABC.

between these two companies discussed in this book stem from the product centered orientation of the parent corporation.

3.3   ORGANIZATION OF THE ABC COMPUTERS COMPANY

Figure 3.2 illustrates the divisional architecture of the ABC Computers Company. At the top of their organization chart is the Office of the President composed of several vice presidents who make policy and strategy decisions as a committee, but who each have functional areas of responsibility where they are nearly autonomous. Reporting to the Office of the President are four divisions that perform the day-to-day work of the company: Marketing, Research and Development, Plans and Administration, and Manufacturing.

ABC Computers is aware of the problems of being product centered in a market place that is dominated by market centered companies, and has set up sales based on industrial rather than on geographical lines. Other marketing functions shown in Figure 3.2 are services to all of the sales organizations.

Research and Development is organized primarily according to the type of product: computers and interface electronics in the Hardware Products Department; peripheral equipment devices and terminal

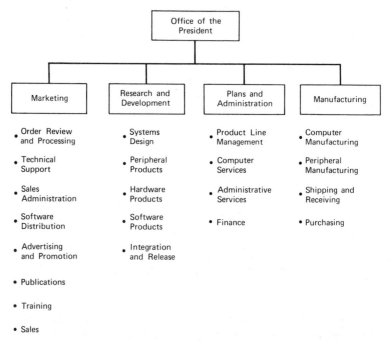

Figure 3.2 Divisions of ABC Computers Company.

devices in the Peripheral Products Department; and software and firmware in the Software Products Department. Systems design, product integration, and product release are functions provided for all types of products.

Plans and Administration is a collection of staff functions for the company. Product Line Management is the seat of division-level planning and budgeting. Finance stewards the sources and sinks of capital within the company, and Administrative Services stewards other essential resources: personnel, facilities, insurance, employee benefits, communications, transportation, etc. Computer Services started as a data processing subfunction of Finance, but when Administrative Services became a bigger user, a separate function was established. After a few years during which costly computers and computer services were being acquired by other operations, all closed-shop computing was centralized in Computer Services, including coordination of outside services.

Manufacturing, like Research and Development, is divided along product lines. This is partly historical and partly functional: computer manufacturing is almost purely fabrication, assembly, and packaging of electronics; peripheral manufacturing requires additional skills to deal with complex electromechanical devices like disc files and line printers. Two services used by the entire company are included in Manufacturing because they are the dominant user: purchasing, and shipping and receiving.

3.4 ORGANIZATION OF RESEARCH AND DEVELOPMENT

Look deeper into ABC in Figure 3.3 to see how Research and Development is organized. Functional specifications for new products and systems of products enter the division through the Systems Design Department where feasibility studies and performance analyses are made and where make-or-buy decisions are managed.

Products, and systems of products, leave Research and Development via the Integration and Release Department, which provides quality control and documentation services for the division. Included are standards and procedures, the document control subfunction of configuration management, and the preparation of publications such as reference and maintenance manuals. Only the writing and editing of engineering publications is done here. Production and printing are done by Marketing to assure consistency of presentation and to take advantage of economies of scale. Quality assurance includes monitoring development to assure adherence to standards and accepted

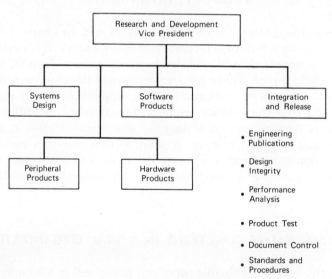

Figure 3.3 The Research and Development Division of ABC Computers Company.

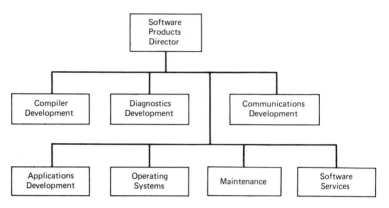

Figure 3.4   The Software Products Department of ABC Computers Company.

design and construction practices, collectively called design integrity; and product test, which provides verification of adherence to design specifications independent of development. The three remaining departments each deal with a type of product, as mentioned in the previous section.

3.5   ORGANIZATION OF THE SOFTWARE PRODUCTS DEPARTMENT

Take a still deeper look into the structure of ABC in Figure 3.4, to see how the Software Products Department is organized. This department reflects the organizational philosophy of its parent division, subdivision by product type. There are five functional development units for compilers, diagnostics, communications, applications, and operating systems. To free these units for new development, maintenance of products is turned over to a separate maintenance unit as soon as possible after product release. A services unit provides liaison with division, company, and corporate services and provides services peculiar to software development, like an open-shop development laboratory.

3.6   STEREOTYPE FUNCTIONS IN A REAL ORGANIZATION

How do the seven stereotypic functions presented in Chapter 2 relate to the ABC Corporation? Look at them one by one.

Planning, as it relates to software development, permeates the structure of ABC. Corporate headquarters provides each division with a mission and a budget. Within ABC Computers, Product Line Management provides strategy and Systems Design supplies tactics. ABC Computers is a strong proponent of matrix organization, and Systems Design provides several matrix program managers. Software Services takes charge of plans management to bring it all together for the Director of Software Products, who otherwise might be bewildered.

Development is entirely contained in the five development units of the Software Products Department, except for a very small amount of microcode developed in the Peripheral Products and Hardware Products departments.

Services is the most heterogeneous function, and as you might expect, it is the most widely dispersed within ABC. Services includes provision of functions specific to software product development and liaison with needed functions that are not specific. At ABC, non-specific services are provided by Computer Services and Administrative Services. Software distribution is handled by Marketing; document control and standards and procedures, by Integration and Release; and all others, including liaison, by Software Services.

Publications writing and editing is provided by Integration and Release, while production and printing are handled by Marketing. Test is handled entirely by Integration and Release; Support, entirely by Marketing.

You may have thought that these functions would be organized into one department, and that it would be the Software Products Department. It might well be so in some companies. In fact it was so at ABC in the early 1960s, but as the company evolved, so did the concept of software as a product, and many of these functions were spun off and placed with similar functions from other product development organizations. This was an appropriate organizational response to the need to build heavy-duty software. For example, in 1967 a combined Product Test Function was organized into a separate department to provide quality assurance for hardware and software. A year later peripherals were added, and in 1970 it became the present Integration and Release Department with the addition of full responsibility for product handoff from Research and Development. The net result of this organizational structure is that software products are treated in every major respect just like other products, with the notable exceptions of Manufacturing and Distribution.

Chapter

4

The
Sample
Product:
A$K

By becoming familiar with one product—how it is born, how it is developed, and how it may be retired—you should be able to see how naturally the management concepts and tools offered in this book fit the life cycle of a product. You will be able to anticipate what is coming next as you accompany this sample product through its life, and you can gain additional insight into the problems posed by comparing your solutions with those offered by this book.

4.1 HOW THE PRODUCT CAME TO BE

Late in 1976 a Financial Services Task Force of ABC Services Company, which included representation from the planning office of its corporate parent, concluded that the company should offer an interactive, remote access financial analysis system to the financial community. The host computer should be a large configuration of the top-of-the-line Stella 100 computer, the major product of ABC Computers Company. The task force recommended offering the system initially only to the New York City financial community, and based on experience there, setting up several processing centers throughout the United

States over a period of five years. They estimated that the service could be developed in six months; be on the air in New York before the end of 1977; and by the end of the fifth year of operation (1982), be flourishing and ready for upgrading to the Galaxie computer line. The service was expected to provide feedback on terminal design to the Research and Development Division of ABC Computers Company and thus contribute substantially to determining whether or not the company should enter the terminal market rather than continue marketing terminals from another manufacturer.

Early in 1977, the ABC Services Company developed a Business Plan for Financial Services. By the middle of the year a Preliminary Plan was circulated for review by the appropriate management throughout ABC Corporation.

The plan called for taking an established financial database, DATABA$E, and coupling it with a powerful on-line information retrieval service. DATABA$E was first introduced in 1973 as a collection of fundamental data for all New York Stock Exchange industrials. Data for 50 common financial parameters (such as price, dividends per share, net income, inventories, and gross plant) were included for 20 years' worth of annual, quarterly, or monthly statistics. The original service was offered as a set of magnetic tapes with periodic tape updates and utility programs for use by the customer on his own computer, and as the same data accessed through a collection of proprietary batch programs at ABC Service Centers, on their ABC computers. In 1976, ABC Services had begun offering updates via data communication, had added several parameters to the data base, and had added utilities to the scope of the service. DATABA$E was highly profitable and plans were approved to add insurance companies and banks to it.

The information retrieval software called for by the Business Plan for Financial Services was called A$K. The interactive service coupling A$K with DATABA$E was called A$K DATABA$E.

The plan took longer than expected to draft, and by the time it was circulated, it no longer seemed possible to market the service before the end of the year if normal funding and approval procedures were followed. The Software Products Department of ABC Computers Company was funded by ABC Services Company to perform a feasibility study, to develop objectives and requirements for A$K, and to provide firm cost and schedule estimates for completion of the product. ABC Services thus hoped to recover development time by overlapping the start of A$K design with corporate approval of their Business Plan.

4.2   THE NEED FOR A$K: WHAT IT IS

A$K is a logical extension of DATABA$E service that embodies the dominant philosophy of ABC Corporation: bring the computer and the ultimate user together via service with as few intermediaries as possible. **A$K** allows a financial analyst—working for a stock broker, bank, insurance company, trust fund, or even for himself—to use a powerful computer to manipulate a massive data base in a language with which he is comfortable. No training or even familiarity with computers is a prerequisite for using A$K DATABA$E. Human engineering studies by the Research Division of ABC Corporation predicted and market studies by ABC Services Company confirmed that to be successful, A$K DATABA$E should conceal the computer at its heart.

Thus the language, syntax, operators, and data structure of A$K were designed to appeal to an economist rather than a logician. The user may, while sitting at a terminal in his office, compare and contrast the fundamental performance of companies or industries either in DATABA$E or as defined by him. A typical query for A$K might be:

> I think a proper investment for my client should be based on an increase over at least the past five years of the sum of the net income and the fixed charges divided by the sum of the long-term debt, the preferred stock value, and the value of the common equity. Only companies not involved in defense contracting are eligible. Show me all companies satisfying these criteria and the value of the screening expression for each, for each quarter of the past two years.

In addition to providing the above tool for analysts, A$K provides tools for computer operators to maintain both A$K and user extensions to DATABA$E.

4.3   A$K AS HEAVY-DUTY SOFTWARE

The purpose of this book, as you will recall, is to define an approach for developing software products, or heavy-duty software. A$K is such an item. It is designed for a long period of use (five years) by persons unfamiliar with the product's internal operation (financial analysts). It has a very high reliability requirement because its users will not tolerate an unforgiving, unresponsive tool. A$K is produced by one company for use by another, necessitating formal, at least quasi-contractual procedures to control development, release, and maintenance. Since A$K is designed specifically to produce revenue, its cumulative and projected costs must be monitored continually and compared with actual and projected revenue. A$K is, in fact, a total, complete business venture.

4.4 TREATMENT OF A$K IN THIS BOOK

As mentioned earlier, whenever possible A$K is used to illustrate the principles and practices advocated by this book. You can be sure the examples of documents pertaining to A$K are complete and consistent in relation to one another. But do not be disarmed by the semblance of reality created by these examples. Be careful that you do not assume you comprehensively cover your own products if you cover the information shown for A$K, and only that information. You can and should rely on the format shown; it is presented in its entirety in Part Three. Do not rely on the content of the A$K examples. The content of examples in the book has been chosen to illustrate specific points and is not intended to be comprehensive. Rigorous examples containing all data would be tedious to read and you might confuse the wheat with the chaff. Programmers among you may be annoyed by this lack of rigor. Keep in mind that such omitted detail is incidental to the objectives set for the examples.

Not all documents pertaining to A$K are covered by examples in this book. This is for two reasons. First, some of the documents deal more with internal design or how the product is programmed. How to document and control coding and debugging is so intimately related to what is good programming practice that it should be covered in treatises on that subject rather than in this book. Second, the other documents barely touch the main subject of this book, being primarily marketing or financially oriented. Including them would contribute little to your understanding of the methodology presented.

Part Two

TECHNIQUES OF SOFTWARE PRODUCT ENGINEERING MANAGEMENT

Chapter
5

Managing Software Product Management

The title of this chapter is not meant to be either tautological or facetious. This chapter truly is about the management of software product management: how to organize for it, how to interface it with other management functions, and how to keep its diverse elements working together.

5.1 THE PRODUCT CONCEPT AS A COMMUNICATIONS TOOL

The first software product, complete with promotion, training, and maintenance probably came into being about 1950. Yet even today the number of people who understand that software can be a product is woefully small. This lack of understanding of software products and the lack of awareness of the need for them is an acute problem when it occurs at high levels in organizations where understanding is most necessary. Even IBM was slow to recognize this problem, and around 1970 closeted several of its top executives for several days of intensive indoctrination on the subject of software as a product. The fact that software as a product is seldom mentioned in widely read literature is one cause for the lack of understanding, but the main cause is the failure of software product managers to educate their superiors. It

Generic Product Development Activity	Software Product Development Activity
Market research	Market research
Planning	Planning
Payback analysis	Requirements contract review
Development	Development
Configuration management	Configuration management
Quality assurance	B-Test
Manufacturing	Replication
Quality control	C-Test
Shipping	Shipping
Installation	Installation
Warranty	Maintenance
Retrofit	Enhancement

Figure 5.1 Generic product development activities and specific software development counterparts.

takes a great deal of effort to get a top-level manager's attention long enough to explain that something like software, which he believes to be intangible, is really a product. His lack of understanding is often at the root of his inability to comprehend why it takes so long or costs so much to produce heavy-duty software.

The product concept on which this book is built is a powerful tool for reaching managers who have not been exposed to heavy-duty software. When you are familiar with the concepts of this book, you will be able to explain clearly to anyone that most generic product development activities have counterparts in software product development, as shown in Figure 5.1 (software product development activities mentioned in this figure will be defined later in this book). Just as it was necessary at IBM, it may be necessary in your organization to start by educating your top management to treat heavy-duty software as a product. Chances are that if you sense your top management's need for enlightenment, so do they. Put together a seminar for them based on the contents of Chapter 2 and Part Two. They will probably welcome an opportunity to have software presented to them in familiar terms.

5.2 A TOP-DOWN VIEW OF SOFTWARE PRODUCT MANAGEMENT

Software product management consists of seven functions: Planning, Development, Services, Publications, Test, Support, and Maintenance.

Figure 5.2 shows a possible hierarchical decomposition of these functions. This idealized organization is unlikely to occur, for it assumes total segregation of software products from other activities and segregation of each function from all others. It does, however, facilitate the discussion that follows. Whether or not there should be an organizational entity for each function depends on your parent organization's mission. If their primary mission is to produce software products, the answer is probably "yes." If, like ABC Computers Company, their primary mission is to sell computer systems, a top-down analysis would produce some distribution of functions across organizations. Indeed, as Figures 6.1 and 11.1 will show, Support and the plans management part of Planning at ABC Computers are quite distributed and remote from Development. Where software products are generated primarily for internal use, as in a bank or insurance company, a top-down analysis would probably show most software product Planning consolidated with other strategic and tactical planning, and software product Services consolidated with other computer services. Software product Test would probably be closely aligned with software Development at a bank because there would be no

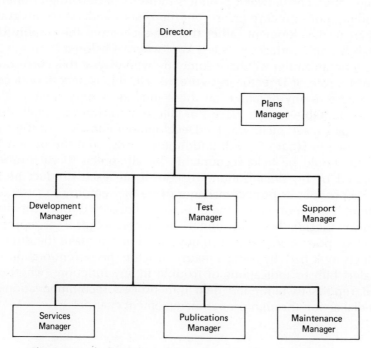

Figure 5.2 Idealized chart of the software products organization.

other test functions with which to combine it to yield a more objective evaluation.

Look at any parent organization, starting from the very top, and ask yourself where each software product development function is provided, or where it should be if it is not already provided. Wherever software product development functions can be performed by organizations existing to perform similar functions without compromising quality, they certainly *may* be. There is nothing about heavy-duty software development that requires special or exclusive treatment, in spite of what the high priests of programming may say to the contrary. Whether or not functions *should* be combined needs to be answered by looking top-down and asking whether combined or separate facilities contribute more to the parent organization's objectives. The answer will vary depending on those objectives and other factors such as organization size, available talent, and geographical distribution.

Keep in mind that a good decomposition is one that minimizes the coupling between partitions of a set. Take software product integration as an example. Sometimes it is combined with product evaluation because none of the individual product development projects is responsible for its ensemble. As a result, the evaluation function debugs interfaces between products rather than devoting its energies to finding more obscure errors. On the other hand, when integration is a part of development rather than of evaluation, the responsibility for debugging interfaces is clearly kept where it belongs.

Every organization will have someone who plays a role corresponding to the role of Director in Figure 5.2. His role is necessary because somewhere in any organization there must be a person who can be held accountable for the success or failure of software products. Some substantial subset, including the Development Function, of the structure shown in Figure 5.2 will undoubtedly exist, and the person who heads it should be held accountable for all aspects of each product generated by his organization. To coordinate each product he may assign a product or project manager or he may employ a matrix organization. It is important for the director to know that functions vital to his own success but not under his direct control are properly managed; poor management of any function can make the director's products look bad. By using a matrix structure his parent organization can alert him to indications of trouble in any function—whether or not it reports to him—and help him process recommendations for remedial action through proper management channels.

5.3 INTERFACE MANAGEMENT

This section is concerned with the management of the interfaces between functions, regardless of where they report. If these interfaces are well defined and well managed, the reporting relationships of the individual functions have little impact on the success or failure of the resulting products. On the other hand, if these interfaces are poorly handled, even a tightly structured line organization will fail to produce good products. The decoupling of partitions within a set is a vital principle, and many of the techniques and tools of the methodology in this book are dedicated to it.

An **organizational interface** is the totality of points at which two organizations meet to interact with one another. An organization can have a single interface at which it interacts with all other organizations. More likely it will have several interfaces because the interactions with other functions differ from one another. Each interface should be well defined, unambiguous, and simple. Interfaces are defined by the totality of written and unwritten plans, policies, and procedures that affect them. The more material you commit to writing the better, for this minimizes ambiguity. The dominant attribute of an interface is the demarcation of responsibility; who does what, with what, to what, with whom, and to whom. Incomplete definition, ambiguity, and complexity all lead to an inability to delineate and then remember the nature of interface relationships. Most notable for their contributions to interface management are the review boards discussed in Chapter 18. By conducting formal phase reviews as suggested in Chapter 6 and by using formal, multifunctional review boards you channel most interface problems into productive resolution. Documents and reviews of them will fail to keep interfaces functioning unless there are frequent face-to-face encounters between functions. Each of the reviews should either be conducted entirely at a meeting or conclude in a meeting. This suggests keeping the geographical distance between functions to a minimum so that other meetings can occur spontaneously. A structured walk-through (23) or inspection (24) will always include Development project members, but it might exclude Publications and Test contributors even if they are only across the street. There is no substitute for proximity to foster communication.

Department charters and mission plans help to define general organizational responsibilities. Product plans define specific responsibilities. Policies provide rationale for the apportionment of responsibility. Procedures define how charters, plans, and policies are to be carried out. Therefore, provide charters, plans, policies, and procedures in standard formats to assure that they are well defined; put them in writing to make them unambiguous; and provide defaults and allow for exceptions to keep them viable. It is particularly important that you clearly define the relations between the organization with prime software product responsibility and other organizations, for these are not as easy to control as if they were all in one organization. Of particular importance are planning functions such as business planning, product line management, and program management; systems organizations that integrate the output of the software products organization with hardware; sister development organizations that make other products comprising systems; and marketing organizations that represent the end users or are the end users themselves.

5.4 SETTING AND MEETING OBJECTIVES

There are a number of management principles to set before all software product development functions. Some of these can be found in classic treatises on management style (25, 26). Others are repeated here for emphasis.

The first step in setting and meeting objectives is selecting the right personnel. As organizations change, the personnel appropriate to them change. Some changes occur periodically, but the most critical change of all usually occurs only once—the change from small to large. This change is characterized by the exponential growth in the number of lines of communication that must be set up and the accompanying need for greater formality in maintaining them. Operating with little structure, little documentation, and predominantly oral communication are useful practices in a small organization. These practices become detrimental in a large organization where a penchant (or at least a tolerance) for structure, thorough documentation, and written communication is essential. In the transition from small to large, the entrepreneurs usually leave and are replaced by organization men. Perceive which management style is most appropriate for you and staff accordingly.

Several periodic changes occur as time passes in an organization. One common cyclical pattern is the oscillation between centralized and decentralized control. To accommodate this change you either need managers who are adaptable, or you must replace managers who are productive in only one form of control when a shift to the other form occurs. Another common cyclical pattern is the oscillation between authoritarian and participative styles. McGregor aptly defined them in his Theory X and Theory Y (25). He noted that these styles clash, and consequently managers surround themselves with managers who share their style. When a new manager of a different style enters an organization, he usually replaces managers of the prevailing style as quickly as he can. Such changes often occur so rapidly and with so much trauma that they are regarded as purges.

Computer programming is a highly technological field that attracts many brilliant and sometimes eccentric people. Such people seldom appreciate the structure appropriate to software product development and often refuse to work in what they consider a confining environment. They want to be free to create and not have to spend time documenting or justifying their designs. Their contribution is needed, however, for as Drucker so well states (26), you must "staff from strength" to obtain their services. This may mean bending a few rules, regarding such things as working hours or office furnishings, or catering to idiosyncracies, such as providing extra help to make up for authors' inabilities to provide clear documentation. Weigh the cost, in the tangible terms mentioned above and in less tangible terms, such as low morale of coworkers who do not receive like treatment, against the benefits that may be achievable in no other way. If you use chief programmer teams, make such adjustments from team to team, making the most of each chief programmer's talents.

The most fundamental principle of the methodology in this book is management by objectives (27). **Management by objectives (MBO)** is a planning and control concept whereby every manager sets his own objectives with the help of his superior, participates in the setting of his superior's objectives, and is measured by his meeting concrete, written objectives. The techniques and tools of the methodology in this book contain many features that are conditioned by MBO; Section 14.3 discusses in detail an MBO system for all software product personnel, integrating it with other tools. As Maslow points out (28), MBO is not suitable for all environments but it is ideally suited to the results-oriented business of software products and the highly skilled and motivated personnel who create them. The day may come when software products can be generated by low-skilled workers, but until then MBO is vital.

Objectives are set in plans at many levels: in mission plans, budgets, product plans, publications plans, and so forth. Each of these plans and others are treated in detail elsewhere in this book. The key plan for a software product, its requirements contract, is rich with concrete objectives that can and should be extracted for inclusion in individual work plans, the vehicles through which an MBO system records contracts between workers and their superiors.

The meeting of objectives is assured in part by incorporating product objectives into individual work plans and monitoring their achievement. Other tools help meet objectives through management by exception techniques. As will be explained later, a requirements contract, a support plan, a budget allocation, and other tools set limits up to which no feedback is required but beyond which immediate management action is required. There are three prime measures of performance: features, time, and cost. Each of these has a threshold that cannot be crossed without precipitating management review. The phase reviews discussed in Chapter 6 provide for periodic checks on progress even if no threshold is passed.

In spite of everything said in this book to promote the idea that software product development is a predictable, controllable human endeavor, you will be quick to observe that it is not perfectly so. Indeed, some people still argue that all computer programming is an art (29). To the degree that this is so, and to the degree that project slippage occurs in spite of our best efforts, the management of software products is an exercise in managing uncertainty. It demands a great ability to foresee problems, to provide contingency plans, and to have the fortitude to defend contingency plans under the pressure of less understanding managers who tell you to "cut out the fat."

5.5 PERSONNEL SELECTION AND TRAINING

The previous section makes a few suggestions for selecting management personnel. But what about technical personnel? What about career paths for all personnel? How do you provide their technical and management training? Here are some techniques that are consistent with the rest of this book's methodology.

First, consider selection. Since you are dealing with heavy-duty software you can take for granted that it is substantially complex and sophisticated; otherwise every user would provide his own and there would be no need to build software products. Dijkstra's observation about system design, that "this type of work is very difficult, and that every effort to do it with other than the best people is doomed to either failure or moderate success at enormous expense" (30) is relevant to all heavy-duty software. Always assign experienced personnel to heavy-duty software projects. This rule applies even to the lowest level jobs. Find people who have already performed similar functions at least moderately well or who have performed slightly lesser functions very well.

Always assign project management responsibility to someone who has had such experience. This is an area where the chief programmer team concept helps; experience as a backup programmer is the next best thing to prior experience as a chief programmer when you are evaluating chief programmer candidates.

It may seem presumptuous to select only experienced personnel. Somewhere, sometime people must get started. How can they if you will hire only experienced people? There is no simple answer. Fortunately, universities are now teaching structured programming and structured design and most of the students are getting some practical experience working while they learn. Thus, new graduates of computer science programs can often be considered as experienced enough for assignment as **task programmers**—programmers who support chief programmers and backup programmers, or who assume the lower level assignments in traditional programming projects.

The best source of truly experienced personnel is among the ranks of the providers of heavy-duty software. Take advantage of every chance you get to actively recruit such people (such as when you are invited to help ease the pain of someone else's layoff), and always advertise heavily in the neighborhoods of organizations where there are people who have the experience you want.

And what is the experience you want? The main thing to look for in candidates is discipline. They must understand the importance of a top-down approach; they must design and document before coding. Unfortunately, university curricula and professional development seminars still put too little emphasis on these crucial elements. Every new employee should receive an in-house seminar on your methodology in which you stress the need to practice discipline. Practice what you preach. If anyone fails to demonstrate sufficient discipline, forcefully remind him that such performance is substandard. Have the willpower to dismiss or at least reassign habitual offenders. These may seem strong words, but remember ". . . every effort to do it with other than the best people is doomed . . ." (30).

Second, consider what you can offer for career paths. Establish several ladders—such as Associate Software Engineer, Software Engineer, Senior Software Engineer, Staff Software Engineer—with alternatives for Engineer such as Evaluator (for the Test Function), Writer (for the Publications Function), and Analyst (for the Support Function). Provide formal descriptions that define increasing responsibility and comparable experience for comparable titles. For example, if a Senior Software Engineer requires the equivalent of 10 years of increasing responsibility, so should a Senior Software Writer.

As you provide vertical mobility for personnel, also provide horizontal mobility. Stimulate breadth of experience and ease the staffing problems for your weaker functions by building into higher-level job descriptions the requirement to have held a lower-level position in one or more other functions.

If you use chief programmer teams, reserve titles like chief programmer, backup programmer, and task programmer for informal rather than for formal titles, just as the title project leader is often reserved. By doing so you can give an ego boost to a Software Engineer who is chief programmer on a moderate-sized project and avoid stigma for a Senior Software Engineer who may be assigned as a task programmer.

If you use development support libraries—tightly controlled documentation and code plus housekeeping and statistics processing services at the project level—consider calling the person who performs the task a **project administrator**. As Cooke points out (31), a stigma and a sex stereotype have become associated with the role of program librarian. He advocates adding some technical responsibilities, such as conducting reviews, and assigning the position to someone with a moderate amount of technical experience. This is an excellent idea, but consider going one step farther: make successful completion of the project administrator function on one project a prerequisite for becoming backup programmer on another. Like the multidisciplinary requirement for advancement mentioned above, this will go a long way toward staffing a sometimes unattractive function.

Third, consider training. At whatever level of experience you hire people, provide them with more training to progress along career paths. Have each function prepare a seminar of at least one-half day's duration which it offers to selected audiences of mixed backgrounds. Have each seminar cover a function in a manner similar to the way it's covered in a chapter of Part Two in this book, emphasizing interactions between functions. Provide similar seminars covering the most significant or unique tools, such as a requirements contract. Offer these as needed to indoctrinate and refresh your staff, and require that everyone, whatever his current function or level, attend each seminar at least once. To stimulate interest make some of these seminars prerequisites to holding specific assignments.

Keep a sharp lookout for external training opportunities. Professional societies like the Association for Computing Machinery and the Institute of Electrical and Electronics Engineers periodically sponsor excellent programs. So do universities, community colleges, and commercial ventures like the American Management Associations. The calendar sections of publications like *Datamation, Communication of the ACM,* and *Computer* publicize many opportunities, as do paid advertisements in the same publications. Always screen such classes by soliciting reviews from previous participants or evaluations from instructors. Such training is very expensive, and, alas, very uneven in quality. Be sure you do all you can to get your money's worth.

Chapter

6

Managing Software Product Planning

There are situations in which computer programs can legitimately be generated without much planning. Some research projects and training exercises yield usable programs, but they never yield products of the type we are discussing in this book. It is just not possible to satisfy enough of the needs of the people involved in product development without preparing and following good plans. Software product plans must cover development, documentation, testing, training, maintenance, marketing, and termination. They must aid decision making with regard to technical, economic, and temporal factors.

Much of the high cost and low productivity of software is due to inadequate planning. Lack of planning is the dominant cause of programming rework which in turn causes schedule slippage, cost overruns, and high maintenance costs. It is true that you cannot plan for every contingency, but you can make reasonable provisions for unexpected events. When software development is as mature as, for instance, building construction, unexpected events will have minimum impact. Until then, only very careful planning will enable you to adequately anticipate the unexpected.

A software product is a piece of software plus documentation, quality assurance, promotional material, training, distribution, and maintenance. Thus, a software product requires a plan or set of plans

52

to cover all aspects of the product and its relationship to its environment. This chapter describes various types of plans, their interrelationships, and how they and the people who produce and use them
affect all phases of the product's life cycle.

6.1 TYPES OF PLAN

Probably the broadest and most abstract plan is a mission plan. Few
companies are willing to be so blunt, but their real objective is to
maximize return on investment. A statement of intent to maximize
return on investment is an example of a mission statement; it is the
mission of the company above all else, to maximize profits. Such a
statement is a **mission plan**, a plan that says *why*. A mission plan says
nothing about how its goal should be achieved, and it seldom states
when. By not stating when, it intentionally implies that the mission is
ongoing. Another example of a goal that might be cited in a mission
statement is improving people's health. Nothing is said about how or
when this should be done. Mission plans seldom stand alone, but they
are needed to provide the *why* for other plans.

Somewhat less abstract is a **strategic plan** which says, basically, *what*
and *when*. Some examples of business strategies are: to integrate
vertically, to finance one operation with profits from another, to enter
markets where competition is minimal, to enter foreign markets after
the domestic market is established, and to make rather than to buy.
The more specific a mission is, the more specific will be the strategies
employed to accomplish it. If the mission is to be number one in the
computer industry, appropriate strategies might be to corner the
market for super computers, and separately, to make super computers
the most cost-effective computers.

More specific still are **tactical plans**; they tell *how*. If your strategy is
to corner the super computers market, a likely tactic is to develop a
bigger and faster machine than any on the market. If your strategy is
also to make super computers the most cost effective, you might also
employ the tactic of integrating data communication hardware and
terminals into your product definition. Tactical plans also tell *who* and
where. In the example, a select team (who) might penetrate very
promising regions (where) to corner the super computers market. In
integrating data communication equipment, you might buy it from a
supplier (who) and integrate it at your plant (where).

Figure 6.1 summarizes these types of plans. A mission plan states
why you are going to do something. A strategic plan states what you

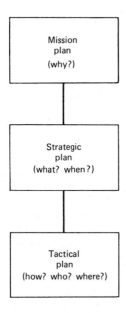

Figure 6.1   The generic hierarchy of plans.

are going to do to accomplish the mission and when you are going to do it. A tactical plan states who is going to do it, how he is going to do it, and where he is going to do it.

To clarify this concept further, take a look at the ABC Corporation and A$K. A mission of ABC is to make the use of computers available to the maximum number of people. A strategy is to vertically integrate products (Stella computers) and services (A$K DATABA$E). Another strategy is to offer services directly to the end user (marketing A$K DATABA$E directly to financial analysts). Still another strategy is to use feedback from A$K DATABA$E to test the market for terminals. Each product offered by ABC is a tactic: Stella 100, A$K, DATABA$E, and, if tests look promising, a terminal. The general case in Figure 6.1 then becomes the specific case in Figure 6.2.

You will seldom see mission, strategic, and tactical plans as separate entities. When you are building a set of plans, however, classify each statement as one of the above to clarify your thinking. You will probably notice that the more refined and effective your organization-wide planning becomes, the more frequently these types of plans will appear as entities.

Consider now some specific plans. A budget is a plan that, in its purest form, does not state why, how, or what. It does, however, place the most highly quantitative constraints on "what." It is also probably the most prevalent and most familiar plan. If no other plans exist, a budget usually does, and the feedback of actual data and the correlation of it with the plan are usually prompt, frequent, and accurate. In fact, the closer a plan can be to a budget, and the more precise and quantitative the feedback can be, the more useful the plan will be.

Another special-purpose plan is a schedule. Time, like money, is a common denominator of diverse activities. Creating a development or production schedule requires much planning effort. Yet the tangible result—one or a few dates—is often so concise that it is not recognized as a plan.

An individual work plan is a fairly recent innovation in planning and it may prove to be the most useful in achieving the goals of product plans. An **individual work plan** is a management-by-objectives tool wherein the objectives of each individual person are worked out in writing by him and his superior, committed to writing with a timetable for completion, and checked off when completed or abandoned. A well-written and well-monitored individual work plan can integrate mission, strategic, and tactical plans with budgets and can even include career planning and work skill improvement! It is a magnificent tool for humanizing product development and making clear to every contributor what his role is. Individual work plans function best when used for all employees, at all levels. The work plans for

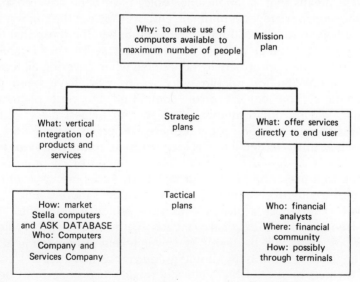

Figure 6.2   Hierarchical plans of ABC Corporation.

a hierarchy of employees are a hierarchical set of strategic and tactical plans, each stating how the objectives of the next higher level are to be met. In a well-integrated matrix organization, program managers can work with line managers to record all objectives of their programs in appropriate work plans, thus reducing much of the friction and confusion of a matrix organization. Individual work plans are discussed in detail in Section 14.3

Another plan, a **network plan**, is predominantly a tactical plan. It states how an objective can be achieved in terms of tasks called activities and who is responsible for performing them. It is also strategic in that it states when each task should be completed in terms of end dates called milestones. Network plans are discussed in detail in Section 14.6

6.2   PLANS DECOMPOSITION

In top-down planning, as in the progression from a family plan to a product line plan to a product set plan and finally to an individual product plan, a complete plan should be presented at each level. The process of doing this meticulously so that each plan is an extension of part of the plan that precedes it is **plans decomposition**. As used here *complete* means that all applicable topics have been covered and at the same, appropriate level of detail. Discuss topics at the highest level of detail (which results in them being complete in the sense that there is no more that could be said) only at the lowest level in the hierarchy.

Keeping to the appropriate level of detail while covering all topics is difficult, especially for people who are or who have been good programmers. The biggest error committed by most planners is omission, leaving out something. The second biggest error, but the one most common among programmer-planners, is commission, getting bogged down in detail that is inappropriate to the decisions that a given plan is designed to support. Avoid the error of omission by adhering to a prescribed format or checklist. Avoid the error of commission by asking over and over, "Of what value is more detail?"

As you decompose a plan, use as your principal guideline, "How much freedom of choice do I want left to the next step?" Typically, succeeding steps will be taken by lower levels of management and their ranges of responsibility should guide you sufficiently.

The formats of several hierarchically related plans need not be the same for the plans to demonstrate decomposition. What is important is that the detail be the same for each topic at any level in the hierarchy and that the detail increase as the scope of the plans narrows to a single product.

By carefully observing this principle of plans decomposition you gain the immeasurable benefit of being able to generate plans appropriate to the level of management that must review and approve them. You have certainly been to meetings where too much time was spent haggling over unnecessary detail. You may have even suffered the worst fate of all, that of failing to gain concensus because all of the participants could not agree at the level of detail presented to them. They would have agreed had they been able to focus on the proper questions.

A second principle of decomposition is that it defines limits for the next lower level. If you say "Give me a COBOL compiler in one year for $300,000," you have set three and only three limits: the compiler will process only COBOL statements; it will not take longer than one year to produce; and it will not cost you more than $300,000. You may not get an ANSI Level III compiler, but the compiler you get might compile faster than anything else on the market. As you decompose your plans farther and farther, you narrow the freedom of choice remaining and therefore progressively complete your plans in the second sense, that of absolute detail. By carefully selecting the parameters to be constrained at each level you control the order in which key decisions are made. This allows delegation of detailed decision making and allows each level of management to concentrate on its proper business. It also implies an obligation on the part of each level not to exceed its authority (i.e., the bounds set by the next higher plan) and to inform higher levels of management, via requests to modify higher-level plans, of their inability to comply with those plans.

6.3 ORGANIZING FOR THE PLANNING FUNCTION

Different types of plans are appropriate to different levels of management. Very seldom are first-level programming managers involved in the preparation, review, or approval of mission plans (except when they are so enlightened as to record and monitor the missions of their own spans of control!). Conversely, a corporate steering committee is not likely to get involved with the test plan for a new communications control program.

Hopefully you have or can create a function in your business organization whose sole responsibility is organization-wide planning and control, and which reports to the same level in your organization as does any function affected by its plans. Someone must assure that plans exist for all functions, that all of those plans are consistent, and that they are followed. To do so requires a broad understanding of the organization and its activities, supreme patience, undauntable perseverance, a high tolerance for frustration, and a reasonable concern for detail. Since few people have all of these attributes and since most managers display them to some degree, staff the function by rotational assignment. The people who staff this function should not simultaneously have other responsibilities. Planning seeks long-range results while other functions seek short-range results. A manager might be tempted to put off planning while "fighting fires."

Plans are like laws, they must be enforced. If you want your plans to be met, arm your planners with adequate weapons. One of the best weapons is a budget. Centralized budget administration can be coupled with incremental release of budgeted funds as plans are reviewed and decomposed to assure that all plans that can be met will be met. In an organization where plans management and budgeting are combined it does not take long for those who seek funds to realize that the best planned products and the organizations performing best in terms of their plans get most of the resources.

Be sure to organize for plans management as well as for planning. **Plans management** is the machinery by which plans are solicited from other functions in a reasonably uniform format; are coordinated with other plans; are checked for consistency with higher level plans (usually mission and strategic plans); and are compared with performance in a fairly formal way. **Plans managers** are the people who perform plans management.

A very small number of high-level, planning-oriented staff managers and support people are needed for mission planning and budget administration, even in large organizations. Putting too many people in these areas breeds bureaucracy. Plans management, on the other hand, is proportional to the variety of products or services produced by the organization. This function can be organized by product line, market area (either geographical or functional), or other attribute that crosses organization lines. The important thing is that it does cross organizational lines, so that it can coordinate and "glue" together the plans of those organizations.

Identify a single point of contact where each function interfaces with plans management. Depending on size and complexity you may want to have several persons working on plans and plans management, organized like the global plans management function, but with one spokesman. The review and approval responsibility sections of Part Two assume such a structure.

If you use or plan to use a matrix organization, have the role of program manager (or project manager) subsume that of plans manager. This will work if your program managers have authority over all functions affecting their programs, including the Planning Function if need be. This is true regardless of the line reporting relationship of the program managers. If you can achieve this authority for them, good plans management will be easier to achieve than if they are part of a staff Planning Function.

Planning must rely on someone to guarantee that sound configuration management is applied to product plans and specifications. Document control—the filing and distribution of design documents—is designed to provide such a guarantee. Document control is classified as a Services activity but you can make it a Planning activity to assure yourself that it is sufficiently objective and thoroughly administered.

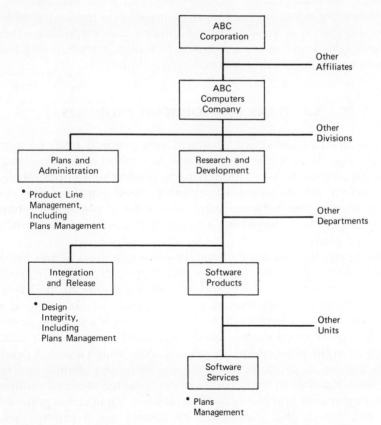

Figure 6.3 Sources of software plans management in ABC Corporation.

Just as you need not put document control into Services, you need not put plans management into Planning. Global plans management can be handled as a Services activity. But place it where its objectivity will not be threatened. Ideally, plans management is done both in Planning and in Services assuming that there is a Planning Function outside of and controlling the software products department and that the Services Function is a part of the software products department. Those elements of plans management that are global (i.e., spanning more than the software products department) should be performed by the Services Function. Recall, for example, the organization of the ABC Corporation. There plans management is performed by Plans and Administration (as a part of their product line management responsibility) and by Software Services (see Figure 6.3).

In summary, there should be a function within any organization producing software products with global responsibility for mission and strategic planning, budget management, and plans management for the entire organization. Each function involved in producing software products—such as product development and marketing—should include in its organization its own tactical planning personnel and an interface with the global plans management function.

6.4 PLANS FOR SOFTWARE PRODUCTS

As you practice top-down planning, you proceed from generic to specific (i.e., from mission to strategic to tactical) and from global to local (i.e., from family to product line to product set to product plans). This section defines several of the more useful plans and the hierarchical relationships between them. The order of presentation here is chronological from beginning to end; it is also top-down until you reach test plans.

Before you try to grasp the types of plans described below, become familiar with a few definitions. A software product (or simply product, for convenience) is a collection of pieces of software and related documentation, quality assurance, promotional material, training, distribution, and maintenance. Whether something is a product or only a part of a product varies, but usually a product is the smallest unit for which all of the above items are present; A$K is such a unit. A **product set** is a group of products that have one or more common interfaces and work together in some combinations as a free-standing group. An operating system and the compilers, utilities, applications generators, and diagnostics, that run under its control are a product set. A

product line is a collection of hardware and software products that have one or more common interfaces and that work together in some combinations as a free-standing group. Univac 90, IBM System 370, Siemens 7000, Burroughs B6800, and Data General Nova are examples of product lines. A **product family** is several closely related software products that do not necessarily have any common interfaces and that need not operate on the same hardware; for example, all FORTRAN compilers produced by a single supplier, for all machines on which they run, could be considered to be a product family.

Several product plans are particularly applicable to the development of software products. Interpret the lack of material devoted to other plans (particularly mission and strategic plans) not as a sign of their unimportance, but as a reflection of their generality, the wide latitude of acceptable alternatives, and the ready availability of other reference material (32–35).

The highest level plans likely to be of much concern in software product management are product family plans and product line plans. As you might infer from the word *product* in their names, they are strategic plans. They broadly state in terms of hardware, software, training, and so on, what will be offered. They contain strategic elements, such as compatibility with competitors to enable market penetration, or phased enhancement to prolong product life. They usually cover a long period of time, say 6 to 10 years, depending on the life of the hardware involved. The input to these plans comes almost equally from all involved functions.

Once a product line plan has been agreed upon, product set plans are developed. Perhaps the best tool for presenting product set plans is a **configurator** (Figure 6.4). This term is used to describe a matrix form of presentation in which several relationships between software operating systems and their subordinate product set members are summarized. Sections 6.6 and 14.5 describe its content and use, both as a predevelopment planning tool and as a postdevelopment communication medium with Support. Its concise form allows it to communicate a great deal of information to high levels of management without confusion. It has even been included in pricing manuals!

When the time comes to investigate developing a specific product, a very preliminary work plan is generated, initial funding is committed, and funds for completion are encumbered. A document designed for this purpose is the **budget allocation**, which is discussed in detail in Section 14.2. It is a vital element of an incremental funding philosophy and as such provides some of the control needed to enforce plans.

STELLA SOFTWARE CONFIGURATOR

VALID UNTIL: 8/1/78		VSOS	2	PRODUCT SET VSOS	3	VSOS	4
PRODUCT NAME	PAGE	STATUS	S/L	STATUS	S/L	STATUS	S/L
VSOS 2	4	S277	3	////		////	
VSOS 3	4	////		S277	2	////	
VSOS 4	5	////		////		7/78	1
BASIC ASSEMBLER 2	5	A117	3	A117	3	////	
ASSEMBLER 1	5	////		A233	1	7/78	1
ASSEMBLER B	6	////		////		10/78	1
COBOL 1	6	C111	3	////		////	
COBOL 2	6	////		C111	2	7/78	2
ANS COBOL 1	7	////		10/78	1	10/78	1
EDIT 1	7	////		U155	1	7/78	1
PERT 1	8	////		7/78	1	7/78	1
ACCESS 2	8	T494	1	T494	1	7/78	1
MANAGE 2	8	////		D655	2	////	
MANAGE 3	9	////		7/78	1	7/78	1
FORTRAN 2	10	////		C050	1	7/78	1

STATUS CODES

PRODUCT # — PRODUCT AVAILABLE

//// — PRODUCT WILL NOT BECOME AVAILABLE

DATE — DATE PRODUCT WILL BECOME AVAILABLE

SUPPORT LEVEL (S/L) CODES

1 — SUPPORT VIA PTR; UPDATES ISSUED; RPE'S WILL BE CONSIDERED

2 — SUPPORT VIA PTR; UPDATES ISSUED; RPE'S WILL NOT BE CONSIDERED

3 — SUPPORT LIMITED TO PTR PROCESSING

A definitive product development plan can be produced only after quite a bit of study and negotiation. The first task usually authorized by a budget allocation is the generation of such a plan. The document that records this development plan is a **requirements statement**, henceforth called a requirements contract to emphasize the contractual relationship it establishes between the developer and the users, including those who must sell or market the product. While the developer usually prepares it, many functions contribute to it and are affected by it—those who test, document, install, distribute, maintain, sell, teach, and support it. Its review, approval, and updating are probably the most crucial activities in the whole development process; it is through the requirements contract that everyone knows what to expect of the product: what it is and is not, what it can and cannot do, and why it should be produced.

Once development gets under way, plans specific to several functions are generated: Test, Publications, and Support. Each of these is covered in Chapter 14, as is a form of network plan that is used throughout Part Two to summarize the activities of each function throughout a product's development.

At this point you might think that every document pertaining to a product's development is some sort of plan. When you carefully catalog documents, you find that this is very nearly true. The other two types of documents discussed in this book are reports, most of which relate progress relative to plans, and specifications, which are plans of a very detailed and precise sort. Planning and control cannot be over emphasized: if you cannot plan it, you cannot do it!

6.5 PILOT SYSTEMS

Even if you can plan it, you may not be able to do it. Therefore, where there is even a moderate chance of failure, plan to give yourself a second chance by including a pilot system. No matter how capable your Development Function is, if the item you plan to build is a new product and not just a new version or variant of an existing product, your whole organization should support Development in producing a pilot system and then *throwing it away!*

A **pilot system** is a nearly complete product. It incorporates all of the principal functions of the final design, includes draft publications, and receives at least a modicum of independent testing to provide constructive criticism for rework and to assure that it is suitable for the minimum user exposure it will get. Very few developers are able to produce a first implementation that is so satisfactory that you can afford to risk delivering it to all users. So plan right from the beginning to build a pilot system. Use it as a basis for setting performance objectives for the final product, and otherwise put it aside. Follow the same management methodology for a pilot that you would for a product, providing the documents, controls, and testing that are appropriate.

A good rule of thumb for deciding how much documentation and control to provide for a pilot is to consider it Version 1 of a product and plan from the start to make your first release Version 2. Carry development of Version 1 through at least one cycle of independent testing, then proceed to the Analysis Phase of Version 2. You will find that generation and review of documents, code, and publications using normal procedures will proceed rapidly and with little wasted effort. Be sure, however, to avoid the **second-system effect** (36) in which architects and implementers alike tend to encumber a possibly clean design with marginally useful frills.

If your proposed product is for many users, select one or two to receive your pilot *free of charge* and fully supported: the pilot users will be so pleased with their selection that they will provide feedback to you worth far more than the cost of providing the pilot to them. Be sure to involve your Test Function in the field trial of the pilot; they can vastly improve their test programs and procedures based on the feedback they get. So, too, for the Publications Function; they will be able to produce far better user publications after field testing their first efforts.

6.6 MANAGING SOFTWARE PRODUCT PLANNING IN THE ANALYSIS PHASE

As Figure 6.5 shows, the Analysis Phase begins when the need for a product is acknowledged and ends when the product requirements are approved. The figure also shows the most intensive planning effort expended in this phase, prior to the start of the Feasibility Phase.

When is the need for a product acknowledged? At some point during the decomposition of plans the need arises to mention specific product offerings. The first suggestion made that a specific product should be offered marks the acknowledgement of a need. This usually occurs in a strategic plan, perhaps a market area, product family, or product line plan.

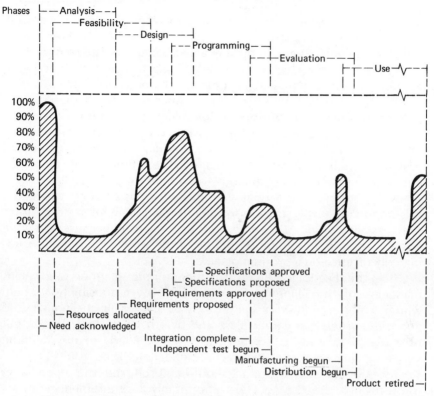

Figure 6.5   Relative manpower loading for the Planning Function.

Once a need is acknowledged a feasibility analysis may begin immediately, but this is not necessarily so. An acknowledged need may be no more than someone's dream that is put on record and escapes deletion during plans review and approval. Weak acknowledgements such as this may be strengthened by emphasizing the need in subsequent plans. The credibility of an idea can often be enhanced merely by having predecessor plans to cite in support of successor plans. The propagation of a product suggestion through plans decomposition builds its own momentum. Anyone who wants to have his idea for a product accepted should remember that the more references that are made to his idea, the more likely it is to win eventual acceptance. A good plans manager, in the Planning Function or elsewhere, will seek support for his plans in every quarter.

Once a need for a new product has been acknowledged, the Planning Function analyzes the possibilities for recouping investment in it. If there is a marketing organization, Planning usually asks it for help in this financial analysis and in making a decision to allocate resources. As stated earlier in this chapter, this marketing activity is not a function of Support. Do not let yourself get confused on points like this.

The second major milestone in the Analysis Phase is the commitment of resources to perform a feasibility study. Here incremental funding is particularly valuable; many feasibility studies may be funded and only the most promising products need to be continued past the Feasibility Phase. Whether by direct funding or merely by encouraging concerned functions to commit funds, a plans manager seeks the issuance of a formal work order such as a budget allocation. It is important at this stage to make a formal commitment to perform the feasibility study. Too many projects overrun because too little effort is spent determining the scope of the work required and gaining concurrence on a product plan.

Once the Feasibility Phase has begun, the planners and plans managers of the Planning Function have a responsibility to help whoever performs the feasibility study to answer all questions raised about the product in earlier plans and by other functions. The output of a feasibility study is a report, directed primarily to the Planning Function, and it makes a clear recommendation. If the results of a feasibility study indicate a product should be produced, the report takes the form of a development plan, preferably a requirements contract to assure thoroughness and avoid duplication of effort should the plan be approved.

Whenever possible a feasibility study should be performed by the function that would have development responsibility should the results of the study recommend that a product be produced. While other types of reports can be written by any function, requirements contracts should be written by probable developers, perhaps under the guidance of the Planning Function. This results in the strongest possible commitment to the contents of a requirements contract, for the developer is then responsible for carrying out his own plans.

The Planning Function always assumes responsibility for assuring consistency of requirements contracts with related tactical, strategic, and even mission plans of the overall organization. This is particularly so in the case of plans of functions outside the software products department, like marketing. This coordination is the key to successful plans management. To guarantee this Planning is a part of the requirements review and approval process.

6.7 MANAGING SOFTWARE PRODUCT PLANNING IN THE FEASIBILITY PHASE

At some time after resources are allocated (the beginning of the Feasibility Phase) and before a requirements contract is approved (the end of the Feasibility Phase), a new product is put into the perspective of its environment. Two tools to achieve this are a configurator and a release schedule. A configurator (Figure 6.4) lists the products with which a proposed product must coexist: those needed to install it or to operate it, those dependent on it for their installation or operation, those with which it may run concurrently, and so forth. A configurator is a high-level interface plan appropriate to communicating with and gaining the concurrence of the management of each of the functions concerned with a product.

VSOS

RELEASE SCHEDULE AS OF 11/1/77

Release G

Planned Product Availability Date 6/19/78
Planned Domestic Field Distribution Date 6/30/78
Planned International Field Distribution Date 6/30/78

Components of Release

Software

VSOS 4.0 . . . . .New version
MANAGE 3.0 . . . . .New version
FORTRAN 2.6 . . . . .Update
PERT 1.0 . . . . .New product

Publications

VSOS Installation Manual (Transmittal G) . . . . .Update
VSOS Programmer's Manual . . . . .Update
VSOS Operator's Manual . . . . .Revision
VSOS Message Manual . . . . .Update
MANAGE User's Manual . . . . .Revision
PERT User's Manual . . . . .New
VSOS Maintenance Manual . . . . .Update
MANAGE Maintenance Manual . . . . .Update
FORTRAN Maintenance Manual . . . . .Update
PERT Maintenance Manual . . . . .New

Figure 6.6 VSOS release schedule.

A **release schedule** has the same communication and commitment attributes as a configurator but it deals only with those items that are to be made available at a single point in time. The Virtual Storage Operating System (VSOS) Release Schedule at the time of A$K requirements contract approval is shown in Figure 6.6. Since A$K was planned for release into this environment, A$K's planners and developers used this release schedule to validate their assumptions. And the Support Function within ABC Computers of course used it to prepare field marketing for the impending release.

Both configurators and release schedules need to be reviewed and updated periodically. While updating is normally the responsibility of a plans manager, review and approval include the Planning Function to assure consistency with other product development. If the organization producing software products is a going concern in the economic sense (i.e., it is engaged in producing an unending stream of products), configurator and release schedule reviews are held on a regular basis to force continual reevaluation and reaffirmation of these plans.

Once Planning receives a draft requirements contract, they can perform a pricing analysis. This is done only if the proposed product will have a price; if it will not, this activity is omitted. How you determine a price depends on your organization's pricing philosophy and policies: Do you seek a profit, and if so, how much; do you seek merely to recover costs; are you willing to suffer a loss to secure a market. The guidelines you follow are highly individual but one that has been publicized for software packages (37) is to keep the price under $50,000, preferably between $5000 and $35,000 and to provide to the user a cost savings ratio of 50:1 between making and buying. If you are building your product for a single user under a contract, obviously you will apply different guidelines. Whatever your guidelines, be sure that your marketing people concur with the final price—even as early as the Feasibility Phase.

The last task performed by Planning in the Feasibility Phase is review and approval of a product's requirements contract. This is also Planning's single most important act, for it sets the course of development and initiates a chain of events over which Planning has no control as long as whatever limits are established in the requirements contract are observed. Among the things Planning looks for is agreement with higher level plans—product set plans and product line plans—because no other function is as concerned with the need for such overall consistency as Planning is.

6.8   MANAGING SOFTWARE PRODUCT PLANNING
IN THE DESIGN AND PROGRAMMING PHASES

After the Analysis Phase, the primary concern of the Planning Function for an individual product or product set is to review and approve supporting plans. During the Design Phase Publications and Test make available for review a publications plan and a test plan. Planning, usually through a plans manager, screens these plans primarily for compliance with prescribed formats and for consistency with the requirements contract, configurator, and release schedule. During the Programming Phase, Support makes its plan available and Planning reviews it as it earlier reviewed the publications and test plans.

6.9   MANAGING SOFTWARE PRODUCT PLANNING
IN THE EVALUATION AND USE PHASES

The next time in a product's life cycle when the Planning Function becomes involved is when the decision to release the product for distribution is made. Either when Test recommends release or when release is sought without Test's consent and Test is asked to report on the condition of a product, Planning reviews a test report and again asks if adherence to the requirements contract is satisfactory. The decision to distribute a product always requires the concurrence of Planning because once a product is released it is very difficult to correct mistakes, not only in the software, but also in the publications, customer preparation, and preparations for maintenance and support. And with more and more software being cast into read-only memories, the correction of mistakes is becoming even more costly. At this time, a plans manager needs assurance that all of the functions have done their jobs and are prepared for the Use Phase. It is very common for Support to press for the earliest possible release, usually to close a sale or to save a customer; for Development to press for early release because it is overconfident in its pride of creation; and for Test to want to run just a few more tests. A management compromise is invariably required, and among the parties involved in a release decision Planning is the most likely to be objective.

Planning monitors a product during its Use Phase, looking continually at the reported errors and requests for enhancement. Someone has to identify the need for an update to incorporate error corrections or a new version to make enhancements available. The support level has to be reviewed and gradually lowered and a recommendation eventually must be made to retire the product. A plans manager can prompt any of these actions and he reviews all recommendations to take such actions.

The recommendation to retire a product may come from any function: Development might want to supersede it with a new product; Maintenance and Support might want to decommit resources. Regardless of the impetus, Planning decides when the end has come. No other function has sufficient breadth of responsibility to make the decision. Therefore Planning decides when to begin a product's life and when to end it.

6.10   PLANNING'S REVIEW AND APPROVAL RESPONSIBILITY

The subdivision of the product life cycle into phases provides several natural checkpoints at which to evaluate a product. The conscious decision, in advance, to reevaluate a product's future at the end of each phase is called **phase planning**. Here is how it works.

First define the phases and what the major milestone at the end of each is. It should be no surprise to you by now to see the milestones shown in Figure 6.7 proposed for this purpose. Conduct a formal review based on at least one document at each milestone. A logical set of documents is shown in Figure 6.8, which shows six reviews called **phase reviews**. The key decisions to be based on the phase reviews are:

Phase I   Should resources be allocated to perform a feasibility study?

Phase II   Does feasibility appear to be proven and should resources be allocated to determine the external design?

Phase III   Does the external design appear to meet the users' needs as currently perceived and should resources be allocated to complete the product?

Phase IV   Is the product complete and ready for independent evaluation?

Phase V   Is the quality of the product sufficient for its release to users?

Phase VI   Is the product ready to be retired?

It is very natural for a plans manager (and even more natural for a program manager) to conduct some of these reviews, but it is certainly feasible for others to do so, particularly those functions responsible

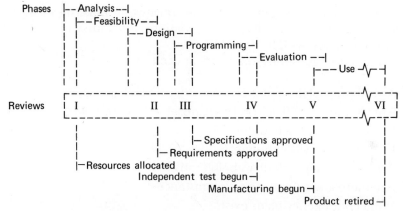

Figure 6.7 Phase plan review milestones.

Phase	Review	Major Milestone	Document(s) Reviewed
			Budget allocation
			: Schedule notice
			: : Requirements contract
			: : : External specification
			: : : : Publications plan
			: : : : : Test plan
			: : : : : : Support plan
			: : : : : : : A-Test report
			: : : : : : : : B-Test report
			: : : : : : : : : Release
			: : : : : : : : : schedule
			: : : : : : : : : : Configurator
			: : : : : : : : : :
			: : : : : : : : : :
			: : : : : : : : : :
Analysis	I	Resources allocated	X X : : : : : : : :
Feasibility	II	Requirements approved	X X X : : : : : : X X
Design	III	Specifications approved	X X : X X X : : : : :
Programming	IV	Independent test begun	X X : : : : X X : : :
Evaluation	V	Distribution entered	: X : : : : : : X X X
Use	VI	Product retired	: : : : : : : : : X

Figure 6.8 Bases for phase reviews.

71

for the primary documents to be reviewed. Regardless of who conducts a review, the Planning Function is included in the formal sign-off for Reviews I, II, V, and VI.

Some of the questions to address at each review are:

- Are all prior plans being observed rigorously?
- Are all prior specifications being observed rigorously?
- Is the project on schedule?
- Is the project within budget?
- Are all interdependencies being satisfied?
- Are there any extenuating circumstances?
- What contingency plans exist?
- What major problems are there?
- What potential solutions exist for major problems?
- What is the risk of proceeding?
- What is the risk of not proceeding?
- Does the product as it is currently defined still meet the needs as they are currently known?

After these and other questions have been explored, actions must be proposed, agreed upon, and taken. Several possibilities are:

- Proceed as planned.
- Revise plans and specifications and proceed along a revised course.
- Invoke contingency plans to return to original plans, specifications, schedules, and costs.
- Terminate the project.

It greatly facilitates phase reviews to conduct them through a standard mechanism. Conduct Review I during a regular or ad hoc budget meeting. Use an interdisciplinary board of the sort presented in Section 18.2 for Reviews II, V, and VI. Conduct Reviews II and VI at regularly scheduled meetings so that thoughtful preparations can be made, but conduct review V at an ad hoc meeting the moment a B-Test report (as defined later in Section 10.8) is available. Review III is best delegated to a technical review board (as presented in Section 18.3) with results reported to the interdisciplinary board for a final decision. Only if technical review board recommendations warrant

Phase	Review	Responsibility
Analysis	I	Review and approve
Feasibility	II	Review and approve
Design	III	Review
Programming	IV	Review
Evaluation	V	Review and approve
Use	VI	Review and approve

Figure 6.9 Minimum responsibilities of the Planning Function at phase reviews.

should the interdisciplinary board have to meet at the end of the Design Phase to debate further action. Lastly, conduct Review IV at an ad hoc meeting as soon as an A-Test report (as defined later in Section 7.9) is available.

Repeat Review VI whenever the question of lowering a product's support level is moot. This may be done on a regular interval (probably no more often than quarterly nor less often than yearly) and it should certainly be done when a warranty expires (assuming, of course, that the product is distributed with a warranty of finite duration). Focus this review on a configurator (Figure 6.4); it is an ideal tool for communicating support levels, and it is well suited to periodic review and revision.

Some of the questions raised at phase reviews pertain to the current validity of previous agreements. Be sure to correct a disagreement whenever you uncover one, either by revising present and future plans or by updating earlier documents. Remember that a requirements contract in particular must reflect reality at all times. Similarly, an external specification is the definitive document describing what a product is and must correspond to the product at all times. Sound configuration management demands also that every extant version of a product have its own external specification or its own unambiguous subset of an external specification. The name of the game in software product management is checks and balances and the Planning Function continually watches for discrepancies between products and their plans and specifications. Review and approval mechanisms must be capable of bringing discrepancies to the surface and then removing them. Technical review boards, interdisciplinary boards, and phase reviews are capable mechanisms.

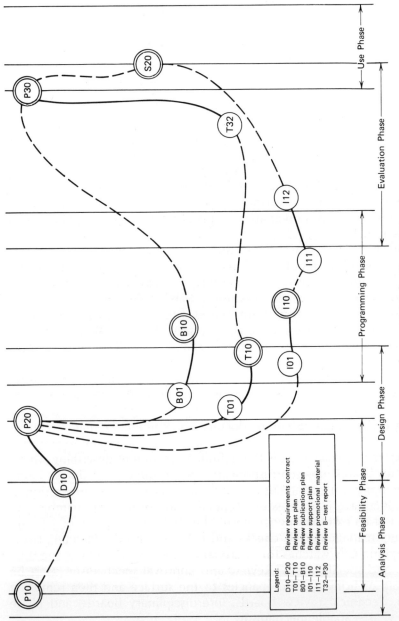

Figure 6.10 Stereotype network for the Planning Function.

Legend:

D10–P20	Review requirements contract
T01–T10	Review test plan
B01–B10	Review publications plan
I01–I10	Review support plan
I11–I12	Review promotional material
T32–P30	Review B—test report

Analysis Phase — Feasibility Phase — Design Phase — Programming Phase — Evaluation Phase — Use Phase

In summary, the role played by the Planning Function at phase reviews, at its simplest, is displayed in Figure 6.9. The role of Planning from the start of the Feasibility Phase until the end of the Evaluation Phase, using the network planning nomenclature of Section 14.6, is shown in Figure 6.10.

Chapter
7

Managing Software Product Development

The Development Function is what most people think of whenever you say *software* or *programming*. This is because the Development Function is responsible for designing, specifying, documenting, coding, and debugging any computer program, including a software product. If you are saying to yourself right now, "But what else is there to creating a software product?" please read Chapter 2 before you go any farther. It is essential to keep the role of the Development Function in perspective. In spite of the lengthy list of responsibilities stated above, much more is required to create a software product.

This chapter is largely a treatise on project management. As viewed by the Development Function, the need for project management is the most significant difference between software product development and programming per se. As in any programming, the prime responsibility for the success or failure of the resulting software lies with the designers and implementers. It is in the Development Function therefore, that prime responsibility for a software product's management is vested.

Since this book is about management and not about programming, the view of development given in this chapter will provide little help on the topics of designing or implementing software. Those topics are vital to a complete understanding of software engineering, and you are encouraged to complement your use of this book with any of the programming references included in the bibliography developed by Sloan (38), or certainly with any of your own choosing.

7.1 ORGANIZING FOR THE DEVELOPMENT FUNCTION

The most important concept to keep in mind when organizing for the software product Development Function is another hierarchical decomposition: **design decomposition,** the process by which a design is always complete—in the sense of covering all aspects—at successive stages of increasing detail. Design decomposition is the second of three decompositions that go hand-in-hand. The first is plans decomposition and the third is program decomposition, or top-down programming as it is frequently called.

As you rigorously employ design decomposition, you decouple the tasks of determining feasibility, external design, internal design, programming, and integration. This suggests vertical structure for your development organization with senior, management-oriented personnel determining feasibility (i.e., developing product objectives and requirements); senior technical personnel working with them to develop external designs; senior technical people developing internal designs; and less senior technical people contributing to the coding, debugging, and integration. This type of labor division brings the correct talent to bear during each phase of development; avoids over-commitment of resources to projects that die prematurely; provides attractive management and technical growth paths for personnel; and, above all, aids project control by providing an orderly transition from phase to phase.

The second most important concept to bear in mind is interface. Every logical entity in software has an interface. An **interface** is the complete description of an entity in its every detail as viewed from without. A product set, a product, a product module, a data file—each has an interface. By decoupling your organization horizontally along software interfaces, you can maximize the clarity and durability of those interfaces. Many projects have faltered because people in separate organizations had different views of the items with which they had to deal. If, for instance, you make one group responsible for compilers, another for logical input/output, and another for physical input/output, you will find a clear-cut, uniform interface between all compilers and the logical input/output system evolves and is not tainted by lapses into physical input/output. Similarly, incorporation of new input/output devices will be easy because a uniform interface between logical and physical input/output is a natural by-product of separate organizational responsibilities. A word of caution is in order here, however; the naturalness and effectiveness of horizontal structuring along interfaces can lead to overorganizing. Be sure the total size of your force warrants all of the organization you provide for it.

What is an appropriate size for a software development unit? The high degree of interaction with other functions, the experience required to perform most of the development activities, and the need to motivate top performance by avoiding overspecialization of duties all suggest a small span of control. First-level projects should have only one to five members. Second-level projects or functional units should have 6 to 15 members, depending on complexity. Third-level projects or units should have 20 to 60 members, again depending on complexity. A manager in software development should seldom try to supervise directly the work of more than seven individuals: otherwise he risks losing the ability to remain sufficiently knowledgeable of the technical content of the work for which he is responsible. In information-theoretical terms, he risks exceeding his channel capacity (9).

The type of person most valuable in software development—highly intelligent, perceptive, aggressive, persistent—responds well to management by objectives. He likes to know what is expected of him, when it is expected, how he can exceed expectations, and why his performance is considered good or bad—all so that he can "get ahead." The basic tool of management by objectives—an individual work plan—is introduced in Section 6.1 as being appropriate to a highly integrated planning methodology and equally important, as a plan that conforms to plans decomposition. The tools of software development described throughout this book provide a multitude of items for inclusion in individual work plans: quantitative statements of product performance by which to measure quality of work performed; milestones by which to measure timeliness of work performed; and economic parameters by which to measure cost of work performed. Couple individual work plans to budget allocations, requirements contracts, test plans, network plans, and other such tools to integrate all of the concepts of this book into an organizational personality highly conducive to successful software product development.

One last concept you should consider while organizing for software product development, which also fits nicely into individual work plans, is standards. Everyone who has done any programming appreciates the need for coding and documentation standards. Equally important are management standards for planning, reviewing, and measuring performance of development projects. A systems and procedures manual covering your Development Function's methodology—and the methodologies of related functions like Support, Publications, and Test—is indispensible for assuring completeness of plans and design decomposition at every stage. And in case you have not yet noticed, there is hardly a better source from which to build your systems and procedures than this book!

7.2 CHIEF PROGRAMMER TEAMS

The use of chief programmer teams as a form of project organization warrants some discussion to compare it with and contrast it to traditional project organization, and to identify how, if at all, the methodology of this book needs adjustment to work with chief programmer teams. They depend on and are intimately related to other modern concepts of programming methodology. Here are some definitions that should help you understand what follows.

Experience at International Business Machines' Federal Systems Division (39) has shown that a chief programmer team is the apex of a hierarchy of techniques that begins with a development support library. It isolates clerical from programming activities to enhance programmer productivity. A **development support library** consists of machine procedures to update source code, object code, and test data libraries; to retrieve programs and data for compilation, link editing, and test running; to back up and restore program and data libraries; and to generate status listings. It also consists of office procedures to maintain program documentation under revision control, to maintain machine procedures, and to maintain status information on all machine and office procedures performed. It is thus a combination of operations and configuration management services.

Next in the hierarchy above the development support library is **structured programming**. It always includes the restriction of program constructs to compounds of composition (sequence), alternation (if-then-else or case), and iteration (do-while or do-until) statements (39, 40). The reason for this restriction is that any program with a single entry and a single exit can be proven to be built from these and only these constructs (19). Since any function can be implemented with a single entry and a single exit, it is possible, using just these constructs, to build a program readable from beginning to end with no control jumps (GO TOs) and thus more easily be comprehended and tested.

Other practices are usually coupled with the above restriction on logic structures. Two are indentation of logic in source code, so that structures can quickly be spotted in listings, and segmentation into functional units, such that none takes more than a page of listing and thus can be fully comprehended within a single visual scan. Together they obviate the need for flow charts in archived documentation. Partly because this technique multiplies the number of modules to be managed, and partly because it is just good practice, structured programming normally requires use of a development support librarian.

Next up in the hierarchy is **top-down development** (39), a process of concurrent internal design, coding, and testing that proceeds from module to module in such an order that testing of no module is ever dependent on modules not yet written nor on data not yet available. This practice leads to continual integration and a system always capable of some level of execution, thus aiding measurement of programming progress. Because early-developed modules are continually exercised as new modules are added, more testing is usually accomplished by the time a system is totally integrated than is usually accomplished through **bottom-up development**, where lowest-level modules are built first and unit tested in harnesses that establish a simulated environment for testing.

Finally, at the apex of the pyramid is the **chief programmer team** consisting of a chief programmer, backup programmer, programming librarian, and, optionally, one to five task programmers. The **chief programmer** is a senior technical expert who manages the team and who, along with the backup programmer, designs, codes, and integrates top-level and critical modules. In addition to assuming primary responsibility for some of the top-level and critical modules, the **backup programmer**, who is also a senior technical expert, is always prepared to assume the role of the chief programmer. The **programming librarian**, who is a high-level clerical person, performs those functions defined for the development support library. Task programmers are lower-level technical persons assigned by the chief programmer to code and test individual, noncritical functions. In addition to employing top-down development and structured programming, and using a development support library, the chief programmer and backup programmer thoroughly review all code generated by task programmers for functional integrity and for adherence to structured programming conventions.

Chief programmer teams fit smoothly into the methodology of this book. A development support library is a precise manifestation of configuration management, albeit at project level. Structured programming is a highly disciplined methodology consistent with the many requirements for high discipline emphasized throughout this book. Top-down development, or **top-down programming** as it is also called, is "an expansion of functional specifications to simpler and simpler functions until, finally, statements of the programming language itself are reached" (14). This is no more and no less than the design decomposition defined in the preceding section. One of the shortcomings of chief programmer team operations noted by Baker (39) is the lack of a ". . . detailed functional specification . . ." that ". . . describes all external aspects of a system . . . but does not address the system's internal design." This is of course the external specification first introduced in Chapter 2. And the chief programmer team, when augmented by a project manager as Baker advocates (41) is capable of fulfilling all requirements of this book's methodology.

Whether you use chief programmer teams or traditionally structured projects, all of the same support functions must be performed, all of the same documents must be generated, and all of the same reviews must be conducted. Only the emphasis placed on particular aspects of the methodology and the characteristic times and efforts needed for several activities differ. Baker (8) suggests that chief programmer team staffing takes 80–90% of the number of total people and total man-months that traditional projects take (recall Figure 2.2).

The functions performed by the programming librarian—or better yet by the project administrator as defined in Section 5.5—may appear suboptimized if they are repeated for each project. This is not so, for the slight loss in redundancy is more than compensated for by the responsiveness of the services rendered and the consolidation of this responsibility with others assumed by the chief programmer. And as Figure 7.1 shows, responsibility shifts from function to function as a product moves from phase to phase such that by the time project materials are entered into archives, they are in the hands of the function best suited to handle them as archives. Figure 7.1 is only a partial matrix, but it shows enough items to demonstrate how archival responsibility is established. The procedures used by custodial functions prior to the product being placed in archives may be local, but the formats of the materials processed are global so that they can easily be passed from one funtion to another.

Another adjustment to make is more an adjustment to the original concept of chief programmer teams than it is to this methodology.

	Phase					
Item	Analysis	Feasibility	Development	Programming	Evaluation	Use
Budget Allocation	D	S	S	S	S	
Requirements Contract		D	S	S	S	S
Network Plan		D	D	D	D	
External Specification		D	D	S	S	S
Internal Specification			D	D	D	
Source Code				D	T	S
Object Code				D	T	S
Project Tests				D	D	
Independent Tests					T	T

Figure 7.1   Functional centers of archival responsibility. *Key:* D = Development Function, S = Services Functon, T = Test Function.

That adjustment is to the management of reviews. Originally, proponents of the chief programmer team advocated **structured walk-throughs** as low-key reviews of documents and code by peers without management feedback. Experience to date has shown there is not enough control of quality without management feedback and the concept of inspections has come into greater use. An **inspection** (24) is a formal, structured walk-through with management feedback similar to the technical review board concept discussed in Section 18.3.

7.3 TIME AND COST ESTIMATING

Estimating is treated here, not because Development makes all estimates, but because it makes key estimates and is often responsible for assembling the estimates of other functions into requests for project budget allocations. The following suggestions and guidelines (note that no hard and fast rules are offered) apply equally to Planning, Support, or whatever function is called upon to make an estimate.

Estimating time and cost are tasks each function performs, seldom with relish. This is because the history made by their predecessors is fraught with notoriously bad estimates. Tales of overruns of hundreds of percent are common.

One of the reasons estimating is so difficult is the tremendous range of programmer productivity. As Figure 7.2 (42) shows, from the 10th to the 90th percentile productivity has ranged over a factor of 10 (from 70 to 900 machine instructions per man-month in 1955) and is not predicted to converge as overall productivity slowly improves. Other reasons are the pervasive optimism of programmers, particularly with respect to documentation and testing efforts; inadequate allowance for reviews and rework in response to reviews; and failure to adequately revise estimates when the scope of a project increases.

Quite a bit can be done to improve estimates. Begin by making a commitment to gathering and preserving statistics on the performance of all activities. It is easy to overlook or deliberately avoid gathering and reviewing performance statistics because they contribute nothing to performance of the activities being monitored, except possibly to slow them down and possibly to aggravate an already overrun budget. The best way to make estimates, however, is to make projections

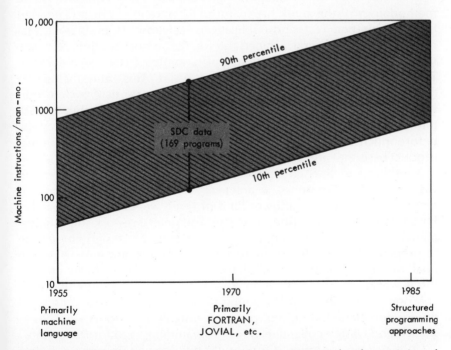

Figure 7.2 Technology forecast: software productivity (Reprinted with permission of Datamation®, copyright 1973 by Technical Publishing Company, Greenwich, Connecticut 06830.)

based on history. You must also develop dedication to recording and reviewing history in order to make good estimates.

The methodology you are studying includes several techniques and tools for gathering, recording, and reviewing performance statistics. The process begins with quantitative plans: time on schedule notices, resources on budgets, budget allocations, and manpower summaries. Several of the reports provide actual data as a function of time: budget request summaries, schedule change summaries, trend charts. Collect these project plans and reports and compile them into project post-mortem reports. Include counts of program statements or modules or whatever you feel is a good measure of product size. Monitor the rates of error detection and correction during the Evaluation Phase. Add computer usage statistics and labor charges from your accounting system. When your methodology is sufficiently uniform from project to project, as it will be after you follow it for two or three product life cycles, you can draw upon your collection of post-mortems to forecast new product developments.

One guideline for estimating that has held fairly constant as the methodology of this book has matured is the ratio of effort expended by Development, Test, and Publications Functions. In budgeting total manpower over several projects, as for the annual staffing of entire functions within an organization, the ratio 10:3:2 (for Development, Test, and Publications, respectively) is valid. This ratio includes a heavier weighting for Development than is appropriate for an individual product because many of Development's efforts either are not intended to yield products or are expended on projects that die before much effort is expended by other functions. On an individual product basis the ratio 10:5:3 is typical.

Another guideline concerns the ratio of calendar time spent in various phases. There is a practical minimum overhead for this methodology that puts a lower limit of three weeks on the Feasibility Phase (one to prepare, one to review, and one to rework the requirements contract); a lower limit of five weeks on the Design Phase (one to prepare, three to iteratively review and rework, and one to do the final reworking of the external specification); and a lower limit of three weeks on the Evaluation Phase (two for independent testing and one for distribution). Assuming these constraints are satisfied and do not dominate, the ratio of phases is roughly 2:1:1 for Analysis, Feasibility, and Design collectively; for Programming; and for Evaluation.

Let your own experience and intuition guide you in using such data as provided above. If you think it will sharpen your intuition, read about quantitative estimating techniques that have worked in a variety of environments. Some particularly good presentations are given by Aron (43, 44), Nelson (45), McNeil (46), Donelson (47), Wolverton (48), and, for a chief programmer team environment, Baker (41). Other authors have reported on programmer productivity such as Brooks (36), Böehm (42), and Scott (49, 50).

7.4   PROJECT MANAGEMENT

The term project management has been widely used for over 20 years. It has been applied to construction projects large and small, to multimillion and even billion dollar space research programs, and to research and development projects in fields as diverse as sociology and economics. The project management dealt with here shares many characteristics with each of these. In the methodology of this book, **project management** is the attainment of a product's requirements and objectives through a matrix of functions and projects. In such a matrix, each function has a management team responsible for performing that function in the best possible manner, and each product has a management team concerned only with that product. Figure 7.3 shows a stylized product-function matrix. In this figure project managers are called product managers to emphasize the concern of each for a single product. Each function is shown to consist of several subprojects; these may or may not actually be organized as projects and they may represent a fraction of one person's full-time effort or up to many persons' full-time efforts. Note that not all functions contribute to all products.

The product manager orchestrates the contributions of all functions toward the success of the product, measured primarily in terms of conformance to predetermined technical requirements and objectives, timeliness, and acceptable cost. He normally exercises his role from the start of the Feasibility Phase until the end of the Evaluation Phase. In a highly developed matrix organization he may be a professional project manager working out of the Planning Function. More likely he will be a member of the Development Function who has demonstrated the ability to get things done through other people. It is often said, and sometimes with a truth that hurts, that a project manager has all responsibility and no authority. Working in a matrix organization is tough not only for him, but also for the functional managers and project members. Everyone has two bosses and the need to continually resolve ambiguity and conflict is the price paid for project accountability. Matrix organizations of the sort shown in

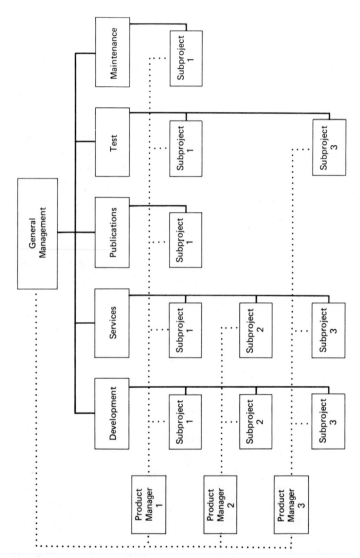

Figure 7.3 A product-function matrix organization.

Figure 7.3 are becoming increasingly more common, and as they do, more and more people learn not only to tolerate them, but to recommend them.

A project manager generates many of the documents discussed in this book, such as requirements contracts, manpower summaries, external specifications, network plans, and schedule notices. Those he does not generate he reviews and approves, such as budget allocations, internal specifications, configurators, publications plans, test plans, and support plans. He also conducts progress reviews, makes presentations, and often provides line management for the development project. In addition to this, he often makes a substantial contribution to the design, coding, and checkout of his product!

Why does he do it? Primarily for the challenge, the chance to be a leader, the exposure to management, and for the sense of satisfaction that accompanies even a qualified success. It is an ego trip, but an eminently worthwhile ego trip.

7.5 MANAGING SOFTWARE PRODUCT DEVELOPMENT IN THE ANALYSIS PHASE

The intensity of activity in the Development Function, for an individual product, is typically distributed as shown in Figure 7.4. The work of the Development Function begins in the Analysis Phase at the moment the need for a product is acknowledged. A plan—perhaps a market area plan, a product line plan, or a budget—specifies when the product is needed. Development's first activity is to determine when work on the product must begin and hence when a project to develop it must commence to provide the product when it is needed. Development carefully coordinates this start time with other functions to be sure that all activities of all functions are accounted for. Development records the proposed start and stop time for all tasks, preferably subdivided into major activities, and requests allocation of enough resources—manpower, computer time, travel expenses, consulting fees—to conduct a feasibility study. It does this with a cost plan like the budget allocation, which specifies persons to be responsible for each task in each function and provides for assignment of an overall project manager. This project, or product, manager requests Phase I Review to take place by soliciting allocation of any of the resources on the budget allocation.

A prudent course of action for management to take at Phase I Review is to allocate only enough resources to complete a feasibility

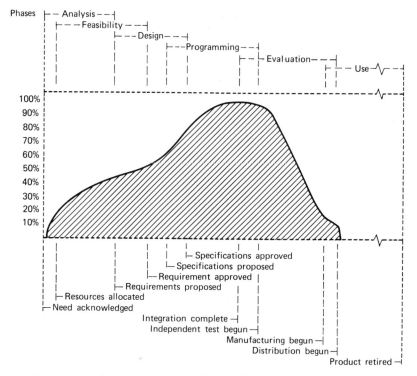

Figure 7.4   Relative manpower loading for the Development Function.

study. You may conveniently do this by including the task of preparing a requirements contract on a budget allocation. This prevents the project from expending resources not needed to determine feasibility and allows management to withhold funding of later tasks until Phase II Review. At that point the magnitude of those tasks is better known and a sound decision on project continuation can be made.

Making a lasting decision at Phase I Review requires evaluation of schedule as well as cost. Someone, therefore, preferably the task leader for requirements contract preparation (who probably becomes the overall project manager, since he will then have a strong commitment to fulfilling the requirements contract should subsequent development be approved), presents an approximate but formal schedule plan like the schedule notice described in Section 14.7. This initial schedule notice records firm commitment for submission of a requirements contract and an objective for availability of the complete product; other milestones may be recorded if they are critical to the planning of any near-term activities.

If at Phase I Review management gives the go-ahead for the Feasibility Phase to begin by allocating resources, Development attempts to prepare a requirements contract. The activities that comprise this task require that enough analysis be performed to demonstrate feasibility. Should the analyst in charge conclude obvious infeasibility or for some reason that the proposed product is undesirable, he abandons his attempt to generate a requirements contract, makes a report of his findings at Phase II Review, and graciously recommends project cancellation. If he feels confident or if he has only mild doubts that a project is feasible, he completes the generation of a requirements contract.

Using the format presented in Chapter 13, writing a requirements contract is easy, but doing the analysis necessary to assure the validity of statements entered into it requires experience and much careful thought. Requirements must be stated clearly and unambiguously. Whether or not they are eventually met must be measurable. "How to" decisions must be avoided wherever possible so as not to preclude options that can be left open until a later stage of development. Other functions will press hard for product features, performance criteria, or other attributes which Development must be prepared to accept or reject with good reasons. Enough analysis must be done to provide those reasons.

A requirements contract, as its name implies, is a development contract between the project manager and his customers, and it contains subcontracts between Development and other functions. Therefore, treat it with all the care and respect a contract deserves, avoiding both overcommitment and undercommitment. Emphasize the contractual aspect by coupling individual work plans to statements made in the requirements contract. And since a requirements contract is binding on several functions, be sure its author informally solicits their concurrence with the document before he submits it for review by anyone, including his own management. This prevents possible confrontation during formal review thereby preventing delay in securing approval.

Create a baseline plan for the whole project. This will show interactions between functions, providing a vehicle for negotiating their participation and commitment to the project. It will also, as its name suggests, provide a baseline for all Development activities. A network presentation such as a Program Evaluation and Review Technique (PERT) or critical path network is ideal for this purpose. Use the stereotype network presented in Section 14.6 as a base from which to build a suitable presentation. The result will look something like the

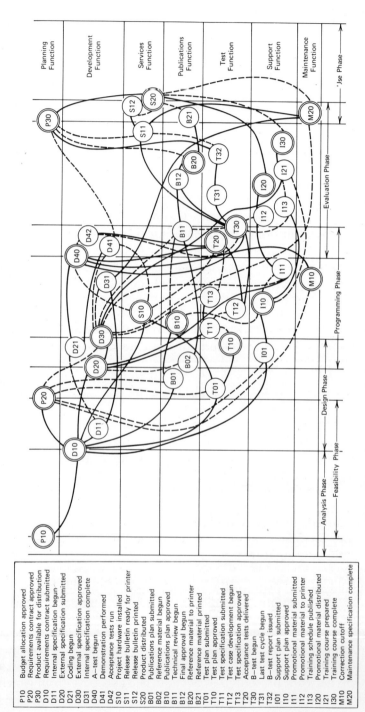

Planning Function
Development Function
Services Function
Publications Function
Test Function
Support Function
Maintenance Function

Analysis Phase · Feasibility Phase · Design Phase · Programming Phase · Evaluation Phase · Use Phase

P10 Budget allocation approved
P20 Requirements contract approved
P30 Product available for distribution
D10 Requirements contract submitted
D11 Internal specification begun
D20 External specification submitted
D21 Coding begun
D30 External specification approved
D31 Internal specification complete
D40 A–test begun
D41 Demonstration performed
D42 Acceptance tests run
S10 Project hardware installed
S11 Release bulletin ready for printer
S12 Release bulletin printed
S20 Product distributed
B01 Publications plan submitted
B02 Reference material begun
B10 Publications plan approved
B11 Technical review begun
B12 Final approval begun
B20 Reference material to printer
B21 Reference material printed
T01 Test plan submitted
T10 Test plan approved
T11 Test specification submitted
T12 Test case development begun
T13 Test specification approved
T20 Acceptance tests delivered
T30 B–test begun
T31 Last test cycle begun
T32 B–test report issued
I01 Support plan submitted
I10 Support plan approved
I11 Promotional material submitted
I12 Promotional material to printer
I13 Training schedule published
I20 Promotional material distributed
I21 Training course prepared
I30 Training course complete
M10 Correction cutoff
M20 Maintenance specification complete

Figure 7.5 A stereotype software product development network.

diagram in Figure 7.5. Use an elaborate, computerized critical path system if it is appropriate, or use a simple manual chart, but by all means use some form of network presentation. It is an unbeatable tool for communicating the complex relationships that exist in a typical software product development project.

7.6 MANAGING SOFTWARE PRODUCT DEVELOPMENT IN THE FEASIBILITY PHASE

Concurrence on feasibility is the result of requirements contract review by all functions. During this review they scrutinize every statement made in the requirements contract. The project manager explains and defends his network plan. As debate on the contract and network proceeds, he modifies and represents them as often as necessary to gain their approval. Time he spends developing his contract and making sure he has a valid plan for fulfilling it pays handsome dividends downstream in the project.

Schedule as many informal reviews of your plans as you like, but be sure to have at least one final, formal Phase II Review. The Interdisciplinary Board described in Section 18.2 is a suitable, formal mechanism for conducting Phase II Review. This formal review puts all functions on record as either approving the requirements contract or not. Hopefully you will not have to seek approval of a requirements contract over the objection of any function. If you must, try to get the dissenters to "agree to disagree"; that is, get them to consent to proceed in spite of their objections.

The many suggestions for change you receive during requirements contract review provide an opportunity to explore design tradeoffs. You have three variables to deal with: features, schedules, and costs. Consider a representation of them in three-dimensional space where each variable is measured along an orthogonal axis as shown in Figure 7.6. You should have no trouble envisioning time and cost along two axes; they are simple, linear variables. Exercise your imagination a bit and think of features as a linear variable also to complete the picture. Then imagine a requirements contract as a rectilinear volume with measurements provided by the cost, schedule, and totality of features represented by the requirements contract. Leave some empty room inside this design space at the time a requirements contract is submitted; that is, be sure that all resources, all time, and all features are not fully allocated. You then have the freedom to make modifications

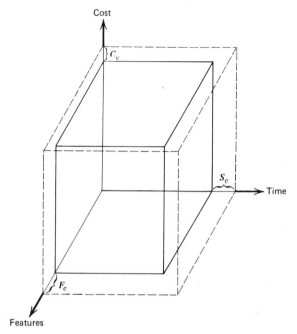

Figure 7.6   The software development design space. C_c = cost contingency allowance; S_c = schedule contingency allowance; F_c = feature contingency allowance.

within the design space and thus to accommodate some changes in the requirements contract without strain and without going outside of the planned design space.

Requirements contract review, rework, and approval may take quite a while. A good project manager overlaps this activity with as much continued development as he can muster resources to cover. Encourage him to "bet on the come," perhaps by allocating funds to develop product specifications at the time he submits his requirements contract, and let him proceed, assuming the requirements contract will be approved as submitted or at least with so little change as can be absorbed within planned contingencies.

Another activity Development undertakes during requirements contract review, or possibly during requirements contract preparation, is development of individual work plans (per Section 14.3) and a manpower summary (per Section 14.4) for prospective project members. This is work to be performed before extensive resource commitments are made to a project, and the relative lull in technical development during requirements contract review is a good time to do it.

7.7 MANAGING SOFTWARE PRODUCT DEVELOPMENT IN THE DESIGN PHASE

The crux of the Design Phase is creation and review of product specifications. Development continues the design decomposition begun in the requirements contract by decoupling specifications into external and internal design components. **External design** is the totality of product attributes visible to any user of a product. **Internal design** is the totality of product attributes not visible to any user of the product. This distinction may at first seem to be artificial, but it is not, and its preservation has distinct advantages. It is consistent with good programming practices such as top-down programming (14), information hiding (15), composite design (16), and structured design (17). From a manager's point of view it has the virtue of allowing users to review features relevant to them without getting involved in a critique of internal design. Said another way, you can describe *what* a product is in an external specification and *how* it is built in an internal specification. You can review an external specification openly and freely, benefiting from user inputs where they are most needed, and you can keep kibitzers from telling Development how to do its job by restricting internal design review to structured walk-throughs or inspections within the Development Function.

To get clearly in your mind the distinction between external and internal design, picture a well-ordered design decomposition such as that shown in Figure 7.7. Such a decomposition is well ordered if it shows every instance of one function invoking another down to whatever level of abstraction you feel is sufficient to control your design. Further, picture each functional module in Figure 7.7 as a "black box" the outside of which you can describe completely, and about the inside of which you (pretend to) know nothing. Define the attributes of a black box, or module, as the totality of its description as viewed from without, including statements describing the conditions under which it is entered and exited (that is, its elements of function and the elements of predication and collection which lead to or from it). Those attributes of those modules which are visible when you describe the product as a whole are the external design. All attributes of invisible modules and all other attributes of partially visible modules are the internal design. Note a corollary of this concept: all control structures that link invisible modules are internal design. Such structures define *how* a product is implemented and are not part of its external design.

To further fix this notion, try another frame of reference—Figures

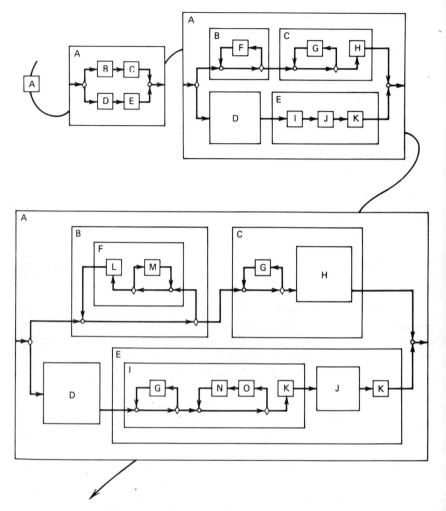

Figure 7.7   A functional design decomposition.

7.8 and 7.9. Figure 7.8 is a transformation of the design represented by Figure 7.7 into a where-used tree structure. Consider the boundary of each block in Figure 7.8 to be the totality of attributes pertaining to the module represented by the block. Boundary P, which in Figure 7.9 includes the projection of all visible attributes onto the surface of the product, is the external design. The internal design is the union of all attributes not so projected. An internal specification covers every other boundary.

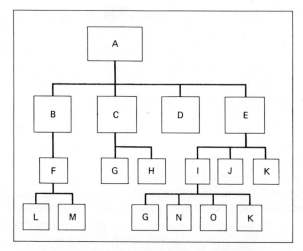

Figure 7.8 A "where-used" tree structure.

Study Figure 7.9 a moment longer before moving on. Notice that the boundary of the top-level module in the tree, Surface A, completely projects to part of the total product's boundary, Boundary P. This is a consequence of top-down design whereby the top-level module merely invokes and terminates a product, handles other communication between the product and the user, and sequences execu-

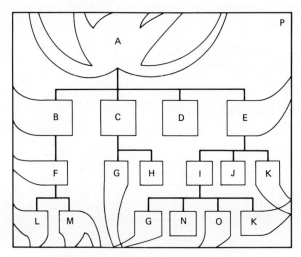

Figure 7.9 Synthesis of external design.

tion of lower-level modules. A corollary of this decomposition is that Module A has no internal design and thus no internal specification.

Notice also in Figure 7.9 that the boundaries of some modules never project to Boundary P (e.g., Boundary D). This is a manifestation of information hiding; no user of the product depicted in Figure 7.9 need know anything about such modules—what they do or what data they deal with.

With the distinction between external and internal design firmly in mind, develop an external specification and an internal specification for your product. As you do so, carefully avoid overlap in design descriptions. The external specification format of Section 15.1 is a rigidly structured design decomposition of the requirements contract format presented in Chapter 13. The internal specification format of Section 15.2 is an even more rigidly structured design decomposition of the external specification format. If the author of each document follows the rules presented in these formats, there is little chance of an overlap occurring. Should a conflict occur, there are built-in rules for resolving it.

The structure of your product may be simple and straightforward or it may be complex and highly convoluted. You may need several documents to completely describe a product. For example the structure of A$K shown in Figure 7.10 requires three external specifications: one each for A$K (L301), the User Interface (L321), and the Update Processor (L331). As noted at the end of Section 7.6, some of this activity may begin before the end of the Feasibility Phase, before the product's requirements contract is approved. As the design

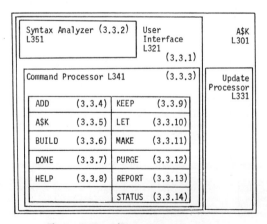

Figure 7.10   A$K program structure.

progresses, Development iterates on both the external specification and the internal specification, with the external specification reaching a high degree of convergence and stability long before the internal specification does.

When Development feels the external specification is relatively stable, it circulates the document, clearly marked preliminary, for review by other functions and by customers if appropriate. Use a formal mechanism such as the technical review board of Section 18.3 to encourage thorough and timely review. A well-constituted technical review board is a valuable asset to a project manager, so be sure to select it carefully. Development should take the board's suggestions seriously and factor them into the external specification.

While Development works on the external specification and the internal specification other functions are busy preparing a publications plan and a test plan. They are circulated for review late in the Design Phase. The project manager personally reviews and approves them. The Development manager approves them too, usually on the project manager's recommendation.

The Design Phase ends with external specification approval which freezes external design and enables internal design to converge. Approving an external specification is not intended to prohibit external design changes but merely to inhibit them and allow all functions to proceed without waiting for further external design to be specified. A mechanism such as an enhancement request (see Sections 16.6 and 18.4) allows last-minute changes to be incorporated into an approved external specification. Watch these carefully to avoid impacting schedules, particularly in functions other than Development which may be unaware of pending changes in time to incorporate them within their contingency allowances.

7.8 MANAGING SOFTWARE PRODUCT DEVELOPMENT IN THE PROGRAMMING PHASE

As Figure 7.4 shows, activity in the Development Function reaches its peak in the Programming Phase. Management of Development in this phase consists mainly of coordinating what might be a large number of people in the Development Function and many interface activities with other functions. It also consists of assuring adherence to programming standards.

Coding begins early in the Programming Phase. Figure 7.11, the subnetwork of the overall stereotype network that covers the activities

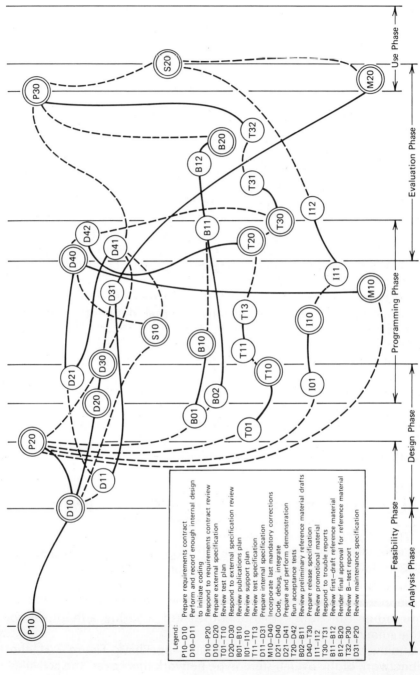

Figure 7.11 Stereotype network for the Development Function.

Legend:

P10–D10	Prepare requirements contract
D10–D11	Perform and record enough internal design to initiate coding
D10–P20	Respond to requirements contract review
D10–D20	Prepare external specification
T01–T10	Review test plan
D20–D30	Respond to external specification review
B01–B10	Review publications plan
I01–I10	Review support plan
T11–T13	Review test specification
D11–D31	Prepare internal specification
M10–D40	Incorporate last mandatory corrections
D21–D40	Code, debug, integrate
D21–D41	Prepare and perform demonstration
T20–D42	Run acceptance tests
B02–B11	Review preliminary reference material drafts
D40–T30	Prepare release specification
I11–I12	Review promotional material
T30–T31	Respond to trouble reports
B11–B12	Review first–draft reference material
B12–B20	Render final approval for reference material
T32–P30	Review B–test report
D31–P20	Review maintenance specification

Analysis Phase — Feasibility Phase — Design Phase — Programming Phase — Evaluation Phase — Use Phase

98

of the Development Function, shows Milestones D21—Coding Begun; D30—External Specification Approved; and D31—Internal Specification Complete occurring in that sequence during the Programming Phase. This is a manifestation of the **wave effect** when external specification generation, internal specification generation, coding, debugging, and integration are all pursued simultaneously at different levels in a product's tree structure. For example, at a point in time well along in the Prgramming Phase for the product shown in Figure 7.7 the status of the modules might be as in Figure 7.12. At such a point in time, the external specification for the whole product might be approved, but the internal specification would not be complete. Similarly, even though coding, debugging, and integration are complete for some modules, they are far from complete for the product as a whole. If you need a more rigid approach, or if your product is too monolithic to proceed as in Figure 7.12, your equivalent of Figure 7.11 might show the sequence D30, D31, D21 rather than D21, D30, D31. That is to say, you might need to complete not only the whole external design, but also the whole internal design before commencing coding.

Be wary of a serious disadvantage of the wave effect; the work of other functions can be impacted by delay in approving the external specification. For example, as shown by the constraints (broken lines) in Figure 7.5, a test specification cannot be approved for Test; promotional material cannot be completed by Support; and reference material cannot be completed by Publications until the external specification is approved.

Other than performing a demonstration of a product late in the Programming Phase, Development activities beyond coding, debugging, and integration consist of managing the interfaces between Development and other functions. First, Support presents its plan for

	Modules														
	A	B	C	D	E	F	G	H	I	J	K	L	M	N	O
ES complete	X	X	—	—	X	X	X	—	—	—	X	X	X	—	X
IS complete	X	X	X	X	—	X	X	X	X	—	—	X	X	—	X
Coding complete	X	X	X	—	—	X	X	X	X	—	—	X	—	—	X
Debug complete	X	X	X	—	—	X	X	X	—	—	—	X	—	—	X
Integration complete	X	X	X	—	—	—	X	X	—	—	—	X	—	—	—

Figure 7.12   The wave effect.

review. Development's main concern is that Support's assumptions about a product's description and schedule are correct; any erroneous feature descriptions or schedules that might reach users through Support's promotional efforts could prove embarassing, or worse yet, costly in terms of nonperformance penalties.

Publications offers several drafts of reference material for review throughout the Programming Phase. Near the middle of the phase Test offers its test specification for review. In its review of publications drafts and a test specification, Development carefully checks for errors introduced by incorrect assumptions. If Development has done a good job building an external specification there should be few and these reviews should be easy, albeit time-consuming. If an external specification has gaps or ambiguities, these reviews will not only be slow but they will be difficult. External specification changes will have to be made and schedule contingency will be eaten up.

Later in the Programming Phase, after its plan is approved, Support presents its promotional material for review. Development makes sure that the representation of the product is technically accurate, again to avoid embarassment and penalty.

As mentioned above, you may want to demonstrate a product at some point, perhaps to show that you can meet your performance requirements for a critical benchmark or to measure progress. Development does this as early as possible to incorporate feedback from observers of the demonstration. Early, however, is probably late in the Programming Phase.

7.9 MANAGING SOFTWARE PRODUCT DEVELOPMENT IN THE EVALUATION PHASE

The start of the Evaluation Phase is heralded by the start of A-Test by Development. **A-Test** is the carefully controlled testing of a total product, after all modules have been tested individually as much as is appropriate and have been integrated into a working system. In many past projects this has been a very visible milestone, accompanied by traumatic simultaneous integration of many modules. Adhering to top-down programming reduces or eliminates the trauma; the start of A-Test is marked merely by the integration of the last module.

During A-Test, Development runs as many of the Test Function's test cases as it can. This speeds eventual completion of Test's independent evaluation and helps debug its test cases, faulty test cases being a frequent source of dispute between Development and Test.

Toward the end of A-Test, Development prepares a **release specification**, a document that ties together the parts of the product with all of their part numbers, installation requirements, and other pieces of information not available earlier such as a final reconciliation of deficiencies and omissions. A format for a release specification is presented in Section 15.4.

When it reaches diminishing returns in A-Test, Development runs the acceptance tests provided by Test. These **acceptance tests** are a subset of Test's total battery of tests designed to screen out poorly prepared products. There is an unfortunate history of Development making last-minute changes under pressure of an "enter Test" deadline which destroys the integrity of a product; running acceptance tests assures everyone, including Development management, that this will not occur.

B-Test is the independent evaluation of a product versus its specifications, notably its requirements contract and external specification. After Development successfully runs acceptance tests, a product is ready for B-Test. Development prepares an **A-Test report** summarizing A-Test results and asserting that it has complied with all B-Test acceptance criteria, such as the successful running of acceptance tests.

The Test Function prides itself on its ability to certify a product and will, as stated above, fire a battery of tests at it. These tests normally are applied in cycles, beginning with a rerunning, by Test, of the acceptance tests (do you really believe they would take Development's word that they ran successfully?!). A **test cycle** consists of running as many tests as possible, as quickly as possible, and reporting the results to Development. Once a cycle is complete, if there are any problems to be resolved before release can be recommended, Development responds as quickly as possible by submitting a revised product to Test for another cycle. An admirable goal for you to set for Development is completing B-Test in one cycle. While this goal is occasionally met, three cycles is more typical and 10 is not unheard of.

While a product cycles through B-Test, Publications presents the reference material for technical review. This is Development's last chance to correct errors in the technical accuracy of the material, so be sure this review is thorough. Publications incorporates Development's response and provides one final review before printing. During final review Development may correct only typographical errors; any other changes cause a delay in the production of finished publications.

The Evaluation Phase ends when Test publishes its findings in a B-Test report. This it does when the criteria, albeit subjective criteria, described later in Section 10.8 are met or when it concludes the criteria cannot be met. Development then hopes that Test will recommend release without any disclaimer. More often there are a few unresolved problems which Development is called upon to review. The decision to release a product is based on Test's report and Development's rebuttal, which usually requires a plan for eventually correcting any deficiencies. Therefore Development reviews the B-Test report carefully and recommends disposition for every outstanding problem. This involves negotiation with Maintenance if it is to be involved in making up any of the deficiencies.

7.10 PROJECT TERMINATION

All development projects end at some time, either normally or prematurely. Whether termination is normal or premature, Development issues a post-mortem report so that future projects can benefit from past experiences. A **post-mortem report** includes contributions from all project members and includes, at the very least, the following information:

- Lessons learned "the hard way."
- Recommendations for future projects, including alternatives.
- A summary of planned versus actual milestones (including all of the project's schedule notices).
- A summary of planned versus actual costs.
- A summary of planned versus actual staffing (including all of the project's manpower summaries).
- A summary of planned versus actual computer usage.
- A chronology of hardware problems and a recommendation for avoiding similar problems in the future.
- A chronology of interface problems (with Test, other Development groups, etc.).
- Tips for planning contingency.
- A history of significant events.

For completed products, include the post-mortem in the maintenance specification, as shown in Section 15.3. Make readily available a file of all post-mortems, for both normally and abnormally terminated projects, and require every project manager at least at the beginning of his project to review it. This is one ingredient of effective planning too often overlooked.

A normal termination occurs at Phase V Review when a decision to release a product is reached. As quickly as possible, before all project members are too engrossed in new assignments, Development generates the post-mortem report. It also generates a final schedule notice and requests closing of the budget allocation account. These last two actions may have to wait for completion of a maintenance specification by Maintenance, but otherwise you can consider a project complete.

Nothing has been said so far about reassigning project personnel. In a normal termination they are phased out gradually, with plenty of advance notice. A premature termination usually catches people by surprise, such as when funding is abruptly withdrawn or the need for a product evaporates. Negotiate a reasonable transition for personnel from a prematurely terminated project. For example, be sure they complete documentation of all work to the current level of knowledge, that they submit to archives all code and documentation, and that they produce an especially thorough post-mortem report. You never can tell when a project will be revived or be used as the basis for something similar, so it pays to salvage all you can. Even if this clean-up cannot be charged to the dead project, do it and charge overhead.

7.11 DEVELOPMENT'S REVIEW AND APPROVAL RESPONSIBILITY

The Development Function participates in five of the six Phase Reviews. At Phase I Review Development presents initial project cost estimates on a budget allocation and initial schedule information on a schedule notice. It reviews all information presented; approves schedule commitments, in particular requirements contract submission; and approves any resource allocations. It is a good idea at this time to allocate only enough resources to carry a project through to expected requirements contract approval, thereby avoiding overexpenditure should the requirements contract not be approved or should it be approved but for a greatly revised product definition.

At Phase II Review the requirements contract is the focus of attention. Development reviews it, the budget allocation, a new schedule notice, and initial preliminary configurator and release schedule entries. It approves the requirements contract, additional resource

Phase	Review	Responsibility
Analysis	I	Review and approve
Feasibility	II	Review and approve
Design	III	Review and approve
Programming	IV	Review and approve
Evaluation	V	Review and approve
Use	VI	None

Figure 7.13 Minimum responsibilities of the Development Function at Phase Reviews.

commitments on the budget allocation, and additional schedule commitments on a schedule notice.

Between Phase II and Phase III Reviews, Development reviews and approves publications and test plans, as mentioned above. At Phase III Review, the external specification is the focal point. Development reviews it, the budget allocation, and a new schedule notice. It approves the external specification, additional resource commitments on the budget allocation, and additional schedule commitments on a schedule notice.

Between Phase III Review and Phase IV Review, Development reviews and approves the support plan, the test specification, and any promotional material. At Phase IV Review, it presents an A-Test report and requests permission to enter B-Test. Once again it reviews the budget allocation and a schedule notice, approving changes as necessary.

Between Phase IV and V Reviews, Development is called on only for technical and final review of publications; final review is accompanied by approval. At Phase V Review, Test's B-Test report is the focal point. Development reviews it and approves any decision based on it. Development also reviews a schedule notice and approves any changes.

This ends Development's review and approval responsibility. In the Use Phase, which begins at Phase V Review, Development is finished except for project clean-up. By the time Phase VI Review comes along, Development is long out of the picture. Figure 7.13 summarizes Development's role at phase reviews.

Chapter

8

Managing Software Product Services

It is easier to say what the Services Function is not than to say what it is. It is not Planning, Development, Publications, Test, or Support. In other words, it is everything needed to keep the other functions running smoothly.

8.1 THE DEFINITION OF SERVICES

Just about any way you organize software development the Services Function includes **operations**: the provision, operation, and maintenance of computer hardware and utility software; **distribution**: the filing and dissemination of software; **systems and procedures**: the provision and maintenance of standards, procedures, and formats; and **configuration management**: the identification of and revision control for all software parts. Services is also responsible for whatever administrative, personnel, and facilities needs you have that are not provided from outside your software development organization.

Some of the above services have major components worth examining separately. Systems and procedures includes plans management, the machinery to assure that plans exist and are followed, as needed within your software development organization. This requires that at least one person, a plans manager, have at least a part-time task of monitoring all plans that relate to each product and assure that they are consistent with one another.

Configuration management includes **document control**—filing and distribution of design documents (as distinguished from the code and publications for which distribution is responsible). At ABC, **Internal Document Distribution (IDD)** is the name given to the document control function. This name was chosen to minimize the stigma of the word *control*; more programmers are willing to turn their documents over to a distribution function than to a control function! A well-organized and adequately staffed document control function relieves other functions of many tedious, routine communications chores and pays for itself many times over in keeping everyone aware of what is happening to each product.

Administration is probably the best term for the mélange of other services. There is no end to the list of items you can include here—clerical and custodial services, accounting, insurance and other benefits, purchasing, and so forth. When these services are adequately covered externally, someone in Services is designated as an interface to each of them so that all functions relying in any way on Services can go to it for help in dealing with outside services. For example, in the ABC Computers Company, Services is a part of the Software Products Department (recall Figure 3.4), but administrative services and computer operations of the service bureau variety are not only not provided by the Software Products Department, they come from another division, Plans and Administration (recall also Figure 3.2).

8.2 ORGANIZING FOR THE SERVICES FUNCTION

The collective size of the functions Services supports and the range of services it provides determine how large Services itself is and how it is subdivided. As mentioned above, plans management can range from using part of one person's time to using several people full time. This is true of each activity. In a growing software development organization, Services is the most dynamic function, constantly rearranging its staff to cover a multitude of demands.

Be guided in organizing Services more by the spirit of service than by any concern for logical grouping of activities. The most important thing for Services to do is to provide whatever is requested, on time, at low cost, and with a minimum of fuss—service with a smile! The other functions have enough headaches meeting the requirements placed on them without having to justify their requests to their Services Function. To ask a conscientious Services manager not to challenge requests he receives may appear to be too demanding. But there is just no room in a results-oriented, project-oriented organization for any bureaucracy that can be avoided. To illustrate this point, if you have software developers housed in two near-by but separate facilities, providing each with separate computer facilities is reasonable if the total software development operation, not just the use of computing tools, is to be optimized. The mistake of locally optimizing where global optimization is needed is common, and Services is often the culprit. The tendency to locally optimize functions such as purchasing by centralizing them is the main reason you need Services to act as an intermediary between them and other software development functions. These functions need to be able to get their work done in spite of local optimization. Your best guideline is to centralize services as much as possible to maximize their efficiency, subject to first making sure that the efficiency of the user of a service is not impaired by such centralization.

Look again at the organization of ABC Computers Company in Figure 3.2. Note that software distribution is located in the Marketing Division, not in the Software Products Department of the Research and Development Division where most of the other elements of the Services Function are located. Also note that document control is located in another department: Integration and Release. This example further illustrates that organizational and functional boundaries need not be aligned. Make sure there is a good reason for it when they are not aligned. In this example ABC Computers management believes all direct customer contact functions should be the responsibility of Marketing. This is a perfectly sound organization, especially if relations with customers are at all strained.

8.3 MANAGING SOFTWARE PRODUCT SERVICES IN THE ANALYSIS PHASE

During the Analysis Phase there is little for Services to do but plan ahead. This is because prudent management calls for avoiding a commitment of significant resources to a project until it is proven feasible; that is, until a requirements contract is approved. The only long-lead item for Services to provide is development hardware and since this is also a high-cost item, its commitment is avoided until requirements contract approval.

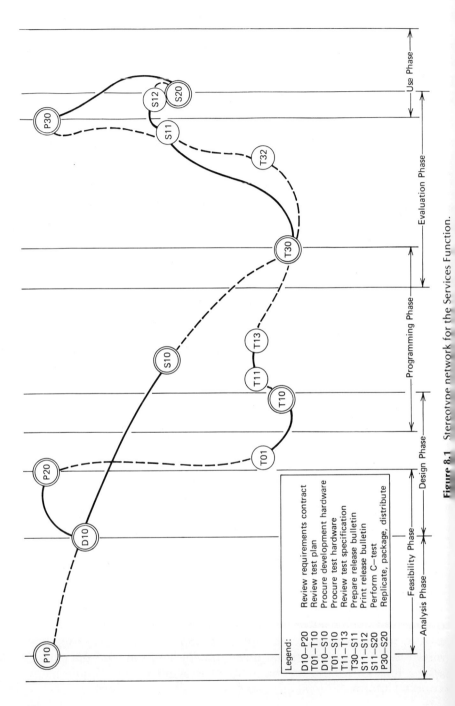

Figure 8.1 Stereotype network for the Services Function.

Legend:

D10–P20	Review requirements contract
T01–T10	Review test plan
D10–S10	Procure development hardware
T01–S10	Procure test hardware
T11–T13	Review test specification
T30–S11	Prepare release bulletin
S11–S12	Print release bulletin
S11–S20	Perform C—test
P30–S20	Replicate, package, distribute

Analysis Phase
Feasibility Phase
Design Phase
Programming Phase
Evaluation Phase
Use Phase

As soon as resources are allocated to a project, that is, when an initial budget allocation is approved, Services works with the project manager to plan computer requirements, clerical requirements, and any other on-going services that affect the success of the project. This sometimes includes office or laboratory facilities.

Approval of a budget allocation also triggers establishment of project accounting records. Every control system needs feedback and Services provides it through summaries of all project charges as a routine part of project accounting. It is appropriate for a project manager to issue an initial schedule notice as soon as a budget allocation is approved. Services provides schedule accounting similar to expense accounting, issuing regular reports on schedule performance; see Section 16.4 for examples.

Configuration management also begins with budget allocation approval. A plans manager assures that a project file is started in document control. From this point on he monitors the file to assure that all planning and design documents for the project are in the file or elsewhere in document control files and pointed to from the project file. Both the budget allocation and the schedule notice are immediately placed under revision control so that all changes receive proper review and approval. Even if a project is killed at the end of its Feasibility Phase, these files are placed in archives so that information is available in the future for reinitiating projects or for providing references for new projects.

Figure 8.1 shows a stereotype network plan for the Services Function. Services continually reviews it as a reminder to watch for the occurrence of events in other functional areas that trigger Services activities.

8.4 MANAGING SOFTWARE PRODUCT SERVICES IN THE FEASIBILITY AND DESIGN PHASES

At the end of the Analysis Phase the project manager submits his proposed requirements contract. The plans manager reviews it for consistency with existing plans and feeds back his findings to the project manager. Services also reviews the requirements contract for developmental hardware requirements and any other project dependencies that must be satisfied by Services. Long-lead procurements are initiated but not committed until requirements contract approval.

Services usually operates a computer center or development laboratory with the appropriate personnel and hardware and software environments to provide C-Test for a product. **C-Test** is a verification of product installability and an assurance that a variety of hardware and software configurations work together with the product. C-Test is most effective when performed by the lowest-level personnel who are least familiar with the product yet can reasonably be expected to configure and install it. A product's requirements contract defines what C-Test will be performed and who will perform it. Thus if Services is to be involved in C-Test it reviews a requirements contract for its concurrence with the statements about C-Test.

Another item of concern to Services during requirements contract review is product distribution—when, to whom, by what means, on what media, and with what components. Services reviews product end items and delivery and installation requirements to assure that no configuration management rules are violated and that Services has (or will have by distribution time) the media, tools, and personnel resources to perform the distribution function.

Make a decision at this time regarding ownership protection. Specify whether the product will be patented, copyrighted, or claimed as proprietary. Experience to date indicates that patenting is expensive and difficult to enforce; copyrighting is easy—especially if you follow the common practice of not registering a copyright until infringement is suspected—and is a reasonable deterrent; and a proprietary claim is easy to make but difficult to enforce. See Section 17.8 for help in making this decision and procedures for enforcing it. Record your decision in a requirements contract and be sure that Services prepares to properly mark all items to be distributed and to appropriately control their distribution.

Immediately after a requirements contract is approved, Services converts tentative hardware acquisition and facilities plans into commitments, because management has expressed its intent to complete the product by approving the requirements contract.

Shortly after requirements contract approval, Test submits a test plan for review. Services reviews this plan primarily to assure that hardware and software requirements for B- and C-Test can be met by Services. Firm commitments are made to acquire and install such tools, again because management has shown sufficient intent to complete the product by already approving the requirements contract.

Certainly by the time a test plan is offered for review, periodic project progress reporting is underway. Services provides help in preparing—as in the case of running PERT analyses on a computer—and distributing reports. Services also consolidates and summarizes project reports by unit, function, department, product line, geographic location—whatever is best for your organization.

8.5 MANAGING SOFTWARE PRODUCT SERVICES IN THE PROGRAMMING PHASE

During the Programming and Evaluation Phases, Development and Test make their heaviest demands on Services, primarily for computer operations. During these phases, schedule slippages due to various reasons within the control of Development may have accumulated, and Development shows little sympathy for or patience with any delays in installing its hardware or keeping it running. This is the time for service with a smile if ever there was one! A prudent operations manager has contingency plans for meeting project needs even if project managers have none, and may even have some in reserve if they do.

Another task performed by Services in the Programming Phase is test specification review. The primary objective is to concur with the details of C-Test, but only if Services is to perform it.

8.6 MANAGING SOFTWARE PRODUCT SERVICES IN THE EVALUATION PHASE

Services activity continues to build as a project moves from the Programming to the Evaluation Phase and peaks near the end of the Evaluation Phase. A stereotype labor distribution curve for the Services Function, such as is shown in Figure 8.2, clearly shows this peak.

Some time after A-Test begins there is likely to be pressure to make some limited release of a product to one or more of its ultimate users. Such a release is called a **prerelease**, for the product is unverified, its publications are incomplete, training is not yet available, and Maintenance is unprepared to support the product. For all of these reasons, carefully control prereleases. Services helps by administering waivers. A **waiver** is a document that records the reason for a prerelease, the recipient, the components, a disclaimer of support, and the approvals which collectively emphasize that a prerelease is an exception to normal procedures and that all participants must carefully weigh the pros and cons of dealing with an incomplete product.

Figure 8.3 is an example of the waiver form used at ABC Computers Company.

As soon as B-Test begins, Services starts to prepare for product distribution. Its main activity here is preparation of a release bulletin which defines for the product's recipients what components they will receive and gives directions on how to install them. A release bulletin is based primarily on data prepared by Development and transmitted to Test as one of the B-Test acceptance criteria. The release specification presented in Section 15.4 serves this purpose.

You may wonder why Services and not Development, Publications, Support, or Test prepares a release bulletin. Any of these functions is capable of performing the task, but Services includes operations; installing and operating software and hardware is one of its routine tasks. Services is exceptionally well qualified to prepare instructions in terms the users of these instructions can understand.

A release bulletin is completed as soon as Test issues a B-Test report recommending release of the product. The release bulletin may not be completed sooner because it must contain descriptions of all product deficiencies that are found during B-Test but that are not

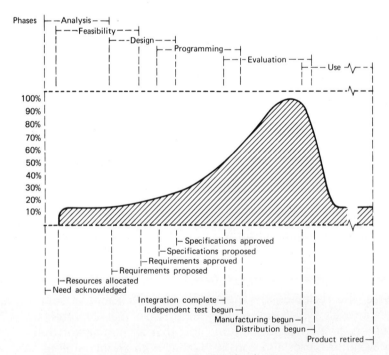

Figure 8.2   Relative manpower loading for the Services Function.

TO BE COMPLETED BY REQUESTOR	
PRODUCT ID #:	PRODUCT NAME:
USER FOR WHOM WAIVER IS REQUESTED:	
REASON FOR REQUESTING WAIVER:	
ITEMS REQUESTED (OBJECT CODE, MANUALS, ETC.):	

SHIP TO:	DATE NEEDED:	REQUEST DATE:
	REQUESTOR SIGNATURE	

TO BE COMPLETED BY SOFTWARE PRODUCTS		
WAIVER #:	RECORD DATE:	SHIP DATE:
☐ APPROVED ☐ DISAPPROVED	IF APPROVED, ITEMS TO BE SHIPPED: IF DISAPPROVED, REASON:	

APPROVALS

FOR MARKETING TECHNICAL SUPPORT

FOR PRODUCT LINE MANAGEMENT

FOR SOFTWARE PRODUCTS

FORM 2455

Figure 8.3   ABC Computers Company's software product waiver form.

serious enough to delay release for correction. These deficiencies include both software and publications.

Completion of a release bulletin is the first step in the manufacturing process. **Software manufacturing** includes preparation of installation instructions; replication of code; packing and shipping; and the quality control function, C-Test. As soon as the release bulletin is complete, Services begins C-Test. It does not begin sooner because the procedures to be followed during C-Test—assembly, system generation, installation, configuration variation—are defined in the release bulletin. One element of C-Test—quality control or evaluation of the software manufacturing process—takes place a bit later.

The decision to release a product triggers several Services activities. It prints the release bulletin in sufficient quantity to make the initial product distribution and to fill all orders anticipated prior to product updating (a product update requires a revised release bulletin if for no other reason than to identify corrected deficiencies and to provide a new list of outstanding deficiencies). Then Services replicates the software in sufficient quantity for the initial distribution plus a few reserves; gathers the software, the release bulletin, and related publications together; and packages them. It completes C-Test by picking a random package (or a few random packages); by verifying the contents against a checklist; and by performing a few simple installation-related procedures to assure things like the readability of tapes.

When distributing a product, Services is responsible for controlling who gets what. It properly labels (see Section 17.8) copyrighted and proprietary materials to enable you to demonstrate at any time that you have exercised control; it assures that recipients sign appropriate disclaimers in which they promise to take precautions against secondary distribution; and it keeps accurate and complete shipping lists of everything sent out. Most importantly, it never allows anyone to "help himself" to any proprietary end items.

Services also assures disaster protection for a product. It duplicates and stores all vital records, which include your entire document control and software code libraries, in fireproof facilities geographically remote from their primary points of reference. It uses a checklist such as the end items matrix of a requirements contract to be sure it knows what is stored for a product and where each piece is located. As a final step in the distribution process, Services reviews the checklist and verifies that all specified items are in secure archives.

8.7 MANAGING SOFTWARE PRODUCT SERVICES IN THE USE PHASE

The Use Phase begins when manufacturing begins, as shown in Figure 8.2. From then until a product is released to all users it remains in its Evaluation Phase because C-Test is in process. The reason for saying the Use Phase begins as soon as manufacturing begins even though C-Test is not complete and even though no user may have received the product, is that the product is complete and a special distribution could be made to a critical user. The subtle distinction is worth making to emphasize the need to be prepared for an exclusive distribution to a critical user.

The part of the Use Phase that gives the phase its name begins as soon as any user receives a product. It is then in use as far as its producers are concerned, and they must be prepared to appropriately support it for the duration of the Use Phase. To Services this means, principally, administering error correction, product updating, and product enhancement procedures.

Some user problems cannot be solved in the field. They must be channeled back to the Maintenance Function for resolution. Services, with the help of Support, provides this channel via a **maintenance request system**. The field procedures for maintenance requests are handled by Support and are covered in Section 11.6. The "in-house" procedures handled by Services are as follows.

As Services receives each maintenance request, it classifies the request, logs it, and acknowledges its receipt directly to the submitter. Requests are classified as corrections, revisions, or enhancements. A suspected error is a **correction request**; a mandatory change to keep a product compatible with its environment is a **revision request**; and a desirable but not necessary new feature is an **enhancement request**. Any of the three is a **maintenance request**. A single form can be used to record all types, with tentative classification made at the source and final classification made by Services when it logs them.

In processing maintenance requests, the acknowledgement is very important for two reasons: first, it assures the user that his problem has been reported; and second, it contains a date by which an answer will be provided. This reply date also is important for two reasons: first, it gives the user an idea of how long he must live with uncertainty; and second, it puts subtle pressure on Maintenance to analyze the problem within a finite amount of time.

In processing a correction request a copy of the acknowledgement is sent to Support for monitoring, and the request with the acknowledgement is sent to Maintenance and Test. Maintenance analyzes the problem and reports the results of the analysis to Test and Services. Services reports the results to the user (this is the previously promised reply) with a copy to Support for monitoring. If the results of the analysis indicate a user misunderstanding that requires no further action, or if they indicate that what the user really wants or needs is an enhancement to the product, no further action on the request is required and this is noted by all functions. If there is a certainty or a high probability that an error exists, Maintenance describes its planned approach to solving the problem and commits a schedule for completing its work on the problem. When Services gets this type of reply from Maintenance, it passes the reply and the correction availability date back to the user and to Support for monitoring.

When Maintenance completes work on a request, it sends its results to Test and Services. Services forwards the results to the user and again to Support for continued monitoring. If the reply promises updated code as part of the solution, Test prepares test cases for subsequent regression testing and Services "keeps the book open" on the request until validated corrective code appears in a product update.

Until Services "closes the book" on each request, it continually reminds Maintenance and Test of their commitments and notifies management of their progress. Services keeps management informed with periodic reports such as the maintenance request summaries described in Section 16.7, and stimulates Maintenance and Test with appropriately timed reminders.

Procedures for handling enhancements and revisions are similar to procedures for handling errors. These requests are logged and acknowledged just as correction requests are. They are routed to someone for review, someone like the enhancement board described in Section 18.4, who provides preliminary responses to Services who in turn responds to the submitters. Final disposition of each request is analyzed and committed under the purview of the enhancement board, and a final response is routed to the submitter by Services. Summary reports and reminders are provided by Services for these requests in much the same manner as for correction requests.

When a correction request turns out to be an enhancement request or a revision request, the centralization of processing for all types of requests in Services makes reclassification easy. Maintenance merely submits an enhancement request or a revision request on behalf of the correction request submitter and returns the new request to Services as part of its reply to the correction request. Services simultaneously makes the appropriate entries in its records and keeps everything moving smoothly.

The updates resulting from error corrections and the new versions resulting from enhancements and revisions cause occasional redistributions of products to come to Services throughout the Use Phase. Each of these is handled just like the initial distribution.

There are several other activities performed by Services in the Use Phase. Recall that plans management is performed by Services. During the Use Phase plans management continues to prepare revised configurators, to monitor change reconciliation in requirements contracts, and to watch for deviations from committed support levels.

Services may provide some user services for items other than your products. A common case is a **user library**—a collection of programs submitted by users for cataloging and distributing to other users. Most computer manufacturers provide such a service through their company-supported user groups like CUBE (Burroughs), FOCUS (Control Data), DECUS (Digital Equipment), and SHARE (IBM). SHARE relieved IBM of responsibility for its user library for political reasons, but this is the exception rather than the rule. User library administration is similar enough to your main distribution function to not require a separate presentation here. Another user-group service is a newsletter. This, too, requires only application of some standard production and distribution techniques.

8.8   SERVICES' REVIEW AND APPROVAL RESPONSIBILITY

Services, like the other functions, has a responsibility to review and approve several key project documents and to participate in some of the phase reviews.

At Phase I Review Services examines a project's budget allocation and discusses the role Services would play in the project should it survive past the Feasibility Phase. It looks primarily for developmental hardware and other facilities requirements that Development would expect Services to provide. Since Services normally makes no irreversible commitments until a requirements contract is approved, its role at Phase I Review is only to review and not to approve.

At Phase II Review Services negotiates commitments to provide hardware and other facilities, to provide C-Test, and to distribute the product. It also reviews, in order to make its own plans, its upcoming obligations in configuration management, ownership protection, filing, and administration of maintenance. Thus, it both reviews and approves at Phase II Review.

Services does not participate in Phase III Review, but between Phase II and IV Reviews it does review and approve the test plan and the test specification to assure its concurrence with C-Test as defined therein. It also reviews and approves its obligation, as stated in the test plan, to provide test hardware and other facilities.

Except for fulfilling the role of plans management and to review and approve schedules, Services does not participate in any other phase reviews. A plans manager reviews the requirements contract at Phase

Phase	Review	Responsibility
Analysis	I	Review
Feasibility	II	Review and approve
Design	III	None
Programming	IV	Review
Evaluation	V	Review
Use	VI	Review

Figure 8.4 Minimum responsibilities of the Services Function at Phase Reviews.

II; the configurator at Phases II, IV, and VI; and the schedule at Phases I–V. His role is entirely advisory and pertains only to plans consistency, so he only reviews and does not approve.

Services reviews all schedule notices and approves any that set or change commitments on Services. With respect to the stereotype milestones presented in Figure 8.1, milestones always of concern to Services are Project Hardware Installed (S10) and Product Distribution Date (S20). It also reviews and approves other minor milestones such as Release Bulletin Ready for Printer (S11) and Release Bulletin Printed (S12) as they are established and modified during network plan reviews. In summary, the role of Services at phase plan reviews, exclusive of purely schedule items, is as presented in Figure 8.4.

Managing Software Product Publications

The word **publications** and the term **reference material** are used to cover those printed documents which have as their audience the end-users of a software product. The word **documentation** is reserved for plans and specifications which have as their audience the planners, developers, writers, testers, supporters, and maintainers who bring the product to the user. Making a distinction such as this improves communication within your software product development organization.

Promotional and reference publications are also differentiated, primarily because their audiences are different and secondarily because they naturally are produced by functions with different objectives. The audience for promotional material is generally management, as contrasted with the operators, programmers, and analysts who use reference material. The Support Function is responsible for promotional material as part of its marketing activity, and as this chapter explains, the Publications Function is responsible for reference material. In practice you may want to combine the production of promotional and reference material, but keep in mind that they are parts of distinctly different functions.

9.1 ORGANIZING FOR THE PUBLICATIONS FUNCTION

Why have a Publications Function? Why not just let developers document their work as they please, have it printed, and leave it at that?

There are many reasons for having a Publications Function and those reasons strongly suggest how that function should be organized.

First of all, you have undoubtedly noticed that few programmers like to write anything but code. While they may relish rewriting their code again and again, making it tighter and more sophisticated, they seldom have the time or the inclination to document their design or to tell someone how to use it. The advent of chief programmer teams has popularized the assignment of technical writers directly to development projects to overcome the programmer's disinclination to write, and the results have been favorable. Where a product has no compatibility constraints or where it need not be used in conjunction with several other products, assignment of writers to development teams may meet your needs. But if you must provide similarity of style and format to make the transition from one publication to another easy for the user, or if you want to convey a professional image of your organization to its customers, you must centralize much if not all of the Publications Function.

Centralized production and planning are essential for achieving consistency from publication to publication. Whether or not you centralize the writing activity may depend on your ability to motivate the writers. Unless you pool their resources, giving them a chance to work not only with programmers but with their peers, you may stifle their professional development, their opportunity to advance in your organization, or ultimately your own ability to retain them long enough to recover your investment in them.

The above objectives can be met by establishing an organizational entity comprised of a writing group and a production group. Writers can be assigned to development projects individually or in teams, with varying degrees of direction by the parent Publications organization and the hosting Development organizations. Whatever produces the smoothest working relationship consistent with Publications' objectives should be your guide. The production group, on the other hand, should be entirely under the direction of the Publications Function. Within the production unit will be editors, proofreaders, typists, illustrators, graphic artists, draftspersons, photographers—a variety of specialists who form a team having far more in common with one another than with anyone else. They need professional guidance in establishing and maintaining a house style, just as the writers do.

The final element of the Publications Function is the provision and maintenance of standards for both writers and the production unit, an activity which one or more publications analysts can perform. A possible Publications Department Organization is shown in Figure 9.1.

Where Publications reports in your organization depends on its scope and size and the nature of your business. As Figure 9.1 shows, there is a Publications Department in the ABC Computers Company that is responsible for both hardware and software products. And, if you will refer back to Figure 3.2, you will see that the department is a part of Marketing. Placing Publications in Marketing at ABC emphasizes the strong customer orientation which has become a competitive forte of ABC.

Staffing the production activity is not peculiar to software engineering but staffing the writing function is. It is not easy to convert a technical writer from another discipline into a software writer because of the complexities and rigors of the subject matter. It is also not easy to convert a programmer into a software writer because so few programmers like to write. The prospective software writer will have demonstrated good writing skills, particularly in dealing with abstract and conceptual processes, and will display a strong interest in technical subjects. He must be specifically trained in your work environment and must be provided with hands-on experience with at least one example of each type of product he must document. The high cost of this type of preparation is one of the reasons you want to provide a suitable career for your writers—to maximize the return on your investment.

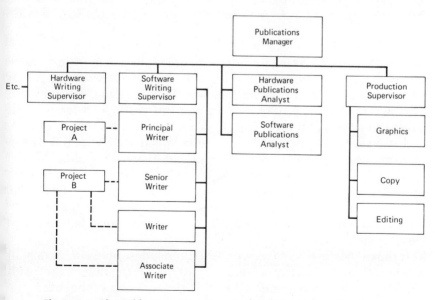

Figure 9.1   The Publications Department of ABC Computers Company.

So much for organization. In the following sections remember that what is described applies to the Publications Function no matter how it is organized, even if it is distributed across several organizational entities.

9.2 STANDARDS AND PRACTICES

Just as programmers will "do their own thing" if not constrained by standards, so will writers and graphic artists. If you want your publications to project a good image among your customers, begin with a good set of standards. Strive to channel creativity without stifling it by involving writers in the preparation and review of standards so that they have a chance to promote their own styles, or have their peers convince them that an alternate style is better.

The first item in a set of standards is a **style guide**. In it you set forth the categories of publication and establish the outline for each category: page size, type font, artistic style, glossary, identification control, proofreading marks, typing format, indexing requirements, format for on-line messages, and anything else you feel is important to the image you want to present.

Categories of publication vary from organization to organization. The following categories, which are used throughout this book, are comprehensive and coherent and can certainly be used for a wide variety of products:

System Description Manual. A system description manual introduces a major software product or system. It provides a prospective user with general, introductory information describing the concepts and capabilities of the product. It discusses the product in terms of its overall functions and highlights its salient features. Its tone is positive and stresses those system characteristics which are competitively significant. The intended audience for this type of manual is not necessarily knowledgeable in program and computer design, but will probably influence computer selection or purchase. The basic source document for the system description manual is the requirements contract supplemented by input from both Support and Development.

Reference Manual. A reference manual describes in detail all external characteristics of a software product. It provides a user with detailed information about what the product does; the hardware required and how this equipment is organized; the program language, including command and message format, input/output forms, codes; and interfaces to other software products. The reference manual assumes that the user has a working knowledge of required hardware and related software products.

The basic source for the reference manual is the external specification. Additional input is provided by Development personnel. The intended audience for this manual is the working programmer or analyst who is the direct user of the product. Normally an experience level of one year is assumed.

Reference Booklet. A reference booklet is a pocket-size compilation of reference information extracted from a reference manual. It provides ready access to such information as statement formats, mnemonics, code conversion tables, and syntax. In its most abbreviated form it is called a **reference card**.

Operator Manual. An operator manual provides information about a product to allow the user to run the program and operate related equipment. It provides equipment specifications, control statements, and operating procedures. The equipment specifications state the minimum equipment configuration, special assignments of equipment, and method of equipment assignment. The control statement descriptions specify the format and rules for using the statements. Examples showing how the control statements are used are also included. Operating procedures specify step-by-step instructions on how to operate the system, including initial loading, job execution, and error recovery procedures.

The basic source material for an operator manual is the external specification. This must be supplemented heavily by input from Development and Test personnel. The intended audience for this publication are operators with little experience appropriate to the complexity of the product.

Message Manual. A message manual describes all messages issued by the product. Descriptions of the conditions that cause the messages to be issued and required user responses, if any, are included. The basic source of information for a message manual is a program listing. A message manual is intended for operator, analyst, and programmer use.

As more people interface with software products interactively there is a growing opportunity to put much documentation on-line. Most interactive systems have (and all should have) sufficient prompting and error messages so that users need not go off-line when they reach an impasse. The Development Function provides the vehicle for such on-line information, but it is the Publications Function that is responsible for the final wording, style, and format. It also assures consistency of on-line material with printed material.

Besides controlling the style of a publication, Publications defines the flow of work from planning through distribution in a procedures manual. In it enough information is provided to schedule a publication and control the schedule. This publications scheduling system interfaces with a stereotype schedule for a complete software product.

Publications may segregate some of the items above as policies, to add emphasis. For example, they might have a policy on copyright that is reviewed and approved by other organizations which have a vested interest such as your legal department. Another example is the binding of manuals; the pros and cons of loose-leaf versus permanent bindings may warrant considerable debate throughout your organization. And there is distribution; if you are multinational you may prefer distributing plates for printing in several countries rather than paying duty on bulky shipments of printed manuals.

9.3 MANAGING SOFTWARE PRODUCT PUBLICATIONS IN THE ANALYSIS PHASE

The Publications Function first becomes involved with a product at Phase I Review by making a preliminary estimate of the cost of providing publications for the product. This implies that some assumptions must be made about what publications to produce, when, and at what standard costs. The better the standards used by Publications are, the more accurate the estimate it renders at this time will be. Deciding to produce a reference manual, an operator manual, and a message manual for a proposed RPG compiler, for instance, should provide enough information to make a "ball-park" estimate of Publications costs.

An initial schedule notice is reviewed at Phase I Review. In your planning and control system provide at least one milestone on the schedule notice for Publications. Whether or not they forecast its schedule at Phase I Review is optional, since its milestones will be sufficiently bounded by other functions' predecessor and successor milestones for early planning purposes. Figure 9.2 shows the relationship of such Publications milestones to other stereotype milestones. After Phase I Review the Publications Function is essentially dormant

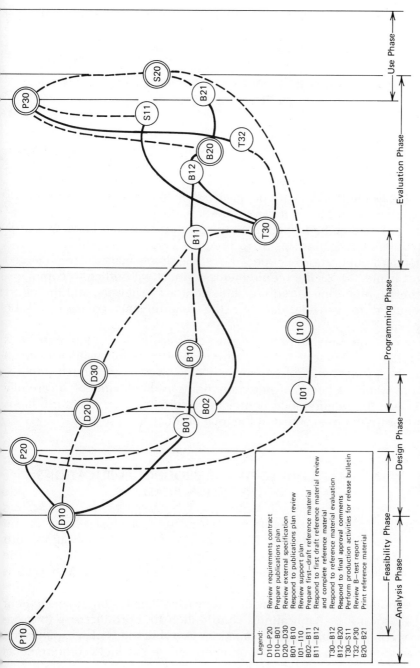

Figure 9.2 Stereotype network for the Publications Function.

Legend:

D10—P20	Review requirements contract
D10—B01	Prepare publications plan
D20—D30	Review external specification
B01—B10	Respond to publications plan review
I01—I10	Review support plan
B02—B11	Prepare first—draft reference material
B11—B12	Respond to first draft reference material review and complete reference material
T30—B12	Respond to reference material evaluation
B12—B20	Respond to final approval comments
T30—S11	Perform production activities for release bulletin
T32—P30	Review B—test report
B20—B21	Print reference material

Analysis Phase — Feasibility Phase — Design Phase — Programming Phase — Evaluation Phase — Use Phase

125

(for an individual product!) until a product's requirements contract is submitted.

9.4 MANAGING SOFTWARE PRODUCT PUBLICATIONS IN THE FEASIBILITY PHASE

When a product's requirements contract is submitted, it includes statements about what publications will be produced, when they will be available, and what exceptional dependencies constrain the Publications Function with respect to its contribution to the product. If Publications wants to be involved in the review of a product's external specification, it can request, as a dependency in the requirements contract, participation on the product's technical review board.

Unless Publications plans to produce a publication other than the standard publications defined above, the simple matrix recommended in Chapter 13 for the requirements contract will suffice to communicate its intentions to requirements contract reviewers, and the effort required to provide data for the requirements contract will be minimal.

From the time a requirements contract is submitted until it is approved at Phase II Review, all interested functions will evaluate all of the product's requirements and objectives. Even though Publications will have been consulted on inputs to the document, it carefully reviews the requirements contract to assure itself that its contributions are proper in the context of the total product.

9.5 MANAGING SOFTWARE PRODUCT PUBLICATIONS IN THE DESIGN PHASE

The Design Phase takes its name from the principal activity of the Development Function at that time. The design of publications also begins here, but it is preceded slightly by a planning activity specific to Publications: preparation, review, and approval of a publications plan.

A publications plan is needed to provide Publications' management with control of Publications' contribution to a product and to make that control visible to other functions. A **publications plan** expands the statements made about publications in a product's requirements

1	PRODUCT DESCRIPTION
1.1	Product Name(s) and Numbers
1.1.1	Product Name(s)
1.1.2	Name Abbreviations
1.1.3	Product Numbers
1.1.4	Project Numbers
1.2	Brief Description of Publications
1.3	Publication End Items
2	MISSION
2.1	Revision Request Reconciliation
2.1.1	Revisions Excluded
2.1.2	Revisions Included
2.2	Enhancement Request Reconciliation
2.2.1	Enhancements Excluded
2.2.2	Enhancements Included
2.3	Correction Request Reconciliation
2.3.1	Corrections Excluded
2.4	Plans Reconciliation
2.4.1	Plans Excluded
2.4.2	Plans Included
2.5	Summary of User Needs
2.6	Alternatives Considered
2.7	Return on Investment
3	STRATEGY
3.1	Conventions
3.1.1	Notations
3.1.2	Terminology
3.2	Publications
3.2.n	(Publication Name n)
3.2.n.1	Constraints
3.2.n.1.1	Standards
3.2.n.1.2	Compatibility Constraints
3.2.n.2	Design Properties
4	BACKGROUND
4.1	References
5	DELIVERY AND INSTALLATION
5.1	Provisions for Protection
5.2	Installation
5.3	Media
6	TACTICS
6.1	Interdependencies
6.1.1	Interdependencies Needed
6.1.2	Interdependencies Provided
6.2	Technical Review
6.3	Product Verification
6.4	Provisions for Support
6.4.1	Provisions for Promotion
6.4.2	Provisions for Training
6.4.3	Provisions for Conversion
7	SCHEDULE

Figure 9.3 Stereotype publications plan contents.

127

contract to cover reconciliation with other plans, incorporation of previously approved changes, applicable standards, characteristics of publications to be produced, and review requirements. Figure 9.3 shows the table of contents for a publications plan derived from the requirements contract format of Chapter 13. There need not be a separate planning document for each product. Indeed, grouping publications for a product set together may reveal interdependencies or conflicts in production. It may also provide needed visibility to program management. Do not infer, however, that a publications plan may ever be omitted or not committed to writing; it must serve the needs of Planning, Development, and Support as well as Publications. Once a publications plan is approved Publications may reinforce it by tying individual work plans to it.

The stereotype network of Figure 9.2 shows major activities of Publications and their relationship to stereotype milestones. Such activities, augmented as necessary for multiple publications and to show reviews of early drafts, can be included in publications plans.

Later in the Design Phase, Development submits an external specification for review by other functions. Publications reviews the external specification to make sure that the document is complete enough to begin drafting reference material. If Publications is going to produce a system description manual, it is begun first because it should be available for distribution about the same time as promotional material produced by the Support Function (refer again to Figure 9.2).

If there is going to be on-line reference material, Publications works closely with Development in preparing a product's external specification, for the form and content of all messages to the user are specified in the external specification. There is not the usual opportunity for Publications to use a different style and format in reference material prepared separately from the external specification. In this situation, having rules for on-line references specified in a publications style guide gets the interaction between Publications and Development off to a good start.

9.6 MANAGING SOFTWARE PRODUCT PUBLICATIONS IN THE PROGRAMMING PHASE

The relative manpower loading curve for Publications (Figure 9.4) peaks in the Programming Phase as the following activities are performed. During the Programming Phase Support's plan is reviewed by other functions. Publications reviews it to be sure that any draft or

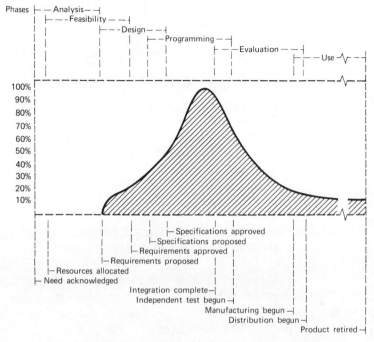

Figure 9.4   Relative manpower loading for the Publications Function.

final publications needed for training or as source or reference material for promotional literature will be available when needed. Drafting of publications begun in the Design Phase reaches its peak of activity during the Programming Phase. Writers are in frequent contact with developers, including attending design review meetings. At one or more times during this phase Publications offers preliminary drafts of reference material to Development for review, primarily to seek affirmation of technical accuracy. Such reviews are kept as informal as is practical to encourage a cooperative relationship between writers and designers. Late in the Programming Phase drafts of training material are offered for review by Support. Publications reviews them to determine if they are consistent in style and content with other publications. If Publications provides production services for training or promotional material this is done in the Programming Phase followed or overlapped by review of the material.

From the time an external specification is first approved early in the Programming Phase until B-Test begins at the very end of the phase, Publications is continually forced to react to changes in the external specification brought about by approved additions and deletions. While Publications is a party to reviewing all such changes prior to approval, it seldom can say "You can't make that change because I can't accommodate it in the reference manual." Instead, Publications agrees to the change and *makes abundantly clear* to management any schedule impact and increases in cost associated with necessary rework. This can be done through a technical review board or enhancement board, where these exist and are appropriate. General management then weighs the design change against the other alternatives such as increased cost, delayed product, and delayed publications. This technique keeps disputes between Publications and Development from delaying progress on a project.

9.7   MANAGING SOFTWARE PRODUCT PUBLICATIONS IN THE EVALUATION PHASE

Fairly early in the Evaluation Phase Publications completes final drafts of all publications, including all illustrations, formatted for production. These drafts are circulated to other functions for their review. At the very least Development, Test, and Support review the material. Test, in particular, evaluates all publications for a product just as it evaluates the software: by comparing the publications to the specifications for accuracy, and by comparing the publications to the software for consistency. Test issues trouble reports (see Section 10.8) for publications deficiencies just as it does for software deficiencies. Publications must respond to them either with corrections or with a rationale for deciding not to provide corrections.

Once Test is satisfied with the accuracy of a publication, it is printed and sent to distribution. This decision to print usually is reached before the software is recommended for release. Publications takes advantage of this lead time to avoid a rush print job.

During the Evaluation Phase Services prepares installation material to accompany a product. This material, called a release bulletin, is produced according to or compatible with standards set by Publications. As for other material, Publications can provide production services for the release bulletin and oversee its printing.

When management makes a decision regarding release of a product near the end of the Evaluation Phase, Publications is involved if there is a recommendation to release the product with publications deficiencies. Such a recommendation is made only if correcting the deficiencies has a negative impact on the release greater than the positive impact of releasing the product sooner at lower cost.

9.8 MANAGING SOFTWARE PRODUCT PUBLICATIONS IN THE USE PHASE

Once a product has entered the Use Phase its publications are maintained just as its code is. In spite of the most careful review and evaluation within a software development organization, some errors will be detected by users. As these errors are reported through maintenance requests, they are corrected by answering these requests and collecting the corrections for publications updates. Updates can be published several ways: reprinting entire publications, printing errata sheets, and printing change-pages. Distribution of corrections can be achieved by directly distributing any of the above forms of correction or by including errata or change-pages in release bulletins for update releases of code or in response to maintenance requests.

Regardless of the form a correction takes or the way it is distributed, adequate configuration management standards are followed. Every edition of a publication, every change-page, and every erratum must correspond to a specific external specification and piece of code, and vice versa. It is usually Services' responsibility to police configuration management, but it is everyone's responsibility to observe it.

9.9 PUBLICATIONS' REVIEW AND APPROVAL RESPONSIBILITY

Just prior to Phase I Review Publications is asked to provide an initial estimate of resources needed, for inclusion in a project budget allocation. As stated earlier in Section 9.3, standard costs may be provided and approval of these estimates may be deferred until Phase II Review at which time they might be revised before approval. Publications will therefore probably want to review only the complete budget allocation at Phase I Review.

At Phase II Review Publications reviews its inputs to the requirements contract in the context of the complete document and approves the document after it is modified during review. Publications' approval is necessary because specific publications are committed at this time. A revision of the project's budget allocation is reviewed and Publications approves the costs for its contributions.

Phase	Review	Responsibility
Analysis	I	Review
Feasibility	II	Review and approve
Design	III	Review
Programming	IV	None
Evaluation	V	None
Use	VI	None

Figure 9.5   Minimum responsibilities of the Publications Function at phase reviews.

Similarly, a schedule notice is reviewed and approved to commit Publications' schedule.

Prior to Phase III Review Publications provides its inputs to the product's external specification. At the actual time of Phase III Review Publications has to review only the external specification as it is recommended for approval by Development—to assure that its interests are accounted for properly.

Phase IV Review is concerned primarily with acceptance of code for evaluation by Test. Publications is concerned only if additional resources are required to complete its work, or if its schedule needs revision. Publications participates in Phase V Review only if there is a recommendation to release a product with deficiencies in any publications. If so, the debate focuses on the relative advantages and disadvantages of meeting schedule at the expense of quality. Phase VI Review is concerned with lowering or dropping support of a product. By this time publications changes are so minimal as to be a routine maintenance activity and Publications is not involved in the review.

In summary, Publications' participation in phase reviews is as shown in Figure 9.5.

Chapter
10

Managing Software Product Test

This chapter is about the Software Product Test Function or, more briefly, the Test Function. Throughout this book the word test, whether used as a noun or as a verb, does *not* mean debugging. **Debugging** is the activity of determining why a program error exists and eliminating the cause of the error. **Testing** is the determination that an error exists and the identification of the discrepancy between a product and its specification.

This book could take the position that software product test is really software **quality assurance**, but that would be presumptuous. Software quality assurance includes a lot more than testing, as defined above. It also includes performance analysis and design analysis aimed at assuring not only freedom from error but also the presence of features and the use of design and programming techniques to enhance reliability, recoverability, usability, maintainability, customizability, and restartability. Quality assurance is really what software engineering *en toto* is all about.

10.1 THE STATE OF THE ART IN ASSURING QUALITY

How much quality assurance can a Test Function provide? Obviously, it can test as defined above. With tools like the review boards of

Chapter 18, the requirements contract of Chapter 13, the specifications of Chapter 15, and the phase reviews introduced in Section 6.10, the Test Function exercises considerable influence over the quality of the whole software production process. It cannot, however, be responsible for assuring quality, since it does not control the production of the elements of a software product: the software, the publications, the training.

This book advocates that the Test Function perform testing as defined above; **evaluation,** defined as measuring the "abilities"— reliability, usability, and so on; and design review, defined as influencing design through phase reviews. Some companies are experimenting with a higher degree of design involvement by quality assurance specialists, but their effectiveness must be proven. The balance between development and test responsibilities is very delicate and must be handled carefully.

Quite apart from the role of the Test Function in producing software products, is the nature of the tests performed. There is a movement in software engineering (51) to certify software—to prove its correctness as compared with its specifications—through independent agencies, or to declare it in compliance with standards in the manner of Underwriters Laboratories or Verband Deutscher Elektrotechniker.

There are also standard tests being developed and circulated, such as United States National Bureau of Standards COBOL tests. There even exist combinations of testing services and standard tests, such as the Federal COBOL Compiler Testing Service operated by the United States Department of the Navy.

Improvements in software quality assurance methodology are appearing at an accelerating rate. A major contributor is structured programming, the advent of which has caught the interest of programmers (more than of designers, testers, and managers) like no other concern for quality previously has. The test methodology you find in this book is fundamentally sound and is integrated into an over-all, top-down, self-consistent methodology for producing software products; as new developments in quality assurance come along, you should have no trouble adding them to this framework.

Unfortunately for those of you who would like to learn more about software quality assurance, it is still considered so vital to manufacturers of heavy-duty software that they consider any improvements in their procedures proprietary and seldom share them. Such a parochial view is still a fact of life.

10.2   TYPES OF SOFTWARE PRODUCT TEST

Just where testing begins and where it ends is hard to define. For the purposes of this book, however, a classification of tests according to who performs them, when, and in what way is useful.

Stages of Software Product Test

Those tests whose time of occurrence varies are called "stages." The first stage is A-Test. A-Test occurs during the latter part of the Programming Phase, after all modules of a product have been individually debugged and integrated. It is accompanied by **system debugging**, the correction of errors in interfaces.

The second stage is B-Test, when an independent (from Development) evaluation of a complete product is performed, both in isolation and in conjunction with other members of its product set. Ideally, B-Test begins when the developers claim their product is ready to distribute to customers. During B-Test a product is compared to its requirements, specifications, publications, and objectives, quite likely in that order of precedence. B-Test may or may not include field testing as well as in-house testing. In either case the products under test are submitted to realistic customer environments.

The third and final stage of testing, C-Test, takes place after the Test Function recommends release of a product and turns it over to distribution. C-Test is akin to a factory quality control test wherein a random package of a software product is taken off the shelf, installed, and briefly exercised.

Typical relative time durations for A-, B-, and C-Tests, their sequence, and their positions in the product's life cycle, are shown in Figure 10.1.

Modes of Software Product Test

Another way to categorize software testing is according to who does it. The categorization that follows assumes the existence of a Test Function that is independent of the Development Function.

Mode I covers full participation by the Test Function—test planning, specifying, building, running, and analyzing. This is normally the highest, most strenuous level of testing and is used for the most heavy-duty products.

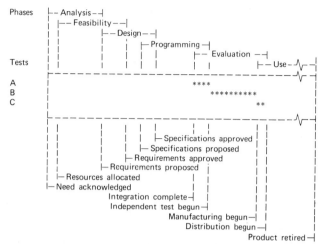

Figure 10.1 The sequence of A-, B-, and C-Tests and their relative positions in the life cycle.

Mode II allows for a short-cut: the Test Function is only responsible for analysis, with its evaluation applied to test plans, test specifications, tests, and test results all produced by developers.

Mode III is testing with no participation by the Test Function. It should be used for software products only in emergencies, such as in a crash, pilot project where the lack of an independent test, or at least the lack of test monitoring, can be tolerated. To be safe, if you ever use Mode III, plan for Development to install and support your "product"; you will have no guarantee that anyone else can do it or that quality is high enough to leave the product unattended in the user's hands.

Categories of Software Product Test

Just as stages define when tests are performed and modes define who performs them, categories define what tests they are. It greatly facilitates communication among the several software development functions to rigorously define a comprehensive set of categories so that everyone concerned knows just by scanning a checklist, whether or not attributes of interest to him are being tested. Such a checklist is presented in the next section.

The list of test categories that follows is comprehensive and designed to facilitate comparing test results to statements of product objectives and requirements. The categories are listed roughly in the order they would be run.

Demonstration. A demonstration uses controlled input to produce expected output. It is normally prepared and run by the Development Function during A-Test to assure management of all interested functions that a product has reached some level of completeness.

Benchmark. A benchmark certifies that a product is capable of processing input from a real user environment and producing correct results. This category of test is often used to satisfy a marketing or customer requirement to demonstrate compatibility or performance attributes of a product. It is usually specified by the Support Function and run by the Development Function near the end of A-Test.

Complete feature test. This category certifies that all features specified in a product's external specification are present and operate as described. If the product to be given a complete feature test is a new version of an existing product, this test checks both old and new features, separately and in conjunction with one another. It is normally performed during A- and B-Tests.

New feature test. A new feature test is used only for new versions of existing products, to evaluate the new features. Only cursory evaluation of previous features is made, primarily to test their interaction with new features. It is normally performed when minor changes are made in a product, as a part of A- and B-Tests.

Performance test. This test evaluates performance characteristics such as execution speed; size; throughput; data transfer rate; compilation, assembly, or generation speed; overhead; response time; and human interface. It is normally a part of A- and B-Tests.

Reliability test. This test evaluates a product under conditions that produce stress to discover its ability to operate without failure or to recover from failure such as parity errors or lost data. Normally included are artificially introduced, controlled errors; an endurance test of several hours of continuous operation; and exercising of all recoverability features. Reliability test is normally a part of A- and B-Tests.

Stability test. Stability testing certifies the successful integration of products into a product set or system. It includes tests to assure that no product causes another product to fail. With respect to an individual product, it includes mean time between failure testing. This is normally a part of A- and B-Tests.

Regression test. This category of test certifies that all errors which should be corrected in a new version or update of a product are corrected and that no new errors are introduced. This is normally a part of A- and B-Tests.

Installability test. This test certifies that a product can be installed as specified: in the time allotted, by personnel trained as specified, from materials distributed off-the-shelf, and with only specified tools. Testing includes several configurations and normally is done during A-, B-, and C-Tests.

Configuration test. This test certifies that a product operates properly on all equipment configurations for which it is designed to operate. Minimum and target configurations plus a reasonable approximation to the maximum configuration are tested, normally during A-, B-, and C-Tests.

Summary of Test Types

The stages, modes, and categories described above can be conveniently presented in matrix format. Indeed, this is precisely the presentation advocated in Chapter 13 for a product's requirements contract. To illustrate this, the matrix from the requirements contract of A$K is shown in Figure 10.2.

Note nesting of stages: The intended implication is that all categories are considered candidates for A-Test, all but two for B-Test, and only two for C-Test. Development will typically run through all stages, Test runs through the second and third, and Services runs the last.

10.3 ORGANIZING FOR THE TEST FUNCTION

The general rule of organizing for quality assurance—having it report as high in the overall organization as possible and as far as possible from development—applies to Software Product Test. The Test Function must serve as a check on other functions, particularly Development and Publications, and a conflict of interest must not be allowed to arise between them. Recall the organization of ABC (Figure 10.3); the Test Function is in the Integration and Release Department, quite separate from the Software Products Department.

The way you organize for software product test must answer the question "Where does evaluation stop and debugging begin?" It is important to keep the product testers from going beyond the identifi-

6.3. Product Verification

6.3.1. Level of Testing

	STAGE		
CATEGORY	A	B	C
Demonstration		/	/
Benchmark	D	/	/
Complete Feature	D	T	/
New Feature			/
Performance	D	T	/
Reliability	D	T	/
Stability			/
Regression			/
Installability	D	T	S
Configuration	D	T	S

TEST MODE

I = Testing performed by Test Function (X)

II = Testing Monitored by Test Function ( )

III = No participation by Test Function ( )

TESTING ORGANIZATION

D = Development   T = Test   S = Services

Services Company will provide two persons with a background
in financial analysis to operate terminals during part of
B-Test.

The Minimum Configuration of Sec. 3.3.1.1.4 will be tested
with real hardware, as will the Target Configuration except

ABC COMPUTERS	A$K POR	SHEET REVISION A	C013/L301A	
			NEXT 17	SHEET 16

MF 1064 APR 1972

Figure 10.2   A$K level of testing matrix.

139

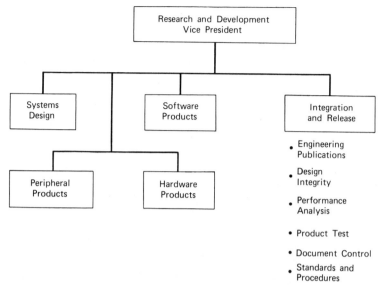

Figure 10.3   The organizational relationships of software product test at ABC Computers Company.

cation of errors; they must not be allowed to diagnose the specific cause of errors or, worse yet, to fix them. If you do not provide this separation, you will never achieve a clean hand-off from Development to Test; the developers will rely on the testers to finish debugging.

You must also think carefully about who you want to be responsible for software integration, or for software, firmware, and hardware integration. On large, multivendor products, integration and test are combined in one organization because combining the outputs of several diverse organizations into a system requires objectivity none of the suppliers is likely to have. Including test with integration reduces the number of different organizations by one without losing objectivity. You want to think carefully, however, about separating integration from Development. A lot of debugging occurs during integration and you want to be sure Development remains responsible for that debugging. You can often minimize the management effort required for successful integration by setting up an integration subfunction in the Development Function. Then any "finger-pointing" is intrafunctional rather than interfunctional and can be resolved at a lower level of management.

Refer again to Figure 10.3. Because hardware—both processors and peripheral equipment—and software are most often released as a system, integration is combined with test. At ABC, the quality assurance function is quite mature and the Integration and Release Department includes a Design Integrity unit which begins the quality assurance in the Planning Phase.

The issue of maturity, mentioned above, is very interesting with respect to many of the functions discussed in this book. Each function evolves as the organization it is part of evolves. A typical evolutionary pattern for software product test is:

1. No test at all; developers debug and release to distribution.
2. Too many bug reports come back from the field, so an entirely separate Test Function is set up, one which has no influence on product design.
3. The Test Function becomes so effective that the management of the Development Function protests, claiming, "How can I be responsible for the schedule of my products if Test keeps picking at nits and never recommends release?" Test is then given to Development, which works sufficiently well because the testers have developed an independence too strong to succumb to contamination.
4. Development and higher management realize that Test is a really professional function and that testers have valuable contributions to make to planning and design. They begin to make substantial contributions to plans and specifications and squabbles arise because they are often overruled by Development management because again, "Schedules and costs can't be met if we do everything Test wants." Test is pulled out from under Development and set up as an independent agent.
5. Similar give and take occurs over the issue of integration; first there is none, then it is separate, then combined with Development, then it's separate again but only if systems of products are too multifaceted to handle objectively in Development.

Wherever you place the Test Function in your overall organization, keep in mind the motivational needs of the people in the function. It is easy to build a case for staffing the Test Function with trainees for and rejects from the Development Function; testing by inexperienced or inept programmers is worse than no testing. Development wastes its efforts helping to debug test cases; communication is carried on inefficiently at a lower than optimal level of mutual understanding; and there is a false sense of confidence given to management which is soon exposed by poor customer acceptance. If a Test Function is to evolve as described above, it must be staffed with at least a nucleus of highly competent, experienced, dedicated testers. What makes good designers and coders seldom makes good testers. Good testers have more in common with systems engineers or applications analysts (or whatever you call the postinstallation customer support personnel of your organization), and with training specialists. A prosperous Test Function offers a self-contained career path for people to run tests, develop tests, develop test plans and specifications, and critique design.

10.4 MANAGING SOFTWARE PRODUCT TEST IN THE ANALYSIS PHASE

During the Analysis Phase, there must be sufficient interaction between the Test Function and other functions to determine which mode (I, II, or III as defined in Section 10.2) of test will be employed; when B-Test will be performed; and with what new techniques or tools. Sufficient analysis must be made to determine how much resource will be needed during each phase and to provide cost and schedule estimates on behalf of Test.

So that higher management can decide whether or not to commit resources to a product development, all resources are identified and collected in a single presentation, the budget allocation. Someone from the Development Function normally solicits cost and schedule inputs from Test and other functions. The actual commitment of resources may be delayed until a later phase, but Test provides its best possible estimate even though little information is available on which to base it. A standard costing algorithm that assumes Test's effort to be proportional to Development's effort is often used.

10.5 MANAGING SOFTWARE PRODUCT TEST IN THE FEASIBILITY PHASE

During the Feasibility Phase, Development defines and commits to writing the requirements and objectives for a product. At this time, Test has its first opportunity to influence a product's quality through its inputs to the requirements contract. In the give-and-take that accompanies requirements contract development, review, and approval, the level of testing to be provided is documented (refer again to Figure 10.2), and definitive statements are made about product features. The Test Function is the biggest gadfly in stimulating Development to agree to quantitative statements about requirements and objectives that can serve as a base of reference in later testing. The requirements contract is a development plan, and as such includes not only what will be done, but enough "how" information to satisfy all functions that the plan is sound. A section is provided specifically for Test to state how it plans to proceed; Figure 10.4 is this section from the A$K requirements contract.

Other items of particular interest to Test in the Feasibility Phase, and which are addressed in a requirements contract, are environmental constraints, ergonomic properties, and restrictions. See the Appendix for such statements about A$K. Test is also interested in critiquing a product's external specification, so it expresses this through the product's requirements contract by requesting to participate on the product's technical review board.

During the Feasibility Phase, Test analyzes a preliminary requirements contract, and, based on the results of that analysis and other inputs, sets schedule objectives for future milestones. Essential milestones are: submission and approval of test plans and specifications, turnover of acceptance tests to Development, start of B-Test, and start of each expected cycle of B-Test. Some of these milestones are included in the schedule section of a product's requirements contract (see Figure 10.5).

Services Company will provide two persons with a background in financial analysis to operate terminals during part of B–Test.

The Minimum Configuration of Sec. 3.3.1.1.4 will be tested with real hardware, as will the Target Configuration except for communications controllers, lines, and terminals. The maximum hardware configuration tested will be M442(1) plus M443(1), probably seven phone lines and terminals. The controller limit is a function of available hardware and the line and terminal limit is a function of available manpower.

Software Product Test will build a terminal simulator and Interface Electronics will build a channel fan to be used with it. With the simulator running in one VSOS partition talking to the apex of the fan, and A$K in another partition talking to the base of the fan, the simultaneous simulation of 144 of 1024 Telcoscopes will be used to test A$K. This simulation will also allow the simulation of one 43–1 per 43.

Figure 10.4 Level of testing description from the A$K requirements contract.

SCHEDULE CHANGE NOTICE

PROJECT NAME: A$K Development		PROJECT NUMBER: C013		
PRODUCT NAME: A$K		PRODUCT NUMBER: L301A		
NAME	OLD	NEW	NOTES
P10 PBR APPROVED	09/29/77 C		
D10 POR SUBMITTED	11/03/77 C		
P20 POR APPROVED	12/15/77 C		
D20 ERS SUBMITTED	01/09/78 C		
T10 TEST PLAN APPROVED	02/09/78		
D30 ERS APPROVED	03/15/78	02/06/78	*
B10 PUBLICATIONS PLAN APPROVED	01/26/78		
S10 PROJECT HARDWARE INSTALLED	03/31/78		
I10 SUPPORT PLAN APPROVED	03/02/78		
D41 DEMONSTRATION PERFORMED	TBS		
T20 ACCEPTANCE TESTS DELIV.	TBS		
T30 B-TEST BEGUN	07/03/78	05/08/78	*
I20 PROMOTIONAL MATERIAL DIST.	TBS		
I21 TRAINING COURSE PREPARED	TBS		
B20 REFERENCE MAT. TO PRINTER	07/17/78	06/05/78	*
P30 PRODUCT AVAILABILITY DATE	08/18/78	07/03/78	*
M20 MAINTENANCE SPEC. COMPLETE	TBS		
S20 PRODUCT DISTRIBUTION DATE	09/01/78	07/17/78	*

EVENT | REASON FOR CHANGE

All | Deferring PLOT and SORT will return project to schedule

PREPARED BY: _Luther Davis_   APPROVED BY: _A OR_

APPROVED BY: _____   APPROVED BY: _____

OLD DATE: 01/06/78   NEW DATE: 1/13/78

FORM 7443a

Figure 10.5 Schedule notice for A$K showing initial Test milestones.

10.6 MANAGING SOFTWARE PRODUCT TEST IN THE DESIGN PHASE

The development of a test plan is the main concern of the Test Function during the Design Phase. A gating item for completing a test plan is the approval of a product's requirements contract, so this activity

1	PRODUCT DESCRIPTION
1.1	Product Name(s) and Numbers
1.1.1	Product Name(s)
1.1.2	Name Abbreviations
1.1.3	Product Numbers
1.1.4	Project Numbers
1.2	Brief Description of Testing to be Performed
1.3	Test End Items
2	MISSION
2.1	Revision Request Reconciliation
2.1.1	Revisions Excluded
2.1.2	Revisions Included
2.2	Enhancement Request Reconciliation
2.2.1	Enhancements Excluded
2.2.2	Enhancements Included
2.3	Correction Request Reconciliation
2.3.1	Corrections Excluded
2.4	Plans Reconciliation
2.4.1	Plans Excluded
2.4.2	Plans Included
3	STRATEGY
3.1	Conventions
3.1.1	Notations
3.1.2	Terminology
3.(2,3)	Test Cases and Procedures for (Generated, Operational) Software
3.(2,3).n	(Name n) (Test Procedure)
3.(2,3).n.1	Constraints
3.(2,3).n.1.1	Standards
3.(2,3).n.1.2	Compatibility Constraints
3.(2,3).n.1.3	Software Constraints
3.(2,3).n.1.4	Hardware Constraints
3.(2,3).n.2	External Properties
3.(2,3).n.3	Ergonomic Properties
3.(2,3).n.4	Internal Properties
3.4	Restrictions
4	BACKGROUND
4.1	References
5	DELIVERY AND INSTALLATION
5.1	Provisions for Protection
5.2	Installation Resources
5.3	Media
6	TACTICS
6.1	Interdependencies
6.1.1	Interdependencies Needed
6.1.2	Interdependencies Provided
6.2	Technical Review
6.3	Product Verification
6.3.1	Level of Testing
6.3.2	Bases of Reference
6.3.3	Method of Testing
6.3.3.1	Demonstration Testing
6.3.3.2	Benchmark Testing
6.3.3.3	Complete Feature Testing
6.3.3.4	New Feature Testing
6.3.3.5	Performance Testing
6.3.3.6	Reliability Testing
6.3.3.7	Stability Testing
6.3.3.8	Regression Testing
6.3.3.9	Installability Testing
6.3.3.10	Configuration Testing
6.4	Acceptance Criteria
6.4.1	A-Test Acceptance Criteria
6.4.2	B-Test Acceptance Criteria
6.4.3	C-Test Acceptance Criteria
7	SCHEDULE

Figure 10.6   Stereotype test plan contents.

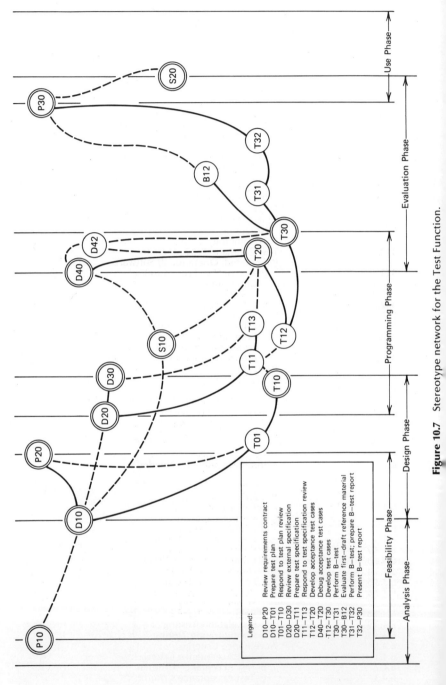

Figure 10.7 Stereotype network for the Test Function.

Legend:

D10–P20 Review requirements contract
D10–T01 Prepare test plan
T01–T10 Respond to test plan review
D20–D30 Review external specification
D20–T11 Prepare test specification
T11–T13 Respond to test specification review
T12–T20 Develop acceptance test cases
D40–T20 Debug acceptance test cases
T12–T30 Develop test cases
T30–T31 Perform B–test
T30–B12 Evaluate first–draft reference material
T31–T32 Perform B–test; prepare B–test report
T32–P30 Present B–test report

146

cannot be completed until after Phase I Review. It can begin, however, as soon as a draft of the requirements contract is available.

The concept of plans decomposition introduced in Section 6.2 is employed when writing a test plan. A **test plan** is an expansion of the requirements contract that provides enough more detail about B-Test for reviewers to determine its adequacy. Figure 10.6 shows the table of contents for a test plan derived from the requirements contract format of Chapter 13.

In developing a test plan, Test takes care that all test activities are accounted for. One way is by using a network diagram. Using the nomenclature of Chapter 14, the activities of Test are as shown in Figure 10.7.

10.7   MANAGING SOFTWARE PRODUCT TEST IN THE PROGRAMMING PHASE

The Programming Phase begins with the appearance of a complete external description of a product, in its external specification. As soon as an external specification is available, Test begins to verify that it is consistent with its preceding requirements contract, inputting to Development any changes needed to achieve consistency. This is done informally or through a formal mechanism like a technical review board. Better still, if the Test Function is sufficiently mature, it reviews a product's internal specification and delivers a critique of it to higher management. The Test Function also provides inputs appropriate to improving the usability, compatibility, reliability, and other attributes of a product.

As soon as an external specification is submitted, Test begins development of a test specification. The relationship of a test specification to a test plan is much like the relationship of an external specification to a requirements contract; it is a further decomposition, one which completely describes all tests to be performed and the results to be expected. Since a test specification depends heavily on an external specification, it must be approved before a dependent test specification can be approved.

You might think that Test has little activity prior to the Evaluation Phase. As Figure 10.8 shows, however, and as this section will explain, Test activity reaches 80% of its peak during the Programming Phase, right at the end of the Design Phase. This is because test case development begins as soon as a test specification is submitted, and continues

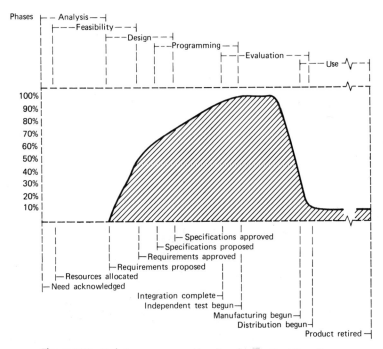

Figure 10.8   Relative manpower loading for the Test Function.

on through the last day of product testing. As soon as a test specification is approved, the scope of the test cases is defined. All tests called for in a test specification are completed by the end of the Programming Phase, however, and only tests suggested by results of testing during the Evaluation Phase are developed later.

It is very important for Development to know what tests its product must pass, both in order for it to be recommended for release and for it to be accepted into B-Test. As early as requirements contract approval, the broad criteria for release are known and they are subsequently refined as the test plan and test specification are approved. The criteria for formally entering B-Test are first defined in the test plan and finalized in the test specification. Following a practice used in contract programming, these threshold criteria are generally called acceptance tests. Again, as in contract programming, they are presented to Development prior to the start of the Evaluation Phase so that they are sure to be found "acceptable." In contract programming, there is little chance of turning back once a product is accepted. This also applies here, for it allows management to plan to selectively release an "acceptable" product to critical customers. To achieve these objectives you should define a subset of test cases as acceptance tests, you should define them early (in a test plan), you should define them precisely (in a test specification), and you should present them to Development with time to spare thereby ensuring their approval. The price paid for poorly managed acceptance into B-Test is proportional to the unacceptability of any release prior to completion of the Evaluation Phase and the field support needed to minimize that unacceptability.

10.8 MANAGING SOFTWARE PRODUCT TEST IN THE EVALUATION PHASE

During the Evaluation Phase the level of activity in the Test Function peaks, and if a project is behind schedule, the pace may be frantic. It is very important that management understand the importance of the Evaluation Phase so as not to slight it under schedule pressure.

Test's first role in this phase is to establish the acceptability of a product for B-Test. This is done very carefully and formally, as stressed in the preceding section, because the commitment to eventually release a product is usually made at this time (with the completion of the Evaluation Phase determining when that release takes place).

Development frequently takes a parochial view of its role, placing maximum schedule emphasis on the start of B-Test. In the final rush to achieve acceptance, the quality of the hand-off from Development to Test can suffer. Control of the quality of this hand-off depends on Test's insistence that acceptance not be recorded as complete until all acceptance tests have been successfully run and a proper release specification as described in Section 15.4 has been prepared.

Test may allow another procedure, acceptance retroactive to the start of an acceptance period, so that Development can receive maximum credit for schedule performance. When following this procedure, it notes the date when a transmittal is made from Development to Test; Test runs all acceptance tests, often taking several days because of their length and complexity; then, at the successful completion of these tests, it retroactively records the date of transmittal as the start of B-Test. If at any time during the running of acceptance tests by the Test Function *any* of them fail, the transmittal is immediately rejected so that Development can prepare for a new transmittal as soon as possible. Rejection is immediate because any delay or even apparent delay by Test may strongly antagonize

Development, since its objective at this time is to record the earliest possible start of B-Test.

Once B-Test has begun, all test cases are run, first in the most logical order, and second in whatever order is required to maximize progress. The need to run tests in other than the most logical order arises from the dependency of some tests on the successful execution of specific functions of the product under test. If those functions are not working properly, tests dependent on them must be delayed until they are working properly.

Seldom will the first transmittal to Test pass all tests. As soon as Test reaches a point of diminishing returns, it terminates testing and asks Development to resubmit the product. Such a period of testing is a cycle. Two or more cycles, separated by intervals of rework by Development, are usually needed to reach a releasable level of quality.

As each problem is found while running tests, Test records and substantiates it with such evidence as console printouts, status settings, output listings, timings, and memory dumps. In so doing, it resists the temptation to debug the product under test. That is Development's responsibility and if Test performs the function, Development will not. If Development does not, the product it transmits to Test will be less carefully designed and integrated; the Evaluation Phase will be protracted due to inefficient use of both Test and Development resources; and, as if that were not enough, the code patched by Test may eventually be distributed to users. Such crudely debugged and patched code is sure to confound Maintenance and may bring the Use Phase to an unnecessarily premature end as further patching eventually becomes impractical. Human nature is such that Development will be all too willing to share its responsibility for debugging with Test unless Test resists the temptation to be helpful. This division of labor is difficult to achieve for two reasons: (1) human nature is also such that people want to be helpful; (2) functions should work together to get products released as quickly and as cheaply as possible. Herein lies a great challenge to the diplomacy of the Test Function!

Administratively, each problem found by Test is treated like an error found after a product is distributed. Giving such error reports a name, such as **trouble reports**, numbering them, ranking them according to severity, and logging them facilitates discussing and disposing of them. As it is found each trouble report is passed on to Development so that Development can get right to work responding to it. Corrections to trouble reports may be accepted into the middle of a test cycle or batched for submission to a subsequent cycle at the discretion of Test. Omission of any trouble report response from the next subsequent cycle should rarely be allowed; the only reasons for doing so should be: (1) another, still subsequent, cycle is assured and the response will be made then; (2) Test plans to recommend release with the problem reported as a deficiency. Otherwise, Development may impede the progress of B-Test by prohibiting the running of tests dependent on such responses.

Both a piece of software and the publications associated with it are evaluated during B-Test. They must correlate and they all must be consistent with a product's requirements contract and external specification. Since problems may be found in publications, plans should never be made to send them to the printer prior to the expected completion of the first cycle of B-Test.

At the end of every cycle, a brief summary report is generated showing the results of testing during the current cycle and cumulatively for all cycles. Figure 10.9 shows such a report.

Sometimes there will be pressure from Support to release a product for limited use before Test makes its recommendation to release it. This sometimes occurs when a project is so far behind schedule that continued unavailability will impact users' plans, or, worse yet, result in liquidated damages or a lost order for the product's supplier. Such a release is called a prerelease and is made only after B-Test has begun. This allows management to know that the product can at least pass acceptance tests. Prereleases are marked as such to warn users of possible problems and they contain all components of the final release, although some may be in draft form. Test adds to each prerelease package a statement of known problems, such as a list of outstanding trouble report descriptions.

Management may elect to overlap the end of B-Test with a field test. In a **field test**, a prerelease is made to a selected user who agrees to help evaluate a product, usually in exchange for an early chance to familiarize himself with it. Personnel from the Test Function may work at the user's site to process trouble reports and expedite any other feedback from the site to their home base.

At some time Test arrives at the moment of truth; it recommends either release or some other disposition of a product. If it concludes that further cycling will not result in a recommendation for release, it calls for a Phase V Review by all functions to decide what to do. Otherwise, it eventually recommends release, albeit with deficiencies.

TEST CYCLE STATUS REPORT

PROJECT NAME: _A $ K DEVELOPMENT_   PROJECT NUMBER: _C 013_

PRODUCT NAME: _A $ K_   PRODUCT NUMBER: _L 301 A_

MODULE	NUMBER OF TESTS IN SET	RUN THIS CYCLE	NUMBER OF PTR'S THIS CYCLE	OPEN	COMMENTS
///////////	74	38	8	6	FROM PREV. PAGE
ADD COMMAND	12	6	1	0	
A $ K COMMAND	5	3	0	0	
BUILD COMMAND	9	3	5	5	2 SEVERE
DONE COMMAND	4	3	0	0	
HELP COMMAND	6	2	1	1	
KEEP COMMAND	6	3	2	1	
LET COMMAND	8	3	2	2	
MAKE COMMAND	7	3	6	5	4 SEVERE
PURGE COMMAND	5	1	0	0	
REPORT COMM.	16	0	0	0	CAN'T REACH YET
SUB—TOTAL	152	65	25	20	TO NEXT PAGE
GRAND TOTAL					LAST PAGE ONLY

NUMBER OF PRODUCT TROUBLE REPORTS TO DATE: _25_   CYCLE NUMBER: _1_

PREDICTED CYCLE END: _5/30/78_   PREDICTED TEST END: _7/11/78_

Figure 10.9 Software product test cycle report.

How does Test know that a product is fully tested? This is a subjective decision based on examination of available information. Questions the Test manager asks his staff are:

- Have you run all available tests?
- Are most known uncorrected errors minor?

- Do you think more testing will uncover no major errors?
- Have the volume and severity of reported errors subsided from cycle to cycle?
- Are known major errors such that they can be adequately explained in the release bulletin?
- Do Development and Publications have reasonable plans for resolving all known deficiencies in the Use Phase?

The answers to all must be "yes" to recommend release.

Whatever Test recommends, it summarizes the results of B-Test both qualitatively and quantitatively (with statistics on trouble reports and measured versus required performance) in a **B-Test report** which becomes the focal point of Phase V Review.

10.9   MANAGING SOFTWARE PRODUCT TEST IN THE USE PHASE

At the start of the Use Phase the role of the Test Function is to monitor the performance of C-Test by the Services Function. As noted earlier, Test will have already executed C-Test cases. Its role now is to assure that C-Test can be performed with off-the-shelf components by nonspecialists.

Once Services has distributed a product to the field, the Evaluation Phase is over and Test plays a new role. When a product is in the field, problems with its installation and use turn up and are reported. As each problem is reported, as through a maintenance request, Test makes a note of it and prepares test cases to validate its correction by the Maintenance Function. Then, before any altered code is distributed as an update to a product, Test certifies by regression testing that not only is each error corrected but that no new errors are introduced.

10.10   TEST'S REVIEW AND APPROVAL RESPONSIBILITY

The Test Function participates in five of the six phase reviews shown in Figure 6.7. Its role is summarized in Figure 10.10 and the following discussion.

At Phase I Review, Test gives a preliminary estimate of resources needed that is consistent with those resources available or reasonably

Phase	Review	Responsibility
Analysis	I	Review
Feasibility	II	Review and approve
Design	III	Review and approve
Programming	IV	Review
Evaluation	V	Approve
Use	VI	None

Figure 10.10 Minimum responsibilities of the Test Function at phase reviews.

expected to be available when needed, and a preliminary estimate of when those resources would be expended. Approval of these estimates can be deferred until Phase II Review, at which time they might be revised before approval.

During Phase II Review, Test must commit to a test mode and to one or more test categories (see Section 10.2). This is also an excellent time to establish the major Test milestones (T10, T20, and T30 in Figure 10.7). Test must also concur with Development's requirements and objectives, particularly those pertaining to performance, reliability, installability, and operability.

At Phase III Review, Test begins to assert its policing function by determining the conformity of the external specification to the requirements contract. There is approval in the role of Test at this review, because it must "blow the whistle" on any discrepancies between the requirements contract and the external specification, and it may, in exercising quality assurance, object to missing or inadequate external attributes of a product.

At Phase IV Review, the focus of the review is on the A-Test report prepared by Development. Test merely reviews the A-Test report and raises little objection, knowing it will have its say later.

At Phase V Review, the focus of the review is a report generated by Test—the B-Test report. For manufacturing to begin (and thus for the Use Phase to begin), Test must recommend release in its B-Test report or be overridden by higher management. Thus, Test must approve (but not review, since it already will have reviewed its report).

Finally, at Phase VI Review, Test probably need not be involved. The decision to lower or drop support has very little impact on the Test Function.

Chapter
11

Managing
Software
Product
Support

The Support Function, like the Services Function, is somewhat of a catch-all function. It is primarily the interface between the users and the developers of a software product. As such, Support gathers user requirements for input to product planning; represents users in design reviews; provides technical support in promoting products; provides training; assists in on-site installation and conversion; performs in-field product maintenance and updating; and feeds back user impressions and requests for product improvement.

These are clearly marketing functions, but they are not all there is to marketing nor need they be construed to be marketing. Marketing includes sales, advertising, market analysis, competitive analysis, pricing strategy, and other activities peculiar to products which are created to seek a profit for the producers. There is a profusion of heavy-duty software which is never offered for sale but which requires all of the elements of Support defined above. Examples include widely used scientific applications like nuclear codes, proprietary reservation systems, actuarial programs, corporate management information systems, process control programs used by conglomerate oil companies, educational resource planning systems—the list is endless.

Examples may come to your mind of heavy-duty software that is not accompanied by the Support activities enumerated above. Ask yourself if such software really is heavy-duty. Better still, ask the users of such software if they are satisfied with it. Chances are they are not and that they only continue to use it because they have no alternative. The support provided for a software product is the key attribute that makes it a product.

11.1 ORGANIZING FOR THE SUPPORT FUNCTION

The many diverse components of Support listed in the preceding section are consistent with several organizational structures. Chapter 5 suggests that most and possibly all functions can be organized into a single department. If your software product development is for a captive user community, that is, if your software products are not marketed, Support can easily be a part of a software products department. If you must combine Support with another function because the demand for Support is not great enough for a separate organizational entity, you will find that it is most compatible with Maintenance. Both functions are remote from the schedule pressures of development and testing, and both are intimately involved with error identification and correction. By all means avoid committing Development resources to Support activities. There is no surer way to miss schedules because the demands on Support are user demands which must be treated with all of the dispatch and courtesy due to customers. These demands must take priority over other work in process or the probity of Support is threatened.

If you do market your software products, even at a null price as in the case of bundled hardware and software, you have a marketing organization. This is the best place for Support to reside, primarily to preserve marketing's control of customer relations. How Support is distributed within marketing is usually a function of organization size and geographical distribution of customers. Customer support is usually divided into pre- and postsales support, with separate cadres of field analysts assigned to each category. Presales analysts, who sometimes are also salespeople, gather user requirements and pass them to Development through a home-office marketing support group. These presales analysts spend most of their time providing technical assistance to product promotion and training. They also sometimes represent users in product design reviews. Post-sales analysts somewhat more often represent users in design reviews. They spend most of their time helping users convert to, install, and use new products, and to identify and compensate for errors. They also feed back user requests for product improvement.

The home-office support group mentioned above is indispensible to Support. This staff is small enough and technically competent enough to interact intimately with Development without being a burden. At the same time it is large enough to handle all field requests expeditiously. Field analysts then do not bypass it to go directly to Development, making a nuisance of themselves. They remain in the field where they belong. Because the home-office support group is so technically competent, it is the first line of defense in fighting fires that get out of control in the field. This is the most important service it performs, for this keeps developers from being distracted. Unfortunately, the home-office staff is seldom popular with anyone it serves. In presenting user inputs, it is accused of presenting biases or incomplete views. It often provides assistance in new product evaluation, and its feedback is often interpreted as highly critical and as contributing to delay in product delivery. When it goes to the field to fight fires, it seldom lives up to the expectation that a savior will come to put everything right. These words of caution are not meant to discourage you from using a home-office support group, but to urge you to use it in spite of difficulty. It is truly indispensible.

What sorts of people make up Support and where do they come from? They are highly competent because they cannot hide their incompetence from users or make up for it with any other attribute. They are generally extroverts because they deal with people at least as much as with things. They frequently bear the brunt of user frustrations and hence are not "thin-skinned." The most successful among them are articulate, diplomatic, and persuasive; these are attributes they have in common with their marketing brethren, salespeople.

Seldom does a neophyte programmer enter the Support Function. Most Support roles are leadership roles: teaching, fire-fighting, consulting. These require experience. Probably the principal source of Support personnel is the rank of user programmers. They are motivated to change roles because Support shows promise of greater career advancement if the main business of Support's parent is computers; because consulting and teaching are more ego-fulfilling than coding; and, in spite of the abuse heaped upon them, Support people are respected.

How is ABC Corporation organized to handle Support, particularly even though it is produced by ABC Computers Company. Therefore,

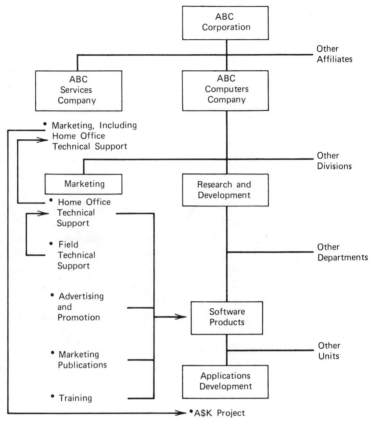

Figure 11.1 Provision for the Support Function at ABC Corporation, showing lines of communication.

customer interface is with ABC Services Company and field support is provided by Services' marketing. In ABC Computers, interface between Software Products and customers is normally buffered by Computers' home-office marketing. A$K is a special case, however. Computers has only one customer for A$K, Services. Therefore, Services' home-office marketing staff is allowed access to Software Products directly—but only for A$K. Services' needs for VSOS and other standard Computers products flow through Computers' home-office just as do any other customer's needs. Computers does allow some privilege to Services for requests relating to standard products, though. Services' home-office staff deals directly with Computers' home-office staff without going through Computers' field staff as do other customers. Figure 11.1 shows sources of Support activities in

ABC and lines of communication, both for A$K and for standard Computers' products. Refer also to Figures 3.1–3.4 for a more complete picture of ABC organization.

11.2 MANAGING SOFTWARE PRODUCT SUPPORT IN THE ANALYSIS AND FEASIBILITY PHASES

Looking chronologically at the development of a software product, the first activity performed by Support is gathering user needs and expressing them, through the Planning Function, as a product need. The acknowledgement by Planning that a product need does exist signals the start of the Analysis Phase. This gathering of inputs is off-scale to the left of Figure 11.2 which shows the level of involvement of Support in a typical software product's life cycle.

Looking at Figure 11.2, notice that Support first gets involved with a product near the end of the Analysis Phase. By this time Development has nearly completed a statement of product goals in a requirements contract. Development calls on Support to assist in preparing several statements. Using the outline in Chapter 13, these statements are:

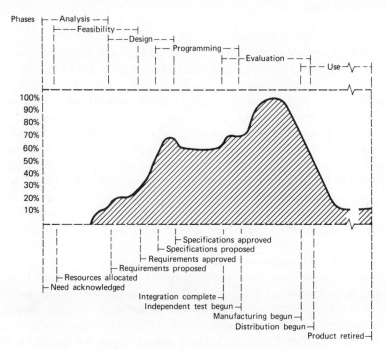

Figure 11.2 Relative manpower loading for the Support Function.

Product Name, Name Abbreviations, Summary of User Needs, Product End Items, Constraints, Ergonomic Properties, Installation Resources, Media, and Provisions for Support. Support may contribute to other sections also but at least for these Support is likely to be more knowledgeable than Development and is always consulted.

Since the reasons for consulting Support may not be obvious in each case, a few words of elaboration are in order. Product naming is always a marketing responsibility because it affects promotion plans and user acceptability; if you have no more appropriate marketing function, Support should provide product names. A clear statement of the reason for building a product, in terms of user benefits, helps everyone who works on the product to appreciate its value. Of all functions, Support is best qualified to recommend a selection of publications to accompany a product. Similarly, it may be best qualified to identify configuration constraints on both hardware and software environments available to users.

During requirements contract review Support carefully reviews every statement for impact on the user or on Support. When all concerned functions, and especially Support, are satisfied with the contents of the requirements contract, they approve it and the Feasibility Phase ends.

11.3 MANAGING SOFTWARE PRODUCT SUPPORT IN THE DESIGN AND PROGRAMMING PHASES

Approval of a requirements contract signals authorization to proceed with product development. To Support this means preparing a support plan. A **support plan** establishes promotion, field test, training, conversion, installation, and support goals in more detail than a requirements contract and with emphasis on the role of Support. Depending on how you are organized and who your users are, a support plan can be either a stand-alone document or a part of a marketing plan. A support plan is a decomposition of a requirements contract and is thus both consistent with and constrained by its antecedent requirements contract. Figure 11.3 shows the table of contents for such a support plan.

While Support is working on its support plan, Publications is working on its publications plan. Figure 11.4 shows a stereotype network plan for Support's activities on a typical software product development project. In this figure you see that Publications submits its plan for review by other functions slightly before Support submits its. Thus

1	PRODUCT DESCRIPTION
1.1	Product Name(s) and Numbers
1.1.1	Product Name(s)
1.1.2	Name Abbreviations
1.1.3	Product Numbers
1.1.4	Project Numbers
1.2	Brief Description of Support Activities
1.3	Support End Items
2	MISSION
2.1	Revision Request Reconciliation
2.1.1	Revisions Excluded
2.1.2	Revisions Included
2.2	Enhancement Request Reconciliation
2.2.1	Enhancements Excluded
2.2.2	Enhancements Included
2.3	Correction Request Reconciliation
2.3.1	Corrections Excluded
2.4	Plans Reconciliation
2.4.1	Plans Excluded
2.4.2	Plans Included
2.5.	Summary of User Needs
2.6	Alternatives Considered
2.7	Return on Investment
3	STRATEGY
3.1	Promotion
3.2	Field Test
3.3	Training
3.4	Conversion and Installation
3.5	Support
4	BACKGROUND
4.1	References
5	DELIVERY AND INSTALLATION
5.1	Provisions for Protection
5.2	Installation Resources
5.2.1	Installation Procedures
6	TACTICS
6.1	Interdependencies
6.1.1	Interdependencies Needed
6.1.2	Interdependencies Provided
6.2	Technical Review
6.3	Product Verification
7	SCHEDULE

Figure 11.3   Stereotype support plan contents.

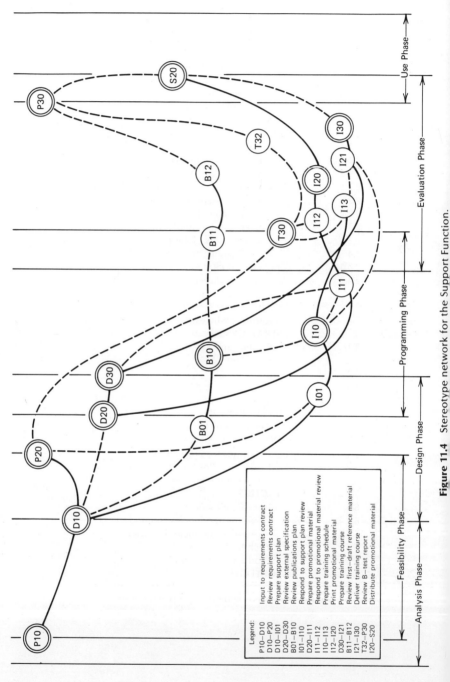

Figure 11.4 Stereotype network for the Support Function.

Legend:
P10–D10   Input to requirements contract
D10–P20   Review requirements contract
D10–I01   Prepare support plan
D20–D30   Review external specification
B01–B10   Review publications plan
I01–I10   Respond to support plan review
D20–I11   Prepare promotional material
I11–I12   Respond to promotional material review
I10–I13   Prepare training schedule
I12–I20   Print promotional material
D30–I21   Prepare training course
B11–B12   Review first–draft reference material
I21–I30   Deliver training course
T32–P30   Review B–test report
I20–S20   Distribute promotional material

Analysis Phase
Feasibility Phase
Design Phase
Programming Phase
Evaluation Phase
Use Phase

the next activity begun by Support is review of the publications plan. In this plan Support looks for assurance that the publications to be offered will meet the training, installation, operation, use, and reference needs both of users and of Support. It pays particular attention to scheduling of both draft and printed publications, as the support plan must be consistent with respect to promotional material and training plans.

Look further at Figure 11.4. Another Support activity, external specification review, begins just after publications plan review and ends before it. Development offers an external specification to Support and to other functions for review to solicit constructive criticism. As this is Support's last chance to influence a product's design, it reviews the external specification thoroughly and offers appropriate suggestions.

Availability of a draft external specification enables Support to begin preparing promotional material and training courses, both of which depend on the external specification as their primary technical reference. The sort of promotional material prepared is usually a short, glossy brochure directed to user management. The objective of promotional material is to convince users that they should use a product if the product is for sale, and to answer key questions about use of the product and overcome objections to it whether or not it is for sale. Such material depends heavily on the nature of intended users, their environments, and their market plans and no standard format is likely to meet enough needs to warrant adoption. This is also true for training course content.

The first peak of Support activity occurs just after it submits its support plan for review by other functions; see Figure 11.2. As Figure 11.4 shows, Support is simultaneously engaged in promotional material preparation, external specification review, and publications plan review. This is a time to carefully watch priorities, for Support must be sure to complete these activities in the proper order. It would be ideal if Support could perform these activities in sequence, but that would lengthen the overall project schedule severely. Each project's schedule is a bit different, but Support strives to complete these tasks in the following order: review external specification, review publications plan, respond to support plan review, and prepare promotional material. This is the sequence most consistent with good plans and design decomposition.

Several logical constraints shown in Figure 11.4 act to aid Support in this scheduling task. Firstly, the schedule of the support plan must be consistent with the schedule of the publications plan, so the latter should be approved first. Secondly, promotional material must be consistent with the support plan, so it should be approved before the promotional material is completely drafted. Thirdly, the promotional material must be consistent with the support plan, so it should also be approved before the promotional material is completely drafted.

When drafts of promotional material are complete, they are offered to other functions for review. This review is primarily to verify technical accuracy and consistency with plans of the reviewing functions; it does not take long and Support's response usually requires little rework. The greatest caution to exert here is to avoid over-commitment. There is a tendency, especially when Support is a part of marketing, to express design goals as though they were commitments. Many products fail to live up to expectations because of undue optimism in the early stages of development.

11.4   MANAGING SOFTWARE PRODUCT SUPPORT IN THE EVALUATION PHASE

Activity in the Support Function shifts into high gear in the Evaluation Phase. This is because many Support activities cannot be performed until a decision to ultimately release a product has been made. This decision is made early in the Evaluation Phase when a product is accepted by the Test Function for B-Test. This decision, made at Phase IV Review, signals Support to publish a training schedule, to print and distribute promotional material, and to complete training course preparation.

Early in the Evaluation Phase is a busy time for many functions as Figure 2.1 shows. This is because tasks completed by each function trigger the initiation of tasks by other functions. One such case is the review of first-draft reference material by Support. This is an intensive review by Support, primarily to determine usability of the material. Many manuals are technically accurate but few are easy to use. Support can offer great assistance to Publications by thoroughly critiquing its work products from this point of view.

The next stereotype activity for Support shown in Figure 11.4 is presentation of training courses. These are given first to Support's field personnel, sometimes with assistance from Development, and then to users. For the early, in-house courses the approved external specification is used as course material; for later in-house and all (hopefully!) user courses, the external specification is replaced by published or at least preprinted reference material. The period of in-house course presentation is usually the one in which Support personnel are most heavily involved in the life cycle of a product (see Figure 11.2) because they either are presenting or receiving the course or are involved in one of the other activities mentioned below.

In addition to the stereotype activities mentioned above, there are a number of tasks occasionally performed by Support during the Evaluation Phase. Chronologically the first of these which might occur is augmented B-Test. **Augmented B-Test** is B-Test performed by Support either along with Test or independent of Test. Augmented B-Test increases the intensity of B-Test, thus testing a product more thoroughly. It also allows Support a chance to gain hands-on familiarity with a product at an early stage and thereby feed back this experience into early training.

A variant of augmented B-Test sometimes employed is field test—user involvement in B-test. Field test is both very valuable and very risky. It is valuable in providing a real-life environment in which to test a product; it is risky because it exposes any weaknesses of your product and your development methodology to users. To avoid as much risk as possible, field test is not started until at least one cycle of B-Test is complete and some measure of product quality, and thus exposure, is known. When field test is employed, Support always selects the user or users and assists them.

A higher-risk variant of field test is prerelease. A prerelease is a transmittal of a product that has not entered distribution to a user who is in such need of the product that he cannot wait for normal distribution. Prereleases are occasioned by development delays that cause normal distribution to fall well beyond at least one user's commitment to have the product operational. It is this need to have the product operational that increases risk; instead of testing the product in a carefully controlled environment as in field test, the user presses it immediately into production. Every prerelease is approved by Support, and then only after determining that the impact of not making the prerelease is probably greater than the impact of making it.

Do not confuse either field test or prerelease with installation of a pilot system, as defined in Section 6.5. A pilot system is planned right from the time its requirements contract is proposed and it has full support not only from Support but from all other functions as well. From Support's point of view, installation and service of a pilot are essentially the same as for a released product.

11.5 MANAGING SOFTWARE PRODUCT SUPPORT IN THE USE PHASE

The Use Phase starts as soon as a decision is made to release a finished product. To Support this means a shift from interfacing with other development functions to interfacing with users. This implies a shift from home-office staff to field staff for much of the work performed. The several activities described below occur in any and every sequence, but they occur predominantly in the sequence of presentation.

First, Support assists users in converting to a new product. This includes training, product customizing, data generation, data conversion, procedure generation, and procedure revision. Then Support assists in installing the product and putting it into operation, perhaps in parallel with a predecessor product. During all of these activities the home-office staff renders assistance to the field staff as needed.

In managing these activities Support minimizes the change of personnel assigned to each user. Users find it very unsettling to see a parade of specialists go by without a chance ever to establish rapport with an on-site expert. There is a psychological advantage to continuity that makes up for some deficiency in expertise. Support keeps home-office visits to the field brief and to the point. Many users are disturbed by exposure to problems that exist but that are not impacting them.

Integrated over time the main activity of Support in the Use Phase is the identification and resolution of software product deficiencies. Each genuine **deficiency** is either an error—a deviation from specification—or an enhancement—something a user would like a product to be which it was never designed to be. You need mechanisms to deal with both types of deficiency.

The mechanism to handle errors is called a maintenance request system. A maintenance request system involves other functions and is discussed in Section 8.7 from the Services point of view, in Section 10.9 from the Test point of view, and in Section 12.5 from the Maintenance point of view. Processing an error through a maintenance request system begins when field Support personnel verify, to the best of their ability, that an error exists and describe the error in a report. They send the report to home office along with supporting documentation such as code or procedures that manifest the problem, memory dumps, and diagnostic messages. Home office solves the problem if it proves to be a misunderstanding or something not requiring action by Maintenance. If home office finds a temporary correction or a way to work around the problem during its analysis, it sends this information back to the field to be relayed to the user. If a problem requires Maintenance action, home office forwards everything it has and knows about the problem to Services. From that point on Support waits for a reply from Services who routes the request through Maintenance, Development, and Test as appropriate. If Maintenance offers a temporary correction, home office forwards it to field personnel for installation. If and when a certified (by Test) correction is offered in a product update, field personnel install the update where and when appropriate to each user. Status of requests in process is continually passed from Services to home office; from home office to field personnel; and, when appropriate, from field personnel to users.

The mechanism for handling enhancements is called an **enhancement request system**. Section 8.7 covers the role of Services in processing enhancement requests, which is primarily an administrative role. Support's role is also administrative. It forwards to Services enhancement requests on forms like those presented in Section 16.6, and at the discretion of field personnel, reports the disposition of enhancement requests to users. Enhancement requests have a way of either disappearing into a queue waiting for review or being approved for a new version of a product which seems never to materialize, so reports to users often have to be made with great diplomacy lest the users feel slighted. Home-office personnel filter out duplicates received by them from field personnel and represent Support in enhancement request reviews. It is usually Support that proposes, based on field experience, each lowering of level. Thus its role is both to review and to approve.

Support levels are normally lowered over a period of time with a reasonable warning—like six months—before each downgrading. They are usually quantized into a small number of standard support services which are defined in detail in the next chapter. It suffices here to note that the amount of effort expended by Support responding to maintenance requests and processing their replies decreases as the level is lowered.

The end of the Use Phase is determined when, at a configurator review meeting, you reach a decision to drop support completely and withdraw a product from distribution. You may argue that some users will continue to use a product beyond the withdrawal of its support. As viewed from your vantage point, however, the Use Phase ends when support ends and the product is withdrawn from distribution.

11.6   SUPPORT'S REVIEW AND APPROVAL RESPONSIBILITY

Although it is often organizationally more remote from Development than other functions, Support plays an active role in phase reviews and in reviewing publications.

At Phase I Review Support looks for assurance that a proposed development schedule will meet known or expected user constraints. It also reviews any cost estimates for Support activities that appear on a budget allocation. Its role is to review only, as shown in Figure 11.5.

At Phase II Review, Support scrutinizes a requirements contract for compliance with both schedule and feature needs of users and approves the requirements contract only when these appear to be addressed satisfactorily. If the requirements contract is approved, Support makes a commitment to schedule and cost parameters which affect it and which are contained in an updated schedule notice and budget allocation.

Support reviews a product's external specification at Phase III Review for consistency with user needs as currently perceived by Support. If user needs have changed such that they cannot be accommodated by Development without a change in project scope, Support must appreciate this and either request a change in scope through a requirements contract revision or settle for the best compromise achievable within the degrees of freedom remaining in the external specification. At this time Support also reviews the budget allocation and schedule notice and updates its inputs as necessary.

Before Phase IV Review Support reviews the publications plan for consistency with its support plan and later reviews first-draft reference material for suitability to user needs.

Support does not take part in Phase IV Review but does take an active part in Phase V Review. Support reviews the B-Test report and

Phase	Review	Responsibility
Analysis	I	Review
Feasibility	II	Review and approve
Design	III	Review
Programming	IV	None
Evaluation	V	Review and approve
Use	VI	Review and approve

Figure 11.5 Minimum responsibilities of the Support Function at phase reviews.

any other data presented at Phase V Review very carefully to be as sure as possible that a product will be acceptable to its users and that Support can support them. Thus, it has a lot at stake at Phase V Review and takes great pains to avoid a bad decision. For the decision to release a product that is made at Phase V Review, Support's approval is mandatory. At configurator reviews it reevaluates the support level provided for a product as it ages.

The decision to be made at the final Phase VI Review—to drop support for a product altogether—is seldom a momentous decision when it is made because little support is usually being provided by that time. Of all functions participating in Phase VI Review, however, the impact is probably greatest on Support, so its approval is mandatory.

12

Managing Software Product Maintenance

The **Maintenance Function** is responsible for correcting errors in released products—corrective maintenance—and for providing minor alterations on them—adaptive maintenance. A distinction is drawn between these two types of product improvement because they have quite different implications for configuration management. For example, a simple error correction brings specifications, code, and publications into agreement. On the other hand, a new feature, however minor, requires specifications, code, and publications all to be revised. New features also may require development of new tests for evaluation and may have compatibility implications.

The minor alterations provided by Maintenance fall into two categories: revisions and enhancements. **Revisions** are changes made necessary by changes in the environment of a product, such as the need in a payroll package to accommodate a revised withholding statement. **Enhancements**, on the other hand, are not mandatory and merely improve attributes of a product such as its usability.

Maintenance—the activity, not the function—consists of processing requests for correction, enhancement, and revision. Most of this chapter deals with the control of changes so that maintenance can be performed routinely, with a minimum of unplanned cost.

12.1 ORGANIZING FOR THE MAINTENANCE FUNCTION

There are three aspects of organizing for the Maintenance Function: who provides maintenance, what maintenance consists of, and how maintenance is accomplished.

Who provides maintenance depends on several factors, including the size of your software development organization, the stability of your work force, the mix of corrections versus enhancements in your product improvements, the length of your warranty, and last but not least, the quality of your Test Function. The size of your software development organization dictates whether or not you can support a group dedicated to maintenance. If you can, you should. Doing so provides a clear interface between Development and Maintenance, encourages preparation of complete maintenance specifications, assures that someone is looking after mature products, provides a training ground for programmers, demonstrates your ability to live up to warranties, and allows easy measurement of the cost of maintenance. If you cannot dedicate a group to Maintenance, the logical alternative is to have each product's developers provide maintenance for it. This has advantages of low overhead, expert talent available to fix errors quickly, and a load-leveling task to fit around new development projects. It has distinct disadvantages, too: it is easy to let maintenance slide; when the developer departs, so does your maintenance capability; error corrections often get a low priority; and thorough analyses of the impact of making or not making a change are often bypassed. If you include many enhancements in your product improvements, you may want experienced developers to provide the enhancements, and you probably will find it most efficient to let them fix bugs, too. If your work force is subject to rapid turnover, a formal maintenance group with good procedures and extensive documentation will minimize the impact of personnel turnover. If your warranty is short or nonexistent, a limited effort by a product's developers may suffice for maintenance. Lastly, if your Test Function is exceptional, there will be little error correction needed and you may be able to staff Maintenance accordingly.

If you do separate Maintenance from Development, be sure that products are not turned over to Maintenance prematurely. The initial surge of maintenance requests should be processed by Development for several reasons. First, developers need to feel a sense of responsibility for the quality and maintainability of their work product. Second, many of the most critical errors or deficiencies are found early in the Use Phase. Development, by virtue of its familiarity with a product, can respond more quickly than can Maintenance. Third, not only are experienced individuals available to correct problems, they are still available as a group if the development project is not disbanded. Last, those who remain on a development project on into the Use Phase are available to clean up any loose ends such as incomplete documentation.

When Maintenance provides enhancements and revisions, the resultant maintenance of documentation and publications dictates that you have someone coordinate maintenance activities, much as a project manager does for a development project. Such a coordinator could belong to the Services Function, if that function provides maintenance administration as advocated in Chapter 8. Also, if you provide enhancements, a word of caution: do not let too many enhancements creep into the work product of the Maintenance Function; you may inadvertently bypass valuable review mechanisms and find that as a result Publications, Test, and above all, Support do not properly prepare for a new version of a product!

If you want to encourage enhancements, you can set up an enhancement board as described in Section 18.4. This will provide a mechanism for soliciting enhancements and for reviewing them in an orderly manner with all concerned functions. An enhancement board can have its own budget to ensure that the work approved by it gets done.

Both the nature and length of your warranty affect the size of your Maintenance Function. Use a three-stage warranty as do several computer manufacturers. The three stages, or **support levels**, are:

Level 1   Periodic releases of new updates (containing only corrections and revisions) and new versions (also containing enhancements).

Level 2   Periodic releases of updates only.

Level 3   No updates or new versions, only written responses to maintenance requests which may or may not offer a solution to the problems reported.

The more products you have at Levels 1 and 2, the larger the organization you need to support them.

12.2 MANAGING SOFTWARE PRODUCT MAINTENANCE IN THE ANALYSIS AND FEASIBILITY PHASES

Most of Maintenance's contribution to a product occurs during the Use Phase, but there are activities performed prior to product release. The effort of Maintenance is distributed as shown in Figure 12.1

The development objectives for a product should state who will provide maintenance and at what level. Such factors as the size of the user base, plans to release new versions, the complexity of the product, and the expertise with such products in Maintenance should be discussed by Maintenance and Development while a requirements contract is being prepared for review and approval. The complete requirements contract for A$K is included in the Appendix. Figure 12.2 shows a page from that requirements contract which defines the initial support level for A$K (i.e., Level 1) and the responsibility of Maintenance to produce a maintenance specification.

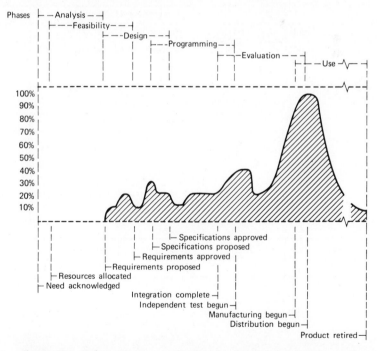

Figure 12.1   Relative manpower loading for the Maintenance Function.

```
    1.3.  Product End Items
------------------------------------  --------------------------------------------------
Key:                                  :                                       Responsibility
     Direct  = Not used to generate   :                                  No Distribution:
               other software         :                                     Distribution:
     Indirect = Used to generate      :                                     Incremental:   :
               other software         :                                        Complete:   :   :
                                      :------------------------------------:---:---:---:---:---
  Support Level 1 = Requests for Product : Specifications:                 :   :   :   :   :
                 correction will be   :------------------------------------:---:---:---:---:---
                 answered; Updates may:   ERS                              : X :   :   : X : D
                 be issued; Requests for:-----------------------------------:---:---:---:---:---
                 Product Enhancement  :   IRS                              : X :   :   : X : D
                 will be considered   :------------------------------------:---:---:---:---:---
              2 = Requests for Product :   Test Specification              : X :   :   : X : T
                 Correction will be   :------------------------------------:---:---:---:---:---
                 answered; Updates may:   Maintenance Specification        : X :   :   : X : M
                 be issued; Requests for:-----------------------------------:---:---:---:---:---
                 Product Enhancement  :   Other:                           :   :   :   :   :
                 will not be considered:-----------------------------------:---:---:---:---:---
              3 = Requests for Product : Publications:                     :   :   :   :   :
                 Correction will be   :------------------------------------:---:---:---:---:---
                 answered             :   System Description Manual        :   :   :   :   :
                                      :------------------------------------:---:---:---:---:---
Responsibility D = Development        :   Reference Manual                 : X :   : X :   : P
               M = Maintenance        :------------------------------------:---:---:---:---:---
               P = Publications       :   Reference Booklet                : X :   : X :   : P
               T = Test               :------------------------------------:---:---:---:---:---
                                      :   Operator Manual                  : X :   : X :   : P
--------------------------------------:------------------------------------:---:---:---:---:---
          : DIRECT   : X :  INITIAL   :   Message Manual                   : X :   : X :   : P
PRODUCT TYPE :--------:---: SUPPORT    :------------------------------------:---:---:---:---:---
          : INDIRECT :   :  LEVEL     :   Software Release Bulletin        :   :   :   :   :
--------------------------------------:------------------------------------:---:---:---:---:---
          :     1    : X :            :   Other:                           :   :   :   :   :
          :---------:---:             :------------------------------------:---:---:---:---:---
          :     2    :   :            : Promotional Material:              :   :   :   :   :
          :---------:---:             :------------------------------------:---:---:---:---:---
          :     3    :   :            :                                    :   :   :   :   :
          :---------:---:             :------------------------------------:---:---:---:---:---
                                      : Software:                          :   :   :   :   :
                                      :------------------------------------:---:---:---:---:---
                                      :   Listings                         : X :   :   : X : D
                                      :------------------------------------:---:---:---:---:---
                                      :   Source Code                      : X :   :   : X : D
                                      :------------------------------------:---:---:---:---:---
                                      :   Object Code                      : X :   : X :   : D
                                      :------------------------------------:---:---:---:---:---
                                      :   Test Material                    : X :   :   : X : D,T
                                      :------------------------------------:---:---:---:---:---
                                      :   Development Tools                :   :   :   :   :
                                      :------------------------------------:---:---:---:---:---
                                      :   Other:                           :   :   :   :   :
                                      :------------------------------------:---:---:---:---:---
```

	SHEET REVISION	C013/L301A
ABC COMPUTERS	A$K POR	A	NEXT 4	SHEET 3

MF 1064 APR 1972

Figure 12.2 Initial support level for A$K and the commitment by Maintenance to produce a maintenance specification.

Maintenance also provides inputs to the design of a product with respect to its maintainability: it urges maximum use of higher-level languages which provide self documentation and easy debugging, it provides interfaces to tracing tools, and it maximizes modularity. Agreements pertaining to maintainability are recorded in the requirements contract.

When Maintenance plans a new version of a product to incorporate enhancements, revisions, and corrections, it prepares a requirements contract for the project. It serves to bring to management's attention how, when, and why a major collection of changes is to be made. All enhancement requests considered for such a new version are identified in this requirements contract, along wich a clear statement of whether or not each is to be implemented.

12.3 MANAGING SOFTWARE PRODUCT MAINTENANCE IN THE DESIGN PHASE

During the Design Phase complete external details of a product are proposed, reviewed, and approved in an external specification. If the product described in an external specification is a new version of a product containing only a limited number of new features, Maintenance is responsible for developing the document. Whether or not Maintenance has this responsibility, it assures that approved enhancement requests are correctly documented in each external specification. This is accomplished through review by a technical review board (see Section 18.3). If an external specification consists solely of enhancement requests, you may want to use the enhancement board (see Section 18.4) rather than a specially constituted technical review board.

12.4 MANAGING SOFTWARE PRODUCT MAINTENANCE IN THE PROGRAMMING AND EVALUATION PHASES

Late in the Programming Phase, the activity of Maintenance increases considerably as it begins to prepare a maintenance specification. The gating item to effectively writing a maintenance specification is the completion of an internal specification. A **maintenance specification** consists of an internal specification augmented with background information and code listings—see Section 15.5. As Figure 12.3 shows,

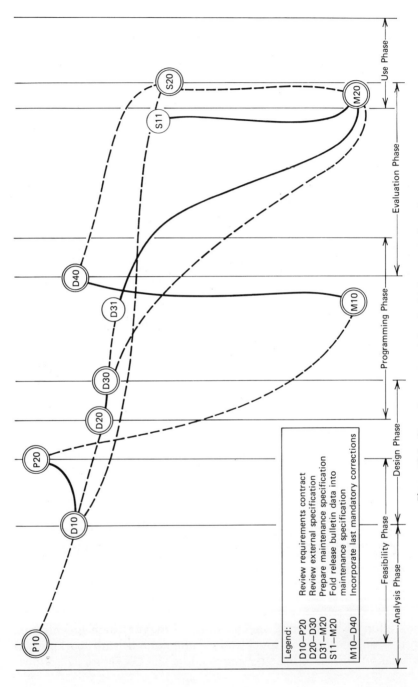

Legend:

D10—P20 Review requirements contract
D20—D30 Review external specification
D31—M20 Prepare maintenance specification
S11—M20 Fold release bulletin data into
         maintenance specification
M10—D40 Incorporate last mandatory corrections

Figure 12.3 Stereotype network for the Maintenance Function.

completion of a maintenance specification is constrained also by approval of the external specification; this assures that both the internal and external design of a product are frozen before the maintenance specification is complete. Figure 12.3 also shows that the installation document, called a release bulletin (see Section 8.6), must be complete so that Maintenance can adjust the maintenance specification to take into account maintenance requests included and excluded, any outstanding deficiencies, and any implications of product installation covered by the release bulletin.

12.5 MANAGING SOFTWARE PRODUCT MAINTENANCE IN THE USE PHASE

As is clearly shown by Figure 12.1, the heaviest activity of the Maintenance Function comes early in the Use Phase, just after a product is put to use by most users. This is true even when early debugging is performed by the Development Function as described in Section 17.1 because Maintenance must work side-by-side with Development to provide a smooth transition. This peak can occur any time from immediately after release until six months or more later, which is common for releases of new operating systems by computer manufacturers; it can take a long time for users to change to new systems.

As stated in Section 12.1, maintenance requests are used to report trouble. You need procedures for processing them: getting them from the users, through Support, through Services or whoever monitors them, into Maintenance for correction and/or reply, and back. Statistics on number, severity, and turn-around time are gathered by Maintenance to measure its performance and to aid in budgeting for future work. It also generates a maintenance request summary to be sent to users periodically, informing them of all known errors, rectified or not. Such a summary also contains corrections, predicts availability of corrections, and describes ways to "work around" errors until corrections are available. As stated at the beginning of this chapter, if no updates containing new code are to be released (as at Support Level 3), the summary is the only feedback users will receive.

In correcting errors and adding enhancements, Maintenance is continually mindful of configuration management. Every time code is released—and this includes code from Maintenance—you assure that all design documents, all publications, and all source and object code agree. This can be burdensome because you need to keep prior sets of code and documents for reference. Simply replacing old end items with new ones in your archives may leave you with serious gaps, should you need to distribute or reconstruct a prior release.

At some time maintenance for each product must be terminated. This can be abrupt, as with the expiration of a simple warranty. It can be gradual, such as by downgrading support levels after reasonable intervals of time and with ample notice to users. Periodically send to all users a configurator (see Section 14.5) to define current support levels and forecast future support levels. Have a configurator reviewed by all functions concerned, including Maintenance, to reach a decision about terminating support altogether.

Once you decide to eliminate support you can withdraw a product from distribution or you can transfer it to an unsupported library like COSMOS, FOCUS, or CUBE. Putting a once-supported product into such a library has disadvantages you should be aware of, however: All tools needed to install the product should be available; you should be prepared to politely say no to requests for information or help; and you should resolve legal complications if any fees were previously charged for use of the product.

12.6 MAINTENANCE'S REVIEW AND APPROVAL RESPONSIBILITY

The Maintenance Function participates in at least three of the six phase reviews presented in Section 6.10. It participates in at least one to input resource requirements for maintenance activities. This can be as early as Phase I and probably should not be later than Phase III. Referring to Figure 12.1 you will see that resources should be approved before the milestone Requirements Proposed unless early maintenance activities like reviewing requirements contracts and

Phase	Review	Responsibility
Analysis	I	None
Feasibility	II	Review and approve
Design	III	Review and approve
Programming	IV	None
Evaluation	V	None
Use	VI	Review and approve

Figure 12.4 Minimum responsibilities of the Maintenance Function at phase reviews.

external specifications are covered by indirect charges (which is very practical).

Maintenance participates in Phase II Review to review and approve a product's requirements contract, since a requirements contract makes commitments for initial support level, maintenance documentation, and maintainability attributes. Maintenance participates in Phase III Review if any enhancement requests are involved, to review requests excluded and included, and to approve requests included if Maintenance must implement them.

Maintenance need not be concerned with other phase reviews until Phase VI which is probably the most significant review for Maintenance. It is at Phase VI Review that the decision to retire a product is made. Since this has a significant impact on Maintenance's budget, Maintenance both reviews and approves retiring it. It also reviews and approves any reduction in support level as this also has significant budget impact on Maintenance. The review and approval responsibilities of Maintenance are summarized in Figure 12.4.

Part Three

TOOLS
FOR
SOFTWARE
PRODUCT
ENGINEERING
MANAGEMENT

13

Requirements Contract

A document called the requirements contract is referenced throughout this book more than any other document and more than any other concept. It is the primary management tool for controlling product development, the master plan. Variations of it are common under other names such as requirements statement, development plan, design objectives, or problem statement; at ABC Computers it is called a **Product Objectives and Requirements (POR)** document. Whatever you call it, you must have a written statement of what you are and are not going to do to produce a product. And there is no reason to restrict the requirements contract concept to software; at ABC Computers Company PORs are used for hardware as well.

It will help you to understand the role of a requirements contract if you think of it as a contract between a customer and a vendor. All of the contributors to a product's requirements contract—Development, Services, Publications, Test, Support—must do what is stated in it or request and gain approval to revise it. Absolutely *no* deviations can be tolerated, for there is no effective way to limit deviations to an acceptable level. If you want to leave an aspect of a product's development to the discretion of a function, either exclude that aspect from discussion in the product's requirements contract or define the limits of that discretion right in the requirements contract.

The responsibilities for preparing, reviewing, and approving a requirements contract are covered in many places in this book. The balance of this section treats the format and content of a requirements contract.

13.1   REQUIREMENTS CONTRACT FORMAT

Every requirements contract you produce should follow whatever format you choose exactly; each topic can then be found in the same place in every requirements contract. Include every title unless your format specifically states conditions under which a title may be omitted. Then the author and all reviewers will be reminded to consider the relevancy of each topic. For example, if a proposed product is not Type Indirect (to be defined shortly), the sections concerned with generated software should state "not applicable." Reviewers will be reminded thereby to ask themselves if any sections truly are not applicable.

Write requirements contracts on forms that allow for adequate configuration management; refer to the A$K POR in the Appendix for representative forms.

Figure 13.1 is a stereotype table of contents for a requirements contract constructed according to the format advocated here. When you follow this specific format you benefit from several years of evolutionary refinement; all major topics are covered; and they are covered in an order that reinforces top-down decision making about a product, both while the requirements contract is being written and reviewed and later when the design is decomposed according to the hierarchy illustrated in Figure 13.2. This will be described in Chapter 15. In Figure 13.2 RC means "requirements contract," ES means "external specification," IS means "internal specification," and MS means "maintenance specification." Further, in both Figures 13.1 and 13.2, each heading is followed by F (for "final"—what is stated may not be changed or extended in a subsequent document), P (for "partial"—what is stated may be extended but not replaced in a subsequent document), G (for "general"—what is stated may be replaced in a subsequent document by a partial or final statement), or T (for "title").

13.2   REQUIREMENTS CONTRACT CONTENTS

Using the format described in the preceding section, the material that follows describes the information you would provide in any requirements contract. All following references to a Requirements Contract (**RC**) refer to a requirements contract constructed according to this section. This approach also presumes design decomposition according to Figure 13.2 and therefore makes references to further detailing to

1	PRODUCT DESCRIPTION	T
1.1	Product Name and Numbers	T
1.1.1	Product Name	F
1.1.2	Name Abbreviations	F
1.1.3	Product Numbers	P
1.1.4	Project Numbers	P
1.2	Brief Description of Product	F
1.2.1	Copyright Notice	F
1.3	Product End Items	F
2	MISSION	T
2.1	Revision Request Reconciliation	T
2.1.1	Revisions Excluded	F
2.1.2	Revisions Included	F
2.2	Enhancement Request Reconciliation	T
2.2.1	Enhancements Excluded	F
2.2.2	Enhancements Included	F
2.3	Correction Request Reconciliation	T
2.3.1	Corrections Excluded	F
2.4	Plans Reconciliation	T
2.4.1	Plans Excluded	F
2.4.2	Plans Included	F
2.5	Summary of User Needs	F
2.6	Alternatives Considered	F
2.7	Return on Investment	F
3	STRATEGY	T
3.1	Conventions	T
3.1.1	Notations	P
3.1.2	Terminology	P
3.(2,3)	(Generated, Operational) Software	G
3.(2,3).n	(Name n) (Function, Module)	G
3.(2,3).n.1	Constraints	T
3.(2,3).n.1.1	Standards	P
3.(2,3).n.1.2	Compatibility Constraints	P
3.(2,3).n.1.3	Software Constraints	P
3.(2,3).n.1.4	Hardware Constraints	P
3.(2,3).n.2	External Properties	T
3.(2,3).n.2.1	Outputs	G
3.(2,3).n.2.2	Processes	G
3.(2,3).n.2.3	Inputs	G
3.(2,3).n.3	Ergonomic Properties	T
3.(2,3).n.3.1	Security and Privacy	G
3.(2,3).n.3.2	Reliability	G
3.(2,3).n.3.3	Restartability	G
3.(2,3).n.3.4	Customizability	G
3.(2,3).n.3.5	Performance	P
3.(2,3).n.3.6	Usability	F
3.(2,3).n.3.7	Portability	F

Figure 13.1 Stereotype requirements contract contents.

3.(2,3).n.4	Internal Properties	T
3.(2,3).n.4.1	Maintainability	G
3.(2,3).n.4.2	Algorithms	G
3.4	Restrictions	F
4	BACKGROUND	T
4.1	References	P
5	DELIVERY AND INSTALLATION	T
5.1	Provisions for protection	G
5.2	Installation Resources	G
5.3	Media	G
6	TACTICS	T
6.1	Interdependencies	T
6.1.1	Interdependencies Needed	F
6.1.2	Interdependencies Provided	F
6.2	Technical Review	F
6.3	Product Verification	T
6.3.1	Level of Testing	F
6.3.2	Bases of Reference	F
6.4	Provisions for Support	T
6.4.1	Provisions for Promotion	F
6.4.2	Provisions for Training	F
6.4.3	Provisions for Conversion	F
7	SCHEDULE	G

Figure 13.1 (Continued)

take place in a product's external specification according to Section 15.1. The material that follows up to the heading entitled "Schedule" is numbered, titled, and printed just as it is in an RC with one exception: each heading is followed by F, P, G, or T as a reminder of the level of detail.

Frequent examples are included, each separated from the text it illustrates by horizontal lines. Everything included in a Requirements Contract is assumed to be a requirement unless it is clearly identified as an objective. The distinction is that a requirement *must* be achieved but an objective will be satisfied if it is merely closely approached.

What follows is laboriously detailed and you may want to skim over it at first reading. When you construct your own format and guide for a requirements contract, however, you may appreciate having this detailed example from which to begin. Also, lest the convolutions of the section headings in Figure 13.1 and the sheer volume of their descriptions obscure the underlying order and simplicity of the resulting document, refer to the complete RC in the Appendix. Again, you probably will not want to read all of the Appendix, but you can first skim over it to get an overall picture of what a typical RC looks like.

Document:	RC	ES	IS	MS
1 PRODUCT DESCRIPTION	T	T	T	T
1.1 Product Name and Numbers	T	T	T	T
1.1.1 Product Name	F	F	F	F
1.1.2 Name Abbreviations	F	F	F	F
1.1.3 Product Numbers	P	F	F	F
1.1.4 Project Numbers	P			
1.2 Brief Description of Product	F	F	F	F
1.2.1 Copyright Notice	F	F	F	F
1.2.2 Hierarchical Precedence		P	F	F
1.2.2.1 Overriding Higher Documents		P	F	F
1.3 Product End Items	F			F
2 MISSION	F	F	F	F
2.1 Revision Request Reconciliation	T	T	T	T
2.1.1 Revisions Excluded	F	F	F	F
2.1.2 Revisions Included	F	F	F	F
2.2 Enhancement Request Reconciliation	T	T	T	T
2.2.1 Enhancements Excluded	F	F	F	F
2.2.2 Enhancements Included	F	F	F	F
2.3 Correction Request Reconciliation	T		T	T
2.3.1 Corrections Excluded	F		F	F
2.3.2 Corrections Included			P	F
2.4 Plans Reconciliation	T			
2.4.1 Plans Excluded	F			
2.4.2 Plans Included	F			
2.5 Summary of User Needs	F			
2.6 Alternatives Considered	F			
2.7 Return on Investment	F			
3 STRATEGY	T	T	T	T
3.1 Conventions	T	T	T	T
3.1.1 Notations	P	P	F	F
3.1.2 Terminology	P	P	F	F
3.1.3 Syntax		P	F	F
3.(2,3) (Generated, Operational) Software	G	F	F	F
3.(2,3).n (Name n) (Function, Module)	G	F	F	F
3.(2,3).n.1 Constraints	T	T	T	T
3.(2,3).n.1.1 Standards	P	P	F	F
3.(2,3).n.1.2 Compatibility Constraints	P	P	F	F
3.(2,3).n.1.3 Software Constraints	P	P	P	F
3.(2,3).n.1.4 Hardware Constraints	P	P	P	F
3.(2,3).n.2 External Properties	T	T	T	T
3.(2,3).n.2.1 Outputs	G	P	F	F
3.(2,3).n.2.2 Processes	G	P	F	F
3.(2,3).n.2.2.1 Invocation		P	F	F
3.(2,3).n.2.2.2 Execution		P	F	F
3.(2,3).n.2.2.3 Termination		P	F	F
3.(2,3).n.2.2.3.1 Normal Termination		P	F	F

Figure 13.2 Nested contents of design documents.

		Document:	RC	ES	IS	MS
3.(2,3).n.2.2.3.2		Abnormal Termination		P	F	F
3.(2,3).n.2.3		Inputs	G	P	F	F
3.(2,3).n.3		Ergonomic Properties	T	T	T	T
3.(2,3).n.3.1		Security and Privacy	G	P	F	F
3.(2,3).n.3.2		Reliability	G	P	F	F
3.(2,3).n.3.3		Restartability	G	P	F	F
3.(2,3).n.3.3.1		Automatic Restart		P	F	F
3.(2,3).n.3.3.2		Manual Restart		P	F	F
3.(2,3).n.3.4		Customizability	G	P	F	F
3.(2,3).n.3.4.1		Parameterization		P	F	F
3.(2,3).n.3.5		Performance	P	P	F	F
3.(2,3).n.3.6		Usability	F			
3.(2,3).n.3.7		Portability	F			
3.(2,3).n.4		Internal Properties	T	T	T	T
3.(2,3).n.4.1		Maintainability	G	P	F	F
3.(2,3).n.4.2		Algorithms	G		F	F
3.(2,3).n.4.3		Internal Data			F	F
3.(2,3).n.4.4		Implementation Strategy			G	F
3.(2,3).n.4.4.1		Function Testing			G	F
3.(2,3).n.4.4.2		Algorithm Testing			G	F
3.(2,3).n.4.4.3		Notes			G	F
3.(2,3).n.4.4.4		Module Status Sheet			P	F
3.(2,3).n.4.4.5		Listings				F
3.4	Restrictions		F			
4	BACKGROUND		T	T	T	T
4.1	References		P	P	P	F
4.2	Post-Mortem					F
4.3	Data Directory					F
4.4	Replacement Cross-Reference					F
5	DELIVERY AND INSTALLATION		T	T		T
5.1	Provisions for Protection		G	F		F
5.2	Installation Resources		G	G		F
5.2.1	Installation Procedures			G		F
5.3	Media		G			F
6	TACTICS		T			
6.1	Interdependencies		T			
6.1.1	Interdependencies Needed		F			
6.1.2	Interdependencies Provided		F			
6.2	Technical Review		F			
6.3	Product Verification		T			
6.3.1	Level of Testing		F			
6.3.2	Bases of Reference		F			
6.4	Provisions for Support		T			
6.4.1	Provisions for Promotion		F			
6.4.2	Provisions for Training		F			
6.4.3	Provisions for Conversion		F			
7	SCHEDULE		G			

Figure 13.2 (Continued)

Then refer to individual sections to find further examples to illustrate what follows.

1 PRODUCT DESCRICPTION (T)

1.1 Product Name and Numbers (T)

1.1.1 Product Name (F)

Enter the proposed full name of the product. Once the RC is approved, use no other name for the product except the abbreviations that follow.

1.1.2 Name Abbreviations (F)

Enter all proposed abbreviations or acronyms to be allowed as substitutes for the name in Section 1.1.1. Use no other abbreviations once the RC is approved.

1.1.3 Product Numbers (P)

Enter a product number or numbers obtained from configuration management as appropriate. If there are to be publications and support plans, assigning product numbers for end items to be produced by Publications and Support can be deferred to those plans.

1.1.4 Project Numbers (P)

Enter all project numbers to which work on the product can be charged.

1.2 Brief Description of Product (F)

Describe briefly and in general terms the major functional features of the product. If the product is an extension of an existing product, describe only the new features.

A$K allows a financial analyst or other person with similar analytic requirements to interactively and remotely "ask" a Stella 100 computer to retrieve and manipulate financial information from DATABA$E which contains twenty years worth of fundamental data and expressions for a large number of corporations and industries. He may also create additional public or private data, corporations, industries, expressions, and items and use his creations along with information from DATABA$E.

1.2.1   Copyright Notice (F)

If you plan to claim statutory copyright protection for the product, begin by copyrighting the RC. Otherwise, state "not applicable."

Copyright © 1977, by ABC Computers Company

1.3   Product End Items (F)

Include a matrix like or equivalent to Figure 12.2. In this example a pre-printed form is used to reduce the time needed to present the information and to assure consistency.

In such a matrix, after Product Type insert X beside either Direct or Indirect. If the product is not used to create other software enter X beside **Direct**. If the product is used to create other software, as in the case of an assembler, compiler, or generator, enter X beside **Indirect**. Under Initial Support Level insert 1, 2, or 3 per the key on the form. For each item insert X under Complete if an entire item will be produced or under Incremental if only an addendum or changes will be produced. Insert X under Distribution (outside of Development) or No Distribution (outside of Development), whichever is correct. Under Responsibility insert D, T, P, or M per the key on the form. If a nonstandard item is to be produced, enter it under Other and define it immediately after the matrix.

For definitions of specifications see Chapter 15. For definitions of publications see Chapter 9. For suggestions for promotional material see Chapter 11. And for a description of a release bulletin see Chapter 8. Software end items are:

Listings.   A listing is the collection of assembly and compilation listings of the product.

Source code.   Source code is all of the statements which must be assembled or compiled to produce the product.

Object code.   Object code is the linkable or loadable output from assembly and compilation of the product's source code or the output of a generator if that output is directly executable or interpretable.

Test material.   Test material is used to assure that the product can be assembled, compiled, linked, loaded, and executed properly. It may consist of listings, source code, object code, and procedures.

Development tools. Development tools are assemblers, compilers, loaders, dump routines, and so forth produced within the development project in order to create the product.

2 MISSION (F)

As noted in Section 1 of Chapter 6, a mission statement is a statement of purpose, an answer to the question "Why?." Therefore accumulate in this section of an RC the reasons for producing the product. Often this will be to fulfill a plan, to satisfy a contract, or to eliminate deficiencies of a predecessor product. Whatever the primary reason or reasons are, state them here.

The Business Plan for Financial Services (Ref. 4.1.a) declares the intent of ABC Services Company to market an interactive, remote access financial analysis system to the financial community. A$K is our proposed response to the software requirements defined in that plan.

2.1 Revision Request Reconciliation (T)

As described in Chapter 12, revision requests represent mandatory product changes resulting from events beyond the control of a product's developers. If no revision requests exist, state it and omit Subsections 2.1.1 and 2.1.2.

2.1.1 Revisions Excluded (F)

Normally enter "none," since inclusion is mandatory. However, you may find it impossible to include a particular revision, in which case the exclusion must be thoroughly justified and documented, beginning here.

2.1.2 Revisions Included (F)

List all revisions that have been approved for implementation and which will be incorporated in the product. If there are none, enter "none."

2.2 Enhancement Request Reconciliation (T)

If no enhancement requests exist, state it and omit Subsections 2.2.1 and 2.2.2.

2.2.1   Enhancements Excluded (F)

List each enhancement considered specifically for implementation in the product, but which will not be, along with the reason for excluding it. If there are none, enter "none."

2.2.2   Enhancements Included (F)

List all enhancements which have been approved for implementation and which will be incorporated in the product. If there are none, enter "none."

2.3   Correction Request Reconciliation (T)

If the subject of the RC is a new product which is not intended to replace another product, there can be no outstanding correction requests; enter "not applicable," and omit Subsection 2.3.1.

2.3.1   Corrections Excluded

If the subject is a product revision or product enhancement or a replacement for a product with known errors, plan to correct all errors identified prior to the latest possible time. Therefore insert a statement like "All relevant errors logged prior to the Correction Request Cutoff Date (Milestone M10) shall be corrected. Relevant requests received between M10 and the Product Availability Date (Milestone P30) will be corrected if possible." Also list all relevant errors logged prior to RC submission that will not be corrected (usually because they cannot be due to technical complexity) along with reasons for exclusion.

As work on the subject product progresses, requests that cannot be corrected may be logged. If they are, this section of the RC must be updated. While this may seem like unnecessary red tape, it is not: willful perpetuation of an error should receive broad management review and approval.

2.4   Plans Reconciliation (T)

2.4.1   Plans Excluded (F)

If any planning references call for specific features or capabilities that will not be available if the product is developed as otherwise described in the RC, describe each one here and state why it will be excluded. If there are none, enter "none." Separately state any other features (not covered by Requests for Product Enhancement) that were seriously considered but were excluded.

The wide range of terminals called for in the Business Plan for Financial Services (see 4.1.a) will not be supported. Only Telcoscope 43 or electrically and functionally equivalent terminals will function properly with A$K.

2.4.2 Plans Included

If the product is justified by a document such as a product plan, a product line plan, or a task force report, cite that document here. Either cite a specific reference in each document or provide an abstract of the appropriate passages. Note that planning references state what you should do in general terms, and why you should do it. They differ from technical references which state or provide background for what you will do, in specific terms. For each cited reference, point to an entry in Section 4.1 of the RC.

2.5 Summary of User Needs (F)

State who the intended users of the product are and why they need it.

The customer for this program is ABC Field Engineering. The customer needs a quick-running test capable of exercising all communications adapter functions to verify proper operation or detect and locate any malfunction. It is desirable to accomplish these actions either with or without use of common carrier facilities.

State how long the product is likely to be used. Generally this will be the length of the hardware usage or until a successor product is released. If the product is to be replaced, identify its successor by name. The purpose of this statement is to give some measure of how heavy-duty the software should be.

2.6 Alternatives Considered (F)

Briefly discuss alternatives to this development that were considered but rejected, including reasons for rejection. If this software is to be purchased, state why it is not to be built in-house, and vice-versa.

Some reviewers of this RC may question the fundamental need for the software, so be sure such questions are answered in this section.

As no present Services product can perform the functions of A$K, a new product must be built. No comparable product is available ready-made. Services has decided to sole-source contract with Computers to build and maintain A$K. They base that decision on past experience contracting with Computers.

2.7 Return on Investment (F)

Quantify the benefits to be gained from creating the product in terms appropriate to the mission of your organization.

Services expects sales to financial customers to increase 10% within three months of release and to reach an increase of at least 170% within one year of release. Based on expected gross profit from such a sales increase, the cost of producing A$K will be recovered within eight months of release and, without a new Version, A$K should produce a cumulative gross margin three times its cumulative cost, including maintenance.

3 STRATEGY (T)

As noted in Section 1 of Chapter 6, a strategy statement answers the question "What?." This section therefore states what the proposed product will be.

3.1 Conventions (T)

In the subsections that follow you may need to develop a special vocabulary to describe your proposed product succinctly. Use this section to introduce readers of your RC to your special vocabulary. You may add to Subsections 3.1.1 and 3.1.2 in your external specifications, but do not alter any statements made here.

3.1.1 Notations (P)

Define all notations used in the RC. If subscripting is used, for example, illustrate its usage and define the method.

3.1.2 Terminology (P)

Clearly define all terminology that may be unique to the product.

3.1.2. *Terminology*
3.1.2.1. *"Blind" Partition*

> *Any partition configured without external communication capabilities other than memory.*

3.2 Generated Software (G) and

3.3 Operational Software (G)

Generated software is what you get as the output from a compiler, assembler, loader, link-editor, or applications generator. It is Type Indirect and is produced by the product being described in the RC. **Operational software** is all other software, including but not limited to operating systems, compilers, utilities, and applications systems. It is Type Direct and is the product being described in the RC.

These two sections and their subsections should be constructed so similarly that they are discussed together here. Where the word "software" or the word "product" appears unmodified, it applies to both generated and operational software. The notation (a,b) means "either a or b." Where it appears twice, as $(a_1,b_1) \ldots (a_2,b_2)$, select a_1 and a_2 or b_1 and b_2.

Because most software products are Type Direct you may be inclined to reverse the order of Sections 3.2 and 3.3 and then omit Section 3.3 for Type Direct products. The reason generated software is listed first here is that, in a true top-down design effort, the generated software is the ultimate goal of the design and should be specified before its generator. Said another way, the design of the generated software should constrain the design of its generator and not vice-versa. If the product is Type Direct, state "not applicable" under the title "3.2 Generated Software" and omit Subsections 3.2.1–3.2.n.4.1.

3.(2,3).n (Name n) Function (G)

Try to treat the entire product as one functional module in order to keep the number of subsections low. If you cannot describe the product adequately without subdividing it into separate functional modules, use a structure diagram to explain how the functional modules relate to one another and number each module. Then create a subsection of Section 3.(2,3) for each functional module using the function name followed by the word "function"; see Figure 13.3.

Note the distinction here of decomposition by *function*. An RC is a *functional* document and is not concerned with *how* the proposed product should be physically modularized. In the internal specifications to be derived from RCs, you do describe physical modularization. To make comparison of internal specifications to their antecedent RCs easier, keep in mind the eventual physical modularization and try to define functional modules that can map simply to physical modules. When doing so, however, remember that clear grouping by function is more important in an RC and that physical modularization can only be implied by an RC and not dictated by it.

Organize Sections 3.(2,3).n hierarchically to cover as many topics as possible in the first set of subsections. Then merely refer to higher-level subsections when no new information is relevant as is done in Section 3.3.2 of Figure 13.3.

Note also in Figure 13.3 that titles are expanded beyond what is shown in Figure 13.1. Such expansion adds clarity and is highly recommended.

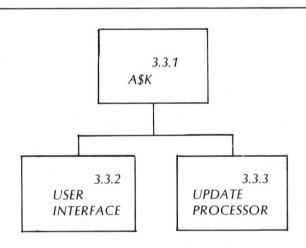

3.3.1. All A$K Functions
3.3.1.1. Constraints on All A$K Functions

Figure 13.3   A structure diagram from the A$K requirements contract.

3.(2,3).n.1   Constraints (T)

List all constraints that have a scope broader than the subject of the RC, such as industry or product line constraints. Allow for additional constraints to be added later to the external specification and internal specification but only those whose scope is restricted to the product, such as memory allocation.

List as many constraints as practical in Section 3.(2,3).1.1, implying that they apply to all functions. However, if the list is long and some constraints apply to some but not all functions, introduce them at the highest appropriate lower level.

3.(2,3).n.1.1   Standards (P)

List all industry and organization standards that are to be included in the product. Be sure that references to them are included in Section 4.1 of the RC.

3.3.1.1.1.   Standards for All A$K Functions
ABC Programming Standard (Ref. 4.1.e.)

3.(2,3).n.1.2   Compatibility Constraints (P)

Always consider several aspects of compatibility: source language, object language, data and message formats, report formats, listing formats, and job formats (control cards, command structure, etc.). Specify compatibility with:

Predecessor products   products that a user may replace with the new product. If the new product lacks a capability that its predecessor had, provide justifiction for the deletion.

Companion products   members of the same product set that are alternatives to the new product. An example is an output formatting program that differs only in format from another output formatting program.

Similar products   products that perform similar functions in other product sets of the same product line. A disc sort and a tape sort could be similar products.

Competitive products   products that perform the same function but
which are provided by a source other than
your organization. If you work for Burroughs,
IBM's COBOL is a competitor of your COBOL.

In each case be sure to state whether your product is a superset or a
subset of another product and be sure to provide a reference in Section 4.1 of the RC. Also discuss provisions for conversion from other
versions or other products.

---

*There are no known software products or databases with which A$K
should be compatible. Files generated by A$K will be VSOS Direct
Access (Ref. 4.1.b), and will thus be readily usable by programs other
than A$K.*

3.(2,3).n.1.3   Software Constraints (P)

Identify the operating systems, if any, under which the proposed
product is to operate. Also identify the other products, if any, with
which this product must interface during execution. Be sure to
include any products required to load the product or to transfer control to or from it.

If there are any significant exclusions from the operating environment
of the product, state them and state why they were excluded.

---

*VSOS, Version 4 (Ref. 4.1.b) is required by A$K. Any VSOS Product Set
Member may run concurrently with A$K as long as the hardware con-
figuration of Sec. 3.3.1.1.4 is not encroached. Update Processor may
run concurrently with User Interface, but no User Interface attempts
to access files currently being used by Update Processor will be
allowed.*

3.(2,3).n.1.4   Hardware Constraints (P)

Tabulate the hardware used by the product during its execution. After
each item, indicate the minimum, target, and maximum number of
units used. The target amount is the value for which the product will
be optimized, or, if no design tradeoffs will be made regarding an
item, the most probable amount.

If other hardware elements must be present in order for the product to execute, reference them indirectly.

In addition to the requirements for VSOS ILSAM (see Ref. 4.1.b), Update Processor will need:

		Minimum	Target	Maximum
M103	*Floating point unit*	1	1	1
M107	*Power fail option*	1	1	1
M1100	*Memory module*	1	2	2
M3100	*Disc module*	1	3	8
M210	*Console*	1	1	1

3.(2,3).n.2   External Properties (T)

Much of this section will be expanded (but not changed) in the external specification; in the RC provide mostly general statements. If the proposed product is an extension of an existing product, comment mainly upon the additional features. Here again treat subtopics in a top-down manner, discussing first what is most vital to the ultimate user.

3.(2,3).n.2.1   Outputs (G)

Describe all outputs from the product or functional module. State their nature and destination—reports, files, records, fields, transactions, tables, flags. Identify all possible media. Do not overlook sense lights, interrupt lines, panel lights, and so forth.

3.(2,3).n.2.2   Processes (G)

Discuss operations performed by the product, looking at the entire product or functional module as a black box (or a collection of black boxes). At the very least, state which inputs are needed for each output, and if the discussion goes to the module or phase level, also state which modules or phases are needed for each output. Discuss all generation or execution parameters that will be provided.

3.(2,3).n.2.3   Inputs (G)

Discuss inputs just as outputs were discussed in Section 3.(2,3).n.2.1.

3.(2,3).n.3   Ergonomic Properties (T)

Ergonomic properties are those design properties that accommodate the safety, comfort, and productiveness of human users and operators. Thus, this section describes the application of human factors engineering to the product and determines how "heavy-duty" the product will be.

3.(2,3).n.3.1   Security and Privacy (G)

Describe in general detail features of the product provided for data and program security and privacy.

No public files, including DATABA$E, will be able to be written into from a terminal. All private files will be password protected using VSOS conventions. All write operations on public files, including DATABA$E, will have to be performed from the console.

3.(2,3).n.3.2   Reliability (G)

Reliability is the ability to recover from data errors and/or failures in the environment. Protection of user data, particularly, is of paramount concern. Note if errors in data can be corrected by an operator, or how processing can continue after an error is detected. Comment on the extent to which user data will be lost under various conditions, including hardware failure.

Discuss the extent to which software is protected from failure if failures in other portions of the system occur. If the environment of the software is a multiprogramming environment, this means failures in other software products as well as equipment failures. If this product does not operate in a multiprogramming environment, this point need not be covered. If it does, the discussion can and should be limited to the isolation of failures that can occur in products that can be coresident.

Discuss how failures in these possibly coresident products can affect the product being described in the RC. Do so in the context of:

(a)   resource allocations where the other products may be allocated space on the same device or partition as this product. Discuss how the isolation between the products is maintained to assure failure does not occur due to overlapping resource usage. If operating system or loader features are used to assure this isolation, reference to such features is sufficient.

(b)   execution errors, discussing how errors in the execution of other products are prevented from affecting the execution of this product. Again, reference to hardware or software features, if they exist, is sufficient.

EDIT executes as a monitor function and observes VSOS requirements for error detection actions. Any transaction that fails editing is put to an error file and EDIT will continue processing to the end of the day's transactions. No user data will be lost due to machine failure except damage to disc recording surfaces.

Programs generated by CPG permit both operator and program input errors to be corrected without loss of previously processed inputs.

3.(2,3).n.3.3   Restartability (G)

Specify capabilities provided to capture and use data to resume operation after voluntary termination, such as checkpoint-restart.

CPG-generated programs can be started at the beginning of any phase.

SORT shall provide automatic or manual checkpointing of parameters and data needed to restart at the last or any previous checkpoint. All restart information shall be stored in nonvolatile media so that power failure will not inhibit restart.

3.(2,3).n.3.4   Customizability (G)

Cover customization features which allow the product or its output to be tailored to meet specific requirements. If possible identify those modules that may or may not be customized.

The internal design of the operational software shall be modular to permit customer-specific modifications of all code concerned with account number identification and expense data accumulation.

State also how much execution-time memory will be reserved for customization and what provisions will be made for user exits.

3.(2,3).n.3.5   Performance (P)

Specify the basic variable or method by which software performance is to be measured and give the value or range of values for the variable. The essential thing is to specify the basic performance measure in actually measurable terms. Do not, for instance, state that "execution speed of generated code will be as fast as if hand-coded in assembler language." Such a statement is not subject to verification nor is it of value in making internal design decisions. Wording should be definite such as "performance will be at least 21 transmissions per minute." Characteristics included here should be measurable by the end user. Address execution speed; throughput; data transfer rate; compilation, generation, or assembly speed; overhead; response time; and so forth.

Each peripheral device shall operate at full rated speed, assuming no other concurrent activity.

Sixteen active terminals shall each be served within a 5-second or less response time for 90% of all trivial interactions, where a trivial interaction is defined as the transmission of a one-character query from a terminal, the look-up on disc of a one-character reply, and the receipt of the one-character reply at the same terminal. Response time shall not degrade more than 100% (to 10 seconds) as the number of active terminals increases from 16 to 180.

This product shall not impose any configuration restrictions beyond those imposed by the hardware.

3.(2,3).n.3.6   Usability (F)

Specify included features that humanize the man-machine interface. Examples are free-form data input, interactivity, syntactical consistency, acceptability of abbreviated commands, and so forth.

If there are other products with which the intended users are likely to be familiar, and that have identical or similar operations or operators, commands, error messages, or other structures, state that corresponding structures of this product will be the same where their functions are the same or similar where their functions are similar.

Also state the types of persons to use the product components and their respective experience levels. Examples of types are: management, commercial analysts, systems programmers, and operators. Try to use a simple, standard method for quoting experience levels, such as high (seven or more years of experience); medium (two to six years of experience); or low (one year or less of experience).

State how the product is to be invoked and terminated. For each appropriate function such as data collection, data entry, output, communications, computation, compilation, or generation state as many of the following modes of operation as apply: batch, interactive, foreground, background, interpretive, diagnostic, continuous, intermittent.

3.(2,3).n.3.7   Portability (F)

Describe requirements and objectives for the transfer of the product from one operating environment to another.

A$K will observe all VSOS interface constraints and will use VSOS Logical Access for all I/O. A$K thus should run unmodified with any operating system which is a superset of VSOS.

3.(2,3).n.4   Internal Properties (T)

The material in this section will be expanded (but of course not changed) in the product's internal specification and some of it may be expanded (but not changed) in the external specification to fully describe related external characteristics.

3.(2,3).n.4.1   Maintainability (G)

Provide a statement guaranteeing identifiability of modules unless you cover the subject in a standard.

The source and object code of each module shall contain the Product Code and Release Level, and if space permits, the Development Code and Product Identity Number. This information shall be so placed that each module can be identified in any disc, tape, or core dump containing it.

Describe any built-in debugging and integration aids, including interfaces to performance monitors, indicating whether or not they may be optionally excluded.

So that ease of maintenance can be evaluated further, state the language(s) of implementation. State how much execution time memory will be reserved for error correction.

A$K will be written entirely in BIL3 (Ref. 4.1.f) with the space reservation factor set to 10%. Per Sec. 1.4, only object code will be distributed. UPDATE (Ref. 4.1.g) will be used to insert object code corrections.

State if anyone outside the Maintenance Function is to insert corrections. If so, state training and resources required.

A Systems Engineer who has successfully completed Marketing's VSOS Basics course should be able to install an object patch at the expense of no more than two hours of his time and one-half hour of machine time.

Be sure that effort expended for maintainability is consistent with the expected life stated in Section 2.4 of the RC.

3.(2,3).n.4.2   Algorithms (G)

If any algorithms or techniques to be employed are particularly significant to success or failure of the product in meeting its reliability or performance requirements, describe the risk to be taken or the advantage to be gained. Otherwise, state "to be specified in the internal specification."

3.4   Restrictions (F)

It is important to state not only what a product is but also what it is not. A **restriction** is any feature or capability a user might logically expect to find present that you elect to exclude. Cross-reference any restrictions mentioned elsewhere in the RC. Include any others that do not belong elsewhere in the RC such as any features or capabilities not present that a user might rightfully expect and the omission of which might evoke his dissatisfaction with the product. Cite such restrictions as incomplete interchangeability of storage media, lack of support for any hardware capabilities, mandatory simulation of an optional hardware feature, or restrictions on the simultaneity of operation or residency with companion products. List as potential restrictions any contingencies that can be left to the discretion of Development.

4   BACKGROUND (T)

This section will be expanded in the maintenance specification. In the RC, it contains only one subsection.

4.1   References (P)

Separately cite every planning or technical reference pointed to elsewhere in the RC. Each cited reference should exist (not be forthcoming) and should be filed with your document control function for configuration management. References to software design documents should include project numbers and product identification numbers to assure accurate reference.

If the product is based on a standard, such as a language or communications code, reference a document defining the standard. If the product is a new version of an existing product, mention all design documents and publications for the product. If the product is concerned with specific hardware, cite here documentation of that hardware.

5   DELIVERY AND INSTALLATION (T)

5.1   Provisions for Protection (G)

State one of the following (see Chapter 17, Section 8 for definitions):
None
Trade Secret

Copyright
Patent

5.2   Installation Resources (G)

Specify the resources required, using materials specified in Section 5.3 of the RC, to install the system in terms of computer time, manpower time, and manpower experience level. The amounts and quality of these resources should be stated as most probable values.

Any VSOS operator with six months experience (or equivalent training) should be able to install A$K using UPDATE in fifteen minutes of console interaction. After studying the verification procedure in the Software Release Bulletin for half an hour, he should be able to execute the verification procedure in ten minutes of terminal interaction.

The above predictions assume all necessary hardware running without malfunction and no concurrent activity on the computer.

Be sure to state the hardware and software environments needed to generate and install the product if they differ from Section 3.(2,3).n.1.4.

5.3   Media (G)

Specify each storage medium for the distributed components (e.g., magnetic tape [specifying number of tracks and density], disc pack, diskette, etc.). If the product is to be packaged with other products, either mention which other products or refer to an RC that does. Be sure that the forms and storage media of release permit installation on each minimum hardware configuration.

6   TACTICS (T)

As noted in Chapter 6, Section 2, tactics deal with how to accomplish a strategy. This section, therefore, tells how the product will be produced.

6.1   Interdependencies (T)

6.1.1   Interdependencies Needed (F)

Define requirements placed on other development projects or on other functions by this product. Include a brief description of each requirement and a precise milestone by which satisfaction of the requirement can be measured unequivocally.

Interface Electronics must make the channel fan, with a diagnostic program, available to Product Test at Milestone S10 (see Sec. 7).

By Milestone D30, the project must have the RPG II compiler modified to provide object programs capable of executing in a blind partition.

6.1.2 Interdependencies Provided (F)

This section is structured like the preceding section but contains requirements this development must satisfy for other products. For every item appearing in Section 6.1.2 for one product there should be a corresponding item in Section 6.1.1 of another product.

Also describe here any impact on other functions produced by this product. State any requirements this product must meet in order for other products to operate. For example, state requirements to provide for or interface with hardware diagnostic and test features, like an error file or aids to on-line diagnosis.

By Milestone D40, the project shall provide a compiler capable of producing object programs that can execute in a blind partition.

6.2 Technical Review (F)

Every RC should recommend a technical review board, specifying each member by name where possible, by organization where not possible, and identifying a chairman. See Chapter 18, Section 3 for technical review board selection criteria and procedures.

Each of the following persons has been contacted and consents to serve in the capacity indicated:

Bob Wilbur (Software Product Test)—Chairman
C. W. Garrison (Services Company)

Robert Wong (Publications)
Bob Sims (Applications Dev.)

6.3   Product Verification (T)

6.3.1   Level of Testing (F)

Testing of software can be organized into three Stages (see Chapter 10, Section 2.1), three Modes (Section 2.2), and ten Categories (Section 2.3). Indicate such information in a matrix. For each Stage and Category indicate who will conduct the test. Summarize the role of Test by indicating a Test Mode. See Figure 10.2 for an example.

6.3.2   Bases of Reference (F)

Specify the base systems against which comparisons will be made. Specify performance relative to the base systems. If there is no base system, provide absolute values.

For any source program, compilation speed shall be no slower than RPG 1, Release B. For test program RPG 43, execution speed of the object code produced by RPG II shall be 10% faster than RPG 1, Release B when run in the same environment.

6.4   Provisions for Support (T)

For each subsection specify what specific provisions will be made, reference a support plan, or state "none."

6.4.1   Provisions for Promotion (F)

Reference, for example, demonstrations to be prepared for trade shows or specific customers.

6.4.2   Provisions for Training (F)

Describe what training will be provided for any audiences, defining the relative point in time (e.g., during the Evaluation Phase) during which each training session will be presented. State who each intended audience is, including any prior training or experience required.

6.4.3   Provisions for Conversion (F)

If appropriate, reference Sections 3.(2,3).n.1.2.

7   SCHEDULE (G)

As the last page of each RC, attach a copy of a current schedule notice, photo-reduced if necessary, to fit on your specification form. Under this title in the document state "see last page." This section is general (G) in the sense that the attached schedule notice probably will be superseded by later schedule notices. There is no need to append subsequent schedule notices to an RC unless new milestones are added that impact any statements made in the RC. In such a case, an RC revision would be necessary and a new schedule notice could be appended to the revision. See Figure 10.5 for an example.

This completes the RC format. Now would be a good time, if you have not already done so, to skim through the Appendix to set in your mind the nature of the document you get when you use this format. Note particularly how much easier to read an actual RC is than the format; this should reassure you that the use of the format is not difficult should it have seemed so to you up until now.

Chapter
14
Other
Plans

Chapter 6 introduced several types of plans. Some it treated generically, such as mission plans and product line plans. It treated others very specifically, such as budget allocations, configurators, and requirements contracts. Chapter 13 details a specific form of master product plan, the Requirements Contract. The present chapter is devoted to arming you with a set of plans consistent with a Requirements Contract and tailored to fit the overall software product engineering methodology. The names of plans presented here are capitalized to emphasize that they follow specific formats and have specific contents.

14.1 BUDGET

A budget is an important type of plan; it is the key to converting desire into action. In the classification scheme of plans, a budget is primarily a tactical plan. It answers the questions, "*How* much will it cost?" and "*Where* will the money come from?."

Many managers view budgeting with disdain as a necessary chore. Enlightened managers view budgeting with relish as an opportunity to gain an almost irrevocable commitment to their plans. Effort spent writing a clear, consistent, and well-justified budget proposal pays handsome dividends when the time comes to compete with other managers for available resources.

The first principle of budgets is to make sure you have one—in writing. A budget tells you where you stand with regard to resources. By comparing actual costs to it you can forecast your ability to meet your commitments. The second principle of budgets is to secure and reaffirm their approval. You may ask for a $6 million budget, but if your management agrees to let you have only $5 million, you will have only $5 million to spend. Your management, by asking you to report actual costs versus an agreed-upon budget, asks you to reaffirm your commitment to the agreed-upon budget. The third principle of budgets is to manage them: maintain a correlation between your current financial plan and your approved budget; record changes in your approved budget as they occur; and report progress versus both your baseline and your working budget so that all concerned know where you stand and how you got there. The fourth principle of budgets is to manage with them. Use historical records of actual costs to forecast future costs, preferably by algorithmically reducing them to standard costs. Know what the key variables are. Incrementally encumber funds so that your subordinates do not overcommit you.

The above four principles apply to two types of budget: project and natural accounts. A **project budget**, or a **program budget** if projects are consolidated into programs, enumerates costs by project with the costs that make up each project usually based on standard costs such as man-days and machine hours. A project budget gathers costs from all functions that contribute to the project. A **natural accounts budget** enumerates costs by type: labor, fringe benefits, rent, utilities, taxes, amortization. Each function or organizational entity has a separate natural accounts budget from which it determines its own standard costs. Usually a manager is required to propose both types of budget for all resources subject to his stewardship. When both budgets exist, they *must* agree in total. Generally, this year's natural accounts are used to develop next year's standard costs which are used to propose next year's project budget from which is derived next year's natural accounts budget. Then, when next year's actual costs are reported, they are totaled by natural accounts and distributed to project accounts, partly direct and the balance pro-rata according to the project budget. The two types of budget thus work together for both planning and reporting.

There is another dichotomy of budgets: expense and capital budgets. Most organizations treat expenditures from income and expenditures from borrowed capital differently, both for tax purposes and for long-range financial planning. A capital project budget is much the same as an expense project budget regarding aggregation into programs. A capital natural accounts budget is usually subdivided into items planned for purchase. In part it is directly allocated to projects, as in the case of contracted software. It is also allocated to amortizing natural expense accounts, as in the case of computer hardware to be used for many projects.

Begin to prepare a budget by analyzing past actual costs. What are the key variables in terms of the cost of a software development project? Which are fixed and which are variable? Which should be direct and which should be indirect? A **key budget variable** is one which the manager submitting the budget can control, and which, as it varies, has a substantial impact on project costs. Key variables are kept to an absolute minimum so that managers can spend their time managing instead of playing accountant. In a company like ABC Computers, the key variables are programming labor and computer time; for contract programming, travel and living expenses are also key. In a project budget, all costs are variable but in a natural accounts budget, items like occupancy costs, taxes, amortization, and administrative costs are fixed over a period of time, usually a year. What is direct and what is indirect is often a matter of policy: Development, Maintenance, Test, and Publications costs might be direct; Services costs, indirect; and Support costs, by virtue of being in marketing, might appear only as a buried component of an administrative allocation.

Other decisions about what is direct and what is indirect affect accurate budgeting. Do direct labor personnel charge directly to a project for time spent in their own training or the training of others? What about reviewing requirements contracts or participating on technical review boards for projects other than the ones to which they are assigned? Where do they charge time when fighting fires for users? Designate direct or indirect accounts to accumulate these costs or merely charge some to overhead, but whatever you do, do it consistently for a long enough period of time to determine the effect, and account for it in your standard cost algorithms.

Once you have isolated your key variables, determine how to distribute all costs over them. Suppose, as at ABC Computers, you conclude there are two key variables: direct labor and computer time in support of direct labor. Allocate all clearly related costs to one variable or the other: to labor allocate fringe benefits, furniture, telephones, travel; to computer time allocate computer depreciation, floor space occupied by computers, burdened personnel costs for computer operations personnel. Distribute remaining costs to both; at ABC, this is done according to the ratio of labor to machine costs prior to this final distribution of indirect costs. Once you have all costs allocated to key variables, determine their unit costs. Use these to prepare a project budget, with each standard cost suitably adjusted for expected inflation. Figure 14.1 shows a trial project budget derived in this manner.

Once you have a project budget, develop a natural accounts budget based on the total cost of the project budget. Be careful to cover the same time interval in both budgets. This requires that only the portion of each project belonging to the time period of the natural accounts budget be included in the natural accounts budget. In decomposing your natural accounts total into individual accounts, reverse whatever algorithms you used to arrive at standard costs. You may need to iteratively refine both budgets if the scale of your new project budget is substantially different from the scale of the total of natural costs used to predict it. For example, if you use this year's actual costs for 50 people to predict next year's budget for 75, you may find some economies of scale appearing in fixed cost allocations. Or, on the contrary, you may find you have to rent additional office space at a higher rate. Figure 14.2 shows a natural accounts budget corresponding to the project budget in Figure 14.1.

In many organizations a long time passes between the submission of first requests and final approvals, particularly in large organizations. During this time, the amount allocated to each request goes up and down. Maintain a clear record of these changes, especially if your allocation decreases. In this way you can easily explain why you later did not do what someone earlier thought you would do. Your management just might forget that you had requested $6 million to do the job properly but under duress you later agreed to do a lesser job for $5 million. Figure 14.3 shows a simple way to maintain a record.

Trial Project Budget
($1000s)

10/7/77

Project Code	Title	Labor	Computers	Total
B	Stella—new development	$ 540	$ 453	$ 993
C	Stella—continuation	1040	772	1812
F	Astros	60	9	69
G	Advanced communications	110	55	165
M	New market penetration	205	92	297
Q	Data entry	60	15	75
U	EFTS	180	58	238
Total	Software Products	$2195	$1454	$3649

Figure 14.1 A trial project budget.

Trial Budget
($1000s)

10/10/77

Software Products

Account Number	Description	Amount
3100	Salaried payroll	$1278
4400	Employee benefits	255
5071	Maintenance, purchased	8
5072	Maintenance, distributed	15
5110	Travel and living, nonproject	9
5111	Travel and living, project	33
5130	Communications	18
5160	Purchased services	14
5165	Administration, distributed	1307
5180	Recruiting	23
5350	Professional development	10
5400	Data processing	127
5910	Intracompany charges	333
7010	Rent, building	22
7030	Rent, equipment	11
7051	Depreciation, machinery	102
7053	Depreciation, software	62
7060	Depreciation, furniture, etc.	8
7110	Taxes	14
	Total	$3649

Figure 14.2   A trial natural accounts budget.

Budgeting is often a contest requiring great skill and diplomacy to win. It also requires good organization of data and perseverance in presenting and representing, justifying and rejustifying the data. To get your fair share at the end of the contest, keep all of your critical budget justification data together and up to date. For example, for every project maintain a concise narrative describing the project, its origin backed by concrete planning references, its dependencies, and its interdependencies. You may not be present when the final cuts are made, so be sure the foundation of one project is not removed by the inadvertant deletion of another project simply because the interrelationship was not made clear. For every line item in your project budget request, there should be a narrative like the one in Figure 14.4. And for every iteration, as shown in Figure 14.3, be sure the increase or decrease in the scope of what you propose to accomplish is clear.

Project Budget History
($1000s)

12/16/77

Project Code	Title	8/19	10/7	12/16
B	Stella—new development	$1249	$ 993	$1021
C	Stella—continuation	2216	1812	2055
F	Astros	226	69	231
G	Advanced communications	125	165	0
H	Research	771	0	731
L	OEM support	0	0	212
M	New market penetration	297	297	297
Q	Data entry	175	75	140
U	EFTS	238	238	238
Total	Software Products	$5337	$3649	$4925

Figure 14.3 Three iterations of project budgeting.

Once a budget is approved, continue to maintain budget records. Develop a working budget or **living budget** which states how you plan to actually spend the money approved in your baseline budget, any monies added to your budget after the baseline is established, and any exbudget authorizations you receive. Your financial managers probably demand official reporting versus the baseline budget in spite of any understandings or agreements you may have regarding deviations from the baseline. As a result, you will often have to explain deviations from your baseline. A well-maintained working budget holds all of the answers. Figure 14.5 shows such a working budget; entries such as "forecast" and "variance" are described in Section 16.1.

Reporting progress versus a budget is always required. Getting

---

#111B *Internal Distribution*
$26K *Capture, catalog, file, retrieve, and distribute firmware prior to availability in ROMs. Includes development of bootstrap FSL system for distribution on cassette, the building of master packs, and the construction and maintenance of tools for distribution via data communication. Depends on #104B. Required for #149B and all F projects.*

Figure 14.4 A project budget narrative entry.

Project Budget Request Summary for Operating Systems Unit
for Calender Year 1977—4/29/77

Budget Reference	Project Number	Base-line Budget	Working Budget	Allo-cated This Year	Spent This Year	Fore-cast	Variance	Notes
039B	B15	410	410	185	161	443	−33	
046B	B00	60	60	64	64	64	−4	1
---B	B40	0	213	80	92	200	13	2
200F	—	120	120	0	0	120	0	
211F	B20	485	300	110	87	305	− 5	
211F	B21	0	185	70	56	180	5	
055L	B10	175	22	22	22	22	0	2, 3
Total		1250	1310	541	490	1334	−24	

Notes:
(1) Complete.
(2) $153K transferred from 055L to B40 per VGM 2/28/77; 60 more authorized by RCM.
(3) Discontinued.

Figure 14.5   A living project budget.

actuals to compare favorably to a budget when all is proceeding according to plan is seldom easy, although it should be. It can be done; the secret is to fully understand the way your accountants distribute actual costs and to develop budgeting algorithms that follow the same rules. If you know, for instance, that posting of payments to your accounts occurs 90 days after you approve invoices for payment, you can budget accordingly.

In summary, budgeting and budget management are activities well worth every moment invested in them. A well-prepared and maintained series of budget requests yields a greater share of available resources than poorly prepared requests. Determining key variables enhances accuracy and responsiveness of work estimates. And a well-maintained working budget eases the burden of reporting inevitable, albeit authorized, deviations from a baseline budget.

14.2   BUDGET ALLOCATION

Once you have an approved budget or an approved contract for an individual project you can and should exert cost control over the project. You should be able to tell quickly how much is available to spend on a project, how much has been spent, how much is yet to be spent. You should also be able to limit the expenditure of resources to approved activities. A tool for achieving these objectives is a **Budget Allocation (BA)**.

A Budget Allocation system consists of a BA form; a BA status summary; and procedures for initiating, amending, reporting against, and canceling BAs. Each of these aspects of a BA system is discussed below.

Figure 14.6 is a BA form filled in as it would be for a project that is about one-half finished. This project, #B21, is the same project as is shown in Figure 14.5. At ABC Computers this particular form of Budget Allocation is called a **Project Budget Request (PBR)**. The fields on the form and their contests, using ABC's nomenclature, are:

PROJECT NAME	The name by which the project will be called; may be the same as a product name; should be the same as a budget project name where a corresponding budget project exists.
PROJECT LEADER	The name of the cognizant project manager, placed here so that a reader knows where to go for more information.
REVISION LEVEL	For each submission after the first, one more letter is crossed out; in the example, Revision D is about to be submitted by CL for approval by VGM.
PROJECT TASKS	Each major activity is named and numbered.
PROJECTS ON WHICH THIS PROJECT IS DEPENDENT	The names and/or numbers of related projects that constrain the completion of this project.
PROJECTS DEPENDENT ON THIS PROJECT	The names and/or numbers of related projects that are constrained from completion by this project; in the example, PAKON and VSOS 4.0 are mutually dependent.
PROJECT END ITEMS	Tasks are defined to produce at least one tangible end item so that task completion can be quickly identified; the end items are listed here.
SPECULATIVE ASSUMPTIONS	Key assumptions which, if proven wrong, may adversely affect project success.

PROJECT NAME: PAKON							REVISION LEVEL				

PROJECT NAME: PAKON

PROJECT LEADER: R. Semovich

REVISION LEVEL: A B C D E F G H I J

PROJECT TASK 5:(Number each task)

This project will yield a product, PAKON (PAcK cONditioner), to initialize disc packs for use by VSOS.
1. Develop POR   4. Code and A-test   7. Develop Maintenance Spec.
2. Develop ERS   5. B-test
3. Develop IRS   6. Develop publications

PROJECTS ON WHICH THIS PROJECT IS DEPENDENT:

VSOS 4.0

PROJECTS DEPENDENT ON THIS PROJECT:

VSOS 4.0

PROJECT END ITEMS: (e.g. plans, reports, documents, code; precede each by corresponding task #)

1. POR   4. Source & object code; listings   7. Maintenance spec.
2. ERS   5. Test report
3. IRS   6. Sections for VSOS manuals

SPECULATIVE ASSUMPTIONS: (e.g. staffing, equipping, parallel activities, contingencies)

Model 9117 disc drive available from one month after POR approval through B-test

---

ITEMS TO BE CAPITALIZED: (e.g. hardware, software, consulting; specify date of capitalization)

None solely for this project; see B17

OTHER EXPENSE ITEMS: (e.g. travel, computing charges, consulting)

Stella computer time at the approximate rate of $100 per manday for Task 4 and $150 per manday for Task 5.

PROJECT BUDGET SUMMARY: (All figures are mandays)

TO BE COMPLETED UPON CLOSING

COMPLETE
DISCONT.

TO BE COMPLETED UPON APPROVAL

SOFTWARE SERVCES BUDGET REMAINING THIS YEAR	ALLOCATED THIS YEAR	SPENT THIS YEAR	COST REMAINING THIS YEAR	THIS REQUEST	TASK #	DEPT. APPRV.	ALLOCATION	SP APPROVED	DATE
185	0	0	170	10	1D	$C \mathcal{L}$	10	$V\mathcal{X}M$	2/28/77
175	10	8	170	20	2D	$C\mathcal{L}$	20	$V\mathcal{X}M$	4/4/77
–	–	–	–	18	5T	ORG	18	$V\mathcal{X}M$	
–	–	–	–	10	6B	$B\mathcal{L}\mathcal{L}$	10	$V\mathcal{X}M$	
127	58	41	182	12	2D	$C\mathcal{L}$	12	$V\mathcal{X}M$	4/18/77
115	70	56	180	15	3D	$C\mathcal{L}$			

ABC COMPUTERS	SOFTWARE PRODUCTS PROJECT BUDGET REQUEST	NEXT SHEET 1	BUDGET REFERENCE #: 211F PROJECT #: B21

FORM NO. 4409 1/71

Figure 14.6 A typical budget allocation.

218

ITEMS TO BE
CAPITALIZED

Capital costs directly attributable to the project, including all or part of the software product itself; in this example, the cost of a Model 9117 disc drive is borne by project B17.

OTHER EXPENSE
ITEMS

Items, other than direct labor, chargeable directly to the project.

PROJECT BUDGET
SUMMARY

As each request for authorization to proceed with a task is made, a row is completed. The project leader enters his first request in the first row, in the second through sixth columns. In the second and third columns, he enters zero. In the fourth, he enters his current estimate of the total cost of the project for the current year; and in the fifth, his request to support the first task. Normally, he requests an amount he expects to cover all work performed on all tasks until the task named in the sixth column is complete. He secures functional management approval in Column 7 for each task from the line manager responsible for it. Then the project leader submits the PBR for approval, through Services. The plans manager in Services enters into Column 1 the available budget and offers the PBR for approval.

The general manager who receives the PBR for approval decides how much manpower, if any, to allocate to requested tasks. He has in front of him enough information to know how much he can safely allocate. He indicates his approval by entering an allocation, his initials, and a date of approval. He returns the PBR through the plans manager who subtracts ALLOCATION from BUDGET REMAINING THIS YEAR and enters the difference in Column 1 of the next row.

When the project leader wants to make another request, he completes Columns 2 through 6 for the task(s). In the example, his second request is for three tasks—one for Development (D), one for Test (T), and one for Publications (B). From Column 8 he obtains the total allocation to date and enters it in Column 2. From Software

Services he obtains the amount SPENT THIS YEAR and enters it in Column 3. In Column 4 he enters his best estimate of the COST REMAINING THIS YEAR, defined as the difference between his current estimate of the whole year's effort minus the amount ALLOCATED THIS YEAR. He obtains functional management approval for each task in Column 7 and submits the PBR again to the plans manager. From here on, steps are followed as for his original request.

SHEET; NEXT
SHEET is the page number; NEXT is the following page number if there is any.

BUDGET REFERENCE #
This number is used for correlation with a budget or contract. When the project leader knows the number, he enters it. Otherwise, the plans manager does.

PROJECT #
As soon as the first allocation is approved, but not until, the plans manager assigns and enters a number against which charges may be recorded.

TO BE COMPLETED UPON CLOSING
When work on a project is to stop, the project leader takes the PBR directly to the general manager and secures his initials and date next to the appropriate type of closing: COMPLETE or DISCONT. (meaning discontinued). The general manager then returns the PBR to the plans manager for project cancellation.

Note that a BA identifies several key variables but that it controls only one—direct labor. The available budget is defined in units of direct labor either by converting money to man-days via a standard cost or by isolating the direct labor component of the total budget and converting that component to man-days via an average burdened labor rate. Unless some other variable is both dominant and not linearly related to direct labor for the aggregate of projects covered by their collective budget, control of direct labor is all you need for adequate control of collective costs. Actual costs are still charged to each project for financial reporting, and resulting financial reports are used to reverify that aggregate costs are proportional to direct labor, or to signal the need to modify budgeting algorithms to restore proportionality. In the case of a contract project or a very large project that dominates a collective budget, variables like machine costs and travel are allocated and controlled in a manner analogous to direct labor.

The fundamental principle underlying a BA system is incremental funding. **Incremental funding** is the authorization of resource expenditure only up to an amount consistent with reaching a particular milestone. If the limit is exceeded, a BA summary (see Section 16.1) shows a negative balance which signals project management to request additional resources and functional management to ask why. The system functions like a bank account, with general management making deposits and functional management making withdrawals. Each deposit encumbers budget funds, assuring that they will not be allocated elsewhere. This encumbrance is performed by recording each allocation in a BA summary. The steps in the BA process, from the beginning to the end of a project, are:

1. A project manager fills in as much of a BA as is appropriate to requesting an allocation; how much information he provides depends on what is needed by managers who must subsequently approve the BA.

2. The project manager seeks concurrence by signature of functional management for each task to be funded.

3. The administrative function notes the budget balance, the amount already spent, and the amount already encumbered on the BA next to the first requested task.

4. General management allocates resources by signature.

5. The administrative function records the allocations in the BA summary.

6. Steps 1 through 5 are repeated as often as necessary to complete the project.

7. When the project is completed or discontinued the project manager submits the BA to the administrative function for appropriate marking, general management approves closing the project, and the administrative function indicates the nature of the closing by a note in the BA summary.

8. When a budget period ends, all encumbrances and balances are zeroed by the administrative function. Project managers submit new BAs or revised BAs depending on how the budget for the new period is treated relative to the previous period.

Note that the BA mechanism described in this section allows several BAs to be open against each budget item so that a fine degree of project control is available. Also, through noting interdependencies, several budget items may contribute to a single project or product.

14.3 INDIVIDUAL WORK PLAN

An **Individual Work Plan (IWP)** is a written statement in which personal goals and accomplishments are stated in objective, measurable terms. An IWP is a tool used in a Management by Objectives program to establish a contract between a worker at any level and his supervisor. A Management by Objectives (MBO) program is a system of mutual goal setting and performance measurement dependent on the existence of tangible objectives achievable over short time intervals—short being three weeks to three months. MBO is thus ideally suited for the development of software products, with their wealth of milestones, end items, and performance criteria. The rest of this section deals with IWPs; for more information about MBO in general, see (52) and (53).

An interesting article appeared in 1972 that demonstrates the synergistic results you can get by setting clear goals before a programming team (54). In the article, Weinberg references an experiment conducted by Schulman in which five teams solved the same programming problem, each with a different objective. As Figure 14.7

	RANKING				
GROUP OBJECTIVE	**Core**	**Output Clarity**	**Program Clarity**	**Statements**	**Hours**
Minimum Core	1	4	4	2	5
Output Clarity	5	1	1-2	5	2-3
Program Clarity	3	2	1-2	3	4
Minimum Statements	2	5	3	1	2-3
Minimum Hours	4	3	5	4	1

Figure 14.7 Programming team performance versus objectives (Reprinted with permission of Datamation®, copyright 1972 by Technical Publishing Company, Greenwich, Connecticut 06830.)

shows, each team ranked first in its stated objective and ranked high in related objectives. Note that program clarity and output clarity appear to be highly correlated, as do minimum statements and minimum core. To get such results through IWPs is easy if you set a comparable goal for a project manager and for his team members.

The use of IWPs, hereafter called **Work Planning**, begins with the translation of mission, strategic, and tactical plans into concrete, tangible objectives for top management. The president or other officer at the apex of an organizational pyramid proposes to his vice-presidents or other subordinates his personal goals for the immediate future— immediate meaning no more than a year. He defines each goal concretely: "Achieve profitability by 4/1/79," "Book $25 million in new business in the second half of the fiscal year," "Implement an affirmative action personnel program before year's end." He reviews his proposal with his subordinates, reworks it as necessary to gain their concurrence, and declares it to be his "contract" for the time period defined in it. The subordinates propose IWPs that translate the president's objectives into objectives for themselves, frequently proposing several of their own for one of the president's. They negotiate their proposals with the president until they and the president concur that all of the president's objectives are covered. The process continues with each manager decomposing his objectives into IWPs for his subordinates. At each level in the hierarchy, other inputs are introduced from other plans: product plans, market plans, policies. When the decomposition reaches project managers, requirements contracts add another source of concrete objectives. For individual project members network plans, external specifications, and publications plans provides still more objective items. The process results in a nested set of plans that becomes more and more specific as the organizational hierarchy is traversed.

In spite of the wealth of available objectives some people argue that they cannot think of suitably concrete objectives for personal situations. In an effort to remove that objection, here are some specific examples of objectives for various levels of responsibility:

Division Manager

- Keep costs for each program from +5% to −10% of budget for the year.
- Revise long-range plan by 4/1.
- Reduce data processing costs for the year by 15% compared to last year.

- Enter at least two of the following markets by midyear: wholesale distribution, hospitals, hotels, education.

Test Manager

- Provide written procedures and formats, by 5/1, for: test plan, test specification, test report.
- Reduce average B-Test duration from 7 to 6 weeks by year's end.
- Automate the Hotel Reservation regression tests by 6/15.
- Initiate use of a performance monitor during B-Test of VSOS 4.0 to demonstrate proficiency with such tools.

Publications Manager

- Have every publication sent to the printer by Field Release Date for the associated software.
- Place one writer in a programming unit and transfer one programmer into a writing assignment by year's end.

Development Programmer

- Complete the external specification for the BASIC syntax analyzer by 2/19; complete A-Test by 11/4.
- Conduct structured walk-through of translator within one week of submitting internal specification.

Maintenance Programmer

- Reduce average error turn-around time 10%.

Plans Manager

- Develop a software data base system to identify classification and responsibility for all software developed by ABC Computers; demonstrate system by 9/1; have all available historical data entered by 12/1.

Support Analyst

- Conduct two SE training classes for CPM II by 3/11.

Project Manager

- Achieve product availability date for COBOL 2 by 8/12.
- Have no cause to report to management any misunderstood commitments.
- Revise and review a network plan for COBOL 2 with manager once a month.
- Keep project costs within 10% of budget.
- Assist Support in one prerelease of COBOL 2 without impacting development schedule.

Most Work Planning systems include self-development plans along with product-oriented plans. Skills to acquire, attitudes to change, and preparation for advancement are covered in a separate Work Plans section. Thus, job-oriented and career-oriented goals are both agreed upon by supervisor and subordinate.

Most MBO programs separate IWPs from salary reviews. Salary reviews should take Work Planning results into account, but should not be conducted simultaneously with IWP review. This adds objectivity to the discussions that take place when the plan is generated and again when it is reviewed and keeps the IWP in its place as a planning tool.

A good Work Planning system can integrate all of your other plans—mission plans, strategic plans, tactical plans; market plans, product plans, budgets; requirements contracts, network plans, schedule notices; test plans, publications plans, support plans. Because of this, an IWP is one of the most valuable tools presented in this methodology.

14.4 MANPOWER SUMMARY

A **Manpower Summary** is a tool for planning and controlling expenditures of direct labor at the individual project level. Where project cost is closely proportional to direct labor, a Manpower Summary is a tool for planning and controlling project cost as well as direct labor. Manpower Summaries are sometimes prepared for nonproject labor categories also: vacation, training. Total manpower planning for an organizational unit is then done by summing up all projects and all nonproject categories.

A Manpower Summary shows at a glance whether or not required labor resources are in place by identifying the need for specific people at specific times. It thus quantifies future requirements and documents the impact of delays in fulfilling them.

A project manager is responsible for preparing a Manpower Summary and reviewing it with functional and general management when and as appropriate. He is aided by administrative services in recording actual data and drafting a new summary as described below. Once he has completed a new summary, a project manager compares it with his budget allocation to determine if an additional allocation is needed to meet the latest milestone for which manpower has been allocated. To this end, he may have separate summaries for different functions such as Support and Test. Alternatively, he may conclude that only Development need be tracked in this way.

The Manpower Summary used by Software Products at ABC Computers is shown in Figure 14.8. This figure shows the same project as is shown in Figure 14.6, at essentially the same point in time. Software Products processes Manpower Summaries as follows:

1. An initial Manpower Summary is prepared just prior to BA initiation to assure that a realistic manpower loading plan exists for a project.
2. After the BA is approved, the initial Manpower Summary is included in the first monthly project progress report.
3. At the end of each month the administrative coordinator in Software Services prepares a draft of a new Manpower Summary for each active project. In these drafts he enters the numbers of man-days of direct labor actually charged to each project by every person, some historical labor statistics, and some housekeeping data; these data are circled for emphasis in Figure 14.8. Then he delivers each draft to its respective project leader.
4. When a project leader receives a new draft, he reforecasts his direct labor requirements for the duration of his project, taking into account the actual data already in his draft and any events that make him want to change his previous forecast. If he spots any erroneous charges to his project, as when a strange name appears in his draft, he excludes the erroneous data from his forecast and simultaneously initiates action to rectify the error.
5. Each project leader correlates his revised Manpower Summary with

PERSON	ACTUAL PAST	(4/77)	(5/77)	(6/77) FORECASTED	(7/77)	FUTURE	NEW TOTAL	OLD TOTAL
RIS	(14)	(17)	20	15	10		76	(76)
DRG	(10)	(15)	20	10	4		59	(59)
X	(0)	(0)	10	10			20	(32)
AMY	(0)	(0)	20	5			25	(15)
TOTAL	////	32	70	40	14		/////	/////
CUM.	(24)	(56)	126	166	180		180	(182)

ABC COMPUTERS COMPANY MANPOWER SUMMARY

PROJECT NAME: *Pakon*   PREPARED BY: *R. S. Semowih*

PROJECT NUMBER: *B21*   DATE PREPARED: *5/5/77*

FORM NO. 4417 REV. 1/76

Figure 14.8   A typical manpower summary.

his current BA, schedule notice, network plan, and other tools, updating any of them that require attention because of his new forecast.

6. When a project leader is satisfied with his new forecast, he includes it in his monthly project progress report.

7. Steps 3 through 6 are repeated for each project until it is complete.

8. In addition to assisting in the preparation of new Manpower Summaries for projects, the administrative coordinator maintains a Manpower Summary for vacations. He treats this summary as a project involving every member of Software Products with himself as project leader. Whenever he spots a discrepancy between his "vacation project" and any other project, he notifies the cognizant project leader and line manager.

9. For nonterminating projects such as program maintenance, a six-month's projection is made.

The columns and rows of the Manpower Summary shown in Figure 14.8 are used as follows:

PERSON	In this column are the names or initials of persons who have charged time to the project or who are expected to prior to its completion. In this example, RIS is the project leader and X is a needed but as yet unidentified person.
ACTUAL	In these columns are the number of man-days of direct labor actually charged to the project during the prior month and for all months prior to it in the current fiscal year.
FORECASTED	In these columns are the number of man-days of direct labor forecasted to be charged to the project prior to its completion. Each column contains one month except for the last, which contains all months remaining in the current fiscal year.
NEW TOTAL	This column contains horizontal sums of all actual and forecasted labor.
OLD TOTAL	This column contains data from the NEW TOTAL column of the previous month's summary. The juxtaposition of the new and old totals highlights changes in manpower loading plans.
TOTAL	This row contains a total of all data in each column.
CUM.(ULATIVE)	This row contains a cumulative total of all columns.

At the bottom of the form are data about the project needed to file the summary and trace its origin.

Note that in the example in Figure 14.8, there is a change of plans relating to X and AMY. This is because X, a new, unidentified project member was to begin in March and did not. Plans were laid in April to compensate for a late start by adding AMY, an experienced, known person. When X did not appear in April, plans were again changed to use more of AMY's time. The reduction in the grand total from 182 to 180 reflects the greater productivity of AMY when compared to X. While all of this information is not contained in the summary, much of it could be deduced by looking at summaries for the two previous months along with this summary.

When using Manpower Summaries it is wise not to allocate more of a person's time than is likely to be available on the average. For example, consider a person who works five days per week for a year except for two weeks vacation, 10 holidays, five days of sickness and excused absence, and a week of training. For him there are 52, five-day weeks in a year, or 260 possible work days. But he is expected to work only 260–10–10–5–5 = 230 days, or 88% of that time. Unless you carefully take into account each of his expected nonworking days, you had best not allocate more than 4.4 days per week, or 18 days in a four-week month, 22 days in a five-week month.

Remember, too, that for a forecast to be accurate, it must be made in units of time comparable to what will be reported as actual time spent. Both casual and scheduled overtime must be treated the same on Manpower Summaries and time-cards.

Lastly, be sure that a person who works on several projects is not forecasted for a total commitment greater than would be made if he worked on a single project. It is wise to reduce the total by, say, 5% for work on each additional project. This compensates some for the compounding of individual forecasting errors.

14.5 CONFIGURATOR

One of the most annoying things about software for people who are not familiar with it is that it is so intangible. It is hard to see it or touch it in a way that conveys much information about it. Yet there is a need to describe a software product in the context of its environment so that people can appreciate its significance and their need for it. A configurator is such a description, one which graphically portrays many software products and their interrelationships, such as: what their most significant component parts are, what hardware is needed to run them, and what their availability and support are.

The earliest configurators were developed to communicate software availability and requirements between Development and Support. Their use was so well established at Control Data Corporation by the middle of the 1960s that they were made a part of the corporate pricing manual. Salesmen were able to make commitments based on those configurators with an understanding of software they and many of their customers never had before. Many product planning and configuration management problems showed clearly when a product was first entered into a configurator. Thus they began to be used to communicate within Development and between Development and Planning. One such early configurator is shown in Figure 14.9.

Just what is a configurator that it can do so much? There are many things you can include and many ways to assemble them into a configurator. A form that covers a variety of needs, henceforth called a **Configurator**, consists of four parts: the Introduction, the Software Matrix, the Hardware Matrix, and the Narrative Matrix. The **Introduction** is a summary of "what's new" since the last Configurator was issued. The **Software Matrix** is a two-dimensional matrix that states what software products can and cannot work together, when they are available, what their support levels are, and where in the Narrative Matrix a description of each can be found. The **Hardware Matrix** is a three-dimensional matrix that defines the hardware and the software needed to run each product contained in the Software Matrix, and what the performance and capability implications of varying configurations are. The **Narrative Matrix** is a one-dimensional list of all products in the Software Matrix; it contains a brief description of each product and a list of its nonsoftware components, such as publications and training courses.

Figure 14.10 is a representative Introduction in the form of a covering memorandum, or **Cover Memo**. Such a memorandum is used to bridge old and new Configurators and to point to changes planned for future Configurators. The Cover Memo establishes the beginning and end of the Configurator's period of validity, in this example from 3/1–8/1/78. It enumerates changes that have occurred, both those predicted by the previous Cover Memo and those which could not be predicted, and changes likely to occur in the future. The Cover Memo states especially carefully all planned and actual changes in support levels, for a Configurator is the primary tool for communicating support levels to the people who must provide first-line user support.

Figure 14.11 is a representative Software Matrix. The data in Figure 14.11 show what will be available from ABC Computers for their STELLA line of computers after release of their VSOS 4 Product Set. The data are shown to be valid until 8/1/78 by which time VSOS 4 should be released and a new Configurator should be issued showing the VSOS Product Set as available. The concepts of product set—an operating system *and* all of the products that work with it; and **product set member**—an operating system *or* any of the products that work with it—are graphically represented by a column in the Software Matrix. In each row the matrix shows the operating environments for a product, points to a page of the Narrative Matrix where a descrip-

CONTROL DATA
PRICING MANUAL
11/30/67

3100 PRODUCT LINE
PAGE 5
3100 SYSTEM TYPE

31/3200 COMPUTER | **SOFTWARE PRODUCT SET HARDWARE CONFIGURATOR FOR REAL TIME SCOPE/E081 VERSION 1.2** | VALID UNTIL 2/29/68

THIS DEFINES THE REQUIRED AND OPTIONAL HARDWARE FOR THE PRODUCT SET OPERATING UNDER THE OPERATING SYSTEM INDICATED IN THE HEADING OF THIS PAGE.

ADDITIONAL HARDWARE OVER AND ABOVE THE OPERATING SYSTEM REQUIREMENTS

SOFTWARE PRODUCT NAME/NO.	VER	VAR	REQUIRED HARDWARE ** (CORE/CHANNELS) PERIPHERAL	OPTIONAL HARDWARE (CORE/CHANNELS) PERIPHERAL C	PERFORMANCE IMPROVEMENT (SPEED / PROBLEM, OPERATING CAPACITY / OPERATING CAPABILITIES)	SPECIFIC NOTES
COMPASS-33 A008	1			A	A / B	
FORTRAN-32 C004	2		1 add'l tape drive (a) / A	B	A / B	Uses Floating Point Option or Software Simulation Package.
COBOL C042	2		1 add'l tape drive (a) / A	C. BCD Option	C / B, A / C	Uses BCD Option or Software Simulation Package.
REPORT GENERATOR C063	1		2 add'l tape drives (a) / A			Footnote (a) applies to 1 of the 2 required additional tape drives.
ADAPT C103	1		see note 2 add'l tape drives / B			Either additional core or a floating point option is required.
TAPE SORT-MERGE SU05	2		2 add'l tape drives / A	C. up to 16 tape drives	A / B, C	
PERT COST TU16	2		2 add'l tape drives / B	C. add'l tape drives	A / C, B	Variant B uses 16K core.
PERT TIME TU17	2	B	2 add'l tape drives / A	C. add'l tape drives	A / C	Variant C uses 32K core.
PERT TIME TU17	2	C	see note 2 add'l tape drives / A	C. 1 add'l tape drive		
SCOPE UTILITY UU03	1			C. add'l tape drive	C	
SIPP UU05	2	A	tape drives as required to perform desired functions / B	C. add'l tape drives, printers, card punches and readers	A / B, C	Operates as a Normal Stacked Job
BSIPP UU05	2	B	see note / A see note	B. C. Add'l tape drives, printers, card punches and readers	A / B, C	To run medium to large problems or to compile during the use of this Interrupt Controlled product an additional 16K is required.
COSY UU07	1		C. add'l tape drives / A, B	C. add'l tape drives	A / C, B	

GENERAL NOTES (a) This satisfies the optional Load & Go requirements specified under Operating System Hardware Requirements (Load and Go System Unit)

LEGEND
A, B, C.—THESE LETTERS IN THE PERFORMANCE IMPROVEMENT COLUMNS INDICATE THAT THE OPTIONAL HARDWARE REFERENCED BY THOSE LETTERS WILL GIVE THE INDICATED KIND OF IMPROVEMENT. THERE IS NO SEQUENTIAL PREFERENCE ATTACHED TO THE LETTERS A, B, C.
*—INDICATED CORE FIGURE IS IN ADDITION TO THE "MINIMUM REQUIRED MACHINE CORE SIZE" SHOWN IN OPERATING SYSTEM CONFIGURATOR.
**—NO ENTRY UNDER REQUIRED HARDWARE INDICATES THAT THE PRODUCT WILL OPERATE WITH OPERATING SYSTEM REQUIREMENTS.

Figure 14.9 A configurator hardware matrix showing the effects of varying hardware. (Courtesy of Control Data Corporation.)

to: STELLA* Software Configurator Recipients

from: C. I. Orwell   3/1/78

subject: Revised STELLA Configurator

The attached Configurator is ABC Computers' way of letting you
know what software is available, off-the-shelf, for customers
of the STELLA computer, and what hardware is needed for its use.

Significant changes from the last Configurator are:

1. VSOS Version 4 Product Set will be released 7/78 which
    includes support for the new Model 2110 Holographic
    Storage Module by both ASSEMBLER and MANAGE, and which
    includes ANS COBOL;

2. The Support Level for VSOS 3 Product Set Members has
    been dropped from 1 to 2 where no enhancements are .
    planned;

3. The Support Level for products unique to the VSOS 2
    Product Set has been dropped from 2 to 3;

4. The VSOS 1 Product Set has been dropped from distribu-
    tion and support for it has been withdrawn;

5. When VSOS 4 is available, support for products unique
    to the VSOS 2 and VSOS 3 Product Sets will be dropped
    to Level 3.

This Configurator is valid until 8/1/78.

C I Orwell

C. I. Orwell, Director
Technical Support
Medium Scale Systems

CIO: rcg
Attach.:   STELLA Configurator

Additional copies of this Configurator may be obtained from:

Technical Support
Medium Scale Systems
ABC Computers Company
1200 Simmons Parkway
Stanton, Pennsylvania 10475
U.S.A.
            * A Trademark of ABC Computers Company

Figure 14.10   A configurator introduction.

STELLA SOFTWARE CONFIGURATOR

VALID UNTIL: 8/1/78		PRODUCT SET					
PRODUCT NAME	PAGE	VSOS STATUS	2 S/L	VSOS STATUS	3 S/L	VSOS STATUS	4 S/L
VSOS 2	4	S277	3	////		////	
VSOS 3	4	////		S277	2	////	
VSOS 4	5	////		////		7/78	1
BASIC ASSEMBLER 2	5	A117	3	A117	3	////	
ASSEMBLER 1	5	////		A233	1	7/78	1
ASSEMBLER B	6	////		////		10/78	1
COBOL 1	6	C111	3	C111	2	////	
COBOL 2	6	////		10/78	1	7/78	2
ANS COBOL 1	7	////		U155	1	10/78	1
EDIT 1	7	////		7/78	1	7/78	1
PERT 1	8	////		7/78	1	7/78	1
ACCESS 2	8	T494	1	D655	1	7/78	1
MANAGE 2	8	////		7/78	2	////	
MANAGE 3	9	////		////		7/78	1
FORTRAN 2	10	////		C050	1	7/78	1

STATUS CODES

PRODUCT # — PRODUCT AVAILABLE

//// — PRODUCT WILL NOT BECOME AVAILABLE

DATE — DATE PRODUCT WILL BECOME AVAILABLE

SUPPORT LEVEL (S/L) CODES

1 — SUPPORT VIA PTR; UPDATES ISSUED; RPE'S WILL BE CONSIDERED

2 — SUPPORT VIA PTR; UPDATES ISSUED; RPE'S WILL NOT BE CONSIDERED

3 — SUPPORT LIMITED TO PTR PROCESSING

Figure 14.11   A configurator software matrix.

233

tion of the product can be found, indicates availability, and commits a support level.

A configurator can show precisely what variants, versions, and updates of a product exist or soon will exist. How much of this information you include depends on the purposes to which you put your configurators. For instance, when the Configurator shown in Figure 14.11 was issued, Version 1 of ASSEMBLER was available in the VSOS 3 Product Set and was planned for inclusion in the VSOS 4 Product Set. Variant B of ASSEMBLER, with support for addressing a trillion bytes of memory, was planned, but for inclusion only in the VSOS 4 Product Set. The complete product number for ASSEMBLER in the VSOS 3 Product Set was A2331G; in the VSOS 4 Product Set, A2331H; and for Variant B, A233BA. At ABC Computers updates have no bearing on product capabilities (updates only correct errors), so update levels are never shown in their Configurators.

Support levels are assigned to software products so that users and potential users may know what to expect in the way of error correction and product enhancement. At ABC Computers a product is assigned to one of three levels, generally according to the following rules:

Support Level 1 A new version or replacement product is planned, so Requests for Product Enhancement (RPEs) will be considered; enough reported errors, by way of Product Trouble Reports (PTRs) are expected to issue updates.

Support Level 2 No new version or replacement product is planned so RPEs will not be considered; enough PTRs are still expected to continue issuing updates.

Support Level 3 Not only is no new version nor any replacement product planned, but so few errors are expected to be reported that no updates will be issued; PTR corrections will continue to be published in summaries as long as the product remains in distribution (and thus in the Configurator).

Note that a separate column or row in the Software Matrix is used for each version of each product. This emphasizes whether or not different versions of a product operate with different versions of their host operating systems. This helps Support to avoid making the commitment to install unworkable combinations of software.

Every column of a Software Matrix yields a two-dimensional Hardware Matrix like the one in Figure 14.12; this is why a complete Hardware Matrix is said to be three-dimensional. Part of the Hardware Matrix corresponding to the VSOS 4 column of Figure 14.11 is shown in Figure 14.12. From this figure you can determine how much of each kind of hardware VSOS 4 and each of its product set members needs to run. Such a tool is invaluable in configuring a system of hardware and software to meet a user's needs.

How much detail you cram into a Hardware Matrix depends on the sophistication of your readers. Unfortunately, the less sophisticated the reader, the more information he needs, and the more complex the matrix must be. You can remove some clutter and confusion from a Hardware Matrix by putting into it references to more detail found in the Narrative Matrix. For instance, Note K in Figure 14.12 points to the narrative for ANS COBOL where the use of an RJE terminal's console as an interactive CRT is explained. You must assume some sophistication, however: Figure 14.12 assumes the reader knows that any disc or combination of discs may be used; that interactive CRTs of various models are intermixable; and that although entries in the matrix are additive, there are absolute limitations on maximum configurations imposed by hardware and practical limitations imposed by intolerable response times. Keep in mind that all four parts of a Configurator should be as self-explanatory as possible. Maintain a proper balance between the simplicity of your configurators and the sophistication of their readers.

Figure 14.9 shows another form of Hardware Matrix. This form was used by Control Data to communicate not only the range of hardware on which a product could run, but also the effect of varying hardware on execution speed or product capability.

The Narrative Matrix is the fourth and last part of a Configurator. For every product in a Configurator, there is an entry in the Narrative Matrix. What you put in the individual narrative descriptions depends partly on how much you have not been able to communicate through the preceding sections. At the very least include a brief description of a product and a list of nonsoftware product end items such as publications and training courses. Figure 14.13 shows a Narrative Matrix entry from a point-of-sale software configurator.

You may have noticed by now that a configurator has many of the attributes of a software catalog. When a software order form is added to a configurator, it may be used as a catalog. The practice at Control Data of including configurators in their pricing manual for both hardware and software led to another use for configurators—order

STELLA HARDWARE CONFIGURATOR

PROCESSOR (A)	RESIDENT MEMORY (B)	ADDRESSABLE MEMORY (C)	COMMUNICATIONS (D)	INPUT/OUTPUT (A)	TERMINALS	CARDS
CPU POOL LOCK	PARTITION COMMON DISC MONITOR	PARTITION COMMON DISC MONITOR	ASCU SDLC ...	CONSOLE MAG TAPE	CRT RJE & TTY	READ PUNCH

NOTES:

A. UNITS ATTACHABLE

B. BYTES RESIDENT

C. BYTES ADDRESSABLE

D. LINES ATTACHABLE

E. COMMON MAILBOX

F. OPTIONAL: MESSAGES MAY BE SPOOLED TO DISC AND INPUT MAY COME FROM JOB STREAM ON DISC

G. EACH LINE REQUIRES 100 BYTES OF COMMON

H. EACH TERMINAL REQUIRES 500–1000 BYTES OF COMMON WHILE ON-LINE

I. EACH TERMINAL REQUIRES 70 BYTES OF COMMON WHILE ON-LINE

J. EACH TERMINAL REQUIRES 200 BYTES OF COMMON WHILE ON-LINE

K. SEE NARRATIVE

LEGEND:
K = 1,000
D = 10K
E = 100K
M = 1,000,000
H = 100M
L = 1MM

VSOS VERSION 4	MINIMUM	0	0	0	0	0	1D	2E	0	6H	1E	6H	0	0	0	0	1	0	0	0	0	0
	MAXIMUM	1	1	1	1	0	2D	6E	0	6H	1E	6H	3L	256	32	32	1	32	32	256	256	4
	NOTES												G	G	G		H	I	J			
ASSEMBLER VERSION 1	MINIMUM					2D	1K	2E		6H	1E	6H					0					
	MAXIMUM					2E	1K	2E		6H	1E	6H					1					
	NOTES							E									F					
ASSEMBLER VARIANT B	MINIMUM					22K	1K	2E		6H	1E	6H					0					
	MAXIMUM					2E	1K	2E		6H	1E	6H	3L				1					
	NOTES							E									F					
COBOL VERSION 2	MINIMUM					25K	1K	3E		0	0	0	0				0					
	MAXIMUM					2E	1K	3E		2H	1E	2H					1					
	NOTES							E									F					
ANS COBOL VERSION 2	MINIMUM	1				2D	1K	3E		0	0	0	0				0					
	MAXIMUM					2E	1K	3E		2H	1E	2H	3L				1			256		1
	NOTES							E									F	K				

CONTINUED . . . .

Figure 14.12 A partial configurator hardware matrix.

237

TOTDRV I (TOTALS DRIVER)

    THE PROGRAM TOTDRV IS DESIGNED TO READ THE RAW TRANS—
ACTION DATA FILE CREATED BY NORMAL SIPOS DATA COLLECTION.
IN GENERAL, EACH TRANSACTION IS READ SERIALLY FROM THE RAW
TRANSACTION FILE AND VALIDATED FOR COMPLETENESS AND
LOGICAL CONSISTENCY. EACH TRANSACTION IS SCANNED FOR
PREDEFINED CONTROL CHARACTERS OR A COMBINATION OF
CHARACTERS THAT DENOTE WHAT TYPE OF TOTALS ACCUMULATION
IS TO BE PERFORMED. THE TOTDRV PROGRAM ACCUMULATES THE
TRANSACTIONS TO A MAXIMUM OF THREE OPTIONAL TOTALS FILES
AND, EITHER BUILDS A FILE OF TRANSACTIONS IN INDIVIDUAL
POINT—OF—SALE TERMINAL SEQUENCE OR BUILDS A POINTER FILE
TO PROVIDE ACCESS TO THE RAW DATA FILE FOR PROGRAMS
OPERATING AT END—OF—DAY. ALL FIVE FILES ARE LINKED
SEQUENTIAL FILES AND MAY BE ACCESSED BY DMF METHODS.

    TOTDRV I MAY EXECUTE CONCURRENTLY WITH POS DATA COLLECTION.

    TOTDRV I EXECUTES ONLY IN A DMF I ENVIRONMENT AND WILL NOT
SUPPORT DATA RECORDED BY THE 910/930 INTERACTIVE TERMINALS.
AS A RESULT, TOTDRV I MAY BE USED ONLY WITH SIPOS 4.2, 4.3,
AND SIPOS 4.4 (WHEN GENERATED IN A DMF I ENVIRONMENT).

    SOFTWARE MANUAL APPLICABLE TO THIS PRODUCT IS:

        TITLE   PUBLICATION NO.

TOTDRV I (TOTALS DRIVER)
REFERENCE MANUAL
EDITION B   64—F758—401—01

Figure 14.13   A configurator narrative matrix entry.

review. A salesman could commit any date, product combination, or hardware configuration contained in a configurator and know that his proposal would pass the corporate order review process.

In Chapter 6, Figure 14.11 is repeated to illustrate a Software Matrix used in a planning configurator. Hardware and Narrative Matrices can also be used for planning. Software Matrices are particularly useful for release planning and Hardware Matrices for configuration management. More than one software product variant was conceived by attempting to construct a Hardware Matrix and finding that a product as originally proposed would not work with all necessary hardware combinations. Figures 14.11 and 14.12 contain such an example: ASSEMBLER Variant B; the need for addressing a trillion bytes of holographic storage forced the creation of an assembler variant capable of manipulating such large numbers.

The uses to which you can put configurators grow as you use them. The uses mentioned above may have already suggested others to you. Try them; they will probably satisfy the needs for which they are designed and suggest still further variations.

14.6 NETWORK PLAN

This book makes prolific use of network diagrams to portray and sum-marize the multitude of activities which comprise the life cycle of a software product. There is probably no better single tool for com-municating such a complex intermingling of activities than a network presentation. This section is dedicated to assuring that you understand this tool well enough to apply it, with appropriate rigor, to every software product development project.

Network plans have their own jargon like most widely accepted technical phenomena. The definitions presented here for terms used throughout this book are consistent with most definitions found elsewhere. Right at the top of the list is the term "network." A **net-work** is an ordered list of activities, an ordered list of events, and a list of constraints. When deviations from it are expected to occur, it is often called a **baseline network**. An **activity** is a task with a well-defined beginning and a well-defined ending that can be performed by a single functional entity (e.g., the Development Function). An **event** is the well-defined beginning or ending of an activity. Another name for an event is a **milestone**. Precedence relationships are specified by pseudoactivities called constraints. A **constraint** simply says that one activity must be completed before another may begin. Figures 14.14, 14.15, and 14.16 comprise a stereotype network for a software product development project. A **network diagram** is a pic-torial representation of a network in which activities and constraints are shown as lines and events are shown as points where the lines begin and end. These points are often referred to as **nodes**, and, because network diagrams are so universally used to portray net-works, events are sometimes referred to as nodes. Figure 14.17 is a network diagram for the network in Figures 14.14 through 14.16. In Figure 14.17 activities are shown as solid lines between nodes and constraints are shown as broken lines between nodes. A network dia-gram is usually drawn large enough to allow placing milestone descriptions in "bubbles" at the nodes and descriptions of activities and constraints on the lines connecting the nodes. While event names are included in Figure 14.17, activity and constraint descriptions are omitted only for clarity; they would be quite obscure if included at the scale necessary to fit on a page of this book. Furthermore, one line of Figure 14.17 may represent more than one activity; for example, D10–P20 represents seven activities (for each of seven different func-tional organizations; see Figure 14.14).

A network diagram takes on added meaning when its horizontal

After	Before	Who	What
D10	P20	P	Review Requirements Contract
T01	T10	P	Review Test Plan
B01	B10	P	Review Publications Plan
I01	I10	P	Review Support Plan
I11	I12	P	Review Promotional Material
T32	P30	P	Review B-Test Report
P10	D10	D	Prepare Requirements Contract
D10	D11	D	Perform and Record Enough Internal Design
		D	to Initiate Coding
D10	P20	D	Respond to Requirements Contract Review
D10	D20	D	Prepare External Specification
T01	T10	D	Review Test Plan
D20	D30	D	Respond to External Specification Review
B01	B10	D	Review Publications Plan
I01	I10	D	Review Support Plan
T11	T13	D	Review Test Specification
D11	D31	D	Prepare Internal Specification
M10	D40	D	Incorporate Last Mandatory Corrections
D21	D40	D	Code, Debug, Integrate
D21	D41	D	Prepare and Perform Demonstration
T20	D42	D	Run Acceptance Tests
B02	B11	D	Review Preliminary Reference Material Drafts
D40	T30	D	Prepare Release Specification
I11	I12	D	Review Promotional Material
T30	T31	D	Respond to Trouble Reports
B11	B12	D	Review First-Draft Reference Material
B12	B20	D	Render Final Approval for Reference Material
T32	P30	D	Review B-Test Report
D31	M20	D	Review Maintenance Specification
D10	P20	S	Review Requirements Contract
T01	T10	S	Review Test Plan
D10	S10	S	Procure Development Hardware
T01	S10	S	Procure Test Hardware
T11	T13	S	Review Test Specification
T30	S11	S	Prepare Release Bulletin
S11	S12	S	Print Release Bulletin
S11	S20	S	Perform C-Test
P30	S20	S	Replicate, Package, Distribute
D10	P20	B	Review Requirements Contract
D10	B01	B	Prepare Publications Plan
D20	D30	B	Review External Specification
B01	B10	B	Respond to Publications Plan Review
I01	I10	B	Review Support Plan

Figure 14.14 Stereotype software product development activities.

After	Before	Who	What
B02	B11	B	Prepare First-Draft Reference Material
B11	B12	B	Respond to First-Draft Reference Material Review,
		B	Complete Reference Material
T30	B12	B	Respond to Reference Material Evaluation
B12	B20	B	Respond to Final Approval Comments
T30	S11	B	Perform Production Activities for Release Bulletin
T32	P30	B	Review B-Test Report
B20	B21	B	Print Reference Material
D10	P20	T	Review Requirements Contract
D10	T01	T	Prepare Test Plan
T01	T10	T	Respond to Test Plan Review
D20	D30	T	Review External Specification
D20	T11	T	Prepare Test Specification
T11	T13	T	Respond to Test Specification Review
T12	T20	T	Develop Acceptance Test Cases
D40	T20	T	Debug Acceptance Test Cases
T12	T30	T	Develop Test Cases
T30	T31	T	Perform B-Test
T30	B12	T	Evaluate First-Draft Reference Material
T31	T32	T	Perform B-Test; Prepare B-Test Report
T32	T30	T	Present B-Test Report
P10	D10	I	Input to Requirements Contract
D10	P20	I	Review Requirements Contract
D10	I01	I	Prepare Support Plan
D20	D30	I	Review External Specification
B01	B10	I	Review Publications Plan
I01	I10	I	Respond to Support Plan Review
D20	I11	I	Prepare Promotional Material
I11	I12	I	Respond to Promotional Material Review
I10	I13	I	Prepare Training Schedule
I12	I20	I	Print Promotional Material
D30	I21	I	Prepare Training Course
B11	B12	I	Review First-Draft Reference Material
I21	I30	I	Deliver Training Course
T32	P30	I	Review B-Test Report
I20	S20	I	Distribute Promotional Material
D10	P20	M	Review Requirements Contract
D20	D30	M	Review External Specification
D31	M20	M	Prepare Maintenance Specification
S11	M20	M	Fold Release Bulletin Data into Maintenance
		M	Specification
M10	D40	M	Incorporate Last Mandatory Corrections

Figure 14.14 (Continued)

Milestone	Definition
P10	Budget Allocation Approved
D10	Requirements Contract Submitted
D11	Internal Specification Begun
P20	Requirements Contract Approved
T01	Test Plan Submitted
B01	Publications Plan Submitted
D20	External Specification Submitted
B02	Reference Material Begun
I01	Support Plan Submitted
D21	Coding Begun
T10	Test Plan Approved
D30	External Specification Approved
T11	Test Specification Submitted
B10	Publications Plan Approved
S10	Project Hardware Installed
T12	Test Case Development Begun
I10	Support Plan Approved
T13	Test Specification Approved
D31	Internal Specification Complete
I11	Promotional Material Submitted
M10	Correction Cutoff
D40	A-Test Begun
D41	Demonstration Performed
T20	Acceptance Tests Delivered
D42	Acceptance Tests Run
B11	Technical Review Begun
T30	B-Test Begun
I12	Promotional Material to Printer
I13	Training Schedule Published
I20	Promotional Material Distributed
B12	Final Approval Begun
I21	Training Course Prepared
B20	Reference Material to Printer
T31	Last Test Cycle Begun
T32	B-Test Report Issued
I30	Training Course Complete
S11	Release Bulletin Ready for Printer
P30	Product Available for Distribution
B21	Reference Material Printed
M20	Maintenance Specification Complete
S12	Release Bulletin Printed
S20	Product Distributed

Figure 14.15 Stereotype software product development milestones.

From	To	Because
P20	T01	The test plan must conform to the requirements contract
P20	B01	The publications plan must conform to the requirements contract
D20	B02	Reference material is based on the external specification
P20	I01	The support plan must conform to the requirements contract
D11	D21	Code is based on the internal specification
P20	D30	The external specification must conform to the requirements contract
T10	T11	The test specification must conform to the test plan
T11	T12	Test cases are based on the test specification
D30	T13	The test specification must conform to the external specification
B10	I10	The support plan depends on publications schedules
D30	I11	Promotional material must conform to the external specification
D30	D31	The internal specification must conform to the external specification
P20	M10	The correction cutoff must be ensurable by management concurrence
I10	I11	Promotional material must conform to the support plan
S10	D40	Project hardware must be available to integrate the product
D30	D41	The demonstration must conform to the external specification
S10	D41	Project hardware must be available to debug and run a demonstration
S10	T20	Project hardware must be available to debug acceptance tests
T13	T20	Acceptance tests are defined in the test specification
D40	D42	Acceptance tests must be run on a fully integrated product
B10	B11	Reference material must conform to the publications plan
D30	B11	Reference material must conform to the approved external specifications
B11	T30	First-draft reference material must be available for comparison with the software
D42	T30	Development must run acceptance tests to assure Test that the product is ready for B-Test
T30	I12	Once B-Test has begun, the probability of ultimately releasing a product is high enough to warrant publishing promotional material
T30	I13	Once B-Test has begun, the probability of ultimately releasing a product is high enough to warrant publishing a training schedule
I10	I21	Training courses must conform to the support plan
I13	I21	Training courses must conform to the training schedule
T32	S11	The release bulletin must report deficiencies identified in the B-Test report
D41	P30	For a demonstration to be most meaningful, it should occur before release is recommended
B20	P30	Reference material must be complete so that rush orders may be processed as soon as release is recommended
S11	P30	The release bulletin must be complete so that rush orders may be processed as soon as release is recommended
D30	M20	The maintenance specification must conform to the external specification
I30	S20	Training should be provided to Support before users receive a product
B21	S20	A product should not be distributed without printed reference material
M20	S20	Correction requests cannot be processed adequately without a maintenance specification
S12	S20	A product should not be distributed without a printed release bulletin

Figure 14.16   Stereotype software product development constraints.

243

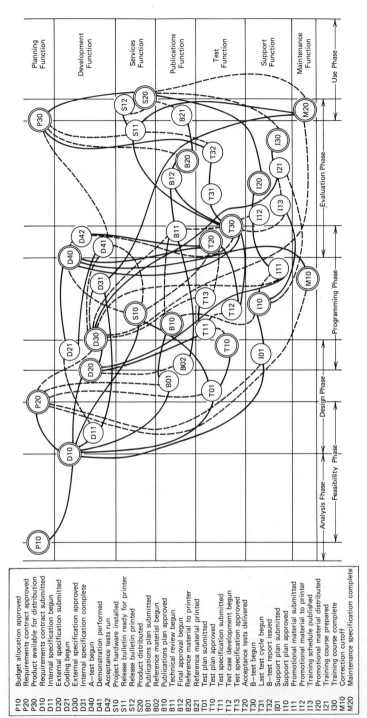

P10 Budget allocation approved
P20 Requirements contract approved
P30 Product available for distribution
D10 Requirements contract submitted
D11 Internal specification begun
D20 External specification submitted
D21 Coding begun
D30 External specification approved
D31 Internal specification complete
D40 A—test begun
D41 Demonstration performed
D42 Acceptance tests run
S10 Project hardware installed
S11 Release bulletin ready for printer
S12 Release bulletin printed
S20 Product distributed
B01 Publications plan submitted
B02 Reference material begun
B10 Publications plan approved
B11 Technical review begun
B12 Final approval begun
B20 Reference material to printer
B21 Reference material printed
T01 Test plan submitted
T10 Test plan approved
T11 Test specification submitted
T12 Test case development begun
T13 Test specification approved
T20 Acceptance tests delivered
T30 B—test begun
T31 Last test cycle begun
T32 B—test report issued
I01 Support plan submitted
I10 Support plan approved
I11 Promotional material submitted
I12 Promotional material to printer
I13 Promotional material distributed
I20 Training schedule published
I21 Training course prepared
I30 Training course complete
M10 Correction cutoff
M20 Maintenance specification complete

Figure 14.17 A stereotype software product development network.

244

axis represents relative time; that is, when every event is positioned to the right of every event required or likely to occur before it. A further refinement of a network diagram is the ordering of events along the vertical axis by the organizations responsible for achieving them. For example, in Figure 14.17 all events for which the Planning Function is primarily responsible are confined to a vertical band devoid of events for which any other function is primarily responsible. A final refinement of a network diagram is the emphasis of major milestones (such as those reported in a schedule notice; see the next section) by such a device as drawing their identifying bubbles with thicker lines than are used for minor milestones. Figure 14.17 includes all of these refinements.

Placing an expected time duration for each activity on a network diagram leads to determining the critical path. By adding the times for activities along all possible (and that obviously implies logically consistent) paths from the first event to the last event of a network, and remembering that constraints are tasks requiring no activity and thus no time to complete, you can determine the longest path. This longest path is called the **critical path** because any delay in any activity on it delays the whole project. As a project progresses and deviations from the baseline are approved and incorporated into the network, the critical path changes. Management of the critical path by altering the network is the most valuable use to which a network plan can be put.

The analysis of networks—including the calculation of paths for alternative plans—can be time consuming. A scientific approach to this task led to the development several decades ago of the now famous **Program Evaluation and Review Technique—PERT** as it is usually called. The mechanization of PERT led to other critical path techniques for management of cost and other resources. There are now many books on the subject and even more computer programs available to reduce the tedium of network analysis.

The classical diagrammatic representation of a network is usually referred to as a PERT chart or PERT network, whether or not PERT is applied to it. In the classical representation care is taken that all activity lines are drawn with their heads to the right of their tails. Said another way, all events occurring later in time than other events are placed to the right of all predecessor events. Constraints are drawn as are activities, usually with a small 0 (for "zero" activity) or c (for "constraint") next to the activity arrowhead or along the activity line if durations are shown for activities. For logical consistency and to facilitate machine analysis of the paths through a network, a PERT network has a single starting event and a single ending event. All paths start at the initial node and end at the final node, even if dummy activities or constraints are required to complete the paths.

The rest of this section deals with the contents of software product development networks and not with their form. If you desire more background in network theory and application consult Archibald (55). Consult the American Management Associations (56) for current trends in the automation of network analysis, and for an intensive application of critical path analysis to software programming management, see Kirk (57). The material that follows is equally relevant and useful whether your networks are simple or elaborate, and whether they are manipulated manually or by a computer.

Many organizations find it easiest to introduce network planning through a stereotype network for their type of project. A **stereotype network** is a standard set of activities, events, and constraints that cover the majority of items of interest in a typical project. Figures 14.15 through 14.17 are such a stereotype network and network diagram for a software development project. Subnetworks of Figure 14.17 appear throughout this book to illustrate many points. Start with these figures and particularize them to a real project by inserting activity times and milestone dates, and by adding and subtracting items as appropriate.

Once you have built a baseline plan, report progress toward it by shading the event bubbles on the network diagram for each milestone as it is met. Draw changes to the baseline plan directly on a baseline diagram, in a different color from the baseline if you wish. Put the baseline and all approved modifications on the same diagram to emphasize that plans are changing.

Effort you expend in defining a good set of stereotype milestones pays compound dividends if you use some of them to report progress on a schedule notice (Section 14.7), a project progress report (Section 16.4), and individual work plans (Section 14.3). The reappearance of these key milestones reinforces their significance, and your ability to visualize them as points on a network diagram makes them easy to remember.

14.7 SCHEDULE NOTICE

A **schedule notice** is a tool for establishing, recording, communicating, and changing a schedule plan. It is a tabular summary of the schedule data contained in a network plan plus brief descriptions of the reasons for any changes that have taken place since the last schedule notice was issued.

A schedule notice is but a part of a system that is built around it. The system works as follows:

1. A project is planned in network form, and forecasted major milestones from the network are transcribed onto a schedule notice form.
2. Management approval of the data is secured and recorded on the schedule notice as signatures.
3. The schedule notice is submitted to document control where it becomes a part of appropriate project and product files, wherefrom it is distributed to all persons concerned with schedule progress, and where it is added to a schedule notice summary (see Section 16.2).
4. When forecasted data no longer appear valid, and when milestones are met, a new schedule notice is generated showing old and new dates and reasons for the changes.
5. Appropriate approvals (there may be none) for changes are obtained and recorded on the schedule notice as signatures.
6. Steps 3, 4, and 5 are repeated until all milestones are reported complete or until the associated project is terminated.

Schedule notices report both project and product schedules, but, since the milestones contained on them are product-oriented, they are normally filed and summarized according to product. Since one project may yield several products and several projects may produce one product, both product(s) and project(s) are identified on each schedule notice. In a situation such as one in which several products are being produced simultaneously for release as a product set, the final schedule notice milestone for each individual product is the start of A-Test and a separate product set schedule notice reports subsequent milestones for all products in the set. In such a case early milestones like those pertaining to the requirements contract review and approval may also be tracked only on a product set schedule notice.

Figure 14.18 is an early schedule notice for A$K, called a **Schedule Change Notice (SCN)**, and uses the milestone nomenclature developed in Section 14.6. The following description of SCN fields and their contents in Fig. 14.18 should give you enough of an understanding of how a schedule notice works to extrapolate to other situations:

SCHEDULE CHANGE NOTICE

PROJECT NAME: A$K Development PROJECT NUMBER: C013			

NAME		OLD	NEW	NOTES
P10	PBR APPROVED	09/29/77 C		
D10	POR SUBMITTED	11/03/77 C		
P20	POR APPROVED	12/15/77 C		
D20	ERS SUBMITTED	01/09/78 C		
T10	TEST PLAN APPROVED	02/09/78		
D30	ERS APPROVED	03/15/78	02/06/78	*
B10	PUBLICATIONS PLAN APPROVED	01/26/78		
S10	PROJECT HARDWARE INSTALLED	03/31/78		
I10	SUPPORT PLAN APPROVED	03/02/78		
D41	DEMONSTRATION PERFORMED	TBS		
T20	ACCEPTANCE TESTS DELIV.	TBS		
T30	B-TEST BEGUN	07/03/78	05/08/78	*
I20	PROMOTIONAL MATERIAL DIST.	TBS		
I21	TRAINING COURSE PREPARED	TBS		
B20	REFERENCE MAT. TO PRINTER	07/17/78	06/05/78	*
P30	PRODUCT AVAILABILITY DATE	08/18/78	07/03/78	*
M20	MAINTENANCE SPEC. COMPLETE	TBS		
S20	PRODUCT DISTRIBUTION DATE	09/01/78	07/17/78	*

Note: the project/product header row spans "PROJECT NAME: A$K Development" / "PRODUCT NAME: A$K" and "PROJECT NUMBER: C013" / "PRODUCT NUMBER: L301A".

EVENT	REASON FOR CHANGE
All	Deferring PLOT and SORT will return project to schedule

PREPARED BY: *Luther Davis*   APPROVED BY: A QR

APPROVED BY: _____   APPROVED BY: _____

OLD DATE: 01/06/78   NEW DATE: 1/13/78

FORM 7443a

Figure 14.18   An early A$K schedule notice.

PROJECT NAME   These names and numbers are used for archival
PRODUCT NAME   reference and for summarizing the schedule data
PROJECT   by both project and product.
NUMBER
PRODUCT
NUMBER

OLD DATE	This is a pointer to the date of record of the preceding SCN.
NEW DATE	This is the date of record of this SCN and is used as a sort key in filing SCNs and to determine when to include the rest of the data from the SCN in a summary.
PREPARED BY	The person who completes the SCN, normally the project manager, signs the SCN here.
APPROVED BY	Each person who needs to approve new data before it becomes a matter of record signs here.
OLD	Every nonblank datum from the NEW column of the previous SCN is transcribed to this column; where the previous NEW datum is blank, the previous OLD datum is transcribed. C indicates "complete"; TBS means "to be scheduled"; blank means "not relevant."
NEW	This is part of the heart of an SCN. Each newly completed (since OLD DATE) milestone is entered, followed by C. Each revised forecast is entered. TBS here with a date on the same row under OLD means that a milestone has been decommitted.
NOTES	An * here is a pointer to EVENT and REASON FOR CHANGE. There is an asterisk here for every nonblank entry under NEW. There is also an asterisk here for other notes, as perhaps when an OLD date is in jeopardy but new date is set.
EVENT	Event numbers from the # column here indicate to which events the neighboring REASONS FOR CHANGE apply.
REASON FOR CHANGE	This is the rest of the heart of an SCN. Approvals are based on the reasons stated here.
BLANK ROWS	These are used to add ad hoc milestones.

The first character of each milestone number indicates the Function (P = Planning, B = Book = Publications, etc.) primarily responsible for milestone completion. Prudent project management demands that functional concurrence accompany NEW data for any of the milestones other than Development (D) milestones; "APPROVED BY" may be used for this purpose.

Chapter

15

Specifications

Documents whose purpose is to state explicitly or *to specify* are **specifications**. They should be readable and concise, but above all they must be accurate and comprehensive. Ambiguity in specifications can be tolerated even less than in plans. In the design decomposition process which for a software product proceeds from a hierarchy of plans through a requirements contract, an external specification, an internal specification, and ends with a maintenance specification, ambiguity is increasingly resolved at each step until, one hopes, none remains.

You achieve accuracy and eliminate ambiguity in specifications through broad and careful review, as through the technical review board of Section 18.3. Making specifications comprehensive is more difficult, but forcing them to conform to standard formats goes a long way toward achieving the objective. This chapter is dedicated to establishing comprehensiveness through rigorous definition of what makes up an adequate specification. Formats for several key specifications are presented, which you may adopt as they are or modify to suit your needs. Their form should also suggest to you how other specifications not included, such as a test specification, might be derived. The relationship between a test plan and a test specification is much the same as the relationship between a requirements contract and an external specification, so you should have little difficulty deriving a test specification once you have studied the external specification format that follows.

Here are two rules worth following for all specifications:

1. Use forms that allow adequate configuration management for all documents.
2. For each type of specification, develop a standard format and adhere to it. In every specification include every section heading from the governing format, entering "not applicable" or "none"

where appropriate. This greatly aids the review process by helping reviewers avoid overlooking any topics.

As mentioned in Chapter 13, the selection of headings to include in a document and their order of occurrence are far from arbitrary. The formats in this chapter are designed to foster top-down design by placing the most important issues first, with minor exceptions where readability for reviewers takes precedence over the natural flow of design decomposition. In the formats that follow, section numbering is ordered to allow nesting of documents for those of you who have adequate facilities to maintain and extract them. For example, recall that Figure 13.2 shows the nested table of contents for a requirements contract (RC), external specification (ES), internal specification (IS), and maintenance specification (MS). The nature of the entry for each document is noted by T for "title," G for "general," P for "partial," and F for "final." Notice that the progression from T to G to P to F is one-directional as decisions are made that freeze the design.

Throughout this chapter, when capital letters are used to begin the name of a document type or stand in place of it, they indicate a document formatted precisely as described here. The abbreviation RC means Requirements Contract, a requirements contract formatted per Chapter 13, and so on. Frequent examples of representative entries are included, each separated from the text it illustrates by horizontal lines to emphasize that it is an example.

15.1   EXTERNAL SPECIFICATION

The uses to which an external specification is put are discussed throughout this book. This section presents a format for an external specification that aids creation of machine code, publications, and test materials and aids evaluation of a product's external design as well. As stressed in Section 7.5, an external specification is restricted to presenting external design, both to encourage a top-down design approach and to prevent legitimate reviewers of external attributes (what a product is) from interfering with internal design (how a product is built).

Parnas (58) has defined a technique for module specification that shares many attributes with an external specification. These attributes are:

1. No information about the structure of a calling module should be conveyed in the external specification for a called module.

2. An external specification should be written in terms familiar to both user and implementer to minimize opportunities for misunderstanding.

3. The implementation of a module should be free to vary, without changing associated modules or procedures.

4. A reviewer of an external specification must assume that only what is specified will work. For example, if an external specification says without qualification "parameter A may have any value between 3 and 14," he is entitled to assume that fractional values such as 5.71 are valid, but he may not assume that end values such as 3 and 14 are valid.

5. Restrictions must be completely and precisely specified, but the reasons for making them need not be. Such reasons may be included in an internal specification if they will help future repairers or enhancers of a module avoid eliminating the restrictions.

6. When a methodology is perfected that can give you a sufficiently precise notation to verify correctness and completeness of an external specification (58–60), this verification should take place before you begin coding. Regardless of your ability to develop such a notation, have users or their representatives thoroughly review an external specification before you begin coding.

Figure 15.1 is the table of contents for an External Specification (**ES**) constructed according to the format that follows. This format is a decomposition of the Requirements Contract (RC) format of Chapter 13. Include every section heading in Figure 15.1 in an ES even if the subject is not relevant to a particular product. Follow such headings by "none," "not applicable," or a pointer to an equivalent RC statement and omit following subsections.

Note in Figure 15.1 that several subsections under STRATEGY (e.g., 3.1.1 and 3.(2,3).n.1.1) are shown to contain partial (*P*) statements. They are partial only in the sense that when a transformation from logical functions in an ES to physical modules in an Internal Specification (IS) and a Maintenance Specification (MS) is made, some interfaces will be exposed that require description. The *entire* description of the product as seen by its *users* and not its implementers must be presented in the ES; withholding those items visible only to implementers until the IS or MS enhances the effectiveness of the ES.

1	PRODUCT DESCRIPTION	T
1.1	Product Name and Numbers	T
1.1.1	Product Name	F
1.1.2	Name Abbreviations	F
1.1.3	Product Numbers	F
1.2	Brief Description of Product	F
1.2.1	Copyright Notice	F
1.2.2	Hierarchical Precedence	P
1.2.2.1	Overriding Higher Documents	P
2	MISSION	F
2.1	Revision Request Reconciliation	T
2.1.1	Revisions Excluded	F
2.1.2	Revisions Included	F
2.2	Enhancement Request Reconciliation	T
2.2.1	Enhancements Excluded	F
2.2.2	Enhancements Included	F
3	STRATEGY	T
3.1	Conventions	T
3.1.1	Notations	P
3.1.2	Terminology	P
3.1.3	Syntax	P
3.(2,3)	(Generated, Operational) Software	F
3.(2,3).n	(Name n) Function	F
3.(2,3).n.1	Constraints	T
3.(2,3).n.1.1	Standards	P
3.(2,3).n.1.2	Compatibility Constraints	P
3.(2,3).n.1.3	Software Constraints	P
3.(2,3).n.1.4	Hardware Constraints	P
3.(2,3).n.2	External Properties	T
3.(2,3).n.2.1	Outputs	P
3.(2,3).n.2.2	Processes	P
3.(2,3).n.2.2.1	Invocation	P
3.(2,3).n.2.2.2	Execution	P
3.(2,3).n.2.2.3	Termination	P
3.(2,3).n.2.2.3.1	Normal Termination	P
3.(2,3).n.2.2.3.2	Abnormal Termination	P
3.(2,3).n.2.3	Inputs	P
3.(2,3).n.3	Ergonomic Properties	T
3.(2,3).n.3.1	Security and Privacy	P
3.(2,3).n.3.2	Reliability	P
3.(2,3).n.3.3	Restartability	P
3.(2,3).n.3.3.1	Automatic Restart	P
3.(2,3).n.3.3.2	Manual Restart	P
3.(2,3).n.3.4	Customizability	P
3.(2,3).n.3.4.1	Parameterization	P
3.(2,3).n.3.5	Performance	P
3.(2,3).n.4	Internal Properties	T
3.(2,3).n.4.1	Maintainability	P
4	BACKGROUND	T
4.1	References	P
5	DELIVERY AND INSTALLATION	T
5.1	Provisions for Protection	F
5.2	Installation Resources	G
5.2.1	Installation Procedures	G

Figure 15.1 Stereotype external specification contents.

253

1 PRODUCT DESCRIPTION

From the RC include verbatim Sections 1 through 1.1.3 and Section 1.2.

1.2.1 Copyright Notice

If you plan to claim statutory copyright protection for the product, be sure to copyright the ES; it is by far the most definitive description of the product. Otherwise, state "none."

Copyright © 1977, by ABC Computers Company

1.2.2 Hierarchical Precedence

Develop a standard statement for this section to remind Development to observe the hierarchical precedence of all relevant RCs and to prevent the design they present in the ES from extending the scope of the product.

All constraints on the external design of this product are defined by this external specification and the requirements contracts and external specifications listed below. The requirements contracts take precedence over this external specification in every instance. Apparent conflicts or ambiguities shall be investigated as soon as they are detected. Confirmed conflicts between and any oversights in any of the documents shall be brought immediately to the attention of the Director, Programming Systems.
This external specification shall detail only features stated or implied in the requirements contracts. As such, it in no way extends the scope of the product.
Omission of features included in the requirements contracts or addition of features not included or implied is not permitted.

1.2.2.1 Overriding Higher Documents

The RCs from which this document is derived and all ESs containing sections pointed to by this document and which are already approved take precedence over this document. List all such documents including product names and numbers. If none, enter "none."

1.2.2.1   Overriding Higher Documents

*System Diagnostics RC (A23) System On-Line Diagnostics RC (G003)
Processor Diagnostics RC (G030)*

2   MISSION

Include the mission statements from the RCs.

2.1   Revision Request Reconciliation

If the governing RCs state that no revision requests exist, state "not applicable" and omit subsections 2.1.1 and 2.1.2. Otherwise include verbatim these subsections from the RCs.

2.1.2   Revisions Included

In addition to the RC statements, for each revision point to section numbers in the ES where the revision is specified. In those sections clearly identify revision descriptions.

2.2   Correction Request Reconciliation

Treat this section in the same manner as Section 2.1.

3   STRATEGY

Repeat Sections 3 through 3.1.2 from the governing RCs, adding items from this ES not present in the RCs.

3.1.1   Notations

3.1.1   Notations

Several notations are used throughout this ERS that have a very specific meaning. They are:
(a)   A character string enclosed by quotation marks means the inputting or outputting of those characters between the quotation marks.
(b)   The symbol b̷ means one blank space. The string b̷ . . b̷ means a string of blanks; the number of periods between the b̷'s is not significant. The number of blanks is determined to maximize readability.
(c)   Any item enclosed by square brackets is optional.

3.1.2 Terminology

3.1.2 Terminology

A$K will operate on several forms of data defined here. When one of the words listed below appears in this ERS with the first letter capitalized, the word carriers the meaning given to it here.

(a) Name. A string of one to eight alphanumeric characters, the first of which must be alphanumeric.

(b) Integer. A string of one to eight digits or the character "–" followed by one to seven digits.

(c) Date. Any of the following strings, where $0 \leq y \leq 9, 1 \leq m \leq 12, 1 \leq q \leq 4$:

$$19yy$$
$$qQ19yy$$
$$yy$$
$$qQyy$$
$$m-yy$$
$$m/yy$$

3.1.3 Syntax

Many computer programs require that specific rules be followed such as word order, punctuation, and mandatory selection from among alternative parameters. Include such rules of syntax here, either in their entirety or by reference (to a document in Section 4.1 of the ES).

3.1.3 Syntax

Curly brackets ({ }) enclose two or more parameters, one of which must be chosen and included. Square brackets ([ ]) enclose an optional parameter string. For brevity period ellipses (. . .) between two terms replace consecutive intervening terms.

3.(2,3) (Generated, Operational) Software

As for an RC, Section 3.2, Generated Software, and Section 3.3, Operational Software, are structured identically and both are present only if the product produces generated software. If the product does not produce generated software, follow the heading of Section 3.2 with "not applicable" and omit subsections.

For whichever sections or subsections are present, insert a hierarchical structure diagram to provide a road map for the subsections that follow. Use a tree-diagram or a nested diagram like the following example. Treat each subsection n as a single functional capability. Organize functions into modules that here, if possible, will have mutually exclusive physical counterparts in the IS so that the process of design decomposition into an IS can continue per Section 15.2. In the process do not lose sight of the overriding requirement to organize an ES according to logical function. It will always be possible to reorganize the material into physical modules when the IS is generated. See Figure 15.2 for an example.

3.(2,3).n   (Name n) Function

For each function identified in Section 3.(2,3) provide a name and use that name in the title above, in place of (Name n). If you wish, follow the title by a few overview words about the function. For functions appropriately described in another ES (as is the case if you use a previously developed module or group of modules), point to the equivalent Section 3.(2,3).n of the definitive ES. If no definitive statement exists for such a function, make sure that one is created and incorporated into the proper document. Do *not*, however, incorporate any descriptions here that more appropriately belong elsewhere; this would lead to serious problems in maintaining such specifications.

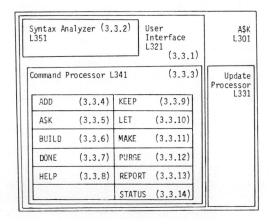

Figure 15.2   An example of a hierarchical structure diagram.

3.(2,3).n.1   Constraints

Add *only* intraproduct constaints, as interproduct constraints are to be specified in the antecedent RCs. List as many constraints as is practical in Section 3.(2,3).1.1, implying that they apply to all functions. However, if the list is long and some constraints apply to some but not all functions, introduce them at the highest appropriate lower level.

3.(2,3).n.1.1   Standards

Include any intraproduct standards, such as a restriction to upper case alphabetic characters for all messages.

3.(2,3).n.1.2   Compatibility Constraints

Include any intraproduct compatibility constraints, such as restricting all output reports to a common format. Describe features to aid conversion from predecessor products.

3.(2,3).n.1.3   Software Constraints

Include any intraproduct software constraints, such as the use of double-precision arithmetic for a class of operations.

3.(2,3).n.1.4   Hardware Constraints

Include any intraproduct hardware constraints, such as avoiding use of an audible alarm.

3.3.1.1.4   Hardware Constraints

In addition to constraints presented in the POR, A$K expects the Telcoscope 43 terminal to be formatted as 25 rows of 80 columns each. The first two rows are called the entry line; the next two rows, the response line; and the last 21 rows, the page.

3.(2,3).n.2   External Properties

These sections are the essence of an ES. They provide the final and complete descriptions of all external attributes of a product.
To maximize the reusability of functional modules in other contexts, define them only once. Therefore, when parameters are merely passed through a function, mention them as inputs to and outputs

from each function they pass through, accompanied by pointers to where they are generated.

If you routinely use input-process-output diagrams (61), insert one for the module here, just before Section 3.(2,3).n.2.1, and number the boxes in the diagram according to the corresponding section numbers as in Figure 15.3.

3.(2,3).n.2.1 Outputs

If there is an RC entry for n, repeat it as an introduction to this section. Then, for all n, list by name every output transmitted outside of the function. For each output that is also input to this function or that is generated by a subordinate function with a separate description, point to the ES of the function where the output is generated. For all other outputs, which are those generated by this function, provide a complete description. For all outputs to be read by humans, such as reports and messages, provide a complete sample.

Include in the description type, structure, format, size, location, and range. Use pictures or diagrams if they are appropriate. Be sure to include:

Index registers	Interrupt lines
Status lines	Condition codes
Tables	Sense lights
Keyboard locks	Messages
Files, records, and fields	

See Figure 15.4 for an example.

3.(2,3).n.2.2 Processes

Repeat the RC entry as an introduction to this section. For each subsection, define precisely all defaults, reported error conditions, and restart and recovery capabilities not covered elsewhere. Use pointers to other sections as appropriate.

3.(2,3).n.2.2.1 Invocation

Describe the way(s) a user can cause the function to be performed. This may be by entering a command, turning a switch, executing a call statement, raising a signal, or any number of other ways. Identify all outputs of the invocation process such as error messages, table entries, and indicator settings.

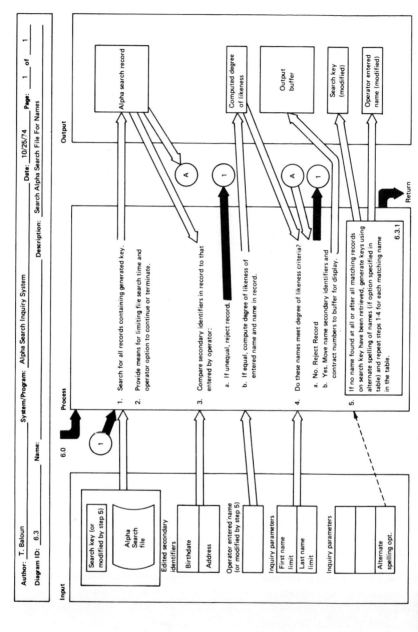

Figure 15.3 An input-process-output diagram. (Reprinted by permission from *HIPO—A Design Aid and Documentation Technique*. © 1974 by International Business Machines Corporation.)

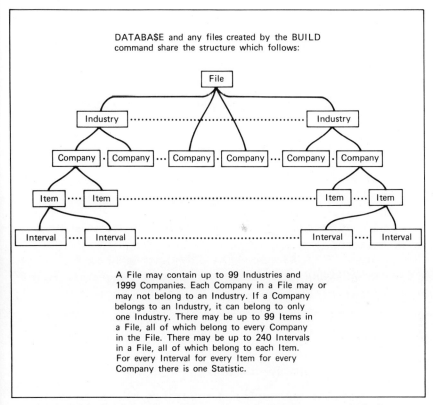

Figure 15.4   The description of outputs from the BUILD command of A$K.

RESTORE [DEV=]n[(mt)] [,SKIP = nn] [,DATE = yy.mm.dd];
Where:

   [DEV=]n[(mt)]   specifies the device number on which the mag-
                         netic tape is mounted,

   [,SKIP = nn]   specifies the number of backup tape files to be
                      skipped before performing the restoration,

[,DATE = yy.mm.dd]   specifies the date the backup tape was created.

In response to the VSOS request "WHAT SYSTEM?" the user may
enter a syntactically correct form of "A$K DATABASE" at the cursor

position set by VSOS. VSOS will either accept the command and pass control to A$K or reject it with a message.

3.(2,3).n.2.2.2   Execution

Describe the data transformation(s) performed by the function.

ADD allows a user to enter data into a file he has created with the BUILD command. Data for as many as 18 Items may be entered with one command. In response to the command, A$K will format the Telcoscope screen with a row for each Item specified and a column for each Interval in the file, displaying six Intervals per page if more than six are in the file. Interval headings by year, quarter, or month will be displayed according to the minimum Interval stored in the file. All data entered by A$K in the matrix will glow steadily; all data entered by the user will blink (to minimize his chance of erroneously changing data). The user may enter data and page forward or backward.

3.(2,3).n.2.2.3   Termination

3.(2,3).n.2.2.3.1   Normal Termination

Specify all ways the function can terminate by itself or be caused to terminate and pass on or return control if all goes well.

3.2.3.2.2.3.1   Normal Termination

If no error is found, the Syntax Analyzer will pass the command to the Command Processor and transfer control to it.
If an error is found that does not require HELP to be called, the user will iterate through the command in process until HELP is called or until the command is successfully passed to the Command Processor.
If HELP is required the Syntax Analyzer passes a correctly formatted HELP command to the Command Processor and transfers control to it.

3.(2,3).n.2.2.3.2   Abnormal Termination

As above, but when anything abnormal occurs at any time during invocation or execution.

If the sector to be read is not a normal, positive disc address, or if the sector read contains "/&" in the first two positions, the end-of-file exit specified by the "eofaddr" in the macro call statement shall be taken.

3.(2,3).n.2.3   Inputs

Repeat the RC entry as an introduction to this section. Then treat every input as you treat outputs in Section 3.(2,3).n.2.1. For inputs that are passed through without being altered in any way, either to become outputs of this function or to become inputs of subordinate functions that have independent descriptions, provide pointers to the corresponding sections of the appropriate ESs.

3.(2,3).n.3   Ergonomic Properties

Some of the subjects treated here are a function of the internal design and may be invisible to users. Then again, they may not be invisible. Require each property to be discussed so that the subject will be considered while the product is being designed. Do this to assure that any external manifestations are not overlooked and that they are described.

3.(2,3).n.3.1   Security and Privacy

Describe access locks, privileged command or terminal restrictions, automatic purging, or other features of a function that contribute to the security or privacy of the user's data and procedures.

When VSOS accepts a valid password it shall blank the user entry on the terminal (or, alternatively, overwrite this entry if his terminal includes hard-copy capability).

Several vital A$K functions are not available to A$K users in operational mode but are available to the A$K supervisor in maintenance mode using a Supervisory Password. Some Telcoscope terminals may be designated as supervisory. The combination of such a terminal and the Supervisory Password are needed to access the Update Processor.

3.(2,3).n.3.2   Reliability

Detail any observable features used to protect the product from failures in its environment and to protect the environment from any failures in the product. Clearly define the status of the data in the event of failure. Include audit trails, error logging, and error correction to the extent that they are visible to a user of the product.

To protect against loss of communications from the terminal to the computer, a user who makes no entry for five minutes will receive an Alarm Light and Alarm Buzzer signal from the computer. These signals will be sent steadily for one minute. If there is still no response from the terminal, the user will be logged-off. Requests for deferred processing will be processed.

3.(2,3).n.3.3   Restartability

Separate the discussion into two subsections, depending upon whether the restart is automatic or manual. Unless restartability of the product is entirely self-contained, describe also the interface to checkpoint and restart utilities.

3.(2,3).n.3.3.1   Automatic Restart

Be sure to state the conditions under which automatic restart will occur and its impact on users and their data.

3.(2,3).n.3.3.2   Manual Restart

Define the conditions under which manual restart will be permitted and the result of attempting it under other conditions. As for automatic restart, state the impact on users and their data.

Users will be unaware that a voluntary restart has been made from a checkpoint except that they may find some of their Private Files, Expressions, and Criteria missing (because they could not be reconstructed from checkpoint data available at the time A$K was terminated). They will be able to determine when the last restart took place, however, through the STATUS command (Section 3.3.14).

3.(2,3).n.3.4   Customizability

Describe the philosophy of any provisions for customization and point to all specific examples that appear elsewhere in the ES. Enumerate all user exits for the addition of user own code or procedures.

All literal values, constraints, etc., shall be located at the area whose label is PARMS. This will facilitate field alteration. No embedded literals shall be permitted.

3.(2,3).n.3.4.1   Parameterization

Discuss the philosophy of using parameters to influence the environment, data, or execution of the product. Include a comprehensive list of parameters if any exist.

3.(2,3).n.3.5   Performance

Describe features of the product that can vary its performance. This includes parameters by which the user can tune the product, such as time-slice, buffer size, and optional error correction. Leave to the IS discussion of parameters available only to the developers.

3.(2,3).n.4   Internal properties

This section is called Internal Properties because the subjects treated are a function of the internal design and may be invisible to users. Then again, they may not be invisible. Require that each property be considered to assure that external manifestations are not overlooked and to encourage coverage of the subject while the product is being designed. Centralize discussion of each property here, or reference other sections where the property is discussed.

3.(2,3).n.4.1   Maintainability

Describe interfaces to debugging tools and any built-in debugging features available to users.

4   BACKGROUND

4.1   References

Repeat the RC statement and add any new references made from within the ES. Use this section to include other documents by reference.

(c)   The document identified below—in the exact date and issue shown—is by this reference made a part of this document:
American National Standard Procedures for the Use of the Communication Control Characters of American National Standard Code for Information Interchange in Specified Data Communication Links, ANSI X3.28–1971, Sections 5.2, 5.4, 5.7.

5   DELIVERY AND INSTALLATION

5.1   Provisions for Protection

Expand the RC statement to show where and how the ownership of the product will be communicated to users. Reference a standard if appropriate.

5.2   Installation Resources

5.2.1   Installation Procedures

Describe in detail how a user places the product in service. Reference all user inputs to and outputs from the installation process. Enumerate all tools and/or features of tools required to install the product by each reasonable alternative procedure. Include any procedures or procedural sequences not detailed by support documentation of the referenced tools.

The following procedure is recommended for installing the new MAINT modules in SYSPOL:
1.   *SELECT M—ALOC; SELECT COPY—; SELECT UNLOC—;*
2.   *SELECT MAINT(M—HOLD);*
3.   *SELECT M—CONS(C—HOLD);*
4.   *RESTORE*
5.   *RENAME MAINT(MAINTC)*
6.   *RENAME M—HOLD(MAINT);*
7.   *EXIT*

15.2 INTERNAL SPECIFICATION

This section presents a format for an Internal Specification (**IS**) which assumes the existence of a Requirements Contract (RC) and an External Specification (ES). This format assumes that all information regarding *what* a product is is contained in its RC and ES and that the IS explains *how* the product is built and *how* it will achieve the requirements and objectives set for it. The reader of an IS need not fully understand the workings of a product without looking at its actual code, but the IS and the code together should suffice.

An IS is a project notebook, growing as the product it describes develops. A subset of an IS is written and approved before coding begins (as at stereotype milestone D11 in Figure 14.16) so that Development management has assurance that a proposed design is sound. Included always is a description of each algorithm to be used; other material to be included is determined project by project. Requiring an ES to be approved before the IS is first reviewed enables the initial IS to be comprehensive. Coding begins when there is enough data and algorithm specification so that coding a portion of the product can result in a testing harness; a skeleton of the final product complete enough to input nontrivial data, process it correctly, and produce nontrivial output. From that time on, the IS and the code are developed concurrently and may reference one another to provide the totality of the internal design description.

As code is generated, it will be both possible and desirable to incorporate much of the internal design documentation in code listings, to delete redundant information from the IS, and to replace deleted data with pointers to the code listings. Just how much you transfer to code listings depends on the capability of your compilers and assemblers to carry meaningful information about the product. Regardless of where information finally resides, it will be included in the maintenance specification because it is a union of the IS and code listings.

An IS has many uses. It begins as a project workbook which shows how a product is built, the product's functional breakdown and the algorithms used to realize its functions. Without this workbook there is little hope of salvaging much internal design if key project personnel are lost or if work on a product is suspended for even a month. As the product develops and the IS grows, it can be used as a subjective indicator of project progress. An IS becomes a maintenance specification (MS—see Section 15.3) and as such is indispensible for rapid error correction. An IS is also an excellent reference document, containing design ideas, algorithms, and even module descriptions which may be useful in later developments.

Figure 15.5 is the table of contents for an IS structured according to the format that follows. This format is a decomposition of the RC and ES formats mentioned above. This type of IS lends itself to describing hierarchical systems, systems organized in a top-down fashion. It is not restricted, however, to top-down structures. When all sections listed in Figure 15.5 are complete, an IS is complete and configuration control is rigorously exercised over it from that point on.

1.	PRODUCT DESCRIPTION	T
1.1	Product Name and Numbers	T
1.1.1	Product Name	F
1.1.2	Name Abbreviations	F
1.1.3	Product Numbers	F
1.2	Brief Description of Product	F
1.2.1	Copyright Notice	F
1.2.2	Hierarchical Precedence	F
1.2.2.1	Overriding Higher Documents	F
2	MISSION	F
2.1	Revision Request Reconciliation	T
2.1.1	Revisions Excluded	F
2.1.2	Revisions Included	F
2.2	Enhancement Request Reconciliation	T
2.2.1	Enhancements Excluded	F
2.2.2	Enhancements Included	F
2.3	Correction Request Reconciliation	T
2.3.1	Corrections Excluded	F
2.3.2	Corrections Included	P
3	STRATEGY	T
3.1	Conventions	T
3.1.1	Notations	F
3.1.2	Terminology	F
3.1.3	Syntax	F
3.(2,3)	(Generated, Operational) Software	F
3.(2,3).n	(Name n) (Function, Module)	F
3.(2,3).n.1	Constraints	T
3.(2,3).n.1.1	Standards	F
3.(2,3).n.1.2	Compatibility Constraints	F
3.(2,3).n.1.3	Software Constraints	P
3.(2,3).n.1.4	Hardware Constraints	P
3.(2,3).n.2	External Properties	T
3.(2,3).n.2.1	Outputs	F
3.(2,3).n.2.2	Processes	F
3.(2,3).n.2.2.1	Invocation	F
3.(2,3).n.2.2.2	Execution	F

Figure 15.5   Stereotype internal specification contents.

3.(2,3).n.2.2.3	Termination	F
3.(2,3).n.2.2.3.1	Normal Termination	F
3.(2,3).n.2.2.3.2	Abnormal Termination	F
3.(2,3).n.2.3	Inputs	F
3.(2,3).n.3	Ergonomic Properties	T
3.(2,3).n.3.1	Security and Privacy	F
3.(2,3).n.3.2	Reliability	F
3.(2,3).n.3.3	Restartability	F
3.(2,3).n.3.3.1	Automatic Restart	F
3.(2,3).n.3.3.2	Manual Restart	F
3.(2,3).n.3.4	Customizability	F
3.(2,3).n.3.4.1	Parameterization	F
3.(2,3).n.3.5	Performance	F
3.(2,3).n.4	Internal Properties	T
3.(2,3).n.4.1	Maintainability	F
3.(2,3).n.4.2	Algorithms	F
3.(2,3).n.4.3	Internal Data	F
3.(2,3).n.4.4	Implementation Strategy	G
3.(2,3).n.4.4.1	Function Testing	G
3.(2,3).n.4.4.2	Algorithm Testing	G
3.(2,3).n.4.4.3	Notes	G
3.(2,3).n.4.4.4	Module Status Sheet	P
4	BACKGROUND	T
4.1	References	P

Figure 15.5 (Continued)

1 PRODUCT DESCRIPTION

Include verbatim Sections 1 through 1.2.1 from the ES.

1.2.2 Hierarchical Precedence

Develop a standard statement for this section to remind Development to observe the hierarchical precedence of all relevant RCs and ESs, and to constrain the design they present in the IS from extending the scope or altering the intent of the product.

All constraints on the design of this product are defined by this IS and the RCs, ESs, and ISs listed below. The RCs take precedence over the ESs and the ESs take precedence over the ISs, including this one. Any previously approved IS takes precedence over this IS. Apparent conflicts or ambiguities shall be investigated as they are detected. Confirmed conflicts between and any oversights in any of the documents shall be brought immediately to the attention of the Director, Programming Systems.

This IS shall detail only properties stated or implied in the·RCs and ESs. As such it in no way extends the scope or intent of the product. Omission of features included in the RCs or addition of features not included or implied therein is not permitted.

1.2.2.1   Overriding Higher Documents

The RCs and ESs from which this document is derived and all ISs containing sections to which this document points and which are already approved take precedence over it. List all such documents, including product names and numbers. If none, enter "none."

2   MISSION

Repeat or point to Sections 2 through 2.2.2 of governing ESs. For included revisions and enhancements point to sections in this IS where the implementations are described. In those sections mark the margin to indicate request descriptions. Some require no IS-level documentation; for them enter "no reference required."

2.2.2   Enhancements Included

(a)   *1314. Display Update level as well as Version level at sign-on. See page 46.*
(b)   *1450. Restructure the Accounts Receivable report per the sample submitted with the RPE. No reference required.*

2.3   Correction Request Reconciliation

2.3.1   Corrections Excluded

Repeat governing RC statements.

2.3.2   Corrections Included

Chapter 13, in the description of RC Section 2.3.1, allows for optional inclusion of corrections developed after a cutoff date which is specified to avoid schedule erosion due to cumulative error-correcting activity. At Development's discretion other corrections may be included, and as they are identified, they are enumerated here. The list is not made final until the maintenance specification is complete.

Include pointers, including pointers to code, and marginal notes as for revisions and enhancements.

3 STRATEGY

Repeat Sections 3 through 3.1.3 from applicable ESs, adding new notations, terminology, and syntax used in the IS.

3.(2,3)   (Generated, Operational) Software

As for an RC and an ES, Section 3.2, Generated Software, and Section 3.3, Operational Software, are structured alike and both are present only if the product produces generated software. If the product does not produce generated software, follow the heading of Section 3.2 with the statement "not applicable" and omit subsection headings.

For whichever section or subsections are present, insert a structure diagram similar to the one in Figure 15.2 to provide a road map for the subsections which follow. Treat a single physical module in each subsection n. The structure diagram presented here is very important; it not only catalogs modules, it describes how they are related: "who calls whom."

Higher-level modules may have attributes that apply to several lower-level modules. Describe such attributes only once, at the highest practical level in your tree structure, and point to the descriptions from lower-level modules. This has two advantages: it saves writing the same thing several times, and it avoids the error of failing to state the same thing at every occurrence. This latter benefit is particularly helpful during the Use Phase when old ISs (in the form of MSs) are updated.

3.(2,3).n   (Name n) Function

For those values of n of the ES for which there *is not* a one-to-one correspondence between logical functions and physical modules, include a list of n's and pointers to where the implementation of each function is described in this IS.

3.2.17   ASSIGN Statement

See Sections 3.2.71, 74, and 101.

3.(2,3).n   (Name n) Module

For each n of the ES where there *is* a one-to-one correspondence between functional and physical modules, in place of a Name n Function heading insert a Name n Module heading and follow it with appropriate subsections as described below. Follow the title by a few overview words about how the module works. Include design objectives such as core minimization or functional independence. For generalized modules state the nature of the modules that use them.

3.3.12   RELREC Module

This module calculates a relative record number in the specified file based upon the input of a record key.

Use a unique new n for each module that has no one-to-one functional counterpart. Note that this allows automated nesting of ES- and IS-level documentation. Specify the name of each module as it is cataloged and referred to by other modules. For example, RPGOI might be the name of an RPG interpreter module. If a module already exists or is to be developed under a separate IS, merely reference it here and omit Subsections 3.(2,3).n.1 through 3.(2,3).n.4.4.4.

3.(2,3).n.1   Constraints

3.(2,3).n.1.1   Standards

Include only implementation of "how to" standards, such as the use of a flow-charting convention. Remember that standards visible to users belong in external specifications.

3.(2,3).n.1.2   Compatibility Constraints

Include any intraproduct compatibility constraints, such as restricting overlays to a maximum size or fixed location, avoiding monopolizing processors, or parameter-passing conventions. Include any statements from RCs that pertain to internal design compatibility constraints.

3.(2,3).n.1.3   Software Constraints

Specify internal, intraproduct constraints imposed by the software environment. If the module being described depends on supporting software being loaded and active, so specify. If some of the software environment is under development at the same time as the product being described, state assumptions about it that are not yet documented. Remove all such assumptions prior to IS final approval. To the degree that code listings have adequate cross-references, do not repeat such information here.

3.(2,3).n.1.4 Hardware Constraints

This section in higher-level documents specifies *what* hardware will or will not be used. Specify here *how* it will be used. For example, if a strappable modem is to be used, specify here the required strapping options.

Temporarily include assumptions about the hardware environment as for software constraints. Permanently include intraproduct, internal hardware constraints such as the number of levels and ranks of interrupts available.

Note that for both software and hardware, constraints may be voluntary as well as imposed. Voluntary constraints are willful decisions to exclude or to use particular features. Once such decisions are made, however, they become constraints.

3.(2,3).n.2 External Properties

As noted in Section 15.1 of this book, Sections 3.2.n.2 and 3.3.n.2 of an ES are its essence. They are vital to an IS, too, insofar as they complete the external description of each module viewed as an entity rather than as a part of a product. To clarify this point, recall Figure 7.9. An ES fully describes Surface P, which includes parts of some surfaces such as B and K, and completely excludes some surfaces such as C and N. Describe here in the IS all of these surfaces and parts of surfaces that are hidden in a product's corresponding ES. For example, still with respect to Figure 7.10, do not describe Surface A here at all, but merely point to its description in its ES. Describe here the part of Surface E that is not described in the ES, referencing the ES for completion of the description. Fully describe Surface J, and so on.

For each of the subsections of 3.(2,3).n.2, follow the ES format of Section 15.1 including pointers to previous IS sections and appropriate ES sections as is necessary.

Specify the flow of control between this module and the next lower level of subordinate modules, preferably in diagram form using only structured programming constructs (21). This will summarize the relationship between this module and other modules described elsewhere. See Figure 15.6 for an example.

3.(2,3).n.3   Ergonomic Properties

Following this title in separate subsections discuss how each key property is provided. Centralize discussion of each property here or point to other sections where the property is discussed.

3.(2,3).n.3.1   Security and Privacy

Describe provisions not visible to users such as file locks and data encryption.

3.(2,3).n.3.2   Reliability

Discuss provisions for reliability not visible to users such as checksumming, retrying reads and writes, and resetting voltage margins. Describe how program status is recovered after power failure in the absence of restart procedures. Explain how data input or output errors are identified. Describe error-correction techniques.

3.(2,3).n.3.3   Restartability

Describe all of the checkpoint and restart provisions and interfaces not visible to users. Separate the discussion into two parts, depending on whether the restart is automatic (Section 3.[2,3].n.3.3.1) or manual (Section 3.[2,3].n.3.3.2).

3.(2,3).n.3.4   Customizability

Describe internal structure that provides for customizing. If customizing is not to be made possible, explain why.

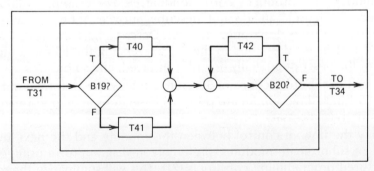

Figure 15.6   A flow-of-control diagram.

3.(2,3).n.3.4.1 Parameterization

Describe parameters used by Development to produce variants of the product and describe resulting variants.

3.(2,3).n.3.5 Performance

Discuss this topic in detail appropriate to the importance of achieving high performance, whether it be measured by speed, size, intelligibility, or a combination of these. Discuss design tradeoffs and alternatives studied and rejected.

3.(2,3).n.4 Internal Properties

3.(2,3).n.4.1 Maintainability

Describe features available to the Maintenance Function to perform its job. Include memory reserved for corrections, built-in debugging aids, interfaces to external debugging aids, and naming conventions that aid in understanding how the product works. Specify the location or the method used to specify the location in code where the module identification is stored, for both mass storage and active memory dumps.

3.(2,3).n.4.2 Algorithms

Describe the algorithm(s) used in the module using whatever notations are appropriate: flowcharts, Nassi-Shneiderman (62) or Chapin Charts (63), state diagrams, or narrative. Be sure to describe algorithms in a clear and natural manner, without allowing idiosyncrasies of the language into which they will be coded to obscure the logic of your descriptions. If appropriate, show an example illustrating the algorithm. For example, if the module is to divide two decimal integers to obtain a quotient and a remainder—without a divide instruction—show step by step how 12/5 = 2 with a remainder of 2.

If alternative algorithms were considered, discuss reasons for rejecting them in favor of the chosen algorithms.

3.(2,3).n.4.3 Internal Data

Some modules operate on data that is neither input to nor output from them. Such data is **internal data**. Describe this data here as completely as external data is described in Sections 3.(2,3).n.2.1 and 3.(2,3).n.2.3 of the ES and the IS. The completeness of this section is crucial to initial coding and subsequent maintenance of the product.

If this data is not described as thoroughly as external data, those who must maintain or enhance the module may not be able to do so without rewriting the whole module.

Observe a note of caution with regard to what is internal data. If a module passes data to or receives data from a subordinate module, even if that subordinate module is used nowhere else, such data is external data. Viewed from the subordinate module such data is clearly external. When in doubt, therefore, always take the subordinate module's view; if data is external to the subordinate module, it is external to the superior module also. As appropriate, discuss why the internal data is organized as it is and what alternatives were rejected.

3.(2,3).n.4.4   Implementation Strategy

This section contains a work plan for product (or module, for n greater than 1) implementation and a history of decisions and events pertinent to the subject product or module. Discuss why the module is organized as it is, with alternatives considered and reasons for rejecting them. For example, if macros or overlays are used, explain the benefits they produce. If design standards are normally followed, such as implementing only one function per module, or having only one entry and one exit point, but are not followed here, state why.

The two subsections that immediately follow describe testing performed by the Development Function prior to turnover of the product to the Test Function. To avoid establishing another document and to keep all developmental data in context, the test plans and test specifications for module and integration testing are placed here.

3.(2,3).n.4.4.1   Function Testing

This section deals with testing the module, listing all those situations that must be tested to determine if the module performs the function it is supposed to perform. For example, "Test that the module works when the identifier table is empty or full as well as partially full." In some cases the actual test data itself may be listed (both input data and expected output data), but in most cases refer to the test file where the test data and results of test runs can be found. Any other relevant information concerning testing should appear in this section (e.g., that a test of a higher-level module also tests this module, or that a special driver is used to test this module in a stand-alone test).

3.(2,3).n.4.4.2   Algorithm Testing

This section is analogous to Function Testing but it deals with test cases that exercise the algorithm. Given a function such as "convert a binary integer to a decimal integer," the test data prepared from the function specification alone probably will not cause every part of the algorithm to be executed, so some additional test data may be needed. If the algorithm is changed later, then new algorithm test data may be needed, but the function test data can still be used with no changes. Therefore, describe here tests that are algorithm-specific.

3.(2,3).n.4.4.3   Notes

Include here any details or remarks that do not conveniently fit elsewhere. This section is particularly useful as a repository for historical notes that might not be included if they had to conform to a structured presentation.

3.(2,3).n.4.4.4   Module Status Sheet

A **module status sheet** is a record of who did what to a module and when. During the Programming and Evaluation Phases, the module status sheets assist project personnel in keeping track of the progress of each module by recording information such as:

- An algorithm is selected.
- An algorithm is later rejected.
- A structured walk-through is conducted.
- Each test run is recorded, along with results.
- The module is integrated into the product.
- The module's ES- or IS-level specification changes, along with a reason.

Module status sheets continue to be updated during the Use Phase, as a part of the product's MS. They also provide valuable data for compilation of a project post-mortem report (see Section 7.10 of this book).

Use a form, such as the one in Figure 15.7, for module status sheets, and allow entries to be handwritten. This will encourage generation of a more thorough record.

PRODUCT NAME:		A $ K	MODULE NAME:		KEEP
PRODUCT NUMBER:		L 432	MODULE NUMBER		3.9
DATE:	NAME		STATUS		
11/25/77	S. Wilson	Algorithm defined			
2/11/78	S. Wilson	IRS OK'd by John			
2/11/78	"	Walk-through with John, Dave, Sam			
3/3/78	"	Coding complete			
3/3/78	"	Assembled, 3 syntax error			
3/4/78	"	Algorithm test data ready			
3/4/78	"	Assembled, no errors			
3/12/78	"	Tested; OK except for abnormal exit			
3/21/78	"	Tested O.K.			
4/4/78	"	Integrated with command processor			
4/24/78	BCL	modified to accomodate change in virtual file structure			
4/24/78	BCL	Reassembled OK			
4/26/78	BCL	Retested OK			
4/26/78	BCL	Reintegrated OK			
ABC COMPUTERS COMPANY			SHEET REVISION	NEXT	SHEET 1

FORM 6006 REV. 4/71

Figure 15.7   A module status sheet.

4   BACKGROUND

4.1   References

Include here, as in an RC or an ES, an entry for each reference document mentioned elsewhere in the IS. At each instance of a reference elsewhere, point to this section.

15.3 MAINTENANCE SPECIFICATION

Once a product enters the Use Phase it must be maintained: errors must be corrected and enhancements may be added. The personnel who designed, coded, and tested a product may be unavailable for consultation when maintenance is required, so a product's documentation must be sufficient to locate and correct errors and to allow enhancements to be made. The basic document used for this purpose is a Maintenance Specification (**MS**).

An MS first comes into being during the Evaluation Phase when the Maintenance Function generates it from a product's Internal Specification (IS). Maintenance does this by adding a few sections to the IS and updating a few sections of it. Figure 15.8 shows the resulting stereotypic table of contents for an MS. What follows is a discussion of the contents of those sections that transform an IS into an MS.

All code for a product will exist prior to completion of an MS. As code comes into existence, some of the documentation originally provided in the IS can better be included in code listings. To the degree this is so, material originally in the IS should be deleted from the MS and be replaced by pointers to the code listings.

1.3 Product End Items

Recall from Chapter 13 that a product's Requirements Contract (RC) first defines the product end items, in matrix form. In an MS, list each of these end items with its identifying name and number.

2.3.1 Corrections Excluded

During the Evaluation Phase the Test Function may issue trouble reports that are not resolved by the time a product is released, due to a management decision to make the product available without Test's concurrence. Such unanswered trouble reports are listed in the product's release specification and again here. Convert each into a correction request and enter it into your maintenance coordinating system.

While this section is shown as final (F) as early in a product's life cycle as the RC entry (recall Figure 13.2), it is really not contradictory to add excluded corrections at this time. The only ones allowable are those that are approved by general management at Phase V Review when the decision to release a product is made. Thus, the level of review

1	PRODUCT DESCRIPTION	T
1.1	Product Name and Numbers	T
1.1.1	Product Name	F
1.1.2	Name Abbreviations	F
1.1.3	Product Numbers	F
1.2	Brief Description of Product	F
1.2.1	Copyright Notice	F
1.2.2	Hierarchical Precedence	F
1.2.2.1	Overriding Higher Documents	F
1.3	Product End Items	F
2	MISSION	F
2.1	Revision Request Reconciliation	T
2.1.1	Revisions Excluded	F
2.1.2	Revisions Included	F
2.2	Enhancement Request Reconciliation	T
2.2.1	Enhancements Excluded	F
2.2.2	Enhancements Included	F
2.3	Correction Request Reconciliation	T
2.3.1	Corrections Excluded	F
2.3.2	Corrections Included	F
3	STRATEGY	T
3.1	Conventions	T
3.1.1	Notations	F
3.1.2	Terminology	F
3.1.3	Syntax	F
3.(2,3)	(Generated, Operational) Software	F
3.(2,3).n	(Name n) (Function, Module)	F
3.(2,3).n.1	Constraints	T
3.(2,3).n.1.1	Standards	F
3.(2,3).n.1.2	Compatibility Constraints	F
3.(2,3).n.1.3	Software Constraints	F
3.(2,3).n.1.4	Hardware Constraints	F
3.(2,3).n.2	External Properties	T
3.(2,3).n.2.1	Outputs	F
3.(2,3).n.2.2	Processes	F
3.(2,3).n.2.2.1	Invocation	F
3.(2,3).n.2.2.2	Execution	F
3.(2,3).n.2.2.3	Termination	F
3.(2,3).n.2.2.3.1	Normal Termination	F
3.(2,3).n.2.2.3.2	Abnormal Termination	F
3.(2,3).n.2.3	Inputs	F
3.(2,3).n.3	Ergonomic Properties	T
3.(2,3).n.3.1	Security and Privacy	F
3.(2,3).n.3.2	Reliability	F
3.(2,3).n.3.3	Restartability	F
3.(2,3).n.3.3.1	Automatic Restart	F
3.(2,3).n.3.3.2	Manual Restart	F

Figure 15.8 Stereotype maintenance specification contents.

3.(2,3).n.3.4	Customizability	F
3.(2,3).n.3.4.1	Parameterization	F
3.(2,3).n.3.5	Performance	F
3.(2,3).n.4	Internal Properties	T
3.(2,3).n.4.1	Maintainability	F
3.(2,3).n.4.2	Algorithms	F
3.(2,3).n.4.3	Internal Data	F
3.(2,3).n.4.4	Implementation Strategy	F
3.(2,3).n.4.4.1	Function Testing	F
3.(2,3).n.4.4.2	Algorithm Testing	F
3.(2,3).n.4.4.3	Notes	F
3.(2,3).n.4.4.4	Module Status Sheet	F
3.(2,3).n.4.4.5	Listings	F
4	BACKGROUND	T
4.1	References	F
4.2	Post-Mortem	F
4.3	Data Directory	F
4.4	Replacement Cross-Reference	F
5	DELIVERY AND INSTALLATION	T
5.1	Provisions for Protection	F
5.2	Installation Resources	F
5.2.1	Installation Procedures	F
5.3	Media	F

Figure 15.8 (Continued)

provided is consistent with RC review and the approval of an RC change at this point in time would be of no practical value.

As time goes by and corrections are provided for these errors, update the MS and move them from here to Section 2.3.2.

ER #289: Delete does not give the full file name in the error message for a file in a generic family for which the correct password is not specified.

2.3.2. Corrections Included

Add any correction requests answered at Development's discretion between IS completion and product release.

3.(2,3).n.1.3 Software Constraints

From the product's release specification, add the correction level required for all supporting software.

3.(2,3).n.1.4   Hardware Constraints

Also from the product's release specification, add the correction level required for all supporting hardware.

3.(2,3).n.4.4   Implementation Strategy

Add to Subsections 3.(2,3).n.4.4.1 through 3.(2,3).n.4.4.4 any data helpful to Maintenance in understanding the inner workings of the product at an indeterminate future date.

3.2.n.4.4.5   Listings

The code listing of each module of a product logically belongs with the description of it. Listings, however, can be cumbersome and bulky to incorporate directly into another document. Either include listings in this section, perhaps on microfiche, or point to them here. If listings are pointed to rather than included, take extreme care to make references precise and to keep them current throughout the Use Phase.

Recall that all of Section 3.2 of an MS deals with generated software. It is probably impractical to include listings of all possible generated software, so do not try. Instead include enough examples to show all formats and representative contents.

3.3.n.4.4.5   Listings

As for generated software, include operational software listings here or point to them here. Be sure to include every subroutine and overlay. Record every enhancement request implementation and correction request solution in the listings through marginal notes and/or sequenced line identifiers coded to indicate changes.

4.2   Post-Mortem

A post-mortem is a record of what went right and wrong during a product's life. This section is a gold mine of planning information for use by Development during early phases of the lives of new products, and provides helfpul background information for use by Maintenance during the Use Phase. Both of these uses capitalize on past experience and save valuable time and expense when exploited.

A post-mortem is as free form as possible so that every item of information that might prove useful can be included. It contains contributions from each Development project member and it is therefore Development's responsibility to produce it as described in Section 10 of Chapter 7. Maintenance incorporates it into the MS, adding or deleting information as appropriate.

4.3 Data Directory

A **data directory** is a list of (1) every data item input to or output from the product or referenced by more than one module, and (2) every module where it is used. For such a list to be used reliably, it must be absolutely complete; a single missed reference can cause an error if a datum is changed by Maintenance.

If you can possibly produce and maintain a data directory, include it here. It can cut maintenance costs substantially.

4.4 Replacement Cross-Reference

As modules are corrected, revised, and enhanced over time the combinations that work correctly together can become quite complex. Therefore for each module that cannot operate correctly with all levels of associated modules, include a list of acceptable (or, alternatively, unacceptable) companion modules. Initiate this section with data from Section 4 of a product's release specification (see Section 15.4, following).

5.1 Provisions for Protection

Define precisely where and how each product end item is marked to provide ownership protection. If you have standards for such markings, merely refer to those standards wherever they apply.

5.2 Installation Resources

For both Section 5.2 and Subsection 5.2.1, Installation Procedures, include the relevant material from the product's release specification. If Maintenance's archival procedures and maintenance tools differ from those presented in the release bulletin for use by Support or by customers, describe them here.

5.3 Media

Include the media statement from the product's release bulletin, being specific about number and length of tape reels or disc packs. If archival media differ, describe them also.

As the Use Phase passes, the MS is continually updated. Good configuration management dictates that changes be controlled and recorded. Therefore no change is made to an MS unless it is the result of revision, enhancement, or correction requests. Mark each such change by a notation such as:

W)DISC I/O ERROR (e), SECTOR sssssss.
where

> *sssssss = sector on which the disc error has occurred*
> *e = error; possible values of e are:*
> *1 = read error*
> *3 = read flag (bad sector or "blot")*
> *4 = read fault (disc drive off-line) (RPE 749)*
> *S = write flag (bad sector)*
> *T = write fault (disc drive off-line) (RPE 749)*

Such a notation is used also in code listings so that the result of each change is fully recorded. Module status sheets and function testing sections are augmented for every change and the product end items list is kept current to show proper version and update levels. Take extreme care in the configuration management of an MS for it is *the* definitive audit trail for a product once it has entered the Use Phase.

15.4   RELEASE SPECIFICATION

When a product is transmitted from Development to Test and again from Test to Services for release to users, it is accompanied by a document called a release specification. It contains precise product identification information, including a complete structure diagram for all modules; hardware requirements, including change levels; a list of relevant publications; and a list of outstanding deficiencies. Services builds a release bulletin from the aggregate of release specifications for products contained in a release. And Maintenance augments each maintenance specification from the corresponding release specification.

Figure 15.9 is a stereotype table of contents for a Release Specification (**RS**) generated according to the following format. Describe only one product in each RS.

1	PRODUCT DESCRIPTION
1.1	Product Name and Numbers
1.1.1	Product Name
1.1.2	Name Abbreviations
1.1.3	Product Numbers
1.2	Brief Description of Product
1.3	Product End Items
1.4	Conversion and Installation Aids
2	PRODUCT DEFICIENCIES
2.1	Product Restrictions
2.2	Correction Request Reconciliation
2.2.1	Corrections Excluded
2.2.2	Corrections Included
3	INSTALLATION
3.1	Hardware Requirements
3.2	Software Requirements
3.3	Installation Procedures
3.4	Verification
4	REPLACEMENT CROSS-REFERENCE

Figure 15.9   Stereotype release specification contents.

1   PRODUCT DESCRIPTION

1.1   Product Name and Numbers

1.1.1   Product Name

State the complete name of the product, per Section 1.1.1 of its Requirements Contract.

1.1.2   Name Abbreviations

State all name abbreviations actually used to mark the product, by the product to identify itself to users, and in publications pertaining to the product. Do not include any names not so used even if they are included in the product's Requirements Contract.

1.1.3   Product Numbers

Enter the top-level product numbers per Section 1.1.3 of the product's Requirements Contract.

1.2   Brief Description of Product

Repeat Section 1.2 of the product's Requirements Contract, paraphrasing as necessary to restrict the information to one product.

1.3   Product End Items

Provide a complete structure diagram for *all* modules of the product, either in block diagram form or as an ordered list with pointers. Indicate each item—source code, object code, listing, macro—and its distribution restrictions. All of this information will be available from a good configuration management system such as a bill of materials processor; see Figure 15.10. In this figure module identifiers and linkages correspond to topics covered in Section 5 of Chapter 17, Configuration Management.

List all publications that describe the product. This list includes but is not limited to the publications end items and appropriate support end items mentioned in the product's publications and support plans. Include full identification numbers.

(a)   Update of System Support Programs Reference Manual, #44-B800-702-1B

(b)   Update of Message Manual, #44-B800-601-1B

Alternatively, include this information in a bill of materials as in Figure 15.10.

1.4   Conversion and Installation Aids

List all conversion and installation aids developed specifically for the product; these are mentioned in the product's support plan. Include other conversion and installation aids that are mandatory or that are described in subsequent procedures even if they are not new. Include full identification numbers.

MAINT (B9914C) is required for installation. PAKON (B8161A) is required to establish the pack-type identification for all drives on a VSOS system prior to building the drive type table with SETCOM (B4322B).

---

2   PRODUCT DEFICIENCIES

2.1   Product Restrictions

Repeat Section 3.4 from the product's Requirements Contract.

ID	Name	Code	Item
#L301AL301A	A$K	ASN	PRODUCT
IL301AL301A	A$K	ASN	IRS
ML301AL301A	A$K	ASN	MAINT. SPEC.
PL301AL301A	A$K	SSN	POR
RL301AL301A	A$K	ASN	SRS
EL301AL301A	A$K	ASN	ERS
+L321AL301A	USER INTERFACE	ASN	ASSEMBLY
EL321AL301A	USER INTERFACE	ASN	ERS
OL331AL301A	UPDATE PROCESSOR	ASN	MODULE–OBJECT
SL331AL301A	UPDATE PROCESSOR	SSN	MODULE–SOURCE
EL331AL301A	UPDATE PROCESSOR	ASN	ERS
+L341AL321A	COMMAND PROCESSOR	ASN	ASSEMBLY
+L351AL321A	SYNTAX ANALYZER	ASN	MODULE
OL371AL341A	ADD COMMAND	ASN	MODULE–OBJECT
SL371AL341A	ADD COMMAND	SSN	MODULE–SOURCE
OL381AL341A	A$K COMMAND	ASN	MODULE–OBJECT
SL381AL341A	A$K COMMAND	SSN	MODULE–SOURCE
OL391AL341A	BUILD COMMAND	ASN	MODULE–OBJECT
SL391AL341A	BUILD COMMAND	SSN	MODULE–SOURCE
OL401AL341A	DONE COMMAND	ASN	MODULE–OBJECT
SL401AL341A	DONE COMMAND	SSN	MODULE–SOURCE
OL411AL341A	HELP COMMAND	ASN	MODULE–OBJECT
SL411AL341A	HELP COMMAND	SSN	MODULE–SOURCE
OL421AL341A	KEEP COMMAND	ASN	MODULE–OBJECT
SL421AL341A	KEEP COMMAND	SSN	MODULE–SOURCE
OL431AL341A	LET COMMAND	ASN	MODULE–OBJECT
SL431AL341A	LET COMMAND	SSN	MODULE–SOURCE
OL441AL341A	MAKE COMMAND	ASN	MODULE–OBJECT
SL441AL341A	MAKE COMMAND	SSN	MODULE–SOURCE
OL451AL341A	PURGE COMMAND	ASN	MODULE–OBJECT
SL451AL341A	PURGE COMMAND	SSN	MODULE–SOURCE
OL461AL341A	REPORT COMMAND	ASN	MODULE–OBJECT
SL461AL341A	REPORT COMMAND	SSN	MODULE–SOURCE
BL471AL301A	REFERENCE MANUAL	ASN	PUBLICATION
BL481AL301A	REFERENCE BOOKLET	ASN	PUBLICATION
BL491AL301A	OPERATOR MANUAL	ASN	PUBLICATION
BL501AL301A	MESSAGE MANUAL	ASN	PUBLICATION

Figure 15.10 Partial bill of materials for A$K.

2.2 Correction Request Reconciliation

2.2.1 Corrections Excluded

List all requests which will still be unresolved when the product is turned over to Test. Hopefully you can state "none," but expediency often dictates leaving a few minor errors uncorrected. Include trouble reports generated during A-Test.

(a) PTR #5561. DISPLAY does not recognize a service request interrupt when skipping records based on the SKIP or IKEY parameters.
(b) PTR #6456. INDEX does not always index the first of a group of duplicate records if a DENSITY parameter greater than 1 is specified.

2.2.2 Corrections Included

List and describe all requests submitted against a preceding release of the product, or previously existing modules used in the product and which are corrected in this release. Do not include trouble reports submitted against new code during A-Test as they will most likely be eliminated during B-Test. If they are not, Test will provide a supplementary list.

3 INSTALLATION

3.1 Hardware Requirements

Sections 3.(2,3).n.1.3 and 3.(2,3).n.1.4 of a product's Internal Specification state hardware and software needed to run a product, and Section 5.2 of its External Specification identifies hardware and software needed for installation. In Section 3.1 of an RS refine the identification of hardware resources to exact revision levels required by customers or to be used during B-Test. Subtle differences can yield future errors and a record of a known-to-be-good environment will aid future error correction.

3.2 Software Requirements

Treat this section like Section 3.1, but for software. Identify resources by exact version and update levels. If any temporary corrections are patched into any of the software (this is a terrible practice, but it does happen), enumerate the patches by correction number.

3.3 Installation Procedures

Refine the statement made in Section 5.2.1 of the product's External Specification to include physical module names and exact locations.

The procedures as stated here must be totally complete; they may, however, point to other documents.

3.4   Verification

Describe a test program or test procedure, including all of its inputs and outputs, to be distributed with the product to verify that it operates correctly once it is installed. If code is to be distributed for this purpose, include complete identification of it.

4   REPLACEMENT CROSS-REFERENCE

For all product end items listed in Section 1.3 specify previous modules that can be directly replaced with new modules with no known impact on users. Maintain this cross-reference at the version or product level, as updates by definition replace their predecessors. Mention modules only where a cross-reference exists; that is, do not list a module and state "none." Note that this replacement applies to publications as well as code.

Generation of all sections of an RS is the responsibility of development at the time a product is transmitted for B-Test, except for Section 2.2.2 which Test updates at the time a product is transmitted to Services for distribution.

16

Reports

Reports serve several purposes. First, they provide status information to keep management informed and to establish communication between several functions. Second, they provide an opportunity to observe an out-of-bounds condition (or one about to go out of bounds) and seek corrective action before much harm is done. Third, they provide a retrospective record from which to predict the future.

16.1 BUDGET ALLOCATION SUMMARY

In Section 14.1 a living budget is defined as a statement of how you plan to spend the money available to your operation. The budget allocation summary described here is such a living budget, one which is easy to maintain if you use Budget Allocations (BAs) for all work as defined in Section 14.2.

In the following description of a BA summary and how it is used, the unit of measure is man-days of direct labor. The rationale for using this unit is presented in Section 14.2. If you need or prefer to use money as a unit of measure, all of the logic presented here remains valid.

Figure 14.5 is repeated here as Figure 16.1. The BA summary in this figure functions as follows:

Column	Use
①	*Budget Reference* The identification number associated with a line item in the approved (baseline) budget. This number will have been associated with the item since the time the item was first proposed and thus is the primary reference number. It may be followed by a descriptive title to aid recollection.

**Project Budget Request Summary for Operating Systems Unit for Calendar Year
1977—4/29/77**

①	②	③	④	⑤	⑥	⑦	⑧	⑨
Budget Reference	Project Number	Base-line Budget	Working Budget	Allocated This Year	Spent This Year	Forecast	Variance	Notes
039B	B15	410	410	185	161	443	−33	
046B	B00	60	60	64	64	64	−4	1
---B	B40	0	213	80	92	200	13	2
200F	—	120	120	0	0	120	0	
211F	B20	485	300	110	87	305	−5	
211F	B21	0	185	70	56	180	5	
055L	B10	175	22	22	22	22	0	2,3
Total		1250	1310	541	490	1334	−24	

Notes:
(1) Complete.
(2) $153K transferred from 055L to B40 per VGM 2/28/77; 60 more authorized by RCM.
(3) Discontinued.

Figure 16.1   A budget allocation summary.

② *Project Number*   The project number assigned to a BA once it is approved.

③ *Baseline Budget*   The approved budget; it does not change.

④ *Working Budget*   The current working budget. The column total may be more or less than the total of Column 1. Items come and go as time passes and conditions change.

⑤ *Allocated This Year*   The sum of all allocations made during the budget period. Due to unauthorized overspending, an entry may be less than the corresponding amount spent. Due to conscious allocation, an entry may be more than either corresponding budget amount.

⑥ *Spent This Year*   The amount spent during the period covered by the baseline budget. An entry may be more or less than any budgeted or encumbered amount on the same row.

⑦ *Forecast*   The current expectation of all costs, both past and future, to be incurred during the budget period; normally the sum of Columns 2 and 4 from a BA; the maximum of Columns 4, 5, and 6 if no other data is provided.

⑧   *Variance*   The difference between Columns 4 and 7. If positive in the Total row, this amount may be allocated without exceeding the current working budget.

⑨   *Notes*   Every exceptional entry is accompanied by one or more notes explaining the exception.

The data contained in the example shown in Figure 16.1 explains further how a BA summary works and why it can be called a living budget:

Budget	Explanation
039B	This item is forecasted to exceed budget by 33 man-days.
046B	This item is complete and the data provided for it in Columns 5 through 7 will not change in the future. Regardless of how much has been allocated prior to closing, Column 5 is set equal to Column 6; this automatically returns any surplus to the allocable pool (Column 4 minus Column 5) or removes from it any overage. The overage remains in Column 8 unless it is cancelled by transferring 4 units from another item in the Working Budget. For example, 4 units could be transferred from 200F in Column 4 if the entry in Column 7 for 200F could honestly be lowered 4 units.
---B	As shown by Note 2, project B40 is exbudget, so a dummy Budget Reference of ---B is used. The origin of its funding is preserved in the BA summary no matter what happens in the future. The project is forecast to be completed 13 units under budget.
200F	The absence of an entry in Column 2 indicates that no BA has yet been initiated. The equality of Columns 3, 4, and 7 indicates an expectation to spend all 120 units before 1977 is over.
211F	This item supports two projects, B20 and B21. Currently B20 is forecast to exceed budget by 5 units and B21 is forecast to be under by 5 for a break-even forecast for all of 211F. Note that 211F was anticipated to fund a single project but that supporting two (or more) simply calls for keeping good records. Note also that B21 is the project shown in Figure 14.6.

055L   This item has been cancelled. At the moment of cancellation the Working Budget was 175 and the Forecast was 22, resulting in a Variance of 153. Per Note 2, this variance was given to project B40. To balance the record, the Working Budget for 055L was reduced to the amount spent.

Total   Note that the Working Budget is 60 units greater than the Baseline Budget and that this difference is accounted for in Note 2. Column 8 carries the most important message: unless corrective action is taken, and assuming forecasts are accurate, there will be a cumulative budget overrun of 24 units at year's end. Most of the problem is in project B15 which is clearly seen by scanning Column 8.

One more note about Figure 16.1 is worth observing. Items in the report are sorted first according to budget program (the terminal letter in each Budget Reference), second according to budget line item (the three-digit number with which each Budget Reference begins), third according to organizational unit identifier (the *B* that begins each Project Number represents the Operating Systems Unit), and fourth according to sequence of BA initiation (the last two digits of each Project Number). Several such reports can be consolidated, either in this sort sequence or another, depending on the needs of the report recipients.

Never lose sight of the fact that a BA summary is a management tool, not a financial accounting tool. It can be used for management status reporting, but not for financial status reporting. Its best use is in decision making, in helping to determine what resources are available for allocation among several projects and in predicting the budget performance of several projects as a group, not individually. For predicting an individual project's budget performance, use a trend chart (Section 16.5) or a manpower summary (Section 14.4).

16.2 SCHEDULE NOTICE SUMMARY

A schedule notice is a plan for a single design-space variable, time. An individual schedule notice is a plan for a relatively short period of time: from the time it is issued until the next schedule notice is issued. In an ideal world a project would proceed from beginning to end according to its original schedule and each schedule notice would merely record completion of each milestone as it is passed. Not many projects proceed as in an ideal world, however, and milestones are

SCHEDULE CHANGE NOTICE SUMMARY

```
'-----------------------------1977----------------------'----1978---'
'                                                                    '
 1   2   3   4    5   6   7    8   9   10  11  12   1   2   3        '
 7...4...4...1....6...3...1....5...2....7...4...2....6...3...3..      '
'                                                                    '
'  P   P   E                       B       P            C            '
'  B   O   R                       T       A            O            '
'  R   R   S                       B       D            N            '
'  -   -   -                       -       -            F            '
'P10 D10   D30                    T30     P30          ----          '
'                                                                    '
'  b   r   e                       t       p                         '
'                                                                    '
06/01 '.B...R.....E....................t.......p                     '
'                          *                                         '
06/29 '...........................................t........p         '
'                                    *                               '
08/03 '...........................................t........p         '
'                                       *                            '
08/31 '...........................................t........p         '
'                                    *                               '
10/05 '...........................................t........p   cccc  '
'                                      *                             '
11/02 '............................................t.......p   cccc  '
'                                        *                           '
11/30 '............................................t......p    cccc  '
'                                         *                          '
01/04 '............................................T......p    cccc  '
'                                          *                         '
02/01 '............................................P    cccc         '
'                                          *                         '
'                                                                    '
 ------------------------------------------------------------ -----
```

        PROJECT: L236   PROJECT MANAGER: C. Linder

Figure 16.2 A schedule notice summary.

frequently rescheduled. As described in Section 14.8, a Schedule Notice (**SN**) is the tool for doing this.

An individual SN or even a stack of them does not quickly convey the trend of a project's schedule plan. This is the job of the schedule notice summary. A **schedule notice summary** graphically traces the schedule history of a project and allows both project and functional management to analyze trends in order to predict the need for corrective action.

Figure 16.2 is a simple, partly automated form of SN summary as used at ABC Computers. At ABC, a word processor is used once a month to record the latest SN data for each active project. Historical data is saved on cassettes so that each time an SN summary is generated, another row is added for each project. One objective of a good SN summary is that it be understandable without reference to an elaborate legend or supporting notes. You may be able to deduce all information contained in Figure 16.2 before you read the following analysis; try it and see.

Figure 16.2 has a horizontal time scale with each division representing one week. Five milestones are plotted: PBR (a PBR is ABC's budget allocation) approved, POR (ABC's requirements contract) approved, ERS (external specification) approved, B-Test begun, and Product Availability Date (PAD). The month shown in the configurator is also included, as a series of Cs spanning the month. Each milestone is assigned a descriptive character. The trail left by each of these

```
                          SCHEDULE CHANGE NOTICE SUMMARY


        '-------------------------1977-----------------------'----1978---'
        '                                                                '
        ' 1   2   3   4    5   6   7    8   9   10  11  12    1   2   3  '
        ' 7..4...4...1....6...3...1....5...2....7...4...2....6...3...3.. '
        '                                                                '
        '   P           P           E                 B           P      '
        '   B           O           R                 T           A      '
        '   R           R           S                 B           D      '
        '   -           -           -                 -           -      '
        '   P10         D10         D30               T30         P30    '
        '                                                                '
        '   b           r           e                 t           p      '
06/01   '...B..........r........e                     t           p      '
        '                        *                                       '
06/29   '..............r.......e...................t                p      '
        '                      *                                         '
08/03   '.......................r......e...........t                p      '
        '                              *                                 '
08/31   '.......................r.......e..........t                p      '
        '                               *                                '
10/05   '............................r.......e............t....p         '
        '                                    *                           '
11/02   '............................R.......e...........t....p          '
        '                                            *                   '
11/30   '...............................e.........t....p                 '
        '                                         *                      '
01/04   '..................................E..............t...p          '
        '                                                 *              '

        -----------------------------------------------------------------
        PROJECT:   C542              PROJECT MANAGER:   T. Wilbur
```

Figure 16.3 A schedule notice summary for a project in trouble.

characters as rows are added to the summary shows the trend of schedule predictions. A vertical line indicates no deviation, while a line sloping down and to the right indicates slippage. The report date is plotted with an asterisk. The slope of the report date locus provides a base of reference for slippage; any line with the same slope represents day-for-day slippage! The column of dates at the left in Figure 16.2 repeats the information given by the asterisks, but it makes the determination of report dates quick and easy without adding much clutter to the summary. The most subtle feature of Figure 16.2, which you may not yet have noticed, is the use of upper and lower case letters for a milestone. A lower case letter indicates a forecasted event and an upper case letter indicates a completed event. How then, you may ask, can a milestone to the left of the report date (e.g., t on line 11/30) be

```
                      SCHEDULE CHANGE NOTICE SUMMARY


        '--------------------------1977---------------------'----1978---'
        '                                                              '
        ' 1   2   3   4   5   6   7   8   9  10  11  12   1   2   3   '
        ' 7...4...4...1....6...3...1....5...2....7...4...2....6...3...3..'
        '                                                              '
        '   P   P           E           B       P   C                  '
        '   B   O           R           T       A   O                  '
        '   R   R           S           B       D   N                  '
        '   -   -           -           -       -       F              '
        ' P10 D10         D30         T30     P30  ----                '
        '                                                              '
        '   b   r           e           t       p                      '
        '                                                              '
 06/01  '..B....R................e.................t........p           '
        '                        *                                     '
 06/29  '.........................E................t........p           '
        '                         *                                    '
 08/03  '.............................................t......p          '
        '                                  *                           '
 08/31  '...........................................t......p cccc       '
        '                                    *                         '
 10/05  '...........................................t......p cccc       '
        '                                     *                        '
 11/02  '..........................................t......p cccc        '
        '                                      *                       '
 11/30  '..........................................T....p cccc          '
        '                                        *                     '
 01/04  '........................................................ccpc   '
        '                                                    *          '
        -----------------------------------------------------------------

    PROJECT:   B266              PROJECT MANAGER:   A. R. Jackson
```

Figure 16.4 A schedule notice summary for a typical project.

shown as forecast? Simple; the SN originator was delinquent in reporting a new, consistent date and the report shows it!

In spite of serious slippage in beginning B-Test, the project shown in Figure 16.2 was completed satisfactorily. How does a project in real trouble look? Figure 16.3 shows such a project. Finally, Figure 16.4 shows a typical project. If you were responsible for releasing the product, would you be comfortable with the configurator date shown in Figure 16.4?

16.3   MILESTONES DUE REPORT

A Milestones due report has as its sole purpose reminding project managers to update their schedule notices (SNs) before any milestones become overdue. If a milestone does become overdue it is only because a project manager is lax in maintaining his SNs. A milestones due report is a tool to help him avoid becoming delinquent.

Unfortunately not every project manager keeps his SNs up to date, even with a milestones due report to remind him. Thus there is a second part to a milestones due report for both project managers and their supervisors: the milestones overdue report. Sending this report to a project manager's supervisor gives the supervisor an opportunity to apply an appropriate reminder to a delinquent project manager. Circulating collective milestones due and milestones overdue reports to all project managers and their supvisors either adds peer pressure to keep SNs up to date or antagonizes recipients; you can do it or not do it as suits your environment.

A milestones due report is issued as frequently as your project managers feel is helpful, but not less often than an SN summary (see Section 16.2). A milestones due report precedes your SN summary by enough time to bring all milestones up to date in the summary.

The essential contents of a milestones due report are, for each milestone included: milestone name, milestone number, forecast date. Include only major milestones and trust that others will be updated when the major milestones are. The forecasted date for each milestone included should lie between the report date and some future date that does not precede the next report date. The time it takes to react to a milestones due report varies from environment to environment, so you will have to experiment with report frequency and the time ahead for milestones to be included. Within a report, sort milestones according to project manager and then according to other keys, such as project and product line. Add a field in the report for each key. Figure 16.5 is an example of a monthly milestones due report at ABC Computers.

A milestones overdue report is the same as a milestones due report except that there is one more datum per milestone: the amount of time by which the milestone is overdue. Figure 16.6 is an ABC Computers milestones overdue report in which the delinquency is measured in days and the primary sort key is due date, earliest first for emphasis. You might want to allow a grace period of, say, five days before including an overdue milestone. This would compensate for possible variations in reporting and processing cycles. The last milestone in Figure 16.6 actually might have been met without the informaton reaching the preparer of the report and there is no need to unnecessarily reprimand D. Malcolm. A few days' grace would save such embarrassment or aggravation.

You may have noticed that both milestones due and milestones overdue can easily be included in a single report formatted like a milestones overdue report but having both positive and negative variances. Such a report might be titled "Milestones Due" with the variance column titled "Days until Due." Whether or not you use such a combined report depends on the relative motivational effects of alternate forms of reporting. Your sole objective in using a milestones

MILESTONES DUE—FEBRUARY 1978

RESPONSIBILITY	MILESTONE NAME	PROJECT #/ MILESTONE #	FORE-CASTED DATE
Z. Albah	POR submitted	E141/D10	2/12
M. Anderson	B-Test begun	E050/T30	2/15
B. Nix	ERS approved	E093/D30	2/15
R. Gandolph	ERS approved	C013/D30	2/15
A. Jeffries	POR submitted	C421/D10	2/12
D. Malcolm	PAD	C336/P30	2/19
G. Becker	PAD	A044/P30	2/17
	PDD	A044/S20	2/17
V. Belcher	B-Test begun	B127/T30	2/15
	B-Test begun	B128/T30	2/15
	B-Test begun	B610/T30	2/15

Figure 16.5 A milestones due report.

MILESTONES OVERDUE—1/27/78

RESPONSIBILITY	MILESTONE NAME	PROJECT #/ MILESTONE #	FORE-CASTED DATE	VAR.
R. Gershon	POR submitted	D410/D10	12/14	−44
D. Malcolm	ERS approved	C336/D30	12/30	−28
M. Anderson	ERS approved	B050/D30	1/12	−15
D. Malcolm	B-Test begun	C336/T30	1/26	−1

Figure 16.6   A milestones overdue report.

due report is to keep SNs up-to-date, so do whatever produces the best results.

16.4   PROJECT PROGRESS REPORT

Trend charts and schedule notice summaries provide visibility of cost and schedule progress but say little about technical progress. They also say little about why more or less progress occurs than is planned. These missing elements of reporting are covered by a **progress report,** a narrative description of activities and events affecting a development project over a period of time significantly shorter than the project's duration.

Before you decide of what a progress report should consist or when it should be generated, think about why you should ask for it. Usually it will be because someone, possibly yourself, has established a habit of reporting all kinds of progress at some periodic interval—weekly, biweekly, monthly, or quarterly. Such reports are designed to communicate status; to let someone in particular or several people in general know that all is going well, or if not, what is being done about it. Such reports should *not* solicit help, and actions by anyone except their authors should *not* be taken as a direct result of them. If this happens, accurate and timely status reporting is undermined by the the author's fear that his readers will interfere. Be sure, therefore, that your progress reporting system is understood by everyone who participates in it—as author or reader—and that it is supportive of open status reporting.

A progress report puts current progress in perspective with past and future progress. Both the writing of it and the reading of it foster a review of requirements and objectives and reaffirm the direction a project is taking. If there is any question about maintaining a course of direction, you raise it in a progress report and simultaneously state what is being done to evaluate continuing on the present course.

Begin a well-structured progress report with a bridge to the past by summarizing milestones that have been met and other events that have occurred since the last report. This is the progress from which the report takes its name, but do not stop there. Go on to evaluate the actual progress versus the planned goals for the reporting period. Mention any threats to successful completion of planned goals for the coming time interval. Acknowledge as problems every missed goal and every threatened goal. For every problem, state a solution that has already been provided, a proposed solution, or a list of alternative solutions under study. Make sure your readers know which problems are under your control and which are not. For those that are not, make sure they know what actions you are taking or plan to take to bring them under control; if you do not, they may offer help you would rather not receive! Conclude a report with a statement of short-range plans to maintain a project's progress according to its long-range plans. Confine the plans reported there to events expected to occur during the next reporting interval and to correcting the problems mentioned earlier.

Maintain continuity in your progress reports. Report each item planned in the previous report as either completed or as a problem because it has not been completed as planned. When reporting an event as completed, unless it occurred as planned, state the implication of the deviation in terms of over- or underrunning budget or schedule or whatever other effect it may have produced. For each problem mentioned, report it as solved or state your plan for solving it. Avoid surprises; mentioning a problem in a progress report first is a sure way to convert a status report into an action request. Accompany each problem description with enough background to remind readers that you warned them of the problem in a previous communication.

In spite of all the recommendations above, keep a progress report as brief as possible. Cover only the most significant happenings and problems. Be sure, however, to include all significant items even if you assume they are of common knowledge. A report must be complete since it becomes a permanent record for future reference, as when you compile a post-mortem for a maintenance specification.

The material discussed above comprises the essence of a progress report. Depending on the frequency with which you generate progress reports and the distribution you give them, you may include as appendices other reports such as manpower summaries, schedule notice summaries, and trend charts.

How often you submit a progress report depnds in part on your reporting environment: who wants status information and how often he wants it. It also depends on the duration of a project. Weekly may not be too often for a critical, three-month project and quarterly may not be too seldom for a low priority eighteen-month project. You may also want to report varying amounts of detail for the same project at different intervals: a basic biweekly status report with a schedule notice summary and trend chart appended monthly, for example.

16.5   TREND CHARTS

Over the years many people have sought ways to graphically portray cost and schedule data such that management could determine progress and approve changes if progress did not meet expectation. Many of their efforts were directed toward presenting some sort of "percentage of completion," based on such assumptions as:

1. If 37% of the *planned* budget is spent, the project is 37% complete.
2. If 48% of the *planned* duration of the project has passed, the project is 48% complete.
3. If some weighted combination of the above *planned* variables reduces to 81%, the project is 81% complete.

Note the emphasis on *planned* and on an *index* (percentage) of completion. This is dangerous, because it leads to oversimplified projections based on data which may bear little resemblance to reality. As Figure 16.7 shows, the expenditure of effort on a typical project is nonlinear, as is the time-spacing of major milestones; attempts to project completion based on simple, usually linear, extrapolations of data at intermediate points can lead to erroneous conclusions.

You can avoid such pitfalls by drawing heavily on experience to predict the future. Figure 16.7 is a set of simple cost versus schedule plots for projects of different sizes. You can build such a set of curves for past projects and use them to plan future projects. As you collect charts of actual data you will note that the curves make up a family as is shown in Figure 16.7. Take the family differences that vary with cost (as measured by manpower assigned) and duration into account as you plan. Note, for instance, that up to the time of requirements

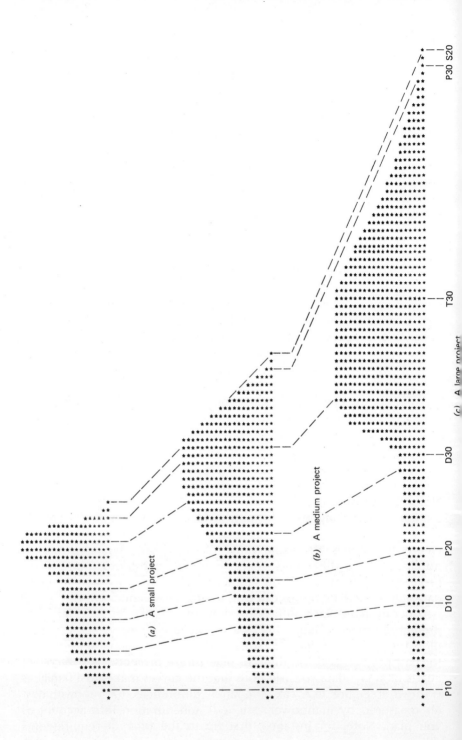

(a) A small project

(b) A medium project

(c) A large project

P10   D10   P20   D30   T30   P30 S20

approval (P20) large and small projects take roughly the same amount of time, but that they differ considerably after that point. If the ordinate were absolute rather than relative manpower, you would also see a similar amount of effort expended. This is due mostly to the relatively fixed overhead associated with both large and small projects that dominates both cost and time at the beginning and end, but not at the middle, of a project.

Declare several of the milestones from your stereotypic network and schedule notice to be standard milestones for reporting progress. The following set (using the same nomenclature as is used in Section 14.6, Network Plan, and Section 14.7, Schedule Notice) are recommended:

P10   Budget Allocation Approved
D10   Requirements Contract Submitted
P20   Requirements Contract Approved
D30   External Specification Approved
T30   B-Test Begun
P30   Product Available for Distribution
S20   Product Distributed

Figure 16.8 shows these milestones for planned data along with partial actual data for A$K plotted in a trend chart. Note that for emphasis a circle is drawn with its center at each planned datum and passes through the corresponding actual datum. Also note that an arrow is drawn from the planned datum to the actual datum. The size of each circle gives a relative, subjective mesure of the magnitude of the cumulative deviation between planned and actual performance. The direction of the arrow defines the nature of the deviation:

Pointing up and to the right, behind schedule and over budget.
Pointing up and to the left, ahead of schedule but over budget.
Pointing down and to the left, ahead of schedule and below budget.
Pointing down and to the right, below budget, but behind schedule.

Such a chart communicates cost and schedule progress simultaneously and shows trends according to both magnitude and direction. It does not, however, quantify trends in a way that has any significant potential for leading to invalid projections. Submit an updated copy of this trend chart with each periodic progress report, to show actual data for each milestone as it is reached. Avoid extrapolation based on partial progress; that is, do not extend your actual curve beyond the last completed milestone. Doing so is more likely to convey false hopes of meeting the next milestone than to indicate true progress. Rely instead on the frequency of milestones to provide sufficient resolution. Ideally you can have at least one planned milestone per reporting period. This is certainly true when you present updated trend charts at each phase review, for by definition they occure at major milestones.

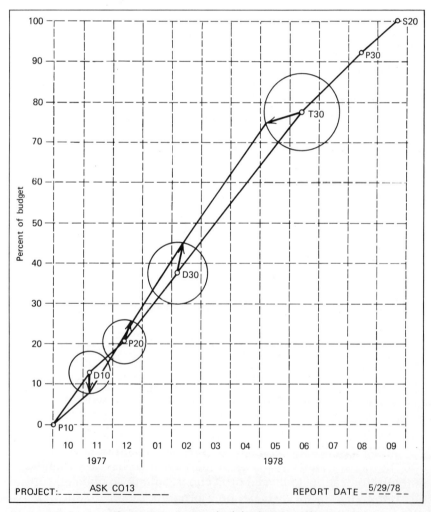

Figure 16.8   A cost-schedule chart for A$K.

The above discussion assumes you are equally interested in cost and schedule performance. If you are more interested in one parameter than the other, as well you might be if a project is under budget but far behind schedule, you can isolate the critical variable and report its trend as shown in Figure 16.3. This type of chart shows the trend of actual data and also the quality of a project manager's ability to make predictions. On this chart, each reported milestone traces a separate curve from the time it is first reported until it is complete. A slope to the right forecasts slippage while a slope to the left forecasts completion ahead of schedule. A straight, vertical line indicates expected performance according to plan. Since each curve ends at an actual datum, the way the curve approaches that datum says a lot about the accuracy (truthfulness?) of the reporting. A nearly veritical curve with a sharp turn to the right at the end is highly suspect. So is a nearly vertical curve just to the right of a curve with a high slope to the right; it is extremely rare for a late milestone to be followed by an on-time milestone when both are compared to the original plan.

16.6   MAINTENANCE REQUEST

Every supplier of warranted or supported software needs a mechanism for communicating user requests to the Maintenance Function, for processing those requests, and for reporting to users actions taken on their requests. Such a mechanism is a maintenance request system that includes a maintenance request form, one or more maintenance request summaries, and attendant procedures.

Chapter 12 defines maintenance as consisting of repair, revision, and enhancement. A claim for any of these elements of support is called a maintenance request (**MR**) and is presented to Maintenance on an MR form. Figure 16.9 shows the best known MR form: IBM's Authorized Program Analysis Report (APAR). The APAR is restricted to repair, to suspected discrepancies between program specification and program operation. Control Data has used an MR called a Programming Systems Report (PSR) that allows requests for enhancement as well as repair. An MR always includes information about its origin and a description of its request. An MR may also contain reply information, routing information, reclassification data, and processing statistics; how much depends on the procedures used to process the MR. In designing an MR, consider each of the following possibilities:

• Do you want your MR to be a turnaround document? If so, provide space for replies as well as requests.

IBM **APAR** AUTHORIZED PROGRAM ANALYSIS REPORT

PREASSIGNED APAR SERIAL NO. | 68354 |

(A) CUSTOMER NAME	CUSTOMER NO.	(E) APAR SUBMITTED	APAR IDENTITY
		MO.	DAY	YR.	
INSTALLATION ADDRESS		(F) SEVERITY CODE	
			ASSIGNED BY APAR CONTROL

(I) SYMPTOMS	TERMINATION CODES MESSAGES/STATUS INDICATORS
WAIT/HALT	

(G) OPERATING JOB ENVIRONMENT	ABNORMAL TERMINATE	
(C) PROGRAM IDENTITY AND CHANGE LEVEL	LOOP	

	NAME AND NUMBER	INSTALLED PROG. LEVEL	SYS-MESSAGE	
COMPONENTS OR PROGRAM IN ERROR/SUSPECTED			SYS-TERMINATE (IPL REQUIRED)	
____FOLD			OTHER	
SPECIAL ACTIVITY				

(B) CPU	CORE SIZE	SYS. RES.	SYS. IN	SYS. OUT

(K) Error Description—Note variations between expected and actual output—differences from previous successful runs—suspected problem area—verify EC level as adequate for program (PSM)—special configuration, teleprocessing, I/O switching, multi-systems, etc.

--------FOLD

IBM REPRESENTATIVE—NAME AND ADDRESS

(L)	FE AREA	BRANCH OFF. NO.	DP REGION	FIELD SYS-CTR.	WORLD TRADE COUNTRY

ITPS	CODE	INSTALLATION PHONE	ORIGINATOR IS
			SE	CE

(M)
NAME

MAILING ADDRESS

(N) AUTHORIZED SIGNATURE   TITLE

(D) SUPPORT GROUP AND INDIVIDUAL CONTACTED

AREA OR FSC	NAME
TEST RUN TIME_____	

MATERIAL SUBMITTED WITH APAR

STORAGE PRINT		CONTROL CARDS/JCL	
STORAGE MAP		CONSOLE LOG	
TAPE PRINT		CONSOLE CONDITIONS	
DASD PRINT		SYSTEM LOG	
SOURCE DECK/TAPE		SYSTEM OUTPUT	
OBJECT DECK/TAPE		TEST DATA	
PROGRAM LISTING		DIAGNOSTIC OUTPUT	
OTHER:		PTF LIST	
		USERS ROUTINE	

MAN HRS.	CE	SE	USER	SYS. HRS.	NO-RETRIES
(J)					

(P) TEMPORARY RELIEF GIVEN   EXPLAIN ABOVE   BYPASS ☐ CORRECTION ☐

DISTRIBUTION: PARTS 1, 2 ....APAR PROCESSING
            4 ....ORIGINATOR
PAGE____OF____ 3 ....APAR PROCESSING/OR AS DIRECTED IN PSM GEN #4

120-0482-8
(U/M-050)

Figure 16.9 A maintenance request form. (Courtesy of International Business Machines Corporation.)

- Do you want to publish an informational summary of reported discrepancies and temporary corrections? If so, you may be able to generate the summary by using a multipart form with administrative information blocked out of the copy to be used for the summary.
- How many copies of the MR are needed and by whom? Candidates are the user, Support, Maintenance, Test, and Services. Each recipient may need copies on the way into your system and again on the way out.
- How many indentifiers are needed on an MR? A preprinted serial number is a good safeguard against failure of any and all handlers to enter their identifiers. In addition to the preprinted serial number, you may want to allow each recipient to assign his own identifier for local tracking. Note the added importance of the preprinted number in this case; only by it can you be precisely assured of uniqueness of request numbers.
- How much environmental definition is needed to identify or reproduce a problem? Computer configuration, software configuration, revision levels, register contents—all are candidates. Unless the MR originator can generate a dump of hardware and software configuration tables, and unless you can get him to submit it in support of his MR, the configuration data on the MR may be all that is available.
- Do you want to record progress of an MR through your system on the MR itself? If so, such data as request type (repair, revision, or enhancement), severity, priority, logging at various checkpoints, other products possibly affected, signatures, and dates will have to appear on one or more copies. Control Data tracks its Programming Systems Reports separately with the routing from as shown in Figure 16.10.
- Are processing statistics important to you? A decision to suspend or increase maintenance may depend on the level of activity or the backlog, or you may evaluate the performance of the Maintenance Function from trends shown by processing statistics. You can include time spent solving a problem or waiting for supporting evidence on your MR or its accompanying routing form.
- Do you want to treat repair, revision, and enhancement all on one form? One advantage in doing this is simpler field procedures, including relieving users of the need to determine what types of requests they are making. Another is simpler reclassification, routing, and logging as the request flows through your system. A disad-

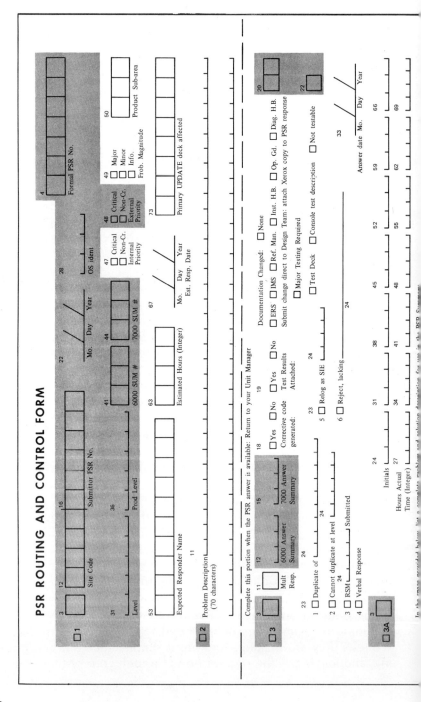

PSR ROUTING AND CONTROL FORM

☐1

Site Code

3 ☐ 12

Submitter FSR No.

16

Prod Level

36

Formal PSR No.

4

31

Level

53

6000 SUM #
41

7000 SUM #
44

Mo. Day Year
22

OS ident
28

47 Internal Priority
☐ Critical ☐ Non-Cr.

48 External Priority
☐ Critical ☐ Non-Cr.

49 Prob. Magnitude
☐ Major ☐ Minor ☐ Info.

50

Product Sub-area

☐2

Expected Responder Name
11

Problem Description
(70 characters)

Estimated Hours (Integer)
63

Mo. Day Year
67 Est. Resp. Date

Primary UPDATE deck affected
73

Complete this portion when the PSR answer is available: Return to your Unit Manager

☐3

3 ☐ 11

Mult Resp.
12

6000 Answer Summary
24

7000 Answer Summary
15

23
1 ☐ Duplicate of
24
2 ☐ Cannot duplicate at level
24
3 ☐ RSM _____ Submitted
4 ☐ Verbal Response

18
Corrective code generated:
☐ Yes ☐ No

19
Test Results Attached:
☐ Yes ☐ No

23
5 ☐ Relog as SIE
24

6 ☐ Reject, lacking

Documentation Changed: ☐ None
☐ ERS ☐ IMS ☐ Ref. Man. ☐ Inst. H.B. ☐ Op. Gd. ☐ Diag. H.B.
Submit change direct to Design Team: attach Xerox copy to PSR response

☐ Major Testing Required
☐ Test Deck ☐ Console test description ☐ Not testable
33

☐3A

3

Initials
24

Hours Actual
27 Time (Integer)

31

34

38

41

45

48

Answer date Mo. Day Year
52 59 66

55

62

69

In the space provided below, list a complete problem and solution description for use in the PSR Summary

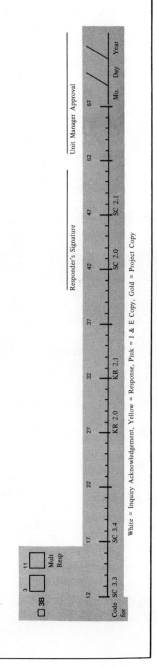

Figure 16.10 A maintenance request routing form. (Courtesy of Control Data Corporation.)

```
 _____
|                                    REQUEST FOR SOFTWARE MODIFICATION
|  PRODUCT I.D. _____
|  PRODUCT NAME _____
|
|  REASON FOR MODIFICATION _____
|  _____
|  _____
|  _____
|  _____
|  _____
|
|  DESCRIPTION OF MODIFICATION _____
|  _____
|  _____
|  _____
|  _____
|  _____
|  _____
|  _____
|
|  REQUESTED BY _____      APPROVED BY _____
|  APPROVED BY  _____      APPROVED BY _____
|
|  DISPOSITION _____      RSM BOARD MEMBERS
|  _____               _____
|  _____               _____
|  _____               _____
|  _____               _____
|  _____               _____
|  _____               _____
|  _____               _____
|  _____               _____
|  _____               _____
|  _____               _____
|  _____               _____
|           Chairman, RSM Board
|  DATE RSM RECEIVED__/__/____    RSM I.D. _____
 _____
```

Form No. 4410 2/75

Figure 16.11 An enhancement request form.

vantage is a more complex and cluttered routing form. If you decide to have separate request forms for repairs, revisions, and enhancements, you can design each optimally for its purpose. The **Request for Software Modification (RSM)** form shown in Figure 16.11 can handle revision and enhancement requests. Control Data has used a similar form not only for revision and enhancement requests in the Use Phase, but also to aid configuration management of an external specification from the time it was first approved: all external specification changes were controlled by enhancement requests.

16.7 MAINTENANCE REQUEST SUMMARIES

Two types of maintenance request summaries are presented here. One is called a discrepancy summary and the other is called a discrepancy activity summary.

A **discrepancy summary** lists all MRs for which a discrepancy is either known or suspected to exist and for which no corrective code, publication change, or other corrective material has been distributed. For a product at Support Level 1 or 2 (as defined in Section 12.1), the purpose of this report is to provide a warning to users about problems they may encounter, and where a temporary correction or circumvention is known, to publish it. Distribution of a discrepancy summary to users is controversial: some software vendors do not want either to alarm users about problems they have not already encountered or to reveal the magnitude of their repair problems. Other vendors feel an obligation to let users know of potential problems. For a product at Support Level 3, a discrepancy summary is the only vehicle for providing error corrections to users. You must, therefore, send to users of Support Level 3 products a discrepancy summary containing at least those MRs for which you acknowledge an error. In such a summary, include all permanent corrections that can be communicated entirely by the summary and declare all others to be permanent restrictions. If you prefer the full disclosure form of summary, also include temporary corrections and circumventions for all support levels.

Compiling and publishing a discrepancy summary can represent a lot of work. If you keep the administrative data required on each MR down to a level where enough room remains on the form to describe both the problem and the response, you can design a multipart form with a copy containing only the problem and the reply. Include this copy directly in the summary. Figure 16.12 is the second part of such a multipart form; the large blank space is used for administrative data on copies other than the discrepancy summary copy.

A **discrepancy activity summary** is used to monitor responsiveness to MRs so you can tell if you are exerting the proper effort in the proper

A B C COMPUTERS	PRODUCT DISCREPANCY REPORT	# 3712

PRODUCT NAME:_____ PRODUCT # (AS IN DUMP): _____

OPERATING SYSTEM:_____ O.S. # (AS IN DUMP): _____

HARDWARE INVIRONMENT: _____

DISCREPANCY: _____

RESOLUTION: _____

REPLY TYPE:_____

FORM 6349 REV. 6/77   PDS COPY

Figure 16.12 A discrepancy summary entry.

COLUMN

	(1)	(2)	(3)	(4)	(5)	(6)	(7)

ROW

PRODUCT NAME: ———————— PRODUCT # : ———— DATE: __/ /__

	TITLE	LAST MONTH COUNT	AGE	THIS MONTH COUNT	AGE	TWELVE MONTHS COUNT	AGE
(1)(2)							
	SUPPORT						
(3)	ON−HAND, BEGIN	####	DDD	####	DDD	####	DDD
(4)	RECEIVED	####		####		####	
(5)	INTO ABEYANCE	####		####		####	
(6)	FROM ABEYANCE	####	DDD	####	DDD	####	DDD
(7)	CLOSED	####	DDD	####	DDD	####	DDD
(8)	FORWARDED TO MAINT.	####	DDD	####	DDD	####	DDD
(9)	ON−HAND, END	####	DDD	####	DDD	####	DDD
	MAINTENANCE						
(10)	ON−HAND, BEGIN	####	DDD	####	DDD	####	DDD
(11)	RECEIVED FROM IMPL.	####		####		####	
(12)	INTO ABEYANCE	####		####		####	
(13)	FROM ABEYANCE	####	DDD	####	DDD	####	DDD
(14)	PERM. CORR. FWD.	####	DDD	####	DDD	####	DDD
(15)	PERM. RESTR. FWD.	####	DDD	####	DDD	####	DDD
(16)	TEMP. CORR. FWD.	####	DDD	####	DDD	####	DDD
(17)	CIRCUMVENTION FWD.	####	DDD	####	DDD	####	DDD
(18)	FROM PROCESS	####	DDD	####	DDD	####	DDD
(19)	ON−HAND, END	####	DDD	####	DDD	####	DDD
	SERVICES						
(20)	ON−HAND, BEGIN	####	DDD	####	DDD	####	DDD
(21)	RECEIVED FROM MAINT.	####		####		####	
(22)	CLOSED	####	DDD	####	DDD	####	DDD
(23)	TEMP. CORR. PUBL.	####	DDD	####	DDD	####	DDD
(24)	CIRCUMVENTION PUBL.	####	DDD	####	DDD	####	DDD
(25)	FROM PROCESS	####	DDD	####	DDD	####	DDD
(26)	ON−HAND, END	####	DDD	####	DDD	####	DDD
	SUMMARY						
(27)	IMPL. BACKLOG	####	DDD	####	DDD	####	DDD
(28)	MAINT. BACKLOG	####	DDD	####	DDD	####	DDD
(29)	TEST. BACKLOG	####	DDD	####	DDD	####	DDD
(30)	TOTAL BACKLOG	####	DDD	####	DDD	####	DDD

Figure 16.13   A stereotype discrepancy activity summary.

places. By tracking such data as number of errors reported, time it takes to route them, and time it takes to correct them, you can determine where to put more or less effort into the concerned functions. Figure 16.13 is a stereotypic discrepancy activity summary for three Functions: Support, Maintenance, and Services. This figure is designed only to illustrate how a discrepancy activity summary works, so do not infer from the omission of Test and Publications that their activities need not also be tracked.

The explanation of Figure 16.13 is quite lengthy, but it tells a lot about how to process those MRs that report errors. In the following discussion, items in the figure are referenced by their row and column positions: (3,1) refers to the title "On-hand, Begin."

(3,1)   The report begins with the number of MRs in the hands of Support at the beginning of the month preceding the report date (3,2), the second month preceding the report date (3,4), and the twelfth month preceding the report date (3,6). For each of these numbers, an average number of days on hand is included (3,3; 3,5; 3,7).

(3,2)   The symbol #### represents a count of the MRs changing status as indicated in Column 1, during the periods indicated by Columns 2, 4, and 6.

(3,3)   The symbol DDD represents the average number of days all MRs, shown by the count in Column 2, were in the status indicated in Column 1.

(4,1)   The number of MRs received during the previous month (4,2), the month prior to it (4,4), and the twelve months prior to the report date (4,7) are given. Age has no relevance in these entries.

(5,1)   Some MRs received provide insufficient information or supply insufficient supporting data. These are recycled to their submitters for augmentation. From the time they are returned to submitters until they are again received by Support they are in abeyance.

(6,1)   For MRs returned from abeyance, the number (6,2) and average time in abeyance (6,3) are included.

(7,1)   MRs determined to be duplicates and others that represent misunderstandings are closed and are not forwarded; that is, they are answered and not processed further.

(8,1)   All other MRs that are not redundant and that appear to be complete are forwarded to Maintenance for correction, even if they appear to require publications rather than code changes. Secondary or multiple routing to obtain corrections is done by Maintenance; in this stereotypic discrepancy activity summary such routings are omitted.

(9,1)   The number of MRs on hand in Support at the end of each of the three reported intervals is included. For each column, this number is Row 3 plus Row 4 minus Row 5 plus Row 6 minus Row 7 minus Row 8. The age is the average of the time each was in Support excluding abeyance time.

(10,1) These entries for Maintenance are analogous to entries for
(11,1) Support.

(12,1) In spite of Support's best efforts to screen out incomplete MRs, some get through to Maintenance. These are put in abeyance until documentation is complete or until a suitable amount of time, such as 90 days, has passed.

(14,1) This row contains statistics on MRs for which a permanent correction has been found and forwarded to Services for inclusion in a discrepancy summary and to Test for inclusion in an update; or in the case of Support Level 3, just to Services for inclusion only in a discrepancy summary.

(15,1) For some errors you may decide to implement no permanent correction. Perhaps the probability of the error recurring is exceedingly low and the impact on users of a correction is detrimental, as in the case of computing a function to the advertised accuracy in the neighborhood of a limit; if implementing the only feasible correction would slow all executions of the function by 20%, you might be better off issuing a warning rather than a correction. For these you must declare a **permanent restriction** and document it accordingly. This row contains statistics on the disposition of such MRs.

(16,1) Temporary corrections often are available, either as submitted with an MR or as generated during Maintenance's early analysis. These are forwarded to Services for inclusion in a discrepancy summary and their statistics are presented here.

(17,1) A **circumvention** is a procedure for avoiding a problem until a correction is generated. Statistics on circumventions forwarded to Services for inclusion in a discrepancy summary go here.

(18,1) MRs for which either temporary correction or a circumvention has been issued are still in process. To keep the statistics balanced, for every permanent correction or permanent restriction forwarded, one MR is taken from process and thus one is added to the count in (18,2), (18,4), or (18,6).

(19,1) The number of MRs on hand in Maintenance at the end of a period is Row 10 plus Row 11 minus Row 12 plus Row 13 minus

Row 14 minus Row 15 minus Row 16 minus Row 17 plus Row 18. The age is the average of the time each was in Maintenance, excluding time in abeyance.

(20,1) These entries for Services also are analogous to entries for
(21,1) Support.

(22,1) Every MR is closed eventually, either by appearing in an update; as a permanent restriction; or, for Support Level 3 products, as a permanent correction in a discrepancy summary. Statistics on closed MRs go here.

(23,1) As temporary solutions (corrections or circumventions) are
(24,1) published, their statistics go in Rows 23 and 24. As they are
(24,1) replaced by closed MRs, Row 25 is incremented to keep the throughput statistics balanced.

(26,1) The number of MRs on hand in Services at the end of a period is Row 20 plus Row 21 minus Row 22 minus Row 23 minus Row 24 plus Row 25. The age is the same as for Maintenance.

(27,1) The backing for each function is the number of MRs on hand
(28,1) at the end of a period minus the number on hand at the
(29,1) beginning of the period.

(30,1) The total backlog of the system is the sum of the individual backlogs, Rows 27, 28, and 29.

You can include more or less in a discrepancy activity summary than is included in this stereotype. One common practice is to subdivide age statistics into brackets, such as: 14 days or less, 15–29 days, 30–44 days, and over 44 days. Another is to prioritize MRs and report each rank separately. Still another variation is to summarize over various levels in a product hierarchy: module, product, product set, product line. You decide by experience what is most useful to you.

A discrepancy activity summary can either be very helpful or very harmful. Use the statistics in it constructively and not to reprimand a function whose trend is unfavorable. Otherwise each function will play games with its statistics to look good on the discrepancy activity summary rather than get the maintenance job done.

Chapter
17
Procedures

To gain maximum benefit from this methodology you must tailor it to your own environment through systems and procedures. All techniques and tools in this book have been tried somewhere, and all have worked. They have not worked because they are intrinsically superior ways to develop software; they have worked because someone took great pains to introduce them in a way that made sense. They were kept relevant by judicious updating and by reindoctrination of their users. This chapter presents a few principles about writing, organizing, presenting, and updating procedures so that you can make the other principles of this book work for you, too.

17.1 WHY PROCEDURES ARE NEEDED

No matter how well you and your co-workers understand the methodology by which your organization works, you will not share the same understanding long enough to get a job done. The business of heavy-duty software production is far too complex for several people to simultaneously hold identical understanding of it in their heads. They need a reference source.

Even if you understand your way of doing business, you may not be able to organize your thoughts well enough to communicate them to others unless you write them down in an orderly manner. You need a reference source.

Business and the ways of doing business are ever changing and they are changing at an ever-increasing rate (64). To keep abreast of how to perform your business today you need an up-to-date reference source.

The reference source in each case is your written procedures. Over several years many books and articles have been printed describing proven and innovative systems and procedures, how to introduce

them, and how to make them work. Among software engineers
Brandon's *Management Standards for Data Processing* (65) is a well-
known work on this topic. Mr. Brandon acknowledges a dichotomy
between methods standards—uniform practices and common techniques—and performance standards—metrics by which to evaluate
performance. The book you are now reading addresses methods
standards and leaves performance standards to other works, such as
Mr. Brandon's.

Within methods standards the methodology of this book recognizes
another dichotomy—management methods and programming
methods. Other than to affirm that written programming methods—
coding conventions, good practices to employ and bad practices to
avoid, input/output formats, communications protocols, character set
standards—are needed, this book leaves them to other works on
software engineering. Management methods—work organization,
what and how to document, feedback control systems, configuration
management—are what this book is all about. Translating them into
procedures is the way to make them work.

When you commit any of these principles to any form of written
instructions or guidelines, you have become convinced that
procedures are needed and that you want people to follow them.
How do you convince others to follow the procedures? Many people,
especially those programmers who consider themselves artists, resent
being told how to do their work. You must present your ideas to them
persuasively so that they themselves become convinced your way is
right. This takes time and patience, but the resulting commitment by
workers to a common way of doing business pays dividends: people
work together smoothly, there is continuity of appearance and performance among products, and you can feel satisfied knowing that a
thorough job has been done.

The answer to the question posed above is this: you not only need
methods procedures, you need a procedure for procedures. This is
not to suggest that you overproceduralize. The way in which you
write, introduce, and enforce procedures requires as much careful
thought as the procedures themselves. Be sure, then, to include the
following points in your procedure for procedures:

• Provide a reason for following every rule, one that can be understood and appreciated by those who must follow it.
• Introduce each new member of your organization to your
  procedures during his orientation discussion, explaining how it is in

his interest to follow them. Cite several examples to show where following procedures paid off and where not following procedures led to problems.

- Introduce each new procedure orally. It is preferable to do this during a monthly communications meeting or other setting not specifically staged for the presentation of procedures so that participants will not anticipate the meeting with aversion.

- Encourage a discussion of each new procedure, particularly to bring out any objections to it or doubts about its effectiveness.

- Keep all procedures up-to-date. Never criticize a worker for following an obsolete procedure unless you are sure he is aware of a new procedure and has had time to adopt it. Conversely, never fail to communicate new procedures, in writing, and to allow time for them to be phased in.

- Make sure your procedures are understood, not only in terms of what is to be done but in terms of how it is to be done.

17.2 POLICIES VERSUS FORMATS VERSUS PROCEDURES

As stated above, a thorough system of procedures makes clear not only what you want but why and how you want it. A convenient and manageable way to organize what, how, and why statements is to cover *what* under **format**; *how* under **procedure**; and *why* under **policy**. When you generate a procedural document, address each topic in the order *why, what, how*. For example, ABC Computers Company has a Product Objectives and Requirements (POR) Policy in which a Purpose paragraph states *why* ABC Computers uses a POR document. The Format section points to a presentation similar to the one in Chapter 13 of this book that states *what* a POR document contains. The Responsibility section summarizes *how* a POR document flows through the steps of generation, review, and approval while pointing to separate documents for details. This allows a hierarchical approach to procedure construction. You may present the three parts in one, two, or three documents depending on the length of the topics and their audiences. For example, the POR Policy just mentioned is intended to apply company-wide with allowance for divisional or even departmental POR Formats and POR Procedures. At ABC, in fact, there are separate POR formats for hardware and software products and there are both divisional and departmental POR procedures.

17.3   PROCEDURES HANDBOOK

As noted in Section 17.1, you will want to keep your procedural information readily available. A sure way to do this, and to keep it all together, is to provide each person with a handbook containing all of the policies, procedures, formats, and standards he needs to get his work done. Depending on how much information each person needs and how you organize it, you may have more than one volume. It is quite appropriate to have separate volumes for corporate, divisional, and departmental data, or for financial, personnel, and technical material. It is equally appropriate to have one binder with separate sections for different scopes of applicability. However you organize your procedural information, the amount you provide should enable a person to carry out his job yet not be oppressive. Never let procedures become an end in themselves rather than a means to an end.

What should you include in your software development methodology handbook? The table of contents of this book suggests many possible entries. You may also want to include background information such as organization charts, department charters, job descriptions; a glossary; a configurator; a summary of your configuration management system; a bibliography of other references, including external standards. Otherwise include anything specific to software development you do as a matter of policy, anything you do according to a procedure, and anything you do following a regular format, even if it seems to be common knowledge. Keep in mind the new employee who has no familiarity with your methodology and the recalcitrant who always seems to do the wrong thing, or at best the right thing the wrong way. Also, committing even the most obvious practices to writing forces you think them through thoroughly and thereby perhaps to improve them.

17.4   PROCEDURES VERSUS STANDARDS

Up to this point no real distinction has been drawn between procedures and standards. In fact any possible distinction has been blurred by the reference to Mr. Brandon's use of standards for what this book calls procedures. There *is* a distinction worth drawing.

A standard differs from a procedure in one or two ways. A standard may be defined outside of your organization, subject to little or none of your influence. Examples are ANSI or ISO standards and de facto industry standards like Synchronous Data Link Control (SDLC) communications protocol introduced by IBM and observed by others in order to interface with IBM computers. Or, even if defined within your organization, a standard may be beyond your control to modify once it is established. For IBM, the Binary Synchronous (BISYNC) communications protocol is an example: it is so wide-spread and so many users and supplementary vendors are dependent upon it that it cannot be altered. Any procedure that cannot practically be altered is called a **standard**. Standards can be revised by addition, but all previous versions must be retained as proper subsets. The sections of this chapter that follow deal with standards; that is, procedures that cannot be modified without severe impact.

17.5 CONFIGURATION MANAGEMENT

There are many references throughout this book to configuration management, the identification and control of what comprises a product. Many people who deal with a small number of product end items and limited distribution of them pay little heed to configuration management. However, anyone who has worked with complex product structures, frequent updating of components, and widespread distribution of them appreciates good configuration management procedures, for they save untold grief in keeping track and control.

There are three key components of a configuration management system: revision control, identification control, and distribution control. The better integrated they are with each other and into your overall software engineering methodology, the easier they are to enforce.

Revision control deals with the classification of product elements according to their differences and interchangeability, and with the control of changes. Revision control, which appears as an example here and there in this book, should be rigorous with regard to both classification and control.

Take classification first. Unless you rigidly define what can or cannot be changed in a product, you run the serious risk of inadvertently obviating a user's programs, data, or procedures; making your own publications obsolete; or confounding your ability to classify support into levels. This is why the concepts of Product, Variant, Version, and Update came into being. Different Products are used to provide different capabilities; different **Variants** are used to provide different environments; different **Versions** provide different features; and different **Updates** provide different degrees of correctness. Deciding whether a proposed change represents a new Product, Variant, Version, or Update is the thorniest problem in configuration management. One reason the problem is thorny is that it is difficult to consider all possible impacts a change might have. Another is that it is hard to apply rules rigorously once they are determined. A good way to make sure you consider most implications of a change beforehand, and that when you break your own rules you do so consciously, is to employ a decision matrix like the one shown in Figure 17.1. Using such a matrix, start at the top and stop as soon as you encounter an N and you will not go astray. For example, if a proposed change requires user programs or data to change, then you need a new Product; a new Version would not suffice because a criterion for a new Version is that it be fully upward compatible. Or, if you propose to increase the speed of a product by 40%, you might produce a new product and tout the speed improvement as a major new feature for which you could charge a higher price; you might merely make a new Version (if your performance were too slow to satisfy your users) and charge the same

	Then You Need a New			
	Product	Variant	Version	Update
If the Proposed Change				
Requires user programs or data to change	N			
Requires user to acquire more or alternate hardware to do the same job as before	N			
Takes away features	N			
Supports alternate hardware		N		
Operates in an alternate software environment		N		
Increases size X% or more		N		
Decreases speed X% or more		N		
Changes features		S	N	
Adds features		S	N	
Increases speed X% or more		S		S	N
Decreases size X% or more				N
Makes end items agree with specification				N

Figure 17.1 A configuration management decision matrix. *Key.* N = necessary; S = sufficient.

Item Impacted	Impact			
	Product	Variant	Version	Update
Release bulletin	N	N	N	N
Release specification	N	N	N	N
Source code	N	N	N	R
Object code	N	N	N	R
Enhancement request		N	N	
Maintenance request				N
Internal specification	N	R	R	R
Maintenance specification	N	R	R	R
Test specification	N	R	R	R
Configurator	N	R	R	R
Plan	N	R	R	
Requirements contract	N	R	R	
External specification	N	R	R	
Test plan	N	R	R	
Publications plan	N	R	R	
Support plan	N	R	R	
Publications	N	R	R	
Courses	N	R	R	
Promotional material	N	R	R	

Figure 17.2 A configuration management impact matrix. *Key.* N = new item required; R = revision required.

price; or you might release a new Update, the smallest possible perturbation of the product, if a 40% speed improvement were needed to meet the product's specification.

Now consider control. Every change has some impact and you must be aware of it and be able to account for it. To make sure you consider all impact implied by changes, use an impact matrix like the one in Figure 17.2. This matrix reminds you what to generate to fully accommodate a change. It may also help you decide whether or not to make a change: if for some reason you cannot generate something required by your impact matrix, do not make the change. In the preceding example, if you decided to make a new Product, you would need much new documentation, new publications, and so on. If you made a new Version, you could get by with merely revising most items. And if you chose the Update route, you could avoid changing most items altogether.

The decision and impact matrices discussed here assume that a new Update or Version replaces an old Update or Version and that a new Variant or Product does not replace an old Variant or Product. If you make different assumptions, your matrices will be different.

Identification control concerns the labeling of product end items and the management of your product structure data base. A structure that meets most needs is referenced throughout this book. This structure, starting from the top of the hierarchy, organizes products according to the diagram in Figure 17.3. In this figure the most likely product end items to be produced at each level are shown. The job of identification control is to uniquely identify each product end item and to associate it, through structure files or diagrams, with every product, product family, product set, and product line of which it is a part.

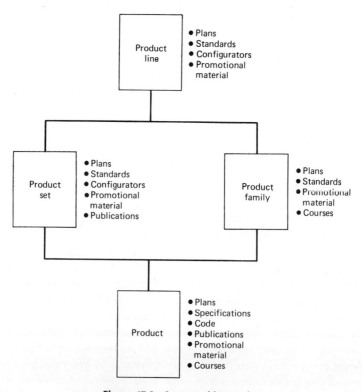

Figure 17.3 Structural hierarchy.

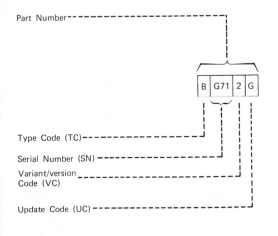

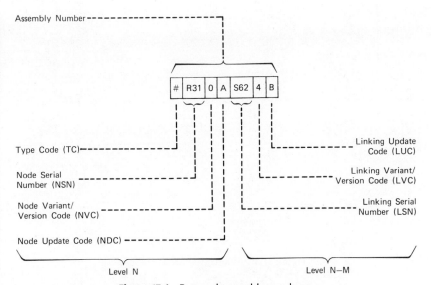

Figure 17.4 Part and assembly numbers.

   Apply identification to products carefully to avoid mixing descriptive and structural information. This is not hard to do if you remember to include in its part number only information about *what* an end item is and in assembly numbers only information about *where* it appears. A fairly simple scheme that meets many needs uses a three-field part number and a seven-field assembly number. This scheme appears frequently in this book and works as follows (refer to Figures 17.4 and 17.5).

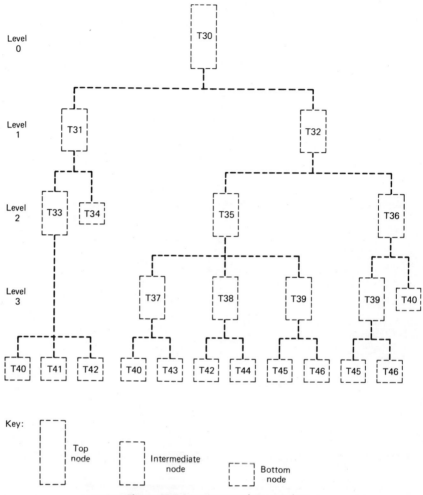

Figure 17.5 A parts tree for a product.

- **Part Number.** Every product end item has a Part Number clearly marked on and sometimes also in it. The meaning assigned to each component of a Part Number may vary from one type of end item to another, but most common meanings are:

  Type Code (TC). This field specifies whether the end item is source code (S), an external specification (E), a publication (B), and so on.
  Serial Number (SN). Once the initial structure of a product is determined, Serial Numbers are assigned to each node in the

physical tree structure of the product. Information about product type (compiler, utility, etc.), origin (department, location, etc.), or product line can be coded into a Serial Number. Sequentiality and proximity of values for Serial Numbers of related nodes help you find your way through structure files, but they are not necessary.

Variant/Version Code (VC). This field is used for revision control. A possible encoding scheme is to use nonalphanumeric values (@, #, etc.) for prototypes, alphabetical values for Variants, and numerical values for Versions.

Update Code (UC). This field is also used for revision control. Its value increments with each Update of a Variant or Version and may either continue to increment or reset when the Variant/Version Code increments.

- **Assembly Number.** Every node of every tree in your structural data base has associated with it one or more Assembly Numbers. Each Assembly Number has two parts, the first of which gives the reason for its existence, and the second of which tells how it is related to each higher-level node to which it is connected. The meanings of the Assembly Number fields are:

Type Code (TC). If the Type Code in an Assembly Number is the same as the Type Code in a Part Number, then a tangible end item exists at that level in the hierarchy and pertains to all nodes below it. For example, in Figure 17.5 one external specification might exist at Node T31 and cover code at and below it. On another branch of the same tree there might be two more external specifications at Nodes T35 and T36, each covering code at and below it. Unless a Node Serial Number pertains to a top node or to a bottom node, there is at least one Assembly Number with that Node Serial Number whose Type Code indicates that the node is a branch point. In this book a Type Code value of + indicates an intermediate node and a value of # indicates a top node.

Node Serial Number (NSN). This is the Serial Number assigned to a node in its structure tree.

Node Variant/Version Code (NVC) and *Node Update Code* (NUC). Whenever a new Variant, Version, or Update is created at any bottom node, all nodes above it on every branch of every tree where it occurs are incremented in the NVC and NUC fields, accordingly. For example, suppose the initial Part Numbers for all bottom nodes in Figure 17.5 had VC = 1 and UC = A. Then for the top node the Assembly Number would be #T301AT301A. If the module at Node T40 were updated (i.e., Part Number = ST401B), then all nodes above it on all branches where it occurs would be incremented until, for the top node, the Assembly Number would become #T301BT301B. Note that unless you purged the structure represented by T301A from your system, you now would have two whole trees for T30.

Linking Serial Number (LSN). This field tells where an element fits in a tree. Some elements, like T40 in Figure 17.5, occur several times and require an Assembly Number for each occurrence: ST401AT331A, ST401AT371A, ST401AT361A; also +T391AT351A, +T391AT361A.

Linking Variant/Version Code (LVC) and *Linking Update Code* (LUC). These fields identify the particular Variant, Version, and Update trees into which an element fits. In case you wonder why this information is necessary, consider the case where an element is used in several products, is updated, but the Update is not applied to all products.

Good identification control requires well thought-out assignment algorithms and thorough record keeping. While you may be able to manage your structural data base manually, you are better off automating it as soon as possible. Consider, for instance, the where-used tree of Figure 17.6 and the inclusive and exclusive external specification trees of Figures 17.7 and 17.8. (An **inclusive tree** includes all modules of an assembly whether or not they are developed as a part of the assembly. An **exclusive tree** excludes those modules not developed as a part of the assembly.) These trees would be difficult to construct manually for even slightly more complex structures. Unless you have resources to build your own data base manager, you will need to adapt an existing bill of materials processor or data base management system. To make such an adaptation you may need to adjust your Part Number and Assembly Number descriptions, so be sure to take available tools into account when designing your identification control system.

The third element of configuration management is distribution control. The functions called document control and distribution are parts of distribution control. So is the issue of ownership dealt with in Section 17.8, the configurator presented in Section 14.5, and the release schedule, prereleases, and waivers discussed at several points. **Distribution control** is the assurance that everyone with a right or a need

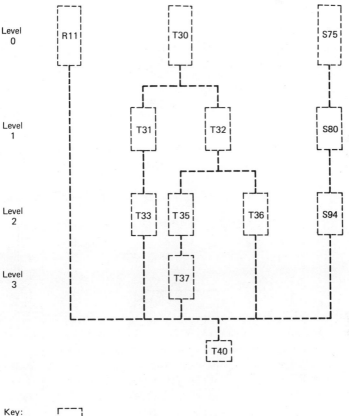

Figure 17.6 A "where-used" tree for module T40.

to know gets what he needs, that only he gets it, and that he can get it as long as it is available. This includes archival of vital records and redundant storage for backup in the event of disaster.

If you fully automate your identification control, it is a simple matter to add retrieval keys for various distribution categories. Some questions to ask yourself when specifying access parameters are:

- Who may have access to items shown in Figure 17.2?
- Shall I distribute listings?

- On what media shall I offer each item?
- When is an item obsolete?
- How long shall I keep obsolete items?
- What supporting documents shall I ask for with requests for exceptional distribution?

Distribution lists and their maintenance can require a great deal of attention. You may have separate lists for domestic and international markets or for different product lines. You may send software releases with associated publications to one list and only the publications to

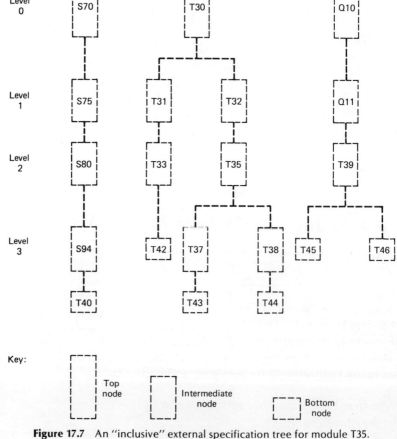

Figure 17.7 An "inclusive" external specification tree for module T35.

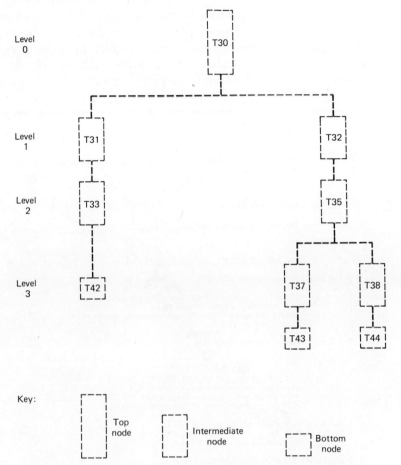

Figure 17.8 An "exclusive" external specification tree for module T35.

another list. The Services Function may perform distribution, but the Support Function may specify who gets what. Regardless of who specifies distribution lists, it is a good idea to reverify each list before using it; distribution lists for far-flung marketing empires have a way of being out-of-date more often than not.

There is some overlap of revision, identification, and distribution control. The Variant/Version Code and the Update Code, for instance, play vital roles in both revision and identification control. Another technique not mentioned previously is the use of preliminary documents. They contribute to both revision and distribution control by clearly differentiating unapproved copies of plans and specifications from approved copies. To use this technique, use "preliminary" and "approved" overlays as in Figure 17.9, when replicating controlled documents. Make document control custodian of all such documents from the time they are first circulated for review, and let only document control make copies. Have document control and only docu-

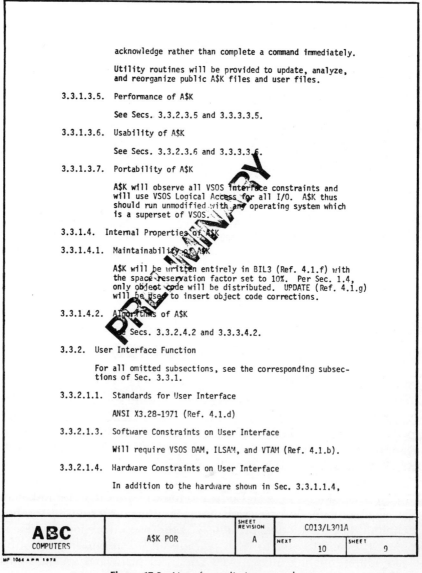

acknowledge rather than complete a command immediately.

Utility routines will be provided to update, analyze, and reorganize public A$K files and user files.

3.3.1.3.5. Performance of A$K

See Secs. 3.3.2.3.5 and 3.3.3.3.5.

3.3.1.3.6. Usability of A$K

See Secs. 3.3.2.3.6 and 3.3.3.3.6.

3.3.1.3.7. Portability of A$K

A$K will observe all VSOS interface constraints and will use VSOS Logical Access for all I/O. A$K thus should run unmodified with any operating system which is a superset of VSOS.

3.3.1.4. Internal Properties of A$K

3.3.1.4.1. Maintainability of A$K

A$K will be written entirely in BIL3 (Ref. 4.1.f) with the space reservation factor set to 10%. Per Sec. 1.4, only object code will be distributed. UPDATE (Ref. 4.1.g) will be used to insert object code corrections.

3.3.1.4.2. Algorithms of A$K

See Secs. 3.3.2.4.2 and 3.3.3.4.2.

3.3.2. User Interface Function

For all omitted subsections, see the corresponding subsections of Sec. 3.3.1.

3.3.2.1.1. Standards for User Interface

ANSI X3.28-1971 (Ref. 4.1.d)

3.3.2.1.3. Software Constraints on User Interface

Will require VSOS DAM, ILSAM, and VTAM (Ref. 4.1.b).

3.3.2.1.4. Hardware Constraints on User Interface

In addition to the hardware shown in Sec. 3.3.1.1.4,

ABC COMPUTERS	A$K POR	SHEET REVISION A	C013/L301A	
			NEXT 10	SHEET 9

MF 1064 APR 1972

Figure 17.9 Use of a preliminary overlay.

ment control use the overlays when making copies, and make sure one overlay or the other is always used. Then each recipient of a document will know if he has an approved, preliminary, or contraband copy.

When you apply all of the tools and techniques mentioned in this section you will have adequate configuration management. Adequate, contrasted to marginal or exceptional. Configuration management is so important that you should provide at least the controls discussed here. The idea of a Development Support Librarian (6) integrates many of these concepts. The Source Code Control System designed by Bell Laboratories (66) is an elegant tool for configuration management. Large military automation projects like navigation and logistics systems use elaborate configuration management: read about such systems (67–73) to gain a feeling for what else you might want to provide in your configuration management.

17.6   PROGRAMMING STANDARDS

In this book programming standards do not include use of requirements contracts, external specifications, and so forth; those are planning and management procedures. In this book **programming standards** refer to enumeration of principles of design and coding that you choose either to follow or to exclude. No attempt is made here to guide you toward or away from specific programming standards; that is another area of software engineering. The message of this book with respect to programming standards is that they are *essential,* more so for software products than for lighter-duty software. Programming standards not only contribute to good design of individual programs, but they also make possible the creation of product sets that can work together harmoniously. They also improve communication among the many, many people who deal with a software product, particularly during the Use Phase. Without good programming standards, performing the Maintenance Function and the Support Function, particularly product customizing, is exceedingly costly and frustrating. So be sure you have a good set of standards that appear in your procedures handbook or somewhere equally accessible and controlled.

17.7   PUBLICATIONS STANDARDS

Chapter 9 mentions the need for standards in the Publications Function. Section 9.2, in particular, mentions a style guide and policies. As

CONTENTS

CATEGORIES
  System Description Manual
  Reference Manual
  Reference Booklet
  Operator Manual
  Message Manual
ORGANIZATION AND FORMAT
  Front Matter
    Covers
    Title page
    Revision Notice
    Preface
    Contents
    Figures
    Tables
  Body
    System Description Manual
    Reference Manual
    Reference Booklet
    Operator Manual
    Message Manual
  Reference Matter
    Appendices
    Glossary
    Index
  Production Standards
    Size
    Materials
    Type
    Artwork
    Photographs
    Use of Color
    Use of Trademarks
    Copyright Notice
    Binding
EXHIBITS
  Page Layout
  Tab Page
  Warning Messages
  Full Page Illustration Layout
  Illustrations Inserted in Text
  Table Layout
  Flow Chart Layout
  Proofreading Marks
  Symbols
  Special Character Notations

Figure 17.10 Contents of a publications style guide.

OWNERSHIP
335

policies, formats, and procedures are defined in Section 17.2, you will probably treat policies and procedures for the Publications Function just as you do for any other Function. Treat publications formats, however, as standards: that is, rigidly follow them and seldom if ever change them so that a consistent image of your organization is projected to all users at all times. If a new idea is so compelling that you must incorporate it in your publications formats, at least introduce it with and only with new product lines.

As Section 9.2 suggests, you can collect all of your publications formats and standards in a publications style guide. Such a style guide might have a table of contents like the one in Figure 17.10.

17.8 OWNERSHIP

The **ownership** of a software product refers to the party with the right to reap economic return from the distribution and use of the product, and who is liable for damages suffered by recipients and users of the product. Ownership was a hotly debated topic during the late 1960s. At that time the computer industry was experiencing the early throes of unbundling, and the patentability of software was contested in the courts. A more recent spin-off from the question of ownership is the taxability of software as tangible personal property. What will probably be the most controversial aspect yet—the privacy of an individual and the liability of software owners for invasions of his privacy—is just being evaluated as this book goes to press.

The reason for discussing ownership among standards is that policies and procedures relating to ownership are difficult and sometimes impossible to change once established. For example, once you put a program in the public domain, there is no way you can take it back. Also, the rules governing ownership—patent, tax, copyright, contract, trade secret, and unfair competition laws—are for practical purposes beyond your ability to control.

You have basically three choices regarding ownership of a software product. It can belong to you, to the user, or to everybody (i.e., it can be in the public domain). The easiest ownership to establish is the third, public ownership. To do so is an easy matter. Simply distribute a product widely with no stated or implied restrictions, or develop it under any of many government contracts that specifically place software in the public domain. Next easiest to establish is the user's ownership. You can do this by stating in a contract that a product belongs to the user for whom you develop it. When doing this also be sure to absolve yourself from future liability for claims suffered due to malfunctioning or to misuse of the product. Note, too, that once you have transferred ownership, the burden of protecting it is that of the new owner. Most difficult to establish is your own ownership, which requires any of three progressively difficult procedures to be followed: proprietary claim, copyright, and patent.

You can gain protection for a proprietary claim under state trade secrets laws in the United States if you can justify that your software gives you an advantage over competitors who do not have access to it. To claim software as a trade secret you must show that access to it is limited and controlled, that it is really valuable, that it was costly to develop, that your company and not an individual developed it and owns it, that you can prove infringement, and that it is fair for you to make your claim (74). You can control distribution via license or contract and by logging all known copies. It is also a good idea to mark all copies with a proprietary notice similar to a copyright notice. One thing worth remembering about this approach to protection is that you have no claim against a third party (i.e., someone who obtained your product from someone other than you) unless he is made aware that he has no right to copy or use it.

You can gain a different measure of protection under national and international copyright laws. Such laws protect the way an idea is expressed rather than the idea itself. What you seek under copyright law is a prohibition against copying, adapting, or translating your software product. To obtain statutory copyright protection in the United States you merely affix an appropriate notice to each end item that can be copied. Since most copyright laws are unclear about what media can be copyrighted and no significant cases have been contested in court, play safe and mark both man- and machine-readable media. Including the symbol © in a United States copyright notice extends protection to all countries subscribing to the Universal Copyright Convention (75). Furthermore, coverage of a copyright observed by the Universal Copyright Convention (U. C. C.) countries is extended to countries subscribing to the Berne Convention for Literary and Artistic Works (76), if the copyrighted work is published in a Berne member country simultaneously with its first publication in a U. C. C. country. As of the Copyright Act of 1976 (77), copyright protection in the United States extends for the life of an author plus 50 years. This is longer than the economic life of most software products. How this will be interpreted for computer software, especially when the author is a corporation, is to be determined by the National Commission on Technological Uses of Copyrighted Works (known as

CONTU [77]). United States copyright law, as of January 1, 1978, calls for registering copyrights within three months of publication (78). Prior to that date the practice had been to register copyrights when infringement was suspected or when a copyright had to be defended (79).

The third and most controversial form of protection is a patent. To obtain patent protection you must have an unobvious and inventive idea, in contrast to the only requirement for copyright protection which is that your work be original. Once you obtain a patent, you can prevent anyone from practicing your invention for 17 years even if another person independently develops it. The U.S. Court of Customs and Patent Appeals has specifically authorized the patenting of software, but the U.S. Supreme Court has disallowed the only patents brought before it (80).

The advantage of patent protection over other forms may only be apparent. Software is not patentable in all countries; it takes about three years to get a patent in the United States at a cost of about $15,000; and due to the precedents of disagreement between the U.S. Court of Customs and Patent Appeals, District Courts, and the Supreme Court a patent dispute could take 15 to 20 years of litigation (81): IBM has estimated that less than 20% of its investment in a program product is in the idea, 25% is in the code, and 50% is in the documentation; it therefore makes broad use of copyright to protect its documentation. IBM has also gone on record favoring a new hybrid form of protection which they call a registration system (82). In addition to requiring registration, it requires a formal disclosure of the principles of operation of the software and a secret filing of a listing of the software.

Regardless of what form of protection you elect, clearly mark all end items with both man- and machine-readable notices. IBM has prepared a useful guideline for applying copyright notices (83) that provides an excellent model for proprietary and patent notices as well.

Claims and counterclaims bearing on ownership and liability as contrasted to whether or not an item can be patented or copyrighted so far have depended mostly on expressed intent to control and restrict distribution and use, rather than on enforcement of specific trade secrets, copyright, or patent laws. As this book goes to press, your best protection is a proprietary claim for narrowly distributed software products, a copyright for broadly distributed products, and a license or contract stating your precise terms of agreement for either type of claim. Ownership and related legal topics are complex and rapidly changing. For fascinating background reading, see (74–86). Wessel's article (74) is frequently referenced as a classic statement of the problem. Goldberg's article (84) is particularly helpful in sorting out the pros and cons of various forms of protection, and the book by Bernacchi and Larsen (85) is excellent for its in-depth analysis. And whatever else you do, be sure to get legal advice before acting! The information above is intended to suggest options open to you rather than to tell you how to exercise them.

17.9 LICENSES AND CONTRACTS

As stated in the previous section, a license or contract may be the best way to establish ownership of a software product. Use a license or contract to define your warranty and any support you provide in addition to it, such as installation, conversion, modification, and consultation on usage. Describe any form of time payment in a license or contract and the limits of your liability due to failure or misuse of your product.

The preceding paragraph assumes that you are a software product seller. You may have someone build a software product for you to deliver to the ultimate user. Then you are a buyer and you need a contract to clarify what you expect, when you expect to get it, how much and when you will pay for it, and what your and your vendor's respective liabilities are. As a buyer you decide whether a time and materials contract or a fixed price contract is best, and you write your contract accordingly. A fixed price contract is usually preferable. This does not hold true, though, if the scope of the work to be performed is unknown, if you need to increase the size of your staff temporarily, or if you temporarily want the expertise of outside people.

Both as buyer and as seller be sure that your licenses and contracts are comprehensive. Your point of view will vary according to which side of an agreement you are on in each specific case, but always be sure to address each of the following topics:

- *Scope.* Enumerate the products covered and whether or not products may be added later. Reference a specification that defines each product. Include all end items to be provided by the seller, such as publications, training, supplies, and developmental computer time.
- *Price.* State any incentives or penalties for early or late delivery and for high or low performance. Include taxes. Guarantee price

stability over the term of the contract. Specify invoicing dates and procedures and progress payments. In the case of multiple copies of a product to be delivered, define quantity discounts.

- *Delivery.* Precisely specify when and where each end item is to be delivered and what constitutes its acceptability.
- *Ownership.* Specify who has title to each end item and any other data or materials transmitted between parties during the term of the contract.
- *Warranty.* Define the term of the warranty, precisely stating its beginning and ending. Identify support levels and specify when and how they might change during the term of the contract.
- *Liability.* Specify any limits to the seller's liability for liquidated damages due to a product's unavailability, consequential damages due to unavailability or erroneous operation, and indemnification for copyright and patent infringement. Limit risk of loss during delivery by a third party and loss by the buyer during use. Where appropriate, include a statement by the seller that all work products are original.
- *Responsibilities.* Define responsibilities of both parties to assure successful fulfillment of the contract. Include schedule commitments, rules governing future employment of the opposite party's personnel, confidential treatment of the other party's data, and a limitation of assignment of responsibilities for both parties. Allow the buyer some control over assignment and replacement of personnel during the contract term.
- *License.* If there are to be any restrictions on where or how a product is to be used, include licensing terms. Specify allowable sites for primary and backup operation, permission to copy product end items, how to redesignate sites of operation, and what to do with end items when the contract terminates.
- *Termination.* State all conditions under which the contract may terminate: time lapse, cancellation, default. State how disputes should be resolved. Describe how terms and conditions can be extended or renegotiated.

The above list is only moderately comprehensive. You can find more suggestions and analyses in (85) and (86). Regarding the issue of ownership, be sure to get professional legal advice on any licenses and contracts you draft or even modify.

Chapter
18

Review
Boards

To assure understanding and to gain commitment, this methodology strongly advocates the use of broad review prior to approval in all aspects of software product management. This chapter describes three specific types of review boards and how they contribute to effective software product management.

18.1 THE NEED FOR FORMAL BOARDS

You may take for granted that design documents, release recommendations, and support decisions are reviewed by line management prior to approval. You may wonder, however, why this methodology places so much emphasis on phase reviews by several functions and on multidisciplinary review of external specifications. The reason goes back to the definition of a software product as heavy-duty software. It must satisfy many needs and contributions from many functions are required to generate it. Many peoples' needs must be incorporated, and unless you provide a formal mechanism for them to express their needs, they may be overlooked or you may inadvertently leave too little time in your development schedules to accommodate them.

Formality has another advantage, it makes reviews less dependent on individuals. When you ask for representation from the Test Function on a review board, you want some assurance that the designated representative speaks for Test and not just for himself. Formality suggests that you keep written records of meetings, decisions, and minority opinions. Good written records encourage continuity of representation as individuals change: if Support is on record favoring perfect bound manuals, a new representative from Support is less likely to influence Publications to begin loose-leaf binding without further review by the body that created the record.

Of the three formal boards detailed below, two are standing committees and one is an ad hoc committee. Employ both types as appropriate in your organization. Use a standing committee where continuity of representation is paramount, and keep to a fairly regular schedule so that the representatives you want can plan well in advance to be available when you need them. Use an ad hoc committee where specific expertise is needed or where the total duration of activity is short. Also use an ad hoc committee where activity is intense but sporadic and continuity or representation over a long period of time are not important. This allows distributing a heavy workload to more people thereby giving those who are interested an opportunity to participate in your decision-making processes.

18.2 INTERDISCIPLINARY BOARD

The **interdisciplinary board** is a standing committee whose job it is to assure the manager responsible for cost, schedule, and features of a software product that it will do the job it is intended to do. Such a committee is usually composed of peers in the management hierarchy to assure that no one is intimidated by a superior manager from another discipline. Unless all concerned functions report to one person, this peer concept applies to the manager responsible for the product as well. He should seek a committee of his peers so that he will not try to "pull rank" on them and they will know that he cannot do so.

Involve an interdisciplinary board early in a product's life cycle and keep it involved and you will maximize the acceptability of the product when it is delivered. This may seem to you like a lot of machinery to do what is clearly the job of the director of software products; indeed it may be so. The formality of regular meetings of a standing committee may be out of place in some organizations, and it may be unnecessary in a very small development group. The review process can be carried on informally in such settings. In other cases the techniques of the review process can be tailored to meet the work habits, management styles, and individual charters of your organizations. Review and approval are essential for good software product management, however, and an interdisciplinary board is a vital tool for carrying out meaningful review and gaining durable approval.

A regular meeting schedule is appropriate for an interdisciplinary board, with an option to call ad hoc meetings when urgent attention is needed. A monthly meeting schedule is well tuned to the software development process: few topics suffer much from one month's delay and once a month is frequent enough to keep communication between functions flowing smoothly.

Topics appropriate for interdisciplinary board meetings are all of those mentioned in Chapters 6 through 12 as being part of the phase review process. All functions need not enter actively into all discussions, but each meeting may cover enough topics to warrant attendance at all meetings by all functions.

Scheduling, running, and documenting interdisciplinary board meetings are responsibilities of the Planning Function. When documents such as plans and requirements contracts are to be reviewed, Planning sends preliminary versions of them to other functions well in advance of a meeting. It is most important to provide plenty of time for each function to thoroughly review any document important enough to bring before the interdisciplinary board. A sure way to break up an interdisciplinary board meeting is for a functional representative to justly claim that he has not had enough time to gather inputs on an important document from his associates!

If you can possibly get the cooperation of all functions, review important documents page by page before approving them. This is the surest way to emphasize the importance of being thorough. Someone familiar with each document should guide the review of it, pointing to controversial elements or asking for opinions where there is some doubt about what is best. Interdisciplinary board members may delegate such detailed review to their associates if necessary, but in a high technology field like software product development, they are better off performing such reviews personally. Plans and requirements contracts are designed to communicate at the level of interdisciplinary board management, so each member should be willing and able to do his own homework.

Use the minutes of interdisciplinary board meetings to record momentous decisions and action items. Give these minutes a wide enough distribution to assure thorough communication. Publish them promptly after meetings are held to assure timely dissemination of information.

18.3   TECHNICAL REVIEW BOARD

A **Technical Review Board** (**TRB**) is an ad hoc committee convened by a manager to review a technical subject and to make a recommendation on the subject to him. The most common use of a TRB is to review an external specification and recommend its approval or disapproval to the manager of the Development Function. TRBs are needed because many managers have too many demands on them to give enough personal attention to each of them, and because some demands require deeper technical expertise than a manager can maintain.

Scheduling, running, and documenting TRB activity is the responsibility of a TRB chairman. Your document control function can provide duplicating and mailing services for documents but the TRB chairman is on his own for everything else. A manager selects a TRB chairman he can trust to get the job done quickly and with minimum disruption of other activities. This latter skill is particularly valuable, for the TRB chairman and all members are asked to perform the TRB's task in addition to whatever else they were doing before joining the TRB.

Because a TRB assignment is added to whatever workload a person already has, selection of TRB members requires a dedication to the role of TRBs by all concerned. Potential TRB members should always be asked, better yet invited, to join. It *is* an honor to be asked to critique a design or plan and TRB members should realize this. Before they are asked their immediate managers should also be consulted, because the demand on a TRB member's time is significant for the duration of the TRB. His manager must be willing to accept the consequences.

If a TRB is asked to recommend approval or disapproval of a document and it makes an affirmative recommendation, the report of the chairman can be simple. If it makes a recommendation to disapprove, the chairman may have to explain the board's rationale. In the case of an external specification and a recommendation to the Development manager, the manager may overrule a TRB recommendation to disapprove and accept the external specification as his subordinates presented it. This is his prerogative, but he is not likely to exercise it without a thorough discussion with both the TRB chairman and his own subordinates.

A TRB can function without holding any meetings, but it usually functions better with them. Most often a TRB chairman will circulate a preliminary document, allow time for TRB members to review it, hold a meeting to discuss their reaction to it, and follow up to make sure all agreed-upon changes get into the document. He will repeat this process until the board agrees or "agrees to disagree"; then he will make a recommendation.

18.4   ENHANCEMENT BOARD

An **enhancement board** reviews maintenance requests for revision or enhancement, but not for repair, and recommends a disposition for each one. It is a sort of standing technical review board. If a product has a technical review board, it can be convened to review revision requests or enhancement requests any time up until product release. After release, maintenance requests for revision and enhancement are turned over to an enhancement board.

Requests for revision can usually be dispatched quickly, since they represent a need that must be acknowledged. For instance, when federal privacy regulations are imposed, many software products will have to be modified to accommodate more stringent protection of customer data. Requests for enhancement are quite different. Their implementation is entirely optional and they deserve considerable analysis, both technical and economical, before you render a decision on implementation. Since the submitter of an enhancement request clearly favors it and the Maintenance Function would probably rather not be bothered with any but the most valuable enhancements, an enhancement board can often tip the scales one way or the other. Many enhancement requests remain "open" for a long time; that is, they are considered for each new release of a product until finally you either implement them or "close" them by clearly stating that you no longer will consider implementing them.

Members of an enhancement board are chosen much as are TRB members. Each serves a term of, say, six months. To provide continuity, terms are staggered. The chairing of an enhancement board requires even more continuity since maintenance requests are often deferred and it is often difficult to reconstruct past analyses without continuity of personnel. A chairman that is permanent works best, perhaps with the role being part of a plans manager's job. A distant second choice is to have one member serve two consecutive terms, the second as chairman.

The Services Function provides clerical help to an enhancement board by routing requests to it, and from it to Maintenance for response. Vesting the clerical function in Services also helps maintain configuration management on maintenance requests, since most configuration management controls are administered by Services.

An enhancement board meets with a frequency commensurate with its workload. Meetings are as periodic as possible to aid planning. Recommendations from the board can emerge at any time, with any frequency, and are acted on according to the workloads of Maintenance and Development.

Product
Objectives
and
Requirements
for
A$K

PRODUCT OBJECTIVES AND REQUIREMENTS FOR A$K

Revision A - Original specification

Revision B - Defer Plot and Sort capabilities to
reestablish original schedule; early
availability is of greater value to
Services Company than delaying initial
release to include these features
(pp. 4,7,10,11,12)

- Correct oversight in statement of
hardware constraints (p. 6)

SHEET REVISION STATUS

SH	REV	SH	REV	SH	REV
1	B				
2	A				
3	A				
4	B				
5	A				
6	B				
7	B				
8	A				
9	A				
10	B				
11	B				
12	B				
13	A				
14	A				
15	A				
16	A				
17	A				
18	B				

REV.	APPROVAL	DATE
A	A OR	11/3/77
A	R c G	12/15/77
A	C E M	12/15/77
B	A OR	1/13/78

ABC COMPUTERS	A$K POR	**COVER**	C013/L301A		
		SHEET	NEXT 2	SHEET	1

MF 1063-1 OCT 1974

1. PRODUCT DESCRIPTION

1.1. Product Name and Numbers

1.1.1. Product Name

A$K (pronounced "ASK")

1.1.2. Name Abbreviations

None

1.1.3. Product Numbers

L301A

1.1.4. Project Numbers

C013

1.2. Brief Description of Product

A$K allows a financial analyst or other person with similar
analytic requirements to interactively and remotely "ask" a
Stella 100 computer to retrieve and manipulate financial
information from DATABASE which contains twenty years worth
of fundamental data and expressions for a large number of
corporations and industries. He may also create additional
public or private data, corporations, industries, expressions,
and items and use his creations along with information from
DATABASE.

The software product A$K plus the DATABASE information comprise
a service called A$K DATABASE, all three of which are propri-
etary to the ABC Services Company.

1.2.1. Copyright Notice

Copyright © 1977, by ABC Computers Company

ABC COMPUTERS	A$K POR	SHEET REVISION	C013/L301A	
		A	NEXT 3	SHEET 2

MF 1064 APR 1972

349

1.3. Product End Items

Key:

Direct = Not used to generate other software
Indirect = Used to generate other software

Support Level 1 = Requests for Product correction will be answered; Updates may be issued; Requests for Product Enhancement will be considered

2 = Requests for Product Correction will be answered; Updates may be issued; Requests for Product Enhancement will not be considered

3 = Requests for Product Correction will be answered

Responsibility D = Development
M = Maintenance
P = Publications
T = Test

PRODUCT TYPE		INITIAL SUPPORT LEVEL	
DIRECT	X		
INDIRECT		1	X
		2	
		3	

	No Distribution	Distribution: Incremental	Complete	Responsibility
Specifications:				
ERS	X		X	D
IRS	X		X	D
Test Specification	X		X	T
Maintenance Specification	X		X	M
Other:				
Publications:				
System Description Manual				
Reference Manual	X	X		P
Reference Booklet	X	X		P
Operator Manual	X	X		P
Message Manual	X	X		P
Software Release Bulletin				
Other:				
Promotional Material:				
Software:				
Listings	X		X	D
Source Code	X		X	D
Object Code	X	X		D
Test Material	X		X	D,T
Development Tools				
Other:				

ABC COMPUTERS	A$K POR	SHEET REVISION A	C013/L301A		
			NEXT 4	SHEET 3	

MF 1064 APR 1972

2.   MISSION

The Business Plan for Financial Services(Ref. 4.1.a) declares
the intent of ABC Services Company to market an interactive,
remote access financial analysis system to the financial community. A$K is our proposed response to the software require-
ments defined in that plan.

2.1.   Request for Product Revision (PPR) Reconciliation

2.1.1.   PPRs Excluded

None

2.1.2.   PPRs Included

None - A$K is a new product.

2.2.   Request for Product Enhancement (RPE) Reconciliation

2.2.1.   RPEs Excluded

None

2.2.2.   RPEs Included

None - A$K is a new product with no similar predecessor.

2.3.   Request for Product Correction (RPC) Reconciliation

2.3.1.   RPCs Excluded

None - A$K is a new product.

2.4.   Plans Reconciliation

2.4.1.   Plans Excluded

The wide range of terminals called for in the Business Plan
for Financial Services (see 4.1.a) will not be supported.
Only Telcoscope 43 or electrically and functionally equivalent terminals will function properly with A$K.

Commands to plot output (rather than tabulate it) and to
sort files are deferred for consideration in a subsequent
version.

2.4.2.   Plans Included

Business Plan for Financial Services, Section 5 -
Ref. 4.1.a.

ABC COMPUTERS	A$K POR	SHEET REVISION B	C013/L301A	
			NEXT 5	SHEET 4

MF 1064 APR 1972

2.5. Summary of User Needs

Intended users of A$K are financial analysts or other persons
with similar analytic requirements, such as portfolio managers. Users are not expected to have familiarity with computer programming nor to be accomplished terminal operators.
See also Section 1.2.

According to Reference 4.1.a, the first Version of A$K should
be marketable for six months to one year. A second Version
should be marketable for at least eighteen months.

2.6. Alternatives Considered

As no present Services product can perform the functions of
A$K, a new product must be built. No comparable product is
available ready-made. Services has decided to sole-source
contract with Computers to build and maintain A$K. They
base that decision on past experience contracting with
Computers.

2.7. Return on Investment

Services expects sales to financial customers to increase
10% within three months of release and to reach an increase
of at least 170% within one year of release. Based on
expected gross profit from such a sales increase, the cost
of producing A$K will be recovered within eight months of
release and, without a new Version, A$K should produce a
cumulative gross margin three times its cumulative cost,
including maintenance.

3. STRATEGY

3.1. Conventions

3.1.1. Notations

No special notations are used in this POR.

3.1.2. Terminology

All special terminology is defined in context in this POR.

3.2. Generated Software

Not applicable

3.3. Operational Software

A$K consists of a collection of operational capabilities

ABC COMPUTERS	A$K POR	SHEET REVISION A	C013/L301A			
			NEXT 6	SHEET 5		

MF 1004 APR 1972

352

called the User Interface and a separate collection of
maintenance utilities called the Update Processor:

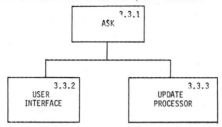

3.3.1. All A$K Functions

3.3.1.1. Constraints on All A$K Functions

3.3.1.1.1. Standards for All A$K Functions

ABC Programming Standard (Ref. 4.1.e)

3.3.1.1.2. Compatibility Constraints on All A$K Functions

There are no known software products or databases with
which A$K should be compatible. Files generated by A$K
will be VSOS Direct Access (Ref. 4.1.b), and will thus
be readily usable by programs other than A$K.

3.3.1.1.3. Software Constraints on All A$K Functions

VSOS, Version 4 (Ref. 4.1.b) is required by A$K. Any
VSOS Product Set Member may run concurrently with A$K
as long as the hardware configuration of Sec. 3.3.1.1.4
is not encroached. Update Processor may run concurrently with User Interface, but no User Interface attempts to access files currently being used by Update
Processor will be allowed.

3.3.1.1.4. Hardware Constraints on All A$K Functions

In addition to the ₍minimum₎ requirements for Ref. 4.1.b and c,
A$K needs:

	Minimum	Target	Maximum
a. M103 Floating point unit	1	1	1
b. M107 Power fail option	1	1	1
c. M1100 Memory module	3	3	6
d. M3100 Disc module	2	3	8

MF 1064 APR 1973

353

```
                                          Minimum Target Maximum
        e. M210  Console                     1       1       1
        f. M442 Communications controller    1       8      16
     or
        g. M443 Communications controller    1       1       2
        h. Switched, 4800 baud, two-wire     1     128     256
           phone line
        i. Telcoscope 43 (or equivalent)     1     512    1024
           terminal (max. 256 on-line
           at one time)
        j. Telcoscope 43-1 (or equivalent) 0 (1/3)/43  1/43
           printer
```

See also Secs. 3.3.2.1.4 and 3.3.3.1.4.

3.3.1.2. A$K External Properties

3.3.1.2.1. A$K Outputs

- Records to public and private A$K files, each VSOS Direct Access (see 4.1.b).

- Records to DATABA$E, a collection of VSOS Indexed Linked Sequential files (see 4.1.b).

- Fields and records transmitted to terminals and the console.

- All output will be VSOS Logical Access

3.3.1.2.2. A$K Processes

Operational Mode will consist of interactive retrieval, computation, reporting, ~~and plotting~~ by financial analysts.

Maintenance Mode will consist of interactive data base analysis, reorganization, and updating by systems analysts trained to maintain the data base.

3.3.1.2.3. A$K Inputs

- Blocks of records from DATABA$E and DATABA$E Update files (also VSOS ILS files).

- Records from public and private A$K files.

- Fields from terminal and console keyboards.

- All input will be VSOS Logical Access.

ABC COMPUTERS	A$K POR	SHEET REVISION	C013/L301A	
		B	NEXT 8	SHEET 7

MF 1064 APR 1973

354

3.3.1.3. A$K Ergonomic Properties

3.3.1.3.1. Security and Privacy of A$K

No public files, including DATABA$E, will be able to be
written into from a terminal. All private files will
be password protected using VSOS conventions. All
write operations on public files, including DATABA$E,
will have to be performed from the console.

3.3.1.3.2. Reliability of A$K

Many failures will be trapped by A$K, logged in an
error file, and referred to whichever VSOS recovery
feature is appropriate.

A$K will not alter DATABA$E; virtual files (see Sec.
5.3.1.1) will be used to pseudo-update DATABA$E.

A$K will obey all VSOS interface constraints and thus
should neither cause a cooperating product to malfunction, nor be caused to malfunction by a cooperating
product which also obeys the conventions.

Each block of records in DATABA$E contains a checksum
which will be computed and compared by A$K to verify
integrity of data.

The Virtual Telecommunications Access Method (VTAM) of
VSOS will be used at Logical Level 4, the highest
available error recovery level (which logs all recover-
able hardware errors.

3.3.1.3.3. Restartability of A$K

See Secs. 3.3.2.3.3 and 3.3.3.3.3.

3.3.1.3.4. Customizability of A$K

A$K will have both assembly time and startup time
parameters to define the configuration on which it is
to run. Assembly parameters will cover number of memory and disc modules, and number and type of communications controllers. Startup parameters will cover
numbers of lines and terminals, and terminal and password identifiers.

Algorithms will be built in to optimize allocation of
disc and to estimate (albeit non-heuristically) when to

ABC COMPUTERS	A$K POR	SHEET REVISION A	C013/L301A	
			NEXT 9	SHEET 8

MF 1064 APR 1972

355

acknowledge rather than complete a command immediately.

Utility routines will be provided to update, analyze, and reorganize public A$K files and user files.

3.3.1.3.5. Performance of A$K

See Secs. 3.3.2.3.5 and 3.3.3.3.5.

3.3.1.3.6. Usability of A$K

See Secs. 3.3.2.3.6 and 3.3.3.3.6.

3.3.1.3.7. Portability of A$K

A$K will observe all VSOS interface constraints and will use VSOS Logical Access for all I/O. A$K thus should run unmodified with any operating system which is a superset of VSOS.

3.3.1.4. Internal Properties of A$K

3.3.1.4.1. Maintainability of A$K

A$K will be written entirely in BIL3 (Ref. 4.1.f) with the space reservation factor set to 10%. Per Sec. 1.4, only object code will be distributed. UPDATE (Ref. 4.1.g) will be used to insert object code corrections.

3.3.1.4.2. Algorithms of A$K

See Secs. 3.3.2.4.2 and 3.3.3.4.2.

3.3.2. User Interface Function

For all omitted subsections, see the corresponding subsections of Sec. 3.3.1.

3.3.2.1.1. Standards for User Interface

ANSI X3.28-1971 (Ref. 4.1.d)

3.3.2.1.3. Software Constraints on User Interface

Will require VSOS DAM, ILSAM, and VTAM (Ref. 4.1.b).

3.3.2.1.4. Hardware Constraints on User Interface

In addition to the hardware shown in Sec. 3.3.1.1.4,

ABC COMPUTERS	A$K POR	SHEET REVISION A	C013/L301A		
			NEXT 10	SHEET 9	

356

User Interface will need the minimum requirements for VSOS ILSAM, DAM, and VTAM (Ref. 4.1.b).

3.3.2.2.1. User Interface Outputs

Same as Sec. 3.3.1.2.1 except for exclusion of records to DATABASE.

3.3.2.2.2. User Interface Processes

User Interface will:

- Create selection criteria and/or expressions

- Create company or industry files

- Add data to files

- ~~Sort data~~

- Report, ~~plot,~~ and/or save results

3.3.2.2.3. User Interface Inputs

Same as Sec. 3.3.1.2.3 except for exclusion of data from DATABASE Update files.

3.3.2.3.3. User Interface Restartability

Status of work in process for all active (including logged out but still processing) users will be saved on disc periodically (on a parametric interval, set at assembly time). Automatic and manual restart procedures will be provided which use this data.

a. Automatic Restart

By use of power fail option M107, User Interface will automatically enter a recovery routine on power-up. All users active when power went down will be notified of the failure. Those still active will be asked to log out or give permission to continue processing from the last checkpoint. Those not still active will be assumed to have given up; their work in process will be purged except for save command results which had been completed prior to power fail. This same procedure will be invoked after any other failure where it can be done reliably.

ABC COMPUTERS	A$K POR	SHEET REVISION	C013/L301A		
		B	NEXT 11	SHEET 10	

MF 1064 APR 1972

357

b. Manual Restart

Each checkpoint will consist of a complete dump
of User Interface memory. Each time User Interface
is started-up, the operator will be asked if he
wants a fresh start or a checkpoint start. If he
selects checkpoint start, User Interface will be
loaded from the checkpoint file and the power fail
procedure will be invoked. Whenever a failure
occurs where the automatic restart cannot reliably
be called, a diagnostic message will be sent to the
VSOS console and the operator will be given a chance
to attempt this manual restart.

3.3.2.3.5. Performance of User Interface

Assuming only A$K active on the computer and the
recovery parameter set for checkpoints once per minute,
every command must be completed or acknowledged within
five seconds of entry, with a goal of three seconds.
All commands acknowledged rather than reported complete
in the initial response must be completed in two seconds per item per period per company.

For the purpose of this section, "completed" means output to the terminal has begun but has not necessarily
completed. All output to the terminal shall be performed at not less than two lines/second, with a goal
of 200 visible characters/second (by judiciously using
the terminal tab feature).

3.3.2.3.6. Usability of User Interface

In a typical session with A$K, an analyst with no
programming experience will log in from a terminal and
enter into a dialog in which he specifies the industries
and companies he is interested in, the types of comparisons he wishes to make, the criteria he wishes to use
for screening and-sorting data, and the reports and
plots he wants. A$K will respond to every command with
either a diagnostic message indicating some error or
ambiguity in the user's entry, an appropriate response
to the command, or an acknowledgement that it is attempting to fulfill the command. The last case occurs when
the appropriate response requires so long to generate
that the user might suspect a malfunction if he received
no acknowledgement (e.g., when a create file command is
entered). When the response to such a command is available, A$K will send it to the terminal unless the user
has logged out, in which case A$K will store the result

ABC	ASK POR	SHEET REVISION	C013/L301A	
COMPUTERS		B	NEXT 12	SHEET 11

MF 1064 APR 1972

358

and inform the user of its availability when next he logs in.

~~Two types of output from files will be available; tabular and graphic.~~ Whenever the data requested exceeds the capacity of the Telcoscope screen, the data will automatically be formatted into pages which can be scanned. Terminals equipped with printers may print pages selectively.

3.3.2.4.2. Algorithms of User Interface

ASK will execute every command interpretively and immediately; stacking of commands will thus not be allowed (except for a save command as explained below).

A virtual file concept will be employed whereby disc space and retrieval time will be conserved. When a user defines a file to be a superset of any existing file, (either user or system defined), no existing data will be stored in the new file. If, at the end of a terminal session, a user wants to preserve such files created during a session, execution of a save command will cause all data elements to be copied and saved. If this command is followed immediatly by a log out command, the save command will be completed after the log out, thus freeing the user and terminal for other activity.

A global syntax analyzer will scan every entry to perform range, character type and number, and other consistency checks before passing control to command or other input processors. This will allow a user to correct erroneous input immediately.

3.3.3. Update Processor Functions

For all omitted subsections, see the corresponding subsections of Sec. 3.3.1.

3.3.3.1.3. Software Constraints on Update Processor

Requires VSOS ILSAM only.

3.3.3.1.4. Hardware Constraints on Update Processor

In addition to the requirements for VSOS ILSAM (see Ref. 4.1.b), Update Processor will need:

ABC COMPUTERS	ASK POR	SHEET REVISION B	C013/L301A		
			NEXT 13	SHEET 12	

MF 1064 APR 1972

359

	Minimum	Target	Maximum
M103 Floating point unit	1	1	1
M107 Power fail option	1	1	1
M1100 Memory module	1	2	2
M3100 Disc module	1	3	8
M210 Console	1	1	1

3.3.3.2.1. Update Processor Outputs

Same as Sec. 3.3.1.2.1 except for exclusion of public
and private files and terminals

3.3.3.2.3. Update Processor Inputs

Same as Sec. 3.3.1.2.3 except for exclusion of public
and private files and terminals.

3.3.3.3.3. Restartability of Update Processor

Will use the audit file capability of UPDATE (Ref. 4.1.g)
to allow checkpoints and restarts.

3.3.3.3.5. Performance of Update Processor

Will use the same concepts as UPDATE and borrow from it
as much code as possible. It is and objective for
Update Processor to be no slower than UPDATE for com-
parable-sized operations.

3.3.3.3.6. Usability of Update Processor

Again, Update Processor will be based on UPDATE and
will have an operator interface as much like it as
possible.

3.3.3.4.2. Algorithms of Update Processor

See Sec. 3.3.3.3.5.

3.4. Restrictions

As mentioned below in Sec. 6.3, it will not be possible within
the scope of the development project to test a maximum hardware configuration.

As noted in Sec. 2.4.2, only Telcoscope 43 terminals will be
supported.

While the following is not a restriction, it is mentioned to

360

avoid misleading anyone. The design of A$K assumes that a user will want to use as many commands interactively as possible and that the report command will be the most heavily used. Thus, he must build all criteria, expressions, and files in advance of issuing a report command which uses them to avoid the frustration of waiting for lengthy procedures to be executed during the heart of his analysis.

See also Sec. 3.3.2.1.3.

4. BACKGROUND

4.1. References

    a. Business Plan for Financial Services, J. A. Auchin-chloss, 6/13/77 (Preliminary), Section 5.

    b. Virtual Storage Operating System Interface Manual, 12-6643-43.

    c. DATABA$E Contents and Format Specification, 1230711, as approved 2/7/77.

    d. American National Standard Procedures for the Use of the Communication Control Characters of American National Standard Code for Information interchange in Specified Data Communication Links, ANSI X3.28-1971, Secs. 5.2, 5.4, 5.7.

    e. ABC Programming Standard, as approved 2/14/73, or as currently approved.

    f. Basic Implementation Language III Reference Manual, 07-5411-67.

    g. UPDATE Operator Manual, 06-4169-3F.

5. DELIVERY AND INSTALLATION

5.1. Provisions for Protection

    Copyright

5.2. Installation Resources

    Any VSOS operator with six months experience (or equivalent training) should be able to install A$K using UPDATE in fifteen minutes of console interaction. After studying the verification procedure in the Software Release Bulletin

ABC COMPUTERS	ASK POR	SHEET REVISION A	C013/L301A	
			NEXT 15	SHEET 14

MF 1064 APR 1972

for half an hour, he should be able to execute the verification procedure in ten minutes of terminal interaction.

The above predictions assume all necessary hardware running without malfunction and no concurrent activity on the computer.

5.3. Media

The object code of A$K will be distributed on Diskette in UPDATE format (see Ref. 4.1.g).

Object code corrections will also be distributed on Diskette.

6. TACTICS

6.1. Interdependencies

6.1.1. Interdependencies Needed

Interface Electronics must make the channel fan, with a diagnostic program, available to Product Test at Milestone S10 (see Sec. 7).

Services Company must provide access to a properly functioning Minimum Configuration (see Sec. 3.3.1.1.4) Stella 100 computer from Milestone D20 to Milestone P30. Items c-i of Sec. 3.3.1.1.4 must be dedicated; all others may be shared.

6.1.2. Interdependencies Provided

The product structure of A$K will be fully described by the following interrelated ERSs:

A$K User Interface ERS (C013/L321)
A$K Update Processor ERS (C013/L331)

The Reference Manual and Reference Booklet must be available in final form, in quantity (quick-print copies acceptable) by Milestone I21 (see Sec. 7) for Services Company to conduct training classes.

6.2. Technical Review Board (TRB)

Each of the following persons has been contacted and consents to serve in the capacity indicated:

Bob Wilbur (Software Product Test) - Chairman
C. W. Garrison (Services Company)
Robert Wong (Publications)   Bob Sims (Applications Dev.)

ABC COMPUTERS	A$K POR	SHEET REVISION	C013/L301A		
		A	NEXT		SHEET
				15	15

MF 1064 APR 1972

362

6.3. Product Verification

6.3.1. Level of Testing

CATEGORY	STAGE		
	A	B	C
Demonstration		/	/
Benchmark	D	/	/
Complete Feature	D	T	/
New Feature			/
Performance	D	T	/
Reliability	D	T	/
Stability			/
Regression			/
Installability	D	T	S
Configuration	D	T	S

TEST   MODE

I   = Testing performed by Test Function   (X)

II = Testing Monitored by Test Function   ( )

III = No participation by Test Function   ( )

TESTING ORGANIZATION

D = Development   T = Test   S = Services

Services Company will provide two persons with a background
in financial analysis to operate terminals during part of
B-Test.

The Minimum Configuration of Sec. 3.3.1.1.4 will be tested
with real hardware, as will the Target Configuration except

ABC COMPUTERS	A$K POR	SHEET REVISION	A	C013/L301A		
				NEXT	17	SHEET 16

MF 1064 APR 1972

for communications controllers, lines, and terminals. The
maximum hardware configuration tested will be M442(1) plus
M443(1), probably seven phone lines and terminals. The
controller limit is a function of available hardware and
the line and terminal limit is a function of available manpower.

Software Product Test will build a terminal simulator and
Interface Electronics will build a channel fan to be used
with it. With the simulator running in one VSOS partition
talking to the apex of the fan, and A$K in another parti-
tion talking to the base of the fan, the simultaneous simulation of 144 of 1024 Telcoscopes will be used to test
A$K. This simulation will also allow the simulation of
one 43-1 per 43.

6.3.2. Bases of Reference

As this is a new product, there is no base of reference for
error correction. The POR and ERSs for A$K shall be the
sole criteria for B-Test.

6.4. Provisions for Implementation

Services Company currently intends to provide and implementation plan; reference it for details. See also Sec. 6.1.2.

7. SCHEDULE CHANGE NOTICE

See next page.

ABC

COMPUTERS

MF 1064 APR 1972

A$K POR

SHEET REVISION	C013/L301A	
A	NEXT	SHEET
	18	17

364

PROJECT NAME: **A$K Development** PROJECT NUMBER: **C013**
PRODUCT NAME: **A$K** PRODUCT NUMBER: **L301A**

	NAME	OLD	NEW	NOTES
P10	PBR APPROVED	09/29/77 C		
D10	POR SUBMITTED	11/03/77 C		
P20	POR APPROVED	12/15/77 C		
D20	ERS SUBMITTED	01/09/78 C		
T10	TEST PLAN APPROVED	02/09/78		
D30	ERS APPROVED	03/15/78	02/06/78	*
B10	PUBLICATIONS PLAN APPROVED	01/26/78		
S10	PROJECT HARDWARE INSTALLED	03/31/78		
I10	SUPPORT PLAN APPROVED	03/02/78		
D41	DEMONSTRATION PERFORMED	TBS		
T20	ACCEPTANCE TESTS DELIV.	TBS		
T30	B-TEST BEGUN	07/03/78	05/08/78	*
I20	PROMOTIONAL MATERIAL DIST.	TBS		
I21	TRAINING COURSE PREPARED	TBS		
B20	REFERENCE MAT. TO PRINTER	07/17/78	06/05/78	*
P30	PRODUCT AVAILABILITY DATE	08/18/78	07/03/78	*
M20	MAINTENANCE SPEC. COMPLETE	TBS		
S20	PRODUCT DISTRIBUTION DATE	09/01/78	07/17/78	*

EVENT	REASON FOR CHANGE
All	Deferring PLOT and SORT will return project to schedule

PREPARED BY: *Luther Davis*   APPROVED BY: *A ØR*

APPROVED BY: _____   APPROVED BY: _____

OLD DATE: 01/06/78   NEW DATE: *1/13/78*

ABC COMPUTERS	A$K POR	SHEET REVISION B	C013/L301A	
			NEXT None	SHEET 18

MF 1064 APR 1972

References

1. J. M. Buxton, Peter Naur, and Brian Randell, *Software Engineering Concepts and Techniques,* Petrocelli/Charter, New York, 1976.
2. Raymond T. Yeh, "Editor's Notice," *IEEE Transactions on Software Engineering,* **SE-2**(4), 265–273 (1976).
3. Richard L. Nolan, "Managing the Computer Resource: A Stage Hypothesis," *Communications of ACM,* **16**(7), 399–405 (1973).
4. Harlan D. Mills, "Software Development," *IEEE Transactions on Software Engineering,* **SE-2**(4), 265–273 (1976).
5. Robert I. Benjamin, *Control of the Information System Development Cycle,* Wiley-Interscience, New York, 1971, p. 29.
6. IBM Corporation, *Federal Systems Center Programming Librarian's Guide,* Version 1, Report FSC 72-5074-1, IBM, Gaithersburg, Md., 1972.
7. Don Leavitt, "ICP Salutes Packages with $1 Million Sales," *Computerworld,* **11**(13), 1–2 (1977).
8. Dr. Victor R. Basili and [F.] Terry Baker, *Structured Programming Tutorial,* Cat. No. 75CH1049-6, IEEE Computer Society, Long Beach, Calif., 1975, pp. 216–217.
9. George A. Miller, "The Magical Number Seven, Plus or Minus Two: Some Limits on our Capacity for Processing Information," *Psychological Review,* **63**, 108 (1956).
10. George A. Miller, Eugene Galanter, and Karl H. Pribram, *Plans and the Structure of Behavior,* Holt, Rinehart & Winston, New York, 1960, p. 16.
11. Nicklaus Wirth, "Program Development by Stepwise Refinement," *Communications of ACM,* **14**(4), 221–227 (1971).
12. E[dsger] W. Dijkstra, "The Structure of 'THE'—Multiprogramming System," *Communications of ACM,* **11**(5), 341–346 (1968).
13. Dr. H. Trauboth, "Guidelines for Documentation of Scientific Software Systems," *1973 IEEE Symposium on Computer Software Reliability,* IEEE Cat. No. 73CH0741-9 CSR, IEEE, New York.
14. Harlan Mills, "Top Down Programming in Large Systems," *Designing Techniques in Large Systems,* presented to the First Courant Computer Science Symposium, 1970, Prentice Hall, Englewood Cliffs, N.J., 1971, pp. 41–55.

15. Dr. L. Parnas, "On the Criteria To Be Used in Decomposing Systems Into Modules," *Communications of ACM,* **15**(12), 1053–1058 (1972).

16. G. J. Myers, "Composite Design: The Design of Modular Programs," *Technical Report No. TR00.2406,* IBM Corporation, Poughkeepsie, N.Y., 1973.

17. W. P. Stevens, G. J. Myers, and L. L. Constantine, "Structured Design," *IBM Systems Journal,* **2**, 115–139 (1974).

18. Christopher Alexander, *Notes on the Synthesis of Form,* Harvard University Press, Cambridge, Mass., 1964.

19. Corrado Böhm and Giuseppe Jacopini, "Flow Diagrams, Turing Machines and Languages with only Two Formation Rules," *Communications of ACM,* **9**(5), 366–371 (1966).

20. C. A. R. Hoare, "Proof of a Program: FIND," *Communications of ACM,* **14**(1), 39–45 (1971).

21. Harlan D. Mills, "Chief Programmer Team Operations," *Mathematical Foundations for Structured Programming,* FSC 72-6012, IBM, Gaithersburg, Md., 1972.

22. Mack Hanan, "Reorganize Your Company Around Its Markets," *Harvard Business Review,* **52**(6), 63–74 (1974).

23. IBM Corporation, *Structured Walk-Throughs: A Project Management Tool,* IBM Corporation, Poughkeepsie, N.Y., 1973.

24. M. E. Fagan, "Design and Code Inspections to Reduce Errors in Program Development," *IBM Systems Journal,* **15**(3), 182–211 (1976).

25. Douglas McGregor, *The Human Side of Enterprise,* McGraw-Hill, New York, 1960.

26. Peter F. Drucker, *The Effective Executive,* Harper & Row, New York, 1966, pp. 71–92.

27. Peter F. Drucker, *The Practice of Management,* Harper, New York, 1954, pp. 121ff.

28. Abraham H. Maslow, "The Superior Person," in Warren G. Bennis, Ed., *American Bureaucracy,* Aldine, Chicago, 1970, pp. 27–37.

29. Donald E. Knuth, "Computer Programming as an Art," *Communications of ACM,* **17**(12), 667–673 (1974).

30. Edsger W. Dijkstra, "The Structure of the 'THE'—Multiprogramming System," *Communications of ACM,* **11**(5), 341 (1968).

31. Lawrence H. Cooke, Jr., "The Chief Programmer Team Administrator," *Datamation,* **22**(6), 85–86 (1976).

32. Merritt L. Kastens, *Long-Range Planning for Your Business,* AMACOM, New York, 1976.

33. David W. Ewing, Ed., *Long-Range Planning for Management,* Harper & Row, New York, 1958, 1964.

34. The Conference Board, *Planning and the Corporate Planning Director,* The Conference Board, Report No. 627, New York, 1974.

35. Harry B. Jones, *Preparing Company Plans,* Halstead Press, New York, 1974.

36. Frederick P. Brooks, Jr., *The Mythical Man-Month: Essays on Software Engineering,* Addison-Wesley, Reading, Mass., 1975.

37. Martin A. Goetz, "Successful Product Has Many Varied Ingredients," *Computerworld,* **10**(8), Software Packages Supplement (1976).

38. M. E. Sloan, "Survey of Electrical Engineering and Computer Science Departments in the U.S.," *Computer,* **8**(12), 41–42 (1975).

39. F. Terry Baker, "Structured Programming in a Production Programming Environment," *IEEE Transactions on Software Engineering,* **SE-1**(2), 241–252 (1975).

40. Harlan D. Mills, "The New Math of Computer Programming," *Communications of ACM,* **18**(1), 43–48 (1975).

41. F. T[erry] Baker, "Chief Programmer Team Management of Production Programming," *IBM Systems Journal,* **1,** 56–73 (1972).

42. Barry W. Boehm, "Software and Its Impact: A Quantitative Assessment," *Datamation,* **19**(5), 48–59 (1973).

43. J. D. Aron, *The Program Development Process: Part I, The Individual Programmer,* Addison-Wesley, Reading, Mass., 1974.

44. J. D. Aron, "Estimating Resources for Large Programming Systems," in *Software Engineering Concepts and Techniques,* Petrocelli/Charter, New York, 1976, pp. 206–217.

45. Edward A. Nelson, *Some Recent Contributions to Computer Programming Management,* SP-3122, Systems Development Corporation, Santa Monica, Calif., April 16, 1968.

46. J. M. McNeil, "Formalizing the Task of Software Estimation," *Software Engineering (International Computer State of the Art Report),* Infotech, Maidenhead, Berkshire, England, 1972.

47. William S. Donelson, "Project Planning and Control," *Datamation,* **22**(6), 73–80 (1976).

48. Ray W. Wolverton, "The Cost of Developing Large-Scale Software," *IEEE Transactions on Computers,* **C-23**(6), 615–636 (1974).

49. Randall F. Scott and Dick B. Simmons, "Programmer Productivity and the Delphi Technique," *Datamation,* **20**(5), 71–73 (1974).

50. Randall F. Scott and Dick B. Simmons, "Predicting Programming Group Productivity—A Communications Model," *IEEE Transactions on Software Engineering,* **SE-1**(4), 411–414 (1975).

51. R. E. Keirstead, *On the Feasibility of Software Certification,* NTIS PB245213/4WC, Stanford Research Institute, Menlo Park, Calif., 1975.

52. John W. Humble, *How to Manage by Objectives,* American Management Association, New York, 1973.

53. J. D. Batten, *Beyond Management by Objectives,* American Management Association, New York, 1966.

54. Gerald M. Weinberg, "The Psychology of Improved Programming Performance," *Datamation,* **18**(11), 82–85 (1972).

55. Russell D. Archibald and Richard L. Villoria, *Network-Based Management Systems (PERT/CPM),* Wiley, New York, 1967.

56. American Management Association, *Basic Project Management: Planning, Scheduling, and Control,* Course 6503–44, American Management Association, New York, 1974, Appendix C.

57. Frank G. Kirk, *Total System Development for Information Systems,* Wiley, New York, 1973.

58. D. L. Parnas, "A Technique for Software Module Specification with Examples," *Communications of ACM,* **15**(5), 330–336 (1972).

59. Barbara H. Liskov and Stephen N. Zilles, "Specification Techniques for Data Abstractions," *IEEE Transactions on Software Engineering,* **SE-1**(1), 7–19 (1975).

60. R. E. Noonan, "Structured Programming and Formal Specification," *Proceedings of the First National Conference on Software Engineering,* IEEE Cat. No. 75CH0992-8C, IEEE, New York, 1975, pp. 75–81.

61. IBM Corporation, *HIPO—A Design Aid and Documentation Technique,* GC 20–1851-1, IBM Corporation, White Plains, N.Y., 1974, p. 86.

62. I. Nassi and B. Shneiderman, "Flowchart Techniques for Structured Programming," *SIGPLAN Notices,* **8**(8), 12–26 (1973).

63. Ned Chapin, "New Format for Flowcharts," *Software—Practice and Experience,* Vol. 4, Wiley, Sussex,.England, 1974, pp. 341–357.

64. Alvin Toffler, *Future Shock,* Random House, New York, 1970.

65. Dick H. Brandon, *Management Standards for Data Processing,* Van Nostrand Reinhold, New York and Canada, 1963.

66. Marc J. Rochkind, "The Source Code Control System," *Proceedings of the First National Conference on Software Engineering,* IEEE Cat. No. 75CH0992-8C, IEEE, New York, 1975, pp. 37–43.

67. US Department of Defense, *Military Standard—Configuration Management Practices for Systems, Equipment, Munitions, and Computer Programs,* MIL–STD–483 (USAF), USG–DOD, Washington, 1970.

68. Burt H. Liebowitz, "The Technical Specification—Key to Management Control of Computer Programming," *AFIPS Conference Proceedings, 1967 SJCC,* Vol. 30, Thompson, Washington, 1967, pp. 51–59.

69. US Department of Defense, "Computer Program Configuration Item Specification," *Military Standard—Configuration Management Practices for Systems, Equipment, Munitions, and Computer Programs,* MIL–STD–483 (USAF), USG–DOD, Washington, 1970, Appendix VI, pp. 39–54.

70. US Department of Defense, "Specification and Support Documentation Maintenance, Computer Program," *Military Standard—Configuration Management Practices for Systems, Equipment, Munitions, and Computer Programs,* MIL–STD–483 (USAF), USG–DOD, Washington, 1970, Appendix VIII, pp. 63–77.

71. US Department of Defense, "Engineering Changes (Computer Programs)," *Military Standard—Configuration Management Practices for Systems, Equipment, Munitions, and Computer Programs,* MIL–STD–483 (USAF), USG–DOD, Washington, 1970, Appendix XIV, pp. 109–115.

72. Lloyd V. Searle and George Neil, "Configuration Management of Computer Programs by the Air Force: Principles and Documentation," *AFIPS Conference Proceedings, 1967 SJCC,* Vol. 30, Thompson, Washington, 1967, pp. 45–49.

73. Milton V. Ratynski, "The Air Force Computer Program Acquisition Concept," *AFIPS Conference Proceedings, 1967 SJCC,* Vol. 30, Thompson, Washington, 1967, pp. 33–44.

74. Milton R. Wessel, "Legal Protection of Computer Programs," *Harvard Business Review,* **43**(2), 97–106 (1965).

75. *Universal Copyright Convention as Revised at Paris on 24 July 1971,* INLA/UCC/42, Conference for Revision of the Universal Copyright Convention, Paris, 1971.

76. Main Commission, Diplomatic Conference for the Revision of the Berne Convention, *The Paris Act,* B/DC/34, World Intellectual Property Organization, Geneva, 1971.

77. Angeline Pantages, "Reminiscences and Predictions," *Datamation,* **23**(1), 156–161 (1977).

78. Robert P. Bigelow, Esq., "Copyright law and your database," *Computer Decisions,* **9**(5), 28–32 (1977).

79. Calvin N. Mooers, "Computer Software and Copyright," *ACM Computing Surveys,* **7**(1), 45–72 (1975).

80. Don Leavitt, "Program Patents Gaining Ground," *Computerworld,* **10**(52)–**11**(1), 14 (1977).

81. Elmer Galbi, "The Protection of Computer Programming in the United States and Throughout the World," presented to the *Japanese Information Processing Association on October 28, 1971,* unpublished, IBM Corporation, Endicott, N.Y., 1971.

82. Elmer Galbi, "Proposal for New Legislation to Protect Computer Programming," *Bulletin, Copyright Society of the USA,* **17**(4), 280–296 (1970).

83. IBM Corporation, *Copyright Instructions,* G120-2083-2, IBM Corporation Data Processing Division, White Plains, N.Y., 1972.

84. David Goldberg, "Legal Protection of EDP Software," *Datamation,* **18**(5), 66–70 (1972).

85. Richard L. Bernacchi and Gerald H. Larsen, *Data Processing Contracts and the Law,* Little, Brown, Boston, Toronto, 1974.

86. Robert P. Bigelow and Susan H. Nycum, *Your Computer and the Law,* Prentice-Hall, Englewood Cliffs, N.J., 1975, pp. 61–95.

87. Oliver R. Smoot, "Development of an International System for Legal Protection of Computer Programs," *Communications of ACM,* **19**(4), 171–174 (1976).

INDEX

Page numbers appearing in **boldface** type indicate the reference for the definition or principle discussion of an item.

ABC Computers Company, 27-33
ABC Corporation, 26-33
ABC Services Company, 27, 35
Abstraction, levels of, 22
Acceptance, retroactive, 149
  test, **101**, 148
Activity, **239**
  dummy, 246
Administration, **106**
Age of Programming, 3
Age of Software Development, 3
Age of Software Engineering, 3
"Agree to disagree," 91, 344
Alexander, Christopher, 22
Algorithm, 267, 275
  testing, 277
Analysis Phase, **16**
APAR, 305
Archival responsibility, 81-82, 329
A$K, 34-37
A$K DATABA$E, 35
Assembly Number, **327**
A-Test, **100**
  report, **101**

Backup programmer, 49, **80**
Baker, F. Terry, 81
Baseline budget, 291
Baseline code, **25**
Baseline network, **239**
Baseline plan, 89
Benchmark test, **137**
Benjamin, Robert I., 16
Bernacchi, Richard L., 338
Black box, 93, 199
Board, enhancement, 116, 130, 172, 344-345
  interdisciplinary, 91, **341-342**
  review, 45, 340-345

Board, Technical Review (TRB), 97, 130, 207, **343-344**
Bottom-up development, **80**
Brandon, Dick H., 318, 320
B-Test, **101**
  report, **153**
  augmented, **165**
Bubble, **239**
Budget, 23, 55, 58, 210-216
  administration, 58
  allocation, **61**, 88, 109
  Allocation (BA), **217**, 290
  allocation summary, 290-293
  baseline, 291
  capital, 211
  expense, 211
  key variable, **212**
  living, **215**, 290
  narrative, 214
  natural accounts, 211
  program, **211**
  project, **211**
  working, 291-292

Career path, 49
Channel capacity, 78
Chart, PERT, 245
  trend, 301-305
Chief programmer, 49, **79-82**
Chief programmer team, 50, **79-82**
Circumvention, **315**
Code, baseline, **25**
  listings, 267, 282
  object, 190
  source, 190
Code, Linking Update, **328**
  Linking Variant/Version, 328
  Node Update, 327
  Node Variant/Version, 327

Type, 326, 327
Update, 327
Variant/Version, 327
Committee, ad hoc, 341
  standing, 341
Compatibility constraints, 197
Complete feature test, 137
Composite design, 22, 93
Configuration management, 8, 59, 75, 79,
    81, **105**, 109, 131, 177, 250, 321-333
Configuration test, **138**
Configurator, **61**, 68
  review, 75, 178
Configurator, **229-238**
  Cover Memo, **230**
  Hardware Matrix, **230**, 235
  Introduction, **230**
  Narrative Matrix, **230**, 235
  Software Matrix, **230**, 238
Constraints, 197, **239**, 245-246, 258
  compatibility, 197, 258, 272
  hardware, 198, 258, 273, 282
  software, 198, 258, 272, 281
Contingency plan, 48, 52, 72, 92, 102, 111
Contracts, 338-339
Control, distribution, 321, **328**
  document, 59, **106**, 247
  identification, 321, **324**
  quality, 15, 114
  revision, **321**
Control Data Corporation, 229, 235, 305,
    307, 311
Conversion aids, 286
Cooke, Lawrence H., Jr., 50
Copyright, 206, 335
  notice, 337
Copyright Act of 1976, 336
Correction request, **115**, 279
Cost, standard, 220
Coupling, 44, 93
Cover Memo, Configurator, **230**
Critical Path, **245**
C-Test, **110**
Customizability, 201, 265, 274
Cycle, test, **101**, 150

DATABASE, 35
Data directory, **283**
Debugging, **133**
  system, **135**

Decision matrix, 322
Decomposition, design, 77, 94, 184, 251
  hierarchical, 8, **22**, 43, 77
  modular, 22
  phase, 16
  plans, **56**, 77
  program, 77
Deficiency, **166**
Demonstration test, 100, **137**
Design, composite, 22, 93
  external, 21, **93**
  internal, 21, **93**
  structured, 22, 49, 93
Design decomposition, 77, 94, 184, 251
Design Phase, **18**
Design space, 91-92
Development, bottom-up, 80
  top-down, 80
Development Function, 20, 76-104
Development support library, 50, **79**, 81,
    333
Development tools, 23-25, 191
Diagram, input-process-output, 259
  nested, 257
  network, **239**
  structure, 257, 284
  tree, 257
Dijkstra, Edsger W., 48
Direct, Type, **190**, 195
Disaster protection, 114, 329
Discipline, importance of, 49
Discrepancy activity summary, **312**
Discrepancy summary, **311**
Distribution, **105**
  control, 321, **328**
  media, 206, 283
Documentation, **119**
Document control, 59, **106**, 247
Drucker, Peter F., 47
Dummy activity, 246

Encumbrance, 221
End items, 23-25, 174, 217, 279, 286
Enhancement, **170**
Enhancement board, 116, 130, 172,
    344-345
Enhancement request, 97, **115**, 167
Enhancement request system, **167**
Ergonomic properties, **200**, 263, 274
Estimating, time and cost, 82-85

Evaluation, 134
Evaluation Phase, 18
Event, 239
Exclusive tree, 328
External design, 21, 93
External specification, 25, 96, 251-252
External Specification (ES), 252-266

Feasibility, economic, 17
  marketing, 17
  operational, 17
Feasibility Phase, 17
Feasibility study, 66
Field test, 151, 165
Format, 319
  standard, 56, 250
Function, Development, 20, 76-104
  Maintenance, 20, 170-179
  Planning, 20, 52-75
  Publications, 20, 119-132
  Services, 20, 105-118
  Support, 20, 155-169
  Test, 20, 133-154
Functions, life cycle, vii
  marketing, 155
  organizational, 20-21
Function testing, 276

Galaxie product line, 35
Generated software, 195, 256, 271
Goldberg, David, 338

Hardware Matrix, Configurator, 230
Hierarchical decomposition, 8, 22, 43, 77
Hierarchical precedence, 254, 268
Hierarchical structure diagram, 257
HIPO diagram, 259, 260
Human engineering, 36. See also Ergonomic
    properties

Identification control, 321, 324
Impact matrix, 323
Implementation strategy, 276, 282
Inclusive tree, 328
Incremental funding, 221
Indirect, Type, 190, 195
Individual work plan, 48, 55, 78
Individual Work Plan (IWP), 110, 222
Information hiding, 93
Input-process-output diagram, 260

Inspection, 82
Installability test, 138
Installation aids, 286
Installation procedures, 266
Interdependencies, 206
Interdisciplinary board, 91, 341-342
Interface, 77
  organizational, 45, 77
  product, 21
  software, 77
Interface management, 45
Interface problems, 45, 102
Internal data, 275
Internal design, 21, 93
Internal Document Distribution (IDD),
    106
Internal properties, 265
Internal specification, 25, 95
Internal Specification (IS), 267-278
International Business Machines, 79, 305,
    321, 337
International Computer Programs, 14

Key budget variable, 212

Larsen, Gerald H., 338
Levels of abstraction, 22
Liability, 339
Licenses, 338-339
Life cycle, viii, 16-20
Life cycle functions, vii
Life cycle phases, vii, 6
Linking Serial Number, 328
Linking Update Code, 328
Linking Variant/Version Code, 328
Listings, code, 267, 282
Living budget, 215

McGregor, Douglas, 47
Maintainability, 175, 203, 265, 275
Maintenance, 170
  adaptive, 170
  corrective, 170
Maintenance administration, 172
Maintenance capability, 171
Maintenance Function, 20, 170-179
Maintenance procedures, 177
Maintenance request, 115, 177, 305-311
Maintenance request summary, 177,
    311-316

Maintenance request system, 115, 166
Maintenance specification, 175, 267,
    279-284
Maintenance Specification (MS),
    279-284
Management, interface, 45
    plans, 58, 105
    project, 76, 85
Management by exception, 48
Management by objectives (MBO), 46-48,
    222
Management Standards for Data Processing,
    318
Manpower Summary, 225-229
Manual, message, 123
    operator, 123
    reference, 122
    system description, 122
Market-centered, 28
Marketing functions, 155
Maslow, Abraham H., 47
Master plan, 8, 183. See also Requirements
    contract
Matrix, decision, 322
    impact, 323
Matrix, Hardware, 230, 235
    Software, 230, 238
Matrix organization, 44, 56, 59, 85
Media, distribution, 206, 283
Message manual, 123
Methods, management, 318
    programming, 318
Milestone, 239
Miller, George A., 22
Mills, Harlan D., 5
Mission, 53, 191
Mission Plan, 53
Module status sheet, 277

Naming, product, 160
Narrative budget, 214
Narrative Matrix, Configurator, 230
NATO, 1
Natural accounts budget, 211
Nested diagram, 257
Network, 239
    baseline, 239
    stereotype, 246
Network diagram, 239
Network plan, 239-246
New feature test, 137

Node, 239
Node Serial Number, 327
Node Update Code, 327
Node Variant/Version Code, 327
Nolan, Richard L., 3
Notes on the Synthesis of Form, 22
Number, Assembly, 327
    Linking Serial, 328
    Node Serial, 327
    Part, 326

Object code, 190
Objective, 25, 186
Open shop, 20
Operational software, 195, 256, 271
Operations, 105
Operator manual, 123
Organizational functions, 20, 21
Organizational interfaces, 45, 77
Overlays, preliminary and approved, 332
Ownership, 110, 328, 335-339
Ownership protection, 114, 205-206, 266,
    283

Parameterization, 265, 275
Parnas, D. L., 251
Part Number, 326
Patent, 206, 335, 337
Performance test, 137
Personnel, reassigning, 103
Personnel selection, 50. See also Staffing
PERT, 89, 245
PERT chart, 245
Phase, life cycle, viii, 6
Phase, Analysis, 16
    Design, 18
    Evaluation, 18
    Feasibility, 17
    Programming, 18
    Use, 20
Phase decomposition, 16
Phase planning, 70
Phase reviews, 70-71, 342
Pilot system, 63
Plan, baseline, 89
    contingency, 48, 52, 72, 92, 102, 111
    master, 8. See also Requirements contract
    mission, 53
    network, 239-246
    product, 23, 52

product line, 23
publications, 126-127
strategic, 53
support, 160
tactical, 53
test, 147
types of, 53-56, 60-63
Planning, Work, 222-225
Planning Function, 20, 52-75
Plans decomposition, 56, 77
Plans management, 58, 105
Plans manager, 58, 69
Policy, 45, 319
Portability, 203
Post-mortem report, 102, 282
Prerelease, 111, 165
Pricing, 69, 338
Privacy, 263, 274, 335
Procedures, 45, 319, 317-339
    installation, 266
    maintenance, 177
    procedure for, 318
    systems and, 105
Procedures handbook, 320
Product, software, 1, 52, 60
Product-centered, 28
Product concept, vii, 14-16, 41-42
Product family, 61
Product-function matrix, 85-86
Product interface, 21
Product line, 61
Product manager, 85
Product naming, 160
Product Objectives and Requirements
    (POR), 183
Product plan, 23, 52
Product set, 60, 230
Product set member, 230
Program budget, 211
Program decomposition, 77
Program manager, 59
Programming, structured, 49, 79
    top-down, 81, 93, 100
Programming librarian, 80
Programming methodology, 1, 21, 37, 76
Programming methods, 318
Programming Phase, 18
programming standards, 333
Programming Systems Report (PSR), 305,
    307
Project administrator, 50, 81

Project budget, 211
Project Budget Request (PBR), 217
Project management, 76, 85
Project manager, 87
Project notebook, 267
Project size, 78
Project workbook, 267
Promotional material, 163
Proof of correctness, 22
Properties, ergonomic, 200, 263, 274
    internal, 265
Proprietary claim, 336
Protection, disaster, 114, 329
    ownership, 114, 205-206, 266, 283,
        335-338
Publications, on-line, 124, 128
Publications Function, 20, 119-132
Publications plan, 126-127
Publications standards, 119-124, 333-335

Quality assurance, 31, 133
Quality control, 15, 114

Reference booklet, 123
Reference card, 123
Reference manual, 122
Regression test, 138, 153
Release bulletin, 25, 112, 114
Release schedule, 67
Release specification, 101
Release Specification (RS), 284-289
Reliability, 200, 264, 274
Reliability test, 137
Replacement cross-reference, 283, 289
Report, A-Test, 101
    B-Test, 101
    milestones due, 297-299
    milestones overdue, 298
    post-mortem, 102, 282
    progress, 299-301
    trouble, 150
Request, correction, 115, 279
    enhancement, 97, 115, 167, 344
    maintenance, 115, 177, 305-311
    revision, 115, 344
Request for Software Modification (RSM),
    311
Requirement, 25, 186
Requirements contract, 25, 63, 66, 183,
    184

Requirements Contract (RC), **184-209**
Requirements statement, **63**
Restartability, 201, 264, 274
Restriction, **205**
   permanent, **315**
Review boards, 45, 340-345
Reviews, ad hoc, 72
   phase, **70-71**, 342
   regular, 72
Revision, **170**
Revision control, **321**
Revision request, 115, 344

Schedule, 55
   release, **68**
Schedule Change Notice (SCN), **247**
Schedule notice, 109, 144, **246-249**
Schedule notice summary, 247, **293-297**
Schulman, Ed, 222
Second-system effect, **64**
Security, 263, 274
Self-consistency, vii, viii, 7
Services Function, **20**, 105-118
Software, generated, **195**, 256, 271
   heavy-duty, vii, **13**, 340
   operational, **195**, 256, 271
Software catalog, 235. *See also* Configurator
Software constraints, 198, 258, 272, 281
Software engineering, **1**
Software integration, 140
Software interfaces, 77
Software manufacturing, **113**
Software Matrix, Configurator, **230**, 238
Software product, **1**, 52, 60
Source code, 190
Source Code Control System, 333
Specification, **250**
   external, **25**, 96, 251-252
   internal, **25**, 95
   maintenance, 25, **175**, 267
   release, **101**
   test, 147
Specification, External (ES), **252-266**
   Internal (IS), **267-278**
   Maintenance (MS), **279-284**
   Release (RS), **284-289**
Stability test, 137
Staffing, 46-51, 58, 77, 121, 141, 157
   from strength, 47
Stage theory, 3
Standard(s), 78, 197, 258, 272, **321**

programming, **333**
   publications, 119-124, 333-335
Standard cost, 220
Standard format, 56, 250
Stella product line, 27
Stepwise refinement, 22
Stereotype network, **246**
Strategic plan, **53**
Strategy, 53, 194
   implementation, 276, 282
Structural data base, 328
Structure, tree, 95
Structured design, 22, 49, 93
Structure diagram, 257, 284
Structured programming, 49, **79**
Structured walk-throughs, 45, **82**
Style guide, **122**
Support, home-office, 157
Support Function, **20**, 155-169
Support level, **172**
Support Level, 70, 75, 113, 167, 172, 178
   311
Support plan, **160**
Syntax, 256
System debugging, **135**
System description manual, **122**
Systems and procedures, **105**

Tactic, 53, 206
Tactical plan, **53**
Task programmer, 49
Taxability, 335
Technical Review Board (TRB), 97, 130,
   207, **343-344**
Telescope terminal, 28
Test, acceptance, **101**, 148
   A-Test, **100**
   benchmark, **137**
   B-Test, **101**
   categories, 136-138
   complete feature, 137
   configuration, **138**
   C-Test, **110**
   demonstration, 100, **137**
   field, **151**, 165
   installability, **138**
   modes, 135-136
   new feature, **137**
   performance, **137**
   regression, **138**, 153
   reliability, **137**

stability, **137**
stages, 135
Test cycle, **101**, 150
Test Function, 20, 133-154
Testing, **133**
  algorithm, 277
  function, 276
Testing harness, 267
Test material, 190
Test plan, **147**
Test specification, 147
Theory X and Theory Y, 47
Top-down development, **80**
Top-down programming, **81**, 93, 100
Trade secrets, 205, 335
Training, personnel, 50
  product, 14, 164
Tree, exclusive, **328**
  inclusive, **328**
Tree diagram, 257
Tree structure, 95, 257
Trend charts, 301-305
Trouble report, **150**
Type Code, 326, 327

Type Direct, **190**
Type Indirect, **190**
Type of plan, 53-56, 60-64

Unbundling, **14**, 335
Update, 234, **322**
Update Code, 327
Usability, 203
Use Phase, **20**
User library, **117**, 178

Variant, 234, **321**
Version, 234, **322**
Virtual Storage Operating System (VSOS),
  68

Waiver, **111**, 113
Warranty, 171-172, 339
Wave effect, **99**
Weinberg, Gerald M., 222
Wessel, Milton R., 338
Work Planning, **222-225**

Yeh, Raymond T., 1